The Economics of International Environmental Agreements

International Library of Environmental Economics and Policy
General Editors: Tom Tietenberg, Theodore Panayotou, Wendy Morrison

Titles in the Series

Fisheries Economics
Lee G. Anderson

The Economics of International Environmental Agreements
Amitrajeet A. Batabyal

International Trade and the Environment
Judith M. Dean

The Implementation and Evolution of Emissions Trading Programs
Tom Tietenberg

The Theory and Design of Emissions Trading Programs
Tom Tietenberg

The Economics of International Environmental Agreements

Edited by

Amitrajeet A. Batabyal

Utah State University

Routledge
Taylor & Francis Group
LONDON AND NEW YORK

First published 2000 by Ashgate Publishing

Reissued 2018 by Routledge
2 Park Square, Milton Park, Abingdon, Oxon OX14 4RN
711 Third Avenue, New York, NY 10017, USA

Routledge is an imprint of the Taylor & Francis Group, an informa business

Publisher's Note
The publisher has gone to great lengths to ensure the quality of this reprint but points out that some imperfections in the original copies may be apparent.

A Library of Congress record exists under LC control number: 99042545

ISBN 13: 978-1-138-70522-7 (hbk)
ISBN 13: 978-1-138-70521-0 (pbk)
ISBN 13: 978-1-315-20231-0 (ebk)

Contents

Acknowledgements

The editor and publishers wish to thank the following for permission to use copyright material.

Academic Press for the essays: Michael Hoel (1991), 'Global Environmental Problems: The Effects of Unilateral Actions Taken by One Country', *Journal of Environmental Economics and Management*, **20**, pp. 55–70. Copyright © 1991 Academic Press; Zhiqi Chen (1997), 'Negotiating an Agreement on Global Warming: A Theoretical Analysis', *Journal of Environmental Economics and Management*, **32**, pp. 170–88. Copyright © 1997 Academic Press; Olli Tahvonen, Veijo Kaitala, and Matti Pohjola (1993), 'A Finnish–Soviet Acid Rain Game: Noncooperative Equilibria, Cost Efficiency, and Sulfur Agreements', *Journal of Environmental Economics and Management*, **24**, pp. 87–99. Copyright © 1993 Academic Press.

Amitrajeet A. Batabyal (1999), 'The Effects of Collusion and Limited Liability on the Design of International Environmental Agreements for Developing Countries', in Amitrajeet A. Batabyal (ed.) *The Economics of International Environmental Agreements*, Aldershot: Ashgate Publishing Limited, pp. 1–25. Copyright © 1999 Amitrajeet A. Batabyal.

Blackwell Publishers for the essays: Jane Black, Maurice D. Levi and David De Meza (1993), 'Creating a Good Atmosphere: Minimum Participation for Tackling the "Greenhouse Effect"', *Economica*, **60**, pp. 281–93. Copyright © 1993 The London School of Economics and Political Science; James C. Murdoch, Todd Sandler and Keith Sargent (1997), 'A Tale of Two Collectives: Sulphur versus Nitrogen Oxides Emission Reduction in Europe', *Economica*, **64**, pp. 281–301. Copyright © 1997 The London School of Economics and Political Science.

Elsevier Science for the essays: Carlo Carraro and Domenico Siniscalco (1993), 'Strategies for the International Protection of the Environment', *Journal of Public Economics*, **52**, pp. 309–28. Copyright © 1993 Elsevier Science; Emmanuel Petrakis and Anastasios Xepapadeas (1996), 'Environmental Consciousness and Moral Hazard in International Agreements to Protect the Environment', *Journal of Public Economics*, **60**, pp. 95–110. Copyright © 1996 Elsevier Science; James C. Murdoch and Todd Sandler (1997), 'The Voluntary Provision of a Pure Public Good: The Case of Reduced CFC Emissions and the Montreal Protocol', *Journal of Public Economics*, **63**, pp. 331–49. Copyright © 1997 Elsevier Science.

Helbing & Lichtenhahn for the essays: Johan Eyckmans, Stef Proost and Erik Schokkaert (1993), 'Efficiency and Distribution in Greenhouse Negotiations', *Kyklos*, **46**, pp. 363–97; Werner W. Pommerehne, Lars P. Feld and Albert Hart (1994), 'Voluntary Provision of a Public Good: Results from a Real World Experiment', *Kyklos*, **47**, pp. 505–18.

MIT Press Journals for the essay: Roger D. Congleton (1992), 'Political Institutions and Pollution Control', *Review of Economics and Statistics*, **74**, pp. 412–21. Copyright © 1992 by the President and Fellows of Harvard College.

Oxford University Press for the essays: Scott Barrett (1990), 'The Problem of Global Environmental Protection', *Oxford Review of Economic Policy*, **6**, pp. 68–79. Copyright ©1990 Oxford University Press; Scott Barrett (1994), 'Self-Enforcing International Environmental Agreements', *Oxford Economic Papers*, **46**, pp. 878–94. Copyright © 1994 Oxford University Press.

Every effort has been made to trace all the copyright holders, but if any have been inadvertently overlooked the publishers will be pleased to make the necessary arrangement at the first opportunity.

Series Preface

The *International Library of Environmental Economics and Policy* explores the influence of economics on the development of environmental and natural resource policy. In a series of twenty five volumes, the most significant journal essays in key areas of contemporary environmental and resource policy are collected. Scholars who are recognized for their expertise and contribution to the literature in the various research areas serve as volume editors and write an introductory essay that provides the context for the collection.

Volumes in the series reflect the broad strands of economic research including 1) Natural and Environmental Resources, 2) Policy Instruments and Institutions and 3) Methodology. The editors, in their introduction to each volume, provide a state-of-the-art overview of the topic and explain the influence and relevance of the collected papers on the development of policy. This reference series provides access to the economic literature that has made an enduring contribution to contemporary and natural resource policy.

TOM TIETENBERG
THEODORE PANAYOTOU
WENDY MORRISON
General Editors

Introduction

Preliminaries

The doctrine of utilitarianism tells us that the rational pursuit of self-interest by individual economic agents is likely to lead to the greatest good for the greatest number. Although this line of reasoning has exerted a powerful influence on a number of prominent Western thinkers, as Oran Young (1989: 1) has pointed out, it is important to recognize that this line of reasoning runs 'counter to some of the most powerful findings produced by social scientists working in ... international relations'. Indeed, in the world of international environmental affairs, it is now well known that the pursuit of self-interest, in the absence of efficacious institutions and rules is more likely than not 'to produce collective outcomes that are socially undesirable ...' (Young, 1989: 2).

Given this state of affairs, the general purpose of this volume is to study a class of problems that typically arise in the world of international environmental affairs. In particular, the chapters in this volume seek to document the theoretical and empirical contributions that rigorous economic analysis can make in improving our understanding of the causes of and the solutions to a variety of international environmental problems.[1]

There are at least three distinguishing features of international environmental problems. First, the detrimental environmental effect on each affected country depends largely on the *global* discharge of some hazardous material or materials. Examples of such problems include the effects of chlorofluorocarbon (CFC) emissions on the earth's ozone layer and the effects of carbon dioxide (CO_2) and other greenhouse gas emissions on the world's climate.

Second, as the perspicacious work of Demsetz (1967) has made clear, one way to deal with global environmental problems is to require effective intervention by an apposite regulatory institution. Indeed, if one could design and empower an international institution to intervene for the good of all, then international environmental problems would be easy to redress. However, as Krasner (1983), Keohane *et al.* (1993), and Batabyal (1996, 1997, 1999) have noted, national sovereignty considerations have generally proved to be an effective stumbling block in the design of international institutions with teeth.

This leads to the third distinguishing feature of international environmental problems – that is, the necessity of agreements in solving these vexing problems. As Keohane *et al.* have put it, 'organized international responses to shared environmental problems will occur through *cooperation* among states, not through the imposition of government over them' (Keohane *et al.*, 1993: 4). This is also the position taken in this volume. Recognizing the salience of international environmental agreements (IEAs) in solving global common property problems, the essays in this volume explore, from an economic standpoint, many of the issues that are germane to increasing our knowledge of the ways in which IEAs work and the ways in which they can be made to work even better.

What can economic *theory* tell us about the design of IEAs that will protect the world's fragile environmental resources? This is the general question that is addressed by the eight chronologically arranged chapters that comprise Part I of this book. The tools of microeconomic and game theory are used effectively by the different chapters to analyse diverse issues such as:

1. the effects that unilateral environmental actions have on the outcome of IEAs;
2. the optimal number of countries that are needed to make an IEA viable; and
3. the effect of limited liability on the design of IEAs.

The six chronologically arranged chapters of Part II *apply* the economic theory of IEAs to practical situations to determine, *inter alia*, the extent to which this theory can inform actual policy decisions about international environmental problems. This part of the book focuses on topics such as:

1. the determinants of environmental cooperation between Finland and the former Soviet Union;
2. the voluntary provision of a public good in the German state of Saarland; and
3. the role of collective action considerations in reducing sulfur and nitrogen oxide emissions in Europe.

International Environmental Agreements: Theory

Before asking and attempting to answer interesting theoretical questions about the functioning of IEAs, one must first comprehend 'the nature of the beast'. This issue is tackled by the opening essay. Here, Scott Barrett takes the reader on a guided tour of the global environmental protection problem. He points out that one reason for the lack of simple solutions to global international problems is the lack of a 'world government' that is empowered to intervene for the benefit of all citizens and he rightly suggests that IEAs provide the only reasonable way of solving global environmental problems. Combining the study of the putative gains from cooperation with a formal model of an IEA, Barrett points out that, relative to the non-cooperative outcome, the benefits from cooperation are sometimes small. Consequently, even when it is needed, cooperation may *not* be forthcoming.

This saturnine conclusion leads to a number of questions, one of which relates to the efficacy for unilateral environmental actions. In particular, if the prospects of achieving global cooperation are limited, what, if anything, can one say about instituting environmental policy unilaterally?[2] This question is addressed lucidly by Michael Hoel in Chapter 2. Hoel constructs a two-country game-theoretic model to study two instances of the institution of unilateral environmental policy. In the first instance, a positive and 'unselfish' unilateral action is taken by one country in the absence of, or prior to, the establishment of an IEA. Hoel shows that, in this instance, the pursuit of unilateral environmental policy has a salubrious effect on the environment. However, recognizing that an unselfish unilateral action may jeopardize subsequent negotiations on an IEA, Hoel then goes on to study this. Here, he shows that an unselfish unilateral action may compromise negotiations on an IEA and ultimately lead to *more* pollution emissions than would have occurred had both countries acted 'selfishly' and not taken unilateral actions.

Because Hoel's analysis is based largely on a two-country model, it is possible to question the generality of his results. For instance, one can ask what happens to his results when the analysis involves more than two countries. More generally, one can ask whether a *minimum number* of countries is necessary to successfully negotiate an IEA. This question is addressed ably by Jane Black, Maurice Levi, and David de Meza in Chapter 3. The authors focus on two salient aspects of the 'minimum numbers' issue. First, they demonstrate that, if the goal is to effect a viable IEA, then it is better to include a 'minimum agreement level or n-rule' rather than permit nations to take independent actions. This minimum agreement level refers to the minimum number of nations that are needed to participate in an IEA before action is taken by any one participant. Second, they point out that, although signatories to an IEA may have their own country-specific n-rules, signatories will often lose little by adopting the social welfare-maximizing n-rule, instead of their own n-rule. This finding has the optimistic implication that countries may, in fact, be quite willing to put sovereignty questions aside and let an international institution set the participation level required to consummate an IEA.

Black *et al.*'s n-rule can also be thought of as the minimum size of a *coalition* necessary to sustain an IEA. This coalition-theoretic view of IEAs has been adopted by a number of scholars and hence there is now a sizeable literature on coalition formation in the context of IEAs (for example, Bohm and Larsen, 1993; Kverndokk, 1993; Chander and Tulkens, 1995, 1996; Welsch, 1995; Finus and Rundshagen, 1998). In Chapter 4, Carlo Carraro and Domenico Siniscalco present a coalition-theoretic account of IEAs in which the signatories to an agreement may choose to act either cooperatively or non-cooperatively. Recognizing the difficulty of obtaining universal participation in an IEA, the authors show that it is possible to design profitable and stable IEAs in which only a coalition or subgroup of countries participate. This finding raises a natural question: are there ways of increasing the number of signatories to an IEA? Carraro and Siniscalco point out that the size of the coalition can indeed be expanded by using self-financed welfare transfers and by requiring the coalition participants to display a minimal level of commitment. By explicitly focusing on the *stability* of IEAs, the authors rightly remind us that, in the realm of international environmental affairs in which there is no potent 'world government', unstable IEAs are of little or no interest.

In Chapter 5, Scott Barrett provides an alternative perspective on this stability issue. The reader will note that a country cannot be forced to join an IEA; moreover, once a country has joined an IEA, it can always choose to withdraw from the agreement. Consequently, a useful IEA must accomplish two things. First, it must appear attractive to potential signatories. Second, once a nation has agreed to join an IEA, this nation must want to carry out the terms of the agreement. For these reasons, Barrett rightly observes that, for an IEA to be useful, it must be *self-enforcing*. He then uses two different game-theoretic approaches to analyse the properties of self-enforcing IEAs, concluding that a self-enforcing IEA which institutes rules for managing global common property resources will typically *not* be able to improve substantially upon the non-cooperative outcome. However, it is important to recognize that this potent and negative finding is based on an analysis of models in which there are *no* informational asymmetries of any kind, and in which all countries are *identical*. Acknowledging the restrictiveness of these and other assumptions, Barrett wisely calls for additional research to determine the robustness of his findings.

This call for additional research is taken up by Emmanuel Petrakis and Anastasios Xepapadeas in Chapter 6. Departing from the analytical approach adopted in Chapter 5, these authors provide a stimulating, coalition-theoretic account of IEAs in a world in which countries are *heterogeneous* and informational *asymmetries* between countries are salient. This chapter contains two significant findings. First, consistent with the analysis presented in Chapter 4, Petrakis and Xepapadeas show that, if there exists a coalition of environmentally conscious countries that is committed to environmental protection, then this coalition can use self-financed transfers or side payments fruitfully to attract less environmentally conscious countries into their coalition. Second, it is shown that, as long as global pollution can be measured accurately and without cost, a mechanism can be constructed which, if incorporated into an IEA between environmentally conscious and less environmentally conscious countries, will lead to optimal pollution emissions by all the participating countries.

Asymmetries between countries also comprise the subject matter of Chapter 7 in which Zhiqi Chen analyses a well articulated discrete-time, infinite-horizon, model of an IEA in the context of the global warming problem. Chen explicitly addresses the effects that side payments[3] between countries and population size have on the outcome of an IEA and, interestingly, shows that although side payments are a part of the IEA that he analyses, they do *not* always reflect either the 'polluter pays principle' or the 'victim pays principle'. In particular, parts of these side payments arise because of the differential bargaining power of the two nations in his model. This leads Chen to note that care must be taken to ensure that the actual outcome of a given negotiation process is consistent with a principle such as the 'polluter pays principle'. As far as population size is concerned, this chapter shows that a country with a small population will, in general, gain more from an IEA than will a country with a large population. This enables a small country to successfully take a less compromising stand in its negotiations about an IEA with a large country.

Chen's analysis depends on his assumptions that, first, the world consists of only *two* countries and, second, that governments have *complete* information about the state of the world's climate and the economy. These assumptions are eschewed by Amitrajeet Batabyal in his Chapter 8 analysis of the design of IEAs. Batabyal studies the problem faced by an *imperfectly* informed supranational governmental authority (SNGA) with limited monetary resources that wishes to design an IEA for $N \in \mathbf{N}$ developing countries (DCs). Using a hierarchical principal-agent model, he investigates the properties of the optimal limited liability IEA that can be implemented by the SNGA when polluting firms and national governments in the individual DCs collude to its detriment. His analysis shows that obtaining voluntary participation by the firms and the governments and preventing *ex post* breach of the IEA by these two players is costly for the SNGA. Moreover, it also tells us that, because a SNGA can successfully design collusion-proof IEAs, IEAs are *not* inherently doomed due to a basic monitoring and enforcement problem stemming from national sovereignty. However. the success of IEAs *is* fundamentally contingent on the funds available for environmental protection.

Chapters 1 through 8 of this volume provide us with diverse theoretical perspectives on the economics of IEAs. Collectively, they illustrate the many useful theoretical insights that can be gained by engaging in rigorous microeconomic and game-theoretic analyses of IEAs. A logical question now is this: how can this theoretical knowledge be used to increase our understanding of the practical aspects of IEAs? It is this application issue that is addressed by Part II of this volume.

International Environmental Agreements: Applications

In Chapter 9, Roger Congleton constructs models of democratic and authoritarian environmental policy-making in order to explore the effect that political institutions have on the willingness of governments to control pollution. He notes that, although data and other limitations preclude one from testing whether democratic regimes – relative to authoritarian ones – are more likely to adopt strict environmental regulations, this hypothesis can be tested using data on IEAs. As such, using national area as a proxy for natural resources, Congleton analyses a data set consisting of 118 countries. This helpful analysis shows that a nation's environmental policy decisions *are* determined primarily by its political institutions and that, in comparison with authoritarian nations, liberal democracies are considerably *more* likely to participate in IEAs.[4] These two findings lead Congleton to conclude that IEAs will attract more signatories as the number of democratic regimes in the world increases.

This issue of international participation in an IEA is examined from the perspectives of efficiency and equity by Johan Eyckmans, Stef Proost and Erik Schokkaert in Chapter 11. The authors divide the world into 12 homogeneous blocks of countries and then examine the CO_2 emissions reduction strategies employed by each of these 12 players (blocks). In the benchmark non-cooperative game in which players behave in Cournot fashion, there is almost no reduction of CO_2 emissions. This pessimistic conclusion changes in the first-best and in the second-best solutions of an international carbon emissions game. In particular, while there is virtually no worldwide pollution abatement in the benchmark game, there is almost 17 per cent pollution abatement in the first-best game. The extent of pollution abatement in the second-best game depends on the magnitude of a parameter called the degree of inequality aversion. Interestingly, Eyckmans *et al.* show that, in the context of their modeling framework, there is no game outcome in which the net pay-offs of *all* the nations is positive. From this, they conclude that an analysis of realistic IEAs will need to pay attention to side payments and incorporate participation constraints[5] explicitly into the analysis.

Why are side payments so important? This question is addressed by Olli Tahvonen, Veijo Kaitala and Matti Pohjola in their Chapter 11 analysis of an acid rain game between Finland and the former Soviet Union. The authors focus on the terms of a 1987 IEA between Finland and the Soviet Union that called for a 50 per cent reduction in sulphur emissions throughout Finland and in adjacent regions of the Soviet Union. After calculating the cost-effective and the non-cooperative sulphur abatement policies for these two countries, they show that the 1987 IEA is *not* cost-effective. Moreover, they demonstrate that the abatement costs implied by the agreement are higher than those in the non-cooperative equilibrium. Interestingly, Tahvonen *et al.* show that, although there are significant potential gains from cooperation between these two countries, this cooperation is unlikely to arise because, in general, cost-effective sulphur IEAs are likely to benefit Finland but *not* the Soviet Union. This raises the thorny issue of side payments once again. As noted by the authors, the implementation of cost-effective sulphur IEAs is likely to require side payments from Finland to the Soviet Union. However, because, from a political standpoint, it may not be possible to make such payments, other ways of implementing cost-effective IEAs will have to be considered.

In Chapter 12 Werner Pommerehne, Lars Feld and Albert Hart study the question of international cooperation from a public goods perspective. The issue here is the construction of a waste incinerator in Grosbliederstroff (in France) that would have adverse impacts on the residents of Kleinblittersdorf (in Germany). On the basis of direct negotiations, it was determined that Kleinblittersdorf would buy the land in question from Grosbliederstroff and then look for an investor who would be willing to operate a less pollution-intensive incinerator. Bringing this plan to fruition required a certain amount of money. Pommerehne *et al.* analyse the factors that determined the provision of this public good – that is, the construction of an 'environmentally more benign' incinerator. On the basis of an econometric study of a random sample of 400 households in Kleinblittersdorf, they note that non-economic factors play a crucial role in the voluntary provision of public goods. This leads them to conclude that it is important to remember that, as compared to economic factors, *non-economic* factors are often a more important determinant of a citizen's voluntary contribution to a particular public good.

Chapter 13 continues the investigation of the voluntary provision of public goods begun in the previous chapter. Here, James Murdoch and Todd Sandler provide a thought-provoking account of cutbacks in CFC emissions that, for the most part, predated the institution of the Montreal Protocol on Substances that Deplete the Ozone Layer. Their econometric analysis validates a key empirical prediction of the theory of the voluntary provision of public goods. That is, these authors demonstrate that, when tastes are controlled and three outlier nations are excluded from the sample, a statistically significant *linear* relationship emerges between CFC emission cutbacks and national income. On the basis of this demonstration, the authors claim that the Montreal Protocol was initially instituted because it codified reductions in CFC emissions that polluting nations were *voluntarily* prepared to undertake. This leads them to conclude that:

1. the Montreal Protocol may *not* be a good model for other IEAs;
2. foreign aid is likely to speed up the adherence to mandated diminutions in CFC emissions; and
3. the promotion of democracy is likely to increase the number of nations that will take steps to effectively deal with global pollution problems.

How general are the conclusions of Chapter 13? Do they apply to pollutants such as sulphur and nitrogen oxides? This and other questions are analysed by James Murdoch, Todd Sandler and Keith Sargent in Chapter 14. From their theoretical framework, Murdoch *et al.* derive an econometric model of the demand for emission reductions which adjusts for the spatial dispersion of the pollutant in question. This model enables them to explain why European nations have been able to meet, or exceed, mandated reductions in sulphur emissions, but not mandated reductions in nitrogen oxide emissions. They point out that sulphur emissions are easier to control than nitrogen oxide emissions because, *inter alia*, a greater proportion of sulphur emissions falls both within a country's jurisdiction and within an IEA's jurisdiction. Moreover, consistent with the conclusions of Chapters 9 and 13, these authors point out that, because increases in income and political freedoms increase emission reductions, foreign aid and the promotion of democracy can result in a cleaner environment for all nations. Perhaps the most significant conclusion to emerge from this chapter is that collective action problems that seem superficially similar, can in fact be quite *dissimilar*. Consequently, one should be careful in lumping collective action problems together, even if they involve the same participants.

Conclusions

The different chapters in this volume effectively describe the theoretical and empirical contributions that rigorous economic analysis can make in improving our understanding of the causes of, and the solutions to, a variety of international environmental problems. These chapters also provide us with a 'state of the art' perspective on what is currently known about the theoretical and the empirical properties of IEAs. The task for researchers now is to use the findings contained in this volume to better design and implement actual IEAs. With talk of rising disparity between the developed world and the developing world and the increasingly contentious nature of international discussions about the use of environmental resources, IEAs take on particular salience. This is in no small measure due to the fact that the design and the implementation of IEAs will do more to engender and maintain international security than will most unilateral or non-cooperative policy measures.

Acknowledgements

I thank Qing Xu for competent research assistance, and Theo Panayotou and Tom Tietenberg for comments on a previous version of this paper. I acknowledge financial support from the Utah Agricultural Experiment Station, Utah State University, Logan, UT 84322-4810, by way of project UTA 024. The usual disclaimer applies.

Notes

1 International environmental problems have attracted the attention of researchers in a number of fields other than economics. In particular, there is now a sizeable literature in political science on such problems. However, in this volume, we are concerned almost exclusively with the economics of international environmental problems. For more on the relevant political science literature, the reader should consult Krasner (1983), Young (1989), Epstein and Gupta (1990), Benedick (1991), Peterson (1992), Rosenau and Czempiel (1992), Haas *et al.* (1993), Wettestad (1994), Bernauer (1995), and Victor *et al.* (1998).

2 This question has been addressed in the 'trade and the environment' literature as well. For more on this, see Batabyal (1993, 1994, 1998), and Xu and Batabyal (1999).

3 This question has been discussed by a number of scholars. For additional details, see Chapters 1, 8, and 10 in this volume and Maler (1990).

4 This finding is corroborated by the results contained in Chapter 13 and in Olson (1993).

5 Participation constraints and their salience are studied by Amitrajeet Batabyal in Chapter 8 of this volume.

References

Batabyal, A.A. (1993), 'Should Large Developing Countries Pursue Environmental Policy Unilaterally?', *Indian Economic Review*, **28**, pp. 191–202.

Batabyal, A.A. (1994), 'An Open Economy Model of the Effects of Unilateral Environmental Policy by a Large Developing Country', *Ecological Economics*, **10**, pp. 221–32.

Batabyal, A.A. (1996), 'An Agenda for the Design and Study of International Environmental Agreements', *Ecological Economics*, **19**, pp. 3–9.

Batabyal, A.A. (1997), 'Developing Countries and Environmental Protection: The Effects of Budget Balance and Pollution Ceiling Constraints', *Journal of Development Economics*, **54**, pp. 285–305.

Batabyal, A.A. (1998), 'Games Governments Play: An Analysis of National Environmental Policy in an Open Economy', *Annals of Regional Science*, **32**, pp. 237–51.

Batabyal, A.A. (1999), 'Developing Countries and Environmental Protection: Contract Design in Perfectly Correlated Environments', *Open Economies Review*, **10**, pp. 305–23.

Benedick, R.E. (1991), *Ozone Diplomacy: New Directions in Safeguarding the Planet*, Cambridge, MA: Harvard University Press.

Bernauer, T. (1995), 'The Effect of International Environmental Institutions: How We Might Learn More', *International Organization*, **49**, pp. 351–77.

Bohm, P. and Larsen, B. (1993), 'Fairness in a Tradeable-Permit Treaty for Carbon Emission Reductions in Europe and the Former Soviet Union', *Environmental and Resource Economics*, **4**, pp. 219–39.

Chander, P. and Tulkens, H. (1995), 'A Core-Theoretic Solution for the Design of Cooperative Agreements on Transfrontier Pollution', *International Tax and Public Finance*, **2**, pp. 279–93.

Chander, P. and Tulkens, H. (1996), 'The Core of an Economy With Multilateral Environmental Externalities', *International Journal of Game Theory*, **26**, pp. 379–402.

Demsetz, H. (1967), 'Toward a Theory of Property Rights', *American Economic Review*, **57**, pp. 347–59.

Epstein, J.M. and Gupta, R. (1990), *Controlling the Greenhouse Effect: Five Global Regimes Compared*, Washington, DC: Brookings Institution.

Finus, M. and Rundshagen, B. (1998), 'Toward a Positive Theory of Coalition Formation and Endogenous Instrumental Choice in Global Pollution Control', *Public Choice*, **96**, pp. 145–86.

Haas, P.M., Keohane, R.O. and Levy, M.A. (eds) (1993), *Institutions for the Earth: Sources of Effective International Environmental Protection*, Cambridge, MA: MIT Press.

Keohane, R.O., Haas, P.M. and Levy, M.A. (1993), 'The Effectiveness of International Environmental Institutions', in P.M. Haas, R.O. Keohane and M.A. Levy (eds), *Institutions for the Earth: Sources of Effective International Environmental Protection*, Cambridge, MA: MIT Press.

Krasner, S. (ed.) (1983), *International Regimes*, Ithaca, NY: Cornell University Press.

Kverndokk, S. (1993), 'Global Agreements: A Cost-Effective Approach', *Energy Journal*, **14**, pp. 91–112.

Maler, K.G. (1990), 'International Environmental Problems', *Oxford Review of Economic Policy*, **6**, pp. 80–108.

Olson, M. (1993), 'Dictatorship, Democracy, and Development', *American Political Science Review*, **87**, pp. 567–76.

Peterson, M.J. (1992), 'Whalers, Cetologists, Environmentalists, and the International Management of Whaling', *International Organization*, **46**, pp. 147–86.

Rosenau, J.N. and Czempiel, E. (eds) (1992), *Governance Without Government: Change and Order in World Politics*, New York: Cambridge University Press.

Victor, D.G., Raustiala, K. and Skolnikoff, E.B. (eds) (1998), *The Implementation and Effectiveness of International Environmental Commitments: Theory and Practice*, Cambridge, MA: MIT Press.

Welsch, H. (1995), 'Incentives for Forty-Five Countries to Join Various Forms of Carbon Reduction Agreements', *Resource and Energy Economics*, **17**, pp. 213–37.

Wettestad, J. (1994), *Institutional Design and the Effectiveness of International Regimes: A Conceptual Framework*, Lysaker: Fridtjof Nansen Institute.

Xu, Q. and Batabyal, A.A. (1999), 'Price Competition, Pollution, and Environmental Policy in an Open Economy', mimeo, Department of Economics, Utah State University.

Young, O. (1989), *International Cooperation: Building Regimes for Natural Resources and the Environment*, Ithaca, NY: Cornell University Press.

Part I
International Environmental Agreements: Theory

[1]

OXFORD REVIEW OF ECONOMIC POLICY, VOL. 6, NO. 1

THE PROBLEM OF GLOBAL ENVIRONMENTAL PROTECTION

SCOTT BARRETT
London Business School[1]

Suppose that land is communally owned. Every person has the right to hunt, till, or mine the land. This form of ownership fails to concentrate the cost associated with any person's exercise of his communal right on that person. If a person seeks to maximize the value of his communal rights, he will tend to overhunt and overwork the land because some of the costs of his doing so are borne by others. The stock of game and the richness of the soil will be diminished too quickly. It is conceivable that those who own these rights, i.e. every member of the community, can agree to curtail the rate at which they work the lands if negotiating and policing costs are zero . . . [However,] negotiating costs will be large because it is difficult for many persons to reach a mutually satisfactory agreement, especially when each hold-out has the right to work the land as fast as he pleases. [Furthermore,] even if an agreement among all can be reached, we must yet take account of the costs of policing the agreement, and these may be large, also.

Demsetz (1967, pp. 354–5)

I. INTRODUCTION

Demsetz's influential paper on the development of private property rights makes depressing reading for anyone concerned about global common property resources such as the oceans and atmosphere. Demsetz's view—and it is one that is shared by many others—is that users of a communally owned resource will fail to come to an agreement on managing the resource even though it is in the interest of all users to co-operate and reduce their rates of use of the resource. The reason is that if this improved situation is attained, every user will earn even higher returns by free-riding on the virtuous behaviour of the remaining co-operators. As a consequence, united action on the part of users can be expected to be unstable; co-operative agreements, even if they are reached, will not persist. The only

[1] I have benefited greatly from comments made by David Pearce on an earlier draft of this paper.

way out of the common property dilemma, as Demsetz makes clear, is intervention by '*the* state, *the* courts, or the leaders of *the* community' (emphasis added). In Demsetz's example, the intervention manifests itself in the development of private property rights to the resource, but the intervention could just as easily involve regulation.

The reason this view is disquieting is that for global common property resources there is no World Government empowered to intervene for the good of all. To be sure, there do exist international institutions—most notably the United Nations Environment Programme—which have been given the mandate to co-ordinate international environmental protection efforts. But none of these institutions can dictate what is to be done; that requires agreement by the parties concerned. The problem is perhaps best exemplified by the International Whaling Commission (IWC), which was established to conserve whale stocks, but whose best efforts in this regard have been repeatedly foiled. IWC membership is open to any country, and this leaves open the possibility that the whales could be protected for the global good. But any member can object to a majority decision, and hence render that decision meaningless. For example, a 1954 proposal to prohibit the taking of blue whales in the North Pacific was rejected by the only members who hunted blue whales in this ocean—Canada, Japan, the US, and the USSR—and hence did nothing to protect this species. In 1981 the IWC sought to ban the use of the non-explosive harpoon for killing minke whales. The ban was objected to by Brazil, Iceland, Japan, Norway, and the USSR. Since these were the only countries that hunted minke whales, the ban had no effect.[2]

Because national sovereignty must be respected, the problem of conserving global common property resources is no different from that described by Demsetz. The only way out of the global common property dilemma is agreement. Yet, just as in the situation Demsetz describes, there are strong incentives for governments not to co-operate, or to defect from an agreement should one be reached. This is the crux of the problem of managing global common property, and what distinguishes this problem from the long studied one of common property management under the jurisdictional control of a central authority.

Attempts to correct global, unidirectional externalities will encounter similar difficulties. Consider the problem where certain activities by one country harm all others. A good example is deforestation of Amazonia by Brazil. The rain forests play a crucial role in the protection of biological diversity and in the functioning of the carbon cycle. When standing, the rain forests serve as habitat to about a half of all wildife species and absorb carbon dioxide, one of the so-called greenhouse gases. When the forests are burned, masses of species can become extinct and substantial quantities of greenhouse gases are emitted. If the rights to generate these externalities are vested in the one country, as indeed they are in the case of Brazilian deforestation, then the others will have to pay this nation to cease its destructive activities. If the externality affected only one other country, then bargaining might be possible; the externalities might be internalized without outside intervention.[3] But in the case of global externalities, all countries except the generator suffer. All sufferers might be willing to bribe the generator to cease its harmful activities. But a contribution by any one country would confer benefits on all others and not just the one making the compensating payment. The others could therefore do better by free-riding. But then so too could the one that contemplated making the payment. Co-operation would again be foiled.[4] Mechanisms exist that can lead countries to reveal their preferences for global public goods truthfully (see, e.g., Groves and Ledyard, 1977), and hence for correct-

[2] See Lyster (1985).

[3] See Coase (1960). Bargaining has in fact taken place at the bilateral level. A famous example is the Trail Smelter case. The Canadian smelter emitted pollutants that crossed the US border. The case was arbitrated by an international tribunal comprised of an American, a Canadian, and a Belgian. The tribunal found that Canada was liable for damages, and also established emission regulations for the plant. The judicial decisions on this case make fascinating reading. See Trail Smelter Arbitral Tribunal (1939, 1941).

[4] Demsetz (1967, p. 357) argues that in the large numbers case, 'it may be too costly to internalize effects through the market-place'. Elsewhere, Demsetz (1964) argues that it might in fact be optimal for the externality not to be internalized since the costs of internalization should include the costs of transacting the agreement. But even then the free-rider problem would prevail; intervention, were it possible, might still be desired.

OXFORD REVIEW OF ECONOMIC POLICY, VOL. 6, NO. 1

ing global externalities. But in the absence of a World Government these mechanisms cannot be employed without the consent of the sovereign nations themselves. Every country would be better off if it agreed to participate in the revelation exercise. But each would do even better if others participated and it did not. All will therefore choose not to participate. The crux of the problem of correcting global externalities, like that of managing global common property, is that global optimality demands global co-operation, and yet the incentives facing individual countries work in the opposite direction.

The theoretical arguments for supposing that co-operation will not develop are compelling. But they can hardly be complete. Co-operation *does* take place and is often codified in international agreements. Some of these are woefully ineffective—a famous example being the International Convention for the Regulation of Whaling (1946) which established the IWC. Others do appear to have achieved a great deal. Of these last, the Montreal Protocol on Substances that Deplete the Ozone Layer (1987) seems the most impressive, because it demands that its many signatories undertake substantial reductions in their emissions of ozone-depleting chlorofluorocarbons (CFCs) and halons. Though agreements dealing with unidirectional externalities are rare and almost invariably toothless, there is one—the World Heritage Convention—that at least holds some promise. This agreement places responsibility for safeguarding natural environments like the Serengeti and the Galapagos Islands on a community of nations, and could be invoked to protect the remaining tropical rain forests. There is clearly a need to explore why international co-operation might develop, and what the significance of particular forms of co-operation might be.

To make any progress we will need a basis from which to assess whether co-operation can in fact be expected to achieve much. Contrary to Hardin's (1968) famous allegory of the commons, the absence of co-operation need not lead to tragedy. Section II discusses some of the parameters that are important in determining the potential gains to co-operation. Having drawn the boundaries, we then consider how we might move closer to the full co-operative solution, the global optimum. Non-co-operation may sometimes wear the disguise of co-operation, and section III shows that an outcome better than the purely nationalistic one can emerge even where binding agreements are absent. Effective management of global environmental resources does however seem to rely on the more formal institution of international law. Section IV discusses the rudiments of a model that explains why countries would co-operate when the free-rider problem must surely bite, and what international agreements mean for global social welfare and the welfare of citizens of individual countries. Just as failure to co-operate may not lead to tragedy, so co-operation may not buy us very much. Indeed, combining the analysis of the potential gains to co-operation with this model of formal agreements, it can be shown that co-operation is sometimes hardest to obtain when it is most needed.

II. THE POTENTIAL GAINS TO CO-OPERATION

Where a global externality is unidirectional, the country causing the externality will, in the absence of a negotiated settlement, ignore the damages its activities impose on other countries. This is the full *non-co-operative* outcome. The full *co-operative* outcome is found by internalizing the externality. In this case the country inflicting the externality chooses its actions so as to maximize the net benefits of all countries, including itself. Global net benefits will of course be higher in this case. The difference between the global net benefits for the co-operative and non-co-operative outcomes defines the potential gains to co-operation.

Where the externalities of concern are reciprocal in nature, every country has some incentive to take unilateral action even in the absence of a binding agreement. Furthermore, the strength of this incentive will depend on the actions taken by all other countries. An example of a reciprocal externality is the emission of a global pollutant. If one country reduces its emissions, it will benefit from the improved environmental quality, provided other countries do not increase their emissions so as to fully offset the one country's action. The other countries will benefit partly by being able to increase their emissions somewhat and partly by enjoying a cleaner environment (again, provided their increase in emissions does not entirely offset the one country's extra abatement). The extent of the benefit enjoyed by the conserving country will clearly depend on the actions taken by the other countries, and of course all countries are subject to a similar calculus. It is this interdependence which makes calculation of the potential gains to co-operative management of global common property more difficult. It is better, then, that we work with a specific model.

To fix ideas, reconsider the problem of global pollution. Suppose that the relevant number of countries is N. One might think that N would include all the world's countries, but that need not be so, a point we return to later. Let us however suppose for simplicity that N does include all countries and that each is identical. Each, therefore, emits the same quantity of a pollutant *ex ante*—that is, before the game is played—and each faces the same abatement cost and benefit functions. The problem is then perfectly symmetric. To simplify the analysis further, assume that the *marginal* abatement cost and benefit functions are linear. Clearly, the marginal abatement cost schedule for each country must depend on its own abatement level, while each country's marginal abatement benefit function must depend on *world-wide* abatement.

In the absence of any co-operation, each country will maximize its own net benefits of abatement and in so doing will choose a level of abatement at which its own marginal abatement cost equals its own marginal abatement benefit.[5] This is the non-co-operative (Nash equilibrium) solution to this game, and it is shown as abatement level Q^* in Figure 1. Were countries to co-operate fully, they would seek to maximize the global net benefits of abatement. Since we have assumed that all countries are identical, the global net benefits of abatement can be defined as the sum of every country's net benefits of abatement. In maximizing the global net benefits of abatement, each country will choose a level of abatement at which its own marginal costs of abatement equal the global marginal benefits of abatement, or the sum of the marginal abatement benefits enjoyed by all countries.[6] The full co-operative solution to this game is shown as abatement level Q^{**} in Figure 1.

Figure 1
Graphical Illustration of the Potential Gains to Co-operation

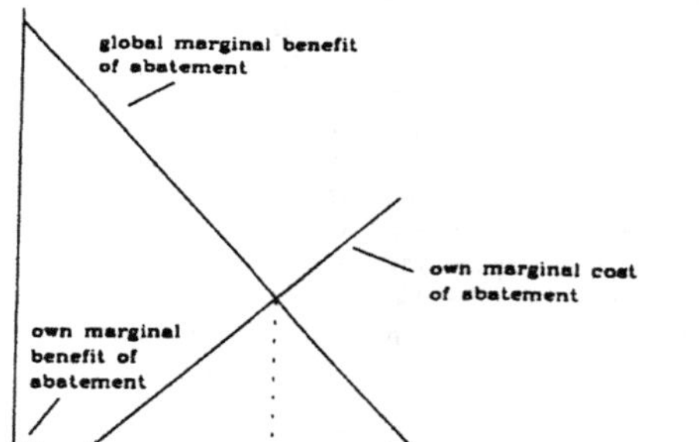

[5] I am assuming here that every country believes that its choice of an abatement level will not alter the choices of the other countries; that is, I am assuming zero conjectural variations. One can impose positive or negative conjectures, but these assumptions would be *ad hoc*. Alternatively, we could determine a consistent conjectures equilibrium—that is, one in whose neighbourhood every country's conjectures are confirmed by the responses of the other countries. Cornes and Sandler (1983) find that consistent conjectures can lead to even greater overuse of the resource compared with the Nash equilibrium.

[6] This is of course nothing but a restatement of Samuelson's (1954) rule for the optimal provision of public goods. For an alternative presentation of these principles, see Dasgupta's (1982) model of a global fishery.

OXFORD REVIEW OF ECONOMIC POLICY, VOL. 6, NO. 1

One sees immediately that the full co-operative solution demands greater abatement but, equally, gives to every country a greater net benefit. For a given size of N, the difference between Q^* and Q^{**} can be shown to depend on the slopes of the marginal abatement benefit and cost curves. Denote the (absolute value of the) slope of each country's marginal abatement benefit curve by the letter b, and the slope of each country's marginal abatement cost curve by the letter c. Then it can be shown that the discrepancy will tend to be small whenever c/b is either 'large' or 'small' (see Barrett, 1989). The approximate implication of this result is that fairly innocuous pollutants (that is, pollutants for which b is small) that are very costly to control (that is, that have a large c) do not cause too great a problem. Nor do extremely hazardous pollutants (that is, pollutants associated with a large b) that are cheap to control (that is, pollutants that have a small c). In the former case, even collective action will not call for large abatement levels. In the latter, countries will want to abate substantial quantities of emissions unilaterally. The real problem is with pollutants whose marginal abatement benefit and cost curves are both either steep or flat—that is, hazardous pollutants that are costly to control, and mildly offensive pollutants that can be controlled at little cost. Of these, the former type naturally causes the greatest concern, for the cost of failing to co-operate in this case is very, very high.

Unidirectional and reciprocal externalities are plainly different in their effects. A country has no incentive to abate its emissions if the externality is unidirectional (provided side payments are ruled out), even if the pollutant is highly toxic. Not so if the externality is reciprocal in nature. For then the emitting country will have strong private incentives to control its emissions.

III. NON-CO-OPERATIVE ENVIRONMENTAL PROTECTION

The politics of global environmental protection are not as sterile as the above models would imply. Once we permit alternative strategies to be chosen, widen the choice sets themselves, and allow motivations other than self-interest (narrowly defined) to guide decision-making, global environmental protection can be enhanced.

(i) Supergames

In the above games, strategies are chosen once, and the games are never repeated. But in the common property game countries are unavoidably locked in a continuing relationship, and this leaves open the possibility that they may retaliate and hence that co-operative strategies may be countenanced. Suppose then that all countries choose one of two strategies: they either choose the full co-operative abatement level Q^{**} initially, and continue to choose Q^{**} in every future period provided all other countries chose Q^{**} in every previous period; or they choose not to co-operate in any period.[7] Then the co-operative trigger strategy will constitute an equilibrium to this supergame provided the rate of discount is sufficiently low (for then the gains to choosing the non-co-operative strategy will be low, too; see Friedman, 1986). Although this supergame equilibrium entails co-operation, the co-operation is tacit and is enforced by means of a non-co-operative mechanism, retaliation; there is no explicit agreement, no open negotiation.[8]

One variant of this game involves countries adopting a convention that says that a subset of countries should co-operate in the face of free-riding by the others (see Sugden, 1986). It may, for example, be believed that the industrialized countries should co-operate to reduce emissions of CFCs or greenhouse gases (because it was their emissions that caused the environmental reservoirs to be filled in the first place), and that the poor countries should be allowed to free ride. In this game, each of the members of the subset could adopt the trigger strategy with respect to the subset, and each of the others could simply choose their optimal non-co-operative responses. This latter possibility may be fragile, because different countries may have different views about which should co-operate and

[7] If countries choose not to co-operate in the initial period, they need not choose Q^* in this period. The reason for this is that the optimal non-co-operative abatement level is contingent on the abatement levels chosen by the other countries.

[8] Axelrod's (1984) tournaments of the repeated prisoners' dilemma game suggest that behaviour in the disguise of co-operation may well emerge. Whether his findings carry over to the common property game with many players, however, is as yet unknown.

which should not. This ambiguity may help explain why unilateral action to reduce CFC emissions was limited (US Environmental Protection Agency, 1988, p. 30576):

> In 1978 the United States restricted the use of CFCs in aerosols. While several nations adopted similar restrictions (e.g. Sweden, Canada, Norway) and others partially cut back their use (European nations, Japan), there was no widespread movement to follow the United States' lead. Concerns existed then that other nations had failed to act because the United States and a few other nations were making the reductions thought necessary to protect the ozone layer. Similar concerns exist today that unilateral action could result in 'free riding' by some other nations.

It is not obvious how sufferers of a unidirectional externality could punish the offending nation. But so long as the countries are engaged in some form of exchange, potent weapons may be at the sufferers' disposal. The Packwood–Magnuson Amendment to the US Fishery Conservation and Management Act (1976) requires the US government to retaliate whenever foreign nationals compromise the effectiveness of the IWC. An offending nation automatically loses half its allocation of fish products taken from US waters, and if the country refuses to improve its behaviour within a year, its right to fish in US waters is revoked.

(ii) Matching

In the one-shot common property game, each country chooses an abatement level and nothing else. There is no reason why a country's choices need be limited in this way. We could, for example, allow countries to choose a 'base' abatement level—that is, a level of abatement which is not explicitly contingent on the abatement levels chosen by other countries—and a 'matching rate'—in our example, a fraction of the sum of all countries' base abatement levels. In effect, countries would then voluntarily subsidize each other's abatement levels. In the original game, one unit of abatement by country i buys country i one unit less of global emission (assuming that the emissions of all other countries are held fixed). In the matching game, one unit of abatement by country i may yield a much greater reduction in global emission. Matching might improve matters—Guttman (1978) shows that under certain conditions matching can sustain the full co-operative solution. But in the management of global common property, matching is rarely invoked. Recently, Norway announced that it would allocate one-tenth of one per cent of its GDP each year to a fund on climate change if other industrial countries matched its contribution (on a GDP percentage basis). The offer has yet to be taken up. Environmental groups in the United States have argued that the US should unilaterally surpass the reductions specified in the Montreal Protocol and at the same time impose restrictions on imports of products containing or made with CFCs from countries that fail to agree to make the same reductions. Their plea was rejected by the authorities (US Environmental Protection Agency, 1988, p. 30574).

(iii) Morality

In the models discussed thus far, the welfare of every country is assumed to depend solely on its *own* net benefits. An alternative way of looking at the problem is to assume that countries act according to some moral principle which requires that they take stock of the effect their actions have on the welfare of other countries. For example, suppose every country but one reduces its emissions of some global pollutant by at least x tonnes. Let us further suppose that the recalcitrant nation would like all others to reduce their emissions by y tonnes each. Then the leaders of the recalcitrant nation might feel compelled to obey the rule: if $y > x$ then we are morally obligated to reduce our emissions by at least x tonnes. If countries obey this rule, then the free-rider problem can be mitigated (see Sugden, 1984). That moral principles may guide non-co-operative abatement is suggested by the following remarks made by the House of Commons Environment Committee (1984, p. lxxi) in its report recommending that the UK join the Thirty Per Cent Club:[9]

> As our inquiry has progressed the stance of the United Kingdom has become increasingly isolated by its refusal to legislate to reduce SO_2 and NO_x emissions. Since our work began three West European countries

[9] The Thirty Per Cent Club consists of the countries that have signed the Protocol to the 1979 Convention on Long-Range Transboundary Air Pollution on the Reduction of Sulphur Emissions or their Transboundary Fluxes by at least 30 Per Cent (1985). The UK has not joined this 'club' but it has committed itself to substantial reductions in sulphur dioxide and nitrogen oxides emissions by agreeing to comply with the European Community Large Combustion Plant Directive.

> have joined those already in the 30 per cent club, and several Eastern European countries have committed themselves to reduce transfrontier emissions by 30 per cent. SO_2 emissions in the United Kingdom have indeed fallen by 37 per cent since 1970, but the levels of high-stack emissions which affect remote areas have not fallen. In 1970, when the 37 per cent fall began, we were the largest emitter in Western Europe. In 1984, we are still the largest emitter. NO_x emissions have not fallen. In Western Europe only West Germany deposits more SO_2 in other countries than does the United Kingdom, and further significant reductions cannot be achieved by either without controls.

The Committee's concern in this passage lies less with the net benefits to the UK of reducing emissions than with how UK abatement has lagged behind the rest of Europe. Indeed, the Committee's evaluation did not even consider whether the other European countries were abating more simply because it was in their own self interest to do so. The argument seems to be: 'The other European nations are reducing their emissions, so we should, too.' Compared with the supergame problem, co-operation in this case is not instrumentally important—the Environment Committee did not seek to reduce UK emissions so that others would reduce theirs even further—but intrinsically important. Concerns about fairness have been shown to militate against the free-rider problem in experimental tests (Marwell and Ames, 1981). However, in the next section we shall see that in a bargaining situation, obeying moral principles may serve only to undermine the cause of environmental protection.

IV. CO-OPERATIVE ENVIRONMENTAL PROTECTION

In the absence of co-operation, outcomes better than the full non-co-operative one can sometimes develop, at least in principle. But such instances seem to be rare. Even two close neighbours with strong trading ties can fail to arrive at a preferred solution, as the disagreement between the United States and Canada over the exploitation of the North Pacific fur seal illustrates. Following an initial conflict between the two nations over the pelagic seal hunt, a Tribunal Arbitration was convened at the request of the two parties (with Great Britain acting for Canada). In late 1893 the Tribunal decided that the United States did not have territorial jurisdiction over the Bering Sea, and hence could not keep Canadian sealing vessels out of these waters. This effectively sanctioned open-access harvesting of the species, and co-operation proved impossible to secure (Paterson and Wilen, 1977, p. 94):

> Following the decision of the Tribunal, the diplomatic efforts of both Great Britain and the United States had been directed to convincing the other to reduce its sealing in order to allow the herd to recover from earlier depradations. No agreement could be reached and in 1897 the United States unilaterally forbade its citizens to engage in pelagic sealing in the North Pacific. At the same time quota adjustments were made as the herd diminished in size. So strong was the reaction to the declining herd size and the continued Canadian pelagic hunt that a bill reached the [United States] Senate which called for the complete destruction of the herd. It did not pass . . .

Better management of the population had to await the signing of the North Pacific Fur Seal Treaty by Great Britain, the United States, Japan, and Russia in 1911—a remarkable agreement that remains in force today.[10] Effective management of global environmental resources seems to demand that countries co-operate openly and put their signatures on international agreements, treaties, and conventions. Explanations for why co-operation of this kind might emerge are offered below.

(i) International Environmental Agreements

Consider the following modification to the common property game described earlier. Suppose a subset of the N identical countries 'collude' by signing an international environmental agreement and that the remaining countries continue to act non-co-operatively. Suppose further that the signatories to the agreement choose their collective abatement level while taking as given the abatement decision functions of the non-signatories, while the latter countries continue to behave atomistically and choose their abatement levels on the assumption that the abatement levels of all other countries are fixed. That is, the signatories act as 'abatement leaders', and the non-signatories as 'abatement followers'. Quite clearly, we would

[10] For legal background on this treaty and its successors, see Lyster (1985).

like the number of signatories, the terms of the agreement, and the abatement levels of all non-signatories to be determined jointly. We also require that the agreement itself is stable. A stable agreement is one where non-signatories do not wish to sign the agreement and signatories do not wish to renege on their commitment. Then it can be shown that for identical countries with linear marginal abatement benefit and cost functions a stable international environmental agreement always exists (Barrett, 1989).

The solution to this problem exhibits many of the features of actual agreements. The net benefits realized by both signatories and non-signatories are higher than in the earlier problem where negotiation was ruled out. What is more, the signatories would like the non-co-operators to sign the agreement. However, non-signatories do better by free-riding.

It is important to emphasize that the agreement is *self-enforcing*. Any signatory that renounces its commitment can reduce its abatement level and hence its costs. However, in pulling out of the agreement, the number of co-operators is reduced and the agreement itself is weakened; the remaining co-operators reduce their abatement levels, too. A signatory will want to pull out of an agreement only if the saving in abatement costs exceeds the resulting loss in benefits. Similarly, a country that joins an agreement will have to abate more and hence incur higher costs. But the very act of joining will strengthen the agreement; the other co-operators will also increase their abatement levels. Joining appears attractive if the resulting increase in benefits realized by the new signatory exceeds the increase in costs that this country must incur in committing itself to the terms of the agreement.

Real treaties are not rewritten with every defection or accession, but mechanisms are at work that have a similar effect. It is common for treaties to come into force only after being ratified by a minimum number of signatories. The Montreal Protocol did not come into force until it had been ratified by at least eleven countries representing at least two-thirds of global consumption of the controlled substances. It is also common for treaties to be reviewed and altered when necessary and often at regular intervals. The Montreal Protocol is being reviewed in 1990, and is then expected to be strengthened. That this agreement is self-enforcing is suggested by a comment made by the US Environmental Protection Agency (EPA) (1988, p. 30573):

> EPA judged that the obvious need for broad international adherence to the Protocol counseled against the United States' deviating from the Protocol, because any significant deviation could lessen other countries' motivation to participate.

Self-enforcement is essential in any model of international environmental agreements because nation states cannot be forced to perform their legal obligations. A country can be taken to the International Court of Justice for failing to comply with the terms of a treaty, but only with the defendant's permission. Even then, the disputing countries cannot be forced to comply with the Court's decision.[11]

What are the gains to having international environmental agreements? The answer depends partly on the number of relevant and potential signatories. When N is large, international environmental agreements can achieve very little no matter the number of signatories. The reason, quite simply, is that when N is large, defection or accession by any country has only a negligible effect on the abatement of the other co-operators.

Determination of N is not always a trivial matter. Some treaties do not restrict participation, but in these cases many of the signatories may have no effective say in environmental protection. Over 100 countries have signed the 1963 Partial Nuclear Test Ban Treaty, but only a few signatories possess nuclear weapons technology. The 1967 United Nations Treaty on Principles Governing the Activities of States in the Exploration and Use of Outer Space including the Moon and Other Celestial Bodies has been ratified by scores of countries but not by the two with space technology capabilities—the US and USSR. Other treaties explicitly restrict participation. The Agreement on the Conservation of Polar Bears can only be signed by five circumpolar countries (Canada, Denmark (including Greenland), Norway, the US, and the

[11] See Lyster (1985) for a discussion of other compliance mechanisms.

USSR). To become a signatory to the Antarctic Treaty of 1959 a country must maintain a scientific research station in the Antarctic and be unanimously accepted by existing parties to the agreement. In these cases non-signatories may quite clearly be affected by how the signatories manage the resource. Signatories to the Antarctic treaty voted recently to allow mineral exploration, despite appeals by non-signatories to designate Antarctica a nature reserve.

In the above model, N was assumed to represent both the number of countries that emit a (uniformly mixed) pollutant into the environment and the number harmed as a consequence. However, for some problems the number of emitters may be less than the number of sufferers (for global pollutants, all countries). When the number of emitters is small, an international environmental agreement signed by a subset of emitters may well have a significant effect on the welfare of these countries. However, the effect on global welfare may still be small because the emitters have no incentive to take into account the welfare losses suffered by non-emitting nations. The appropriate way to account for countries that do not emit the pollutant but nevertheless suffer the consequences of others' emissions is to admit side payments—payments which induce emitting nations to undertake greater abatement but which leave all parties no worse off compared to the situation where side payments are forbidden. We return to the side payments issue later.

The gains to international co-operation can also be shown to depend on c, the slope of each country's marginal abatement cost curve; and b, the (absolute value of the) slope of each country's marginal abatement benefit curve. For a given size of N, the number of signatories to a treaty increases as c/b falls. This suggests that we should expect to observe a large number of signatories (in absolute terms) when N is 'large', the marginal abatement cost curve is flat, and the marginal abatement benefit curve steep. However, we already know that when c/b is 'small' the benefit of having an agreement is diminished. It is commonly asserted that treaties signed by a large number of countries accomplish little of substance: 'The greater the number of participants in the formulation of a treaty, the weaker or more ambiguous its provisions are likely to be since they have to reflect compromises making them acceptable to every State involved' (Lyster, 1985, p. 4). This analysis suggests that the reason treaties signed by a large number of countries appear to effect little additional abatement is not that the signatories are heterogeneous—although that may be a contributing factor. Nor is the reason solely that in these cases N is also large. A major insight of the model is that a large subset of N will sign an agreement only when the non-co-operative and full co-operative outcomes are already close.

This latter observation may not seem consistent with all the evidence. The Montreal Protocol, for example, demands of its signatories significant reductions in the production and consumption of the hard CFCs and halons, and about 46 countries have already signed the agreement—a fairly large number by any standard. As Table 1 shows, the effect of the agreement on ozone depletion is estimated to be very significant. Percentage ozone depletion is estimated to be reduced from 50 to 2 per cent in 2075 as a result of the agreement. But of course each country has some incentive to take unilateral action in reducing emissions; in doing so all other countries will benefit, but so too will the country taking the action. Furthermore, non-signatories to the agreement may well face an incentive to abate less than they would otherwise for the simple reason that greater abatement on the part of signatories improves the environment for non-signatories as well. Hence it is by no means clear that the agreement necessarily means that the environ-

Table 1
Estimates of the Reduction in Percentage Ozone Depletion Effected by the Montreal Protocol

Case	2000	2025	2050	2075
No controls	1.0	4.6	15.7	50.0
Montreal Protocol	0.8	1.5	1.9	1.9

Source: US EPA (1988), Table 3, p. 30575.

ment and global welfare will be significantly better off, contrary to what the figures in Table 1 imply. What the model does suggest is that so many countries would not have committed themselves to the agreement in the first place unless they already intended to take substantial unilateral action. In other words, although the agreement itself may effect only little additional abatement, the very fact that so many countries have signed the agreement suggests that the potential gains to co-operation were in this instance not very great.

What does the model predict about the prospects of an agreement being reached on global warming? *N* will again be large, and this will militate against significant united action. However, in this case *c/b* will be large, too; the marginal costs of abating carbon dioxide emissions will rise very steeply as fossil fuels must be substituted for and energy is conserved. This suggests that the number of signatories to an agreement would be small, and that little additional abatement could be effected by co-operation. The tragedy is that in the case of global warming fuller co-operation would probably result in huge gains in global welfare.[12]

(ii) Leadership

It is sometimes asserted that countries should, on their own, do more than the non-co-operative solution demands of them. US environmental groups, for example, have argued that the US should have taken greater unilateral action before the Montreal Protocol was drafted, that it should now comply with the terms of the Protocol in advance of the deadlines, and that it should exceed the agreed emission reductions and phase out production and consumption of these chemicals entirely. The House of Commons Energy Committee (1989, p. xvii), in its recent investigation on the greenhouse effect, recommended '... that the UK should ... consider setting an example to the world by seriously tackling its own emission problems in advance of international action, especially where it is economically prudent to do so'.

We have already seen that such 'unselfish' unilateral actions need not be matched by other countries. The United States, Canada, Sweden, and Norway banned the use of CFCs in non-essential aerosols in the late 1970s, and yet other countries did not reciprocate.[13] Unilateral restrictions on pelagic sealing in the North Pacific by the US were not duplicated by Canada. We have also seen that countries may wish to give in to their moral beliefs and embrace a less insular view of their responsibilities. An important question is whether 'unselfish' unilateral action can be expected to have a positive influence on international negotiations. If one country (or group of countries) abates more than the Nash non-co-operative solution demands, and all others choose the abatement levels that are optimal for them in a non-co-operative setting, will the environment be any better protected when international treaties are later negotiated?

In a two-country analysis, Hoel (1989) shows that the answer depends on whether the unilateral action is taken before agreement is reached and is not contingent on that agreement or whether the action is a commitment to abate more than the negotiated agreement requires. Hoel shows that in the former case, 'unselfish' unilateral action may compromise negotiations and lead, ultimately, to *greater* emissions than would have occurred had both countries behaved 'selfishly'. In the latter case, however, the country's announced commitment to overfulfil its negotiated abatement level can be expected to reduce total emissions.

There is an obvious incentive compatability problem with this tactic, for the 'unselfish' country could do better by reneging on its commitment (the agreement is therefore *not* self-enforcing). Nevertheless, the analysis shows that the desire by environmentalists and others to reduce total emissions may not be well served by their calls for 'unselfish' unilateral action, a point that the EPA stressed in defending its ozone depletion policy (1988, p. 30574): 'Unilateral action by the United States would not significantly add to efforts to protect the ozone layer and could even be counter productive by undermining other nations' incentive to participate in the Protocol.'

It is important to note that the US and the European Community announced their intentions to phase out production and consumption of the ozone-

[12] The analysis given here is by necessity over-simplified. For a more detailed analysis, see Barrett (1990).

[13] Reciprocity was certainly not full. The European Community, for example, passed two decisions limiting production capacity of the so-called hard CFCs (CFC-11 and -12) and reducing their use in aerosols by 30 per cent.

depleting chemicals by the end of the century *after* the Montreal Protocol came into force but before re-negotiation talks had started. It would be wrong, however, to ascribe these developments simply to 'unselfish' behaviour. After all, the world's largest manufacturer of CFCs, US-based Du Pont, announced its intention to phase out production of CFCs by the end of the century *before* the phase-out decisions were taken by the US and EC. Three days after the EC decided to phase out CFCs, the chairman of the leading European producer of CFCs, ICI, declared that production of CFCs should cease 'as soon after 1998 as is practicable'. Much more is at work here.[14]

(iii) Efficient Co-operation

Signatories to an international environmental agreement are assumed to maximize the net benefits accruing to the *group*. This means, among other things, that the marginal abatement costs of every signatory must be equal; the abatement undertaken by the group must be achieved at minimum total cost.

How realistic is this assumption? In the case of the Montreal Protocol, the assumption is not very wide of the mark. The Protocol imposes on every industrial country signatory an obligation to reduce its production and consumption of CFCs by an equal percentage. This requirement on its own is inefficient because at the margin the costs of complying with the Protocol will surely vary. For example, the UK can apparently meet its obligations by simply prohibiting the use of CFCs in aerosols—an action that is nearly costless. The US banned the use of CFCs in aerosols many years ago, and hence can meet the terms of the Protocol only by instituting more costly measures. However, the Protocol allows limited international *trading* in emission reductions. For any signatory, CFC production through mid-1998 can be 10 per cent, and from mid-1998 onwards 15 per cent, higher than it would have been without trading provided the increase in production by this signatory is offset by a decrease in production by another signatory. Furthermore, trades of consumption (but, strangely, not production) quotas are permitted by the Protocol within the European Community. These provisions will help increase the efficiency of attaining the total emission reduction implicit in the agreement, although they almost certainly do not go far enough.

(iv) Side Payments

The equilibrium in the model of international environmental agreements is determined by a concept of stability that prohibits side payments. An important question is whether side payments might effect a Pareto improvement. To investigate this issue, reconsider the concept of stability employed in the model. In equilibrium, non-signatories do better than signatories, but no country can do better by changing its status. Signatories want non-co-operators to sign the agreement, because their net benefits would then increase. But non-signatories do worse by signing. Hence, without compensating payments, non-signatories will not want to sign the agreement. It is in this sense that the agreement is stable.

However, the very fact that signatories do better if non-co-operators sign the agreement suggests that trade might be possible. In particular, it might be possible for signatories to make side payments to a subset of non-co-operators to encourage them to sign the agreement. All might be made better off. It is in fact very easy to show that this can happen, that an international environmental agreement that specifies abatement levels *and* side payments can manage the global common property resource better than one that prohibits side payments.

An important feature of the World Heritage Convention is that it does admit side payments. The Convention established a World Heritage Fund that is used to help protect natural environments of 'outstanding universal value'. Each party to the Convention (there are over 90 signatories) is required to provide the Fund every two years with at least one per cent of its contribution to the regular budget of UNESCO.[15] In practice this means that the Fund is almost entirely financed by the industrial countries. Clearly, both the industrial and poor countries benefit from the Convention—otherwise

[14] See Barrett (1990) for an analysis of these developments.

[15] The United States and the UK continued to contribute to the Fund even after withdrawing their funding from UNESCO.

they would not have signed it—but the poor countries may not have signed the Convention were it not for the Fund. Though the Fund is small, the mechanism could prove instrumental in protecting many of the world's remaining natural environments, including the tropical rain forests.

The World Heritage Convention is unique among international environmental agreements for incorporating side payments. But the need for side payments is not unique to the conservation of natural environments and wildlife. It has, for example, become increasingly clear that the success of the Montreal Protocol will ultimately hinge on the accession of non-signatories to the Protocol. Concern has specially been voiced about the need to get the poor countries—and, in particular, China and India—to sign the Protocol. These countries have declared their need for financial assistance, and the issue of setting up a global fund for protecting the ozone layer is likely to dominate discussion at the next meeting of the Protocol's signatories. It would seem to be something that cannot be avoided.

REFERENCES

Axelrod, R. (1984), *The Evolution of Cooperation*, New York, Basic Books.

Barrett, S. (1989), 'On the Nature and Significance of International Environmental Agreements', mimeo, London Business School.

— (1990), *Ozone Holes, Greenhouse Gases, and Economic Policy*, London, Institute of Economic Affairs (forthcoming).

Coase, R. H. (1960), 'The Problem of Social Cost', *Journal of Law and Economics*, 3, 1–44.

Cornes, R. and Sandler, T. (1983), 'On Commons and Tragedies', *American Economic Review*, 73, 787–92.

Dasgupta, P. (1982), *The Control of Resources*, Cambridge, MA., Harvard University.

Demsetz, H. (1964), 'The Exchange and Enforcement of Property Rights', *Journal of Law and Economics*, 7, 11–26.

— (1967), 'Toward a Theory of Property Rights', *American Economic Review*, 57, 347–59.

Friedman, J. W. (1986), *Game Theory with Applications to Economics*, Oxford, Oxford University Press.

Groves, T. and Ledyard, J. (1977), 'Optimal Allocation of Public Goods: A Solution to the "Free Rider" Problem', *Econometrica*, 45, 783–809.

Guttman, J. M. (1978), 'Understanding Collective Action: Matching Behavior', *American Economic Review Papers and Proceedings*, 68, 251–5.

Hardin, G. (1968), 'The Tragedy of the Commons', *Science*, 162, 1243–8.

Hoel, M. (1989), 'Global Environmental Problems: The Effects of Unilateral Actions Taken by One Country', Working Paper No. 11, Department of Economics, University of Oslo.

House of Commons Energy Committee (1989), *Energy Policy Implications of the Greenhouse Effect*, vol. 1, London, HMSO.

House of Commons Environment Committee (1984), *Acid Rain*, vol. 1, London, HMSO.

Lyster, S. (1985), *International Wildlife Law*, Cambridge, Grotius.

Marwell, G. E. and Ames, R. E. (1981), 'Economists Free Ride, Does Anyone Else?', *Journal of Public Economics*, 15, 295–310.

Paterson, D. G. and Wilen, J. (1977), 'Depletion and Diplomacy: The North Pacific Seal Hunt, 1886–1910', *Research in Economic History*, 2, 81–139.

Samuelson, P. (1954), 'The Pure Theory of Public Expenditure', *Review of Economics and Statistics*, 36, 387–9.

Sugden, R. (1984), 'Reciprocity: The Supply of Public Goods through Voluntary Contributions', *Economic Journal*, 94, 772–87.

— (1986), *The Economics of Rights, Co-operation and Welfare*, Oxford, Basil Blackwell.

Trail Smelter Arbitral Tribunal (1939), 'Decision', *American Journal of International Law*, 33, 182–212.

— (1941), 'Decision', *American Journal of International Law*, 35, 684–736.

US Environmental Protection Agency (1988), 'Protection of Stratospheric Ozone; Final Rule', *Federal Register*, 53, 30566–602.

[2]

JOURNAL OF ENVIRONMENTAL ECONOMICS AND MANAGEMENT 20, 55–70 (1991)

Global Environmental Problems: The Effects of Unilateral Actions Taken by One Country*

MICHAEL HOEL

University of Oslo, P.O. Box 1095 Blindern, N-0317 Oslo 3, Norway

Received May 25, 1989; revised August 28, 1989

In global environmental problems, each country's own contribution to worldwide emissions is small, so there is little a country can do by itself. To solve global environmental problems one needs coordinated actions between countries. Environmental groups often advocate that in spite of the global character of the problem, a country ought to take unilateral actions to reduce its environmentally harmful emissions. The argument for such unilateral actions is that they at least give a contribution in the right direction (however small), and also that by "setting a good example" of this type one might affect the behavior of other countries, and/or improve the chances of reaching international agreements of coordinated reductions of harmful emissions. The paper gives an analysis of the consequences of unilateral reductions of harmful emissions. It is shown that such a policy will generally affect the outcome of international negotiations about reduced emissions. The outcome of such negotiations may very well imply *higher* total emissions when one country reduces its emissions unilaterally than if both countries act selfishly.

1. INTRODUCTION

Some of the most serious environmental problems have a global character. Global environmental problems are characterized by the environmental effect on each country only depending on the worldwide aggregate emission of some harmful material, and not on each country's contribution to these total emissions. An example of such a global environmental problem is the effect of emissions of CFC on the ozone layer. Another example is the effect of emission of carbon dioxide and other greenhouse gases on the global climate. The *consequences* of a thinner ozone layer and a warmer global climate may be quite different for different countries, but the environmental changes themselves depend only on worldwide aggregate emissions. (For general discussions of global and transfrontier environmental problems, see e.g., d'Arge [1, 2].)

Environmental problems related to the ozone layer and the global climate are by their nature serious. Moreover, their global character makes them difficult to solve: Each country's own contribution to worldwide emissions is small, so there is

*This paper is part of the research project "Energy and Society" at the Center for Applied Research (SAF), Department of Economics, University of Oslo. The hospitality of the Norwegian School of Management, where this paper was written, is gratefully acknowledged. Participants at seminars at the University of Oslo, the Norwegian School of Management, and the Central Bureau of Statistics have given useful comments and criticism. In particular, I am grateful to K. A. Brekke, R. Golombek, Aa. Hylland, C. Riis, J. Vislie and two anonymous referees for their comments to earlier versions of the paper.

0095-0696/91 $3.00

little a country can do by itself. To solve global environmental problems one needs coordinated actions between countries, which is difficult in the absence of suitable institutions which can make and enforce global decisions.

Understandably, environmental groups are often frustrated by the prisoners' dilemma type of situation which characterizes global environmental problems. They often advocate that in spite of the global character of the problem, a country ought to take unilateral actions to reduce its environmentally harmful emissions. The argument for such unilateral actions is that they at least give a contribution in the right direction (however small), and also that by "setting a good example" of this type one might affect the behavior of other countries, and/or improve the chances of reaching international agreements of coordinated reductions of harmful emissions.

There are examples of governments taking unilateral actions as a step towards improving the global environment: Norway decided to sharply reduce its CFC emissions unilaterally before any international agreement was reached. With less than 1% of the world's GDP, Norway's contribution to global CFC emissions are of course negligible. Recently, most West European countries and the USA have decided to cut back emissions of CFC gases in excess of the standards set by the Montreal convention of 1987 (which is a 50% reduction of the 1986 level by the year 2000).

This paper gives an analysis of the consequences of unilateral reductions of harmful emissions. I do *not* take up the question of whether such action from one country might lead to similar behavior from other countries. Instead I analyze the consequences of one country's reducing its emissions unilaterally when other countries' policy is dictated purely by their self-interest.

To simplify, only two countries are considered in most of the analysis. In practice, each "country" may be a group of countries who have coordinated their policies. The two groups of countries could, e.g., be industrialized countries versus LDCs, or "environmentally concerned countries" versus "material consumption oriented countries." A brief discussion of the n-country case is given in Section 6.

In Section 2, it is shown how harmful emissions are determined as equilibria of noncooperative games in the absence of international agreements of reduced emissions. Sections 3 and 4 describe possible negotiated agreements on reduced emissions of environmentally harmful materials.

Sections 2–4 discuss unilateral actions in the context of the policy followed by a country in the absence of (or prior to) a negotiated agreement. A unilateral emission reduction is defined as a country choosing lower emissions than what follows from its true payoff function. It is shown that in the absence of a negotiated agreement, such a policy will normally lead to lower total emissions than a selfish policy. However, such a policy will generally also effect the outcome of international negotiations about reduced emissions. It is shown that the outcome of such negotiations may very well imply *higher* total emissions when one country reduces emissions unilaterally in the absence of an agreement than if both countries act selfishly. This will *always* be the case if the countries for some reason restrict their negotiations to equal or proportional reductions of harmful emissions.

Section 5 considers a different kind of unilateral action. Here it is assumed that countries negotiate about equal or proportional reductions of their emissions. A unilateral emission reduction is defined as an announced commitment to cut down ones emissions in excess of whatever negotiated agreement one reaches. Provided the country sticks to this commitment, total emissions will most likely be lower in this case than in the case when both countries act selfishly.

The n-country case is considered in Section 6, before some concluding remarks are given in Section 7.

2. NONCOOPERATIVE GAMES

There are two countries, $i = 1, 2$. Each country's reduction of environmentally harmful emissions is X_i $(i = 1, 2)$. The "reductions" X_1 and X_2 are relative to what the emissions would have been in the absence of any environmental concern.

The countries have benefit and cost functions $B_i(X_1 + X_2)$ and $C_i(X_i)$, $B_i' > 0$, $B_i'' < 0$, $C_i' > 0$, $C_i'' > 0$.[1] It is the global character of the environmental problem under consideration which implies that each country's benefit of emission reductions only depends on the *sum* of these reductions. The cost functions give reductions of output associated with the reductions of emissions.[2]

Consider first the Nash equilibrium of the game in which the countries choose their emissions simultaneously.[3] For given emissions from country 2, i.e., a given value of X_2, country 1 maximizes its payoff function $B_1(X_1 + X_2) - C_1(X_1)$ by choosing X_1 so that

$$B_1'(X_1 + X_2) = C_1'(X_1) \tag{2.1}$$

holds (for an interior solution, i.e. for $X_1 > 0$). This defines X_1 as a function of X_2, we call this function the response function of country 1, and denote it by $R_1(X_2)$. From (2.1) we find

$$-R_1'(X_2) = \frac{-B_1''}{C_1'' - B_1''} \in (0, 1). \tag{2.2}$$

Similarly, country 2's optimal reply to country 1's choice of X_1 is given by

$$B_2'(X_1 + X_2) = C_2'(X_2) \tag{2.3}$$

which defines country 2's response function $R_2(X_1)$. From (2.3) we have

$$-R_2'(X_1) = \frac{-B_2''}{C_2'' - B_2''} \in (0, 1). \tag{2.4}$$

These response functions are drawn in Fig. 1, together with some indifference curves for the two countries (denoted I_1 and I_2).[4,5]

[1] For some types of environmental problems, we may have $B_i''(x) > 0$ for some x-values for one or both countries. As we shall see, the main conclusions remain valid also for this case, as long as B_i'' is not too large.

[2] In practice, emission reductions in one country may affect real income in other countries through general equilibrium effects on prices of internationally traded goods. However, this is ignored in the present analysis.

[3] Similar games with "nonzero conjectural variations" have been studied by Cornes and Sandler [3, 4].

[4] A similar figure is used by Cornes and Sandler [4].

[5] Along an indifference curve I_1 (I_2), $B_1 - C_1$ $(B_2 - C_2)$ is constant. The indifference curves I_1 (I_2) are horizontal (vertical) where they intersect the response curve R_1 (R_2). The response curves for country 1 and 2 have the slopes $1/R_1'$ and R_2', respectively. The response curves and the curve L in Fig. 1 (and in Fig. 2) are for convenience drawn as straight lines, although they generally are nonlinear.

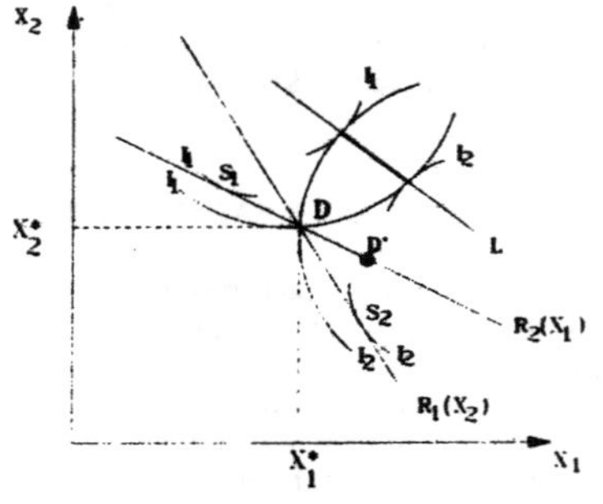

FIGURE 1

The Nash equilibrium of the simultaneous move game is given by the pair (X_1^*, X_2^*) satisfying (2.1) and (2.3), i.e., by $X_1^* = R_1(X_2^*)$ and $X_2^* = R_2(X_1^*)$. In Fig. 1 this equilibrium is given by the intersection of the two response functions, i.e., by the point D in Fig. 1. It follows from (2.2) and (2.4) that the response functions can only intersect once. If the game has an interior Nash equilibrium, this equilibrium is therefore unique.

The response functions need not intersect for any nonnegative (X_1, X_2) contributions. This is illustrated in Fig. 2, where D is the unique Nash equilibrium (given the restriction $X_1 \geq 0$). Note that for the limiting case of $C_i'' = 0$ $(i = 1, 2)$, both response functions have the slope -1. In this case we therefore must get an equilibrium of the type illustrated in Fig. 2, unless the two response functions coincide. The latter case occurs if, e.g., $C_i'' = 0$ and benefit and cost functions are equal for the two countries. In this case there is a continuum of equilibria: All (X_1, X_2)-combinations satisfying $B_i'(X_1 + X_2) = C_i'$ are Nash equilibria for this (rather implausible) special case.

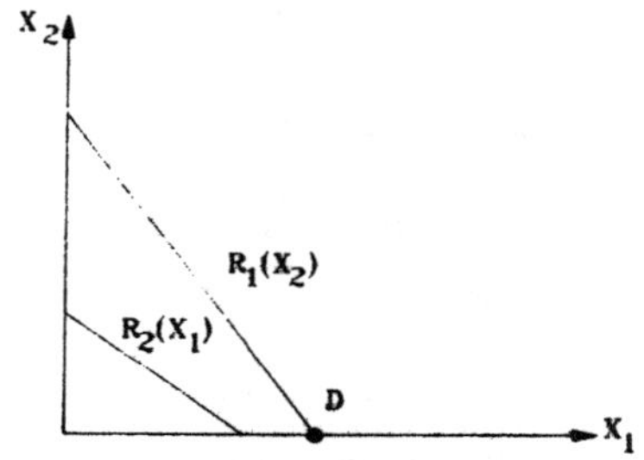

FIGURE 2

In the limiting case of $B_i'' = 0$ for one or both countries, the response function of one or both countries will be horizontal/vertical, but otherwise this limiting case doesn't differ from the general case.[6]

In the subsequent analysis, only interior solutions will be considered. Sufficient conditions for an interior solution are $C_i'(0) = 0$, $C_i'' > 0$, and $B_i'(x) > 0$ for all $x \geq 0$ $(i = 1, 2)$. With these conditions we get $R_i(X_j) > 0$ for all $X_j \geq 0$ $(i, j = 1, 2)$. Note that since X_i is defined as reductions relative to emissions in the absence of any environmental concern, $C_i'(0) = 0$ follows from any smooth production technology.

Our interest is in the consequence of one country (1, say) reducing its emissions in excess of what its true payoff function dictates. In a game theoretical context, it is not obvious how to define unilateral actions by one country, since the Nash equilibrium is completely determined by the payoff-functions of the countries. We shall define a unilateral action by country 1 as a situation in which country 1 plays the game as if it has the payoff function $B_1(X_1 + X_2) - C_1(X_1) + h \cdot (X_1 + X_2)$ where $h > 0$, although its true net benefit is $B_1(X_1 + X_2) - C_1(X_1)$.[7,8] With the payoff function $B_1 + h - C_1$, the behavior of country 1 is given by

$$B_1'(X_1 + X_2) + h = C_1'(X_1) \tag{2.1'}$$

instead of by (2.1). We shall denote the corresponding response function by $\bar{R}_1(X_2)$. Comparing (2.1′) with (2.1) it is clear that $\bar{R}_1(X_2)$ lies further to the right in Fig. 1 than $R_1(X_2)$, so that it also must intersect $R_2(X_2)$ at a point D' to the right of the intersection point D ($\bar{R}_1(X_2)$ is not drawn in Fig. 1). Moreover, it follows from (2.1′) that $\bar{R}_1'$ is given by the same expression as R_1', i.e., by (2.2).

We assume that country 2 plays according to its true payoff function, and that it knows that country 1 plays as if its payoff function is $B_1 + h - C_1$. This means that country 2 acts according to its response function, and that the new equilibrium will be at a point such as D' in Fig. 1. In other words, country 2 will increase its emissions. The reason for this result is that country 1's unilateral reduction of its emissions reduces the marginal benefit of emission reduction for country 2.[9]

Since $-R_2'(X_1) < 1$, it is clear that the unilateral emission reduction by country 1 gives lower total emissions than if country 1 acts selfishly. However, the smaller C_2'' is, the closer will $-R_2'(X_1)$ be to 1, and the less will $X_1 + X_2$ be affected by the increase in X_1. In the limiting case of $C_2'' = 0$ (but $C_1'' > 0$), country 1's choice of X_1 affects only the distribution of $X_1 + X_2$ between the two countries, while total emissions are unaffected by country 1's policy.

It is also of interest to study how country 1's unilateral action affects total welfare $W = B_1(X_1 + X_2) + B_2(X_1 + X_2) - C_1(X_1) - C_2(X_2)$. Differentiating with respect to h (which is 0 in the standard "selfish" case and positive in the case

[6]If $B_i'' > 0$, we see from (2.2) that the response function for country i is upward sloping, since $C_i'' > B_i''$ follows from the second-order condition for (2.1).

[7]It is the true net benefit which is relevant in the bargaining solutions considered in Sections 3–6.

[8]It should be stressed the present analysis does *not* treat h as a choice variable. The analysis simply compares the case of $h = 0$ (i.e., standard behavior as dictated by the country's self interest) with the case of $h > 0$, which represents the behavior of a country which (for whatever reason) reduces its emissions compared with what its self-interest implies.

[9]If $B_2'' > 0$ (and $C_2'' > B_2''$), $R_2(X_1)$ is upward sloping, implying that emissions from *both* countries go down.

of unilateral action) gives

$$\frac{dW}{dh} = \left\{ (B_1' - C_1') + B_2' + [B_1' + (B_2' - C_2')] \frac{dX_2}{dX_1} \right\} \frac{dX_1}{dh}. \tag{2.5}$$

The second term in the square brackets is zero (cf. 2.3), using (2.1′) we therefore have

$$\frac{dW}{dh} = \left\{ -h + B_2' + B_1' \frac{dX_2}{dX_1} \right\} \frac{dX_1}{dh}. \tag{2.6}$$

The first and last terms in the curly brackets in (2.6) are negative, while the second term as well as dX_1/dh are positive. The sign of (2.6) is therefore ambiguous. However, starting at $h = 0$, a sufficient condition for W to increase as h increases is that $B_1' \le B_2'$ (since $-dX_2/dX_1 = -R(X_1) < 1$). If country 1 has a lower marginal benefit of emission reductions than country 2, total welfare therefore increases if country 1 changes its behavior slightly in the direction of unilateral action, when both countries initially follow their self-interests.

From (2.1) and (2.3) we have $B_i' = C_i'$ for $i = 1, 2$ when $h = 0$. The result above may therefore be formulated as follows: Starting from a situation in which both countries follow their self-interests, total welfare will increase if the country which has the lowest marginal cost of reducing its emissions changes its behavior slightly in the direction of unilateral action, by choosing an emission level which is lower than what follows from its true payoff function.

The results in this section are formally derived for a specific change in the payoff function of country 1. However, it is easily verified that *any* change in country 1's payoff function which shifts its response function to the right in Fig. 1 gives the same conclusions.

3. COOPERATIVE SOLUTIONS

The noncooperative equilibria of the games of the preceding section are obviously not Pareto efficient for the two countries. If one allows for side payments between the two countries, the only efficient (X_1, X_2) combination is the one that maximizes $B_1(X_1 + X_2) + B_2(X_1 + X_2) - C_1(X_1) - C_2(X_2)$, giving

$$B_1'(X_1 + X_2) + B_2'(X_1 + X_2) = C_1'(X_1) = C_2'(X_2). \tag{3.1}$$

Without side payments, the conditions for efficiency follows from maximizing $B_1(X_1 + X_2) - C_1(X_1)$ holding $B_2(X_1 + X_2) - C_2(X_2)$ constant. This gives

$$(B_1' - C_1')(B_2' - C_2') = B_1'B_2' \tag{3.2}$$

or

$$B_1'C_2' + B_2'C_1' - C_1'C_2' = 0. \tag{3.2'}$$

Comparing (3.1) and (3.2′), we see that they coincide for (X_1, X_2) values yielding $C_1'(X_1) = C_2'(X_2)$. This is of course the benefit of institutional arrangements allowing side payments: No matter what size of total emissions one chooses, one always distributes the emissions so that the total costs of the reduction of the emissions are minimized, implying $C_1'(X_1) = C_2'(X_2)$.[10]

The (X_1, X_2)-combinations satisfying (3.2) lie on the curve L in Fig. 1. If D is the relevant equilibrium in the absence of any agreement, the potential candidates for a cooperative solution must lie on the heavily drawn segment of L. Negotiations between the two countries will determine exactly which point on this line segment will be the cooperative solution. We shall assume that the outcome of such negotiations is given by the *Nash bargaining solution*.

The Nash bargaining solution is the (X_1, X_2)-combination which solves

$$\max_{(X_1, X_2)} \{\log[B_1(X_1 + X_2) - C_1(X_1) - D_1] + \log[B_2(X_1 + X_2) - C_2(X_2) - D_2]\}. \tag{3.3}$$

In (3.3), (D_1, D_2) represents the "disagreement point," and gives the benefits minus costs to the two countries in the event that a cooperative agreement is not reached. It is assumed that in the absence of a negotiated agreement, the outcome is the noncooperative equilibrium of the simultaneous move game, denoted by D in Fig. 1. In other words, we have

$$D_i = B_i(X_1^* + X_2^*) - C_i(X_i^*), \tag{3.4}$$

where (X_1^*, X_2^*) is the Nash equilibrium of the noncooperative simultaneous move game, i.e., defined by (2.1) and (2.3).

The first-order conditions, of the Nash bargaining solution are

$$\frac{B_1' - C_1'}{B_1 - C_1 - D_1} + \frac{B_2'}{B_2 - C_2 - D_2} = 0 \tag{3.5}$$

$$\frac{B_1'}{B_1 - C_1 - D_1} + \frac{B_2' - C_2'}{B_2 - C_2 - D_2} = 0. \tag{3.6}$$

Dividing (3.5) by (3.6) gives us Eq. (3.2), which was the condition for efficiency (in the absence of side payments).

The Nash bargaining solution is illustrated in Fig. 2. The "disagreement point" D corresponds to the equilibrium D of the noncooperative game illustrated in Fig. 1. The payoff (or "benefit-minus-cost") function EF in Fig. 3 corresponds to the contract curve L in Fig. 1, with the heavily drawn portion of EF corresponding to

[10]Kosobud and Daly [6] give a numerical analysis of a game of CO_2 emissions between South and North America. In the cooperative solution they considered, there is an equal tax on CO_2 emissions in both regions. A suitable uniform tax (combined with side payments) could lead to a first best solution. However, with the tax consired by Kosobud and Daly the sum of net welfare in the two regions is *lower* than in the noncooperative solution of their game. This means that the tax they have considered is too high given their benefit and cost functions.

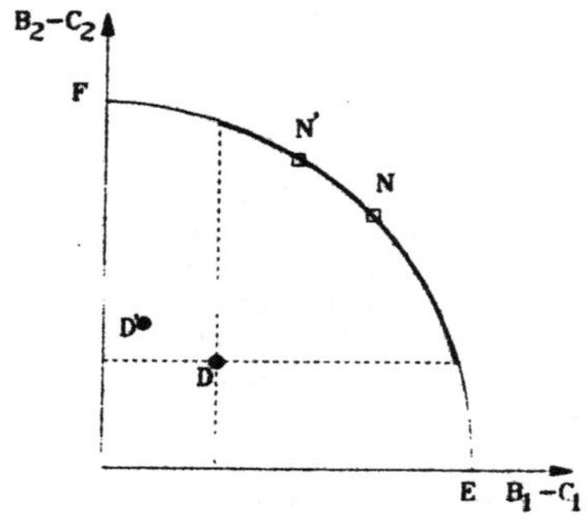

FIGURE 3

the heavily drawn portion of L.[11] The Nash bargaining solution in Fig. 3 is defined by the tangential point between the payoff function EF and a hyperbola with origin D (not drawn in Fig. 3).

Assume that country 1 reduces its emissions in excess of X_1^* in the event of no agreement. From Section 2, we know that this moves the noncooperative equilibrium from D to D' in Fig. 1 (provided country 2 always acts according to its response function). In other words, this behavior of country 1 reduces country 1's utility and increases country 2's utility in the absence of a negotiated agreement. In Fig. 3, this moves the disagreement point from D to D', giving a move of the Nash bargaining solution from N to N'.[12] The move from N to N' in Fig. 3 corresponds to a move along L in Fig. 1 in the south eastern direction, i.e., X_1 goes up and X_2 goes down.

What happens to the total emissions as we move from N to N'? This depends on how $X_1 + X_2$ changes as we move down along the contract L in Fig. 1. From the efficiency condition (3.2′) we find

$$-\frac{dX_2}{dX_1} = \frac{(C_2' - B_2')C_1'' + H}{(C_1' - B_1')C_2'' + H}, \tag{3.7}$$

where

$$H = -B_1''C_2' - B_2''C_1' > 0. \tag{3.8}$$

Since $B_i - C_i - D_i \geq 0$ in the Nash solution and $B_i' > 0$, it follows from (3.5)–(3.6)

[11] The concavity of the curve EF follows from the assumptions $B_i'' < 0$ and $C_i'' > 0$. If instead $B_i'' > 0$ at all points on the EF curve, the EF curve cannot be concave everywhere. Nevertheless, the second-order conditions of the Nash bargaining solution will hold provided B_i'' is sufficiently small.

[12] If $B_2'' > 0$ at the noncooperative equilibrium, the utility of *both* countries would increase, i.e., D' would lie northeast of D. As long as B_2'' is sufficiently small, the path from D to D' will be steep, implying the same relationship between N and N' as in Fig. 3.

that $C_i' - B_i' > 0$ in the Nash solution. It is therefore clear from (3.7)–(3.8) that

$$-\frac{dX_2}{dX_1} < 1 \quad \text{iff} \quad \frac{C_1' - B_1'}{C_1''} > \frac{C_2' - B_2'}{C_2''}. \tag{3.9}$$

For general functions B_i and C_i we do not know whether $X_2/dX_1 < 1$ or not. If $-dX_2/dX_1 > 1$ the move from D to D' will give an *increase* in total emissions in a cooperative agreement (i.e., a reduction in $X_1 + X_2$). To see that both cases $-dX_2/dX_1 < 1$ and $-dX_2/dX_1 > 1$ are possible, consider the case in which the countries have identical benefit and cost functions. In the Nash equilibrium corresponding to D we have $X_1 = X_2$ for this case, and therefore $-dX/dX_1 = 1$ from (3.7) since benefit and cost functions are equal. However, for $X_1 > X_2$ we have $C_1' - B_1' > C_2' - B_2'$, giving $-dX_2/dX_1 < 1$ for $X_1 > X_2$ unless $C_i''' > 0$ and "large." If C_i''' is sufficiently large, we get $-dX_2/dX_1 > 1$ for $X_1 > X_2$. In this latter case the consequence of country 1's unilateral reduction of its emissions in excess of its optimal reply therefore gives *higher* total emissions in a cooperative agreement.

When the countries have different B_i- and C_i-functions $dX_2/dX_1 < 1$ and $dX_2/dX_1 > 1$ are both possible. In particular, it follows from (3.9) that we always get an increase in total emissions in a cooperative agreement as a consequence of the change of the disagreement point from D to D' if C_1''/C_2'' is sufficiently large.

The results above have the following interpretation. When country 1 commits itself to a unilateral reduction of emissions even if an agreement is not reached, this weakens its position in the negotiations.[13] The outcome of the negotiations therefore gives a lower payoff to country 1 and a higher payoff to country 2 (relative to the outcome when D is the disagreement point). This redistribution of net benefits from country 1 to country 2 comes about through lower emissions from country 1 and higher emissions from country 2 (relative to the outcome N in Fig. 3). If C_1'' is "high," the appropriate reduction of $B_1 - C_1$ is achieved by a relatively small increase in X_1; and if C_2'' is "low," the appropriate increase in $B_2 - C_2$ requires a relatively large reduction in X_2. For this case we therefore get an increase in total emissions as a consequence of the unilateral action by country 1. Conversely for the case of a "low" value of C_1''/C_2''; in this case we get a reduction in total emissions as a consequence of the unilateral action by country 1.

For this special case of $C_2'' = 0$ and $C_2'' > 0$, it was shown in Section 2 that total emissions in the absence of a cooperative agreement were independent of the behavior of country 1. From (3.7) it is clear that in this case a cooperative agreement has highest emissions when country 1 reduces emissions unilaterally (since $-dX_2/dX_1 > 1$ in this case).

Finally, consider the effects on total welfare of moving from N to N'. Somewhere along the curve EF total welfare is maximized. This point is given by the conditions (3.1), and at that point the slope of the EF curve is -1. For the general case, this point may lie to the right or the left of N. If it lies to the right, it follows from the curvature of the EF curve that total welfare will decline as we move from N to N'. On the other hand, if the point which maximizes total welfare lies to the left of N, a (small) move leftwards to N to N' will increase total welfare.

[13]As explained in footnote 8, the paper does not address the question of why and how the country can commit itself to reducing its emissions if no agreement is reached, i.e., why $h > 0$.

We showed above that if the countries had equal benefit and cost functions, unilateral emission reduction from country 1 could reduce total emissions in the cooperative solution. However, total welfare will go down in this case, since total welfare is maximized at N in this case.

4. EQUAL EMISSION REDUCTIONS

International negotiations on emission reductions are often restricted to equal (or proportional) reductions for all participating countries. If countries have different benefit and cost functions, a restriction of the type $X_1 = X_2$ will usually imply a welfare loss compared to unrestricted outcomes along the contract curve L in Fig. 1. One of the reasons for restricting oneself to simple cases of the type $X_1 = X_2$ is asymmetric information. Cost functions C_i might be known reasonably well. However, the benefits B_i of a country depend on this country's characteristics and preferences and in many cases also on the subjective probability distribution the country has regarding the uncertain consequences of high global emissions.[14] With unrestricted negotiations, it may be in each country's interest to pretend that its B_i- and B_i'-function is lower-valued than what it really is.

Whatever the reason for a restriction of the type $X_1 = X_2$, it is of interest to consider the consequences of one country taking unilateral action as described in the previous section (i.e., by choosing lower emissions in the absence of a negotiated agreement than follow from its true payoff function).[15]

With bargaining restricted to outcomes where $X_1 = X_2$, the outcome is straightforward if the countries have equal benefit and cost functions: The optimal $X_1 = X_2 = X$ is the one maximizing $B_i(X_1 + X_2) - C_i(X_i) = B_i(2X) - C_i(X)$, giving $2B_i'(2X) = C_i'(X)$.

If benefit (and/or cost) functions differ, the countries will usually have different most preferred X-values. Figure 4 illustrates the case in which country 1 would like a higher X-value than country 2. The line $0P0$ shows how each country's payoff changes as X increases from 0 to X^P and further to X^Q, with X^P and X^Q defined by $2B_2'(2X^P) = C_2'(X^P)$ and $2B_1'(2X^Q) = C_1'(X^Q)$. In the absence of a negotiated agreement the outcome is given by the disagreement point D (where we usually will *not* have $X_1 = X_2$). Country 1's most preferred point is Q, and country 2's is P.[16] Negotiations will be about which point on the segment PQ to choose.[17] The point N in Fig. 4 is the Nash bargaining solution corresponding to the disagreement point D. If the disagreement point is changed from D to D', the Nash bargaining solution changes from N to N', implying a reduction in X. In this case we thus unambiguously find that the total emissions go *up* as a consequence of country 1's unilateral policy of reducing its emissions before a negotiated agreement is reached.

[14] Benefit functions $B_i(x)$ may differ strongly between countries due to differences in the characteristics of the countries. The effects of global climatic changes due to increased atmospheric concentration of CO_2 will for instance vary a lot between countries with different locations.

[15] Although the analysis is restricted to the case of $X_1 = X_2$, similar conclusions hold for the more general case of $X_1 = F(X_2)$ for $F' > 0$.

[16] It is easily verified that $B_i'' < 0$ and $C_i'' > 0$ imply that the curve $0PQ$ is concave over the segment PQ.

[17] If D had been further north-east in the figure, only part of the line segment PQ would have given both parties $B_i - C_i - D_i \geq 0$.

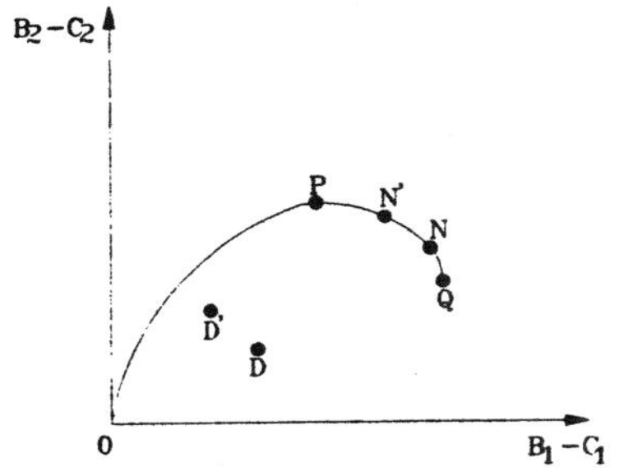

FIGURE 4

5. OVERFULFILLMENT OF NEGOTIATED AGREEMENTS

So far, we have only considered unilateral action that a country may take in the absence of a negotiated agreement, e.g., before the negotiations are finished. When negotiations are restricted to equal emission reductions, an alternative unilateral action would be to overfulfill whatever the negotiated agreement requires of emission reductions. If a country can credibly commit itself to such a unilateral reduction of emissions, and this behavior is predicted prior to the negotiations, we would expect the negotiated outcome to be affected by this behavior. An obvious question is whether or not this type of unilateral reduction of emissions will reduce total emissions. There are of course several different commitments a country can make which all imply an overfulfillment of a negotiated agreement. Here we shall consider one simple example of such a commitment.

Let $X = X_1 = X_2$ be the negotiated agreement, and assume that if an agreement is reached country 1 will reduce its emissions by $X + k$. It is assumed that k is independent of X, and that country 1's behavior is correctly predicted by country 2 in the negotiations. In other words, the issue of the negotiations is the size of the variable X, and both countries know that if an agreement is reached country 1 will reduce its emissions by $X + k$, while country 2 will reduce its emissions by X.

The choice of X is determined as a Nash bargaining solution, i.e.,

$$\max_X \{\log[B_1(2X + k) - C_1(X + k) - D_1] + \log[B_2(2X + k) - C_2(X) - D_2]\} \tag{5.1}$$

or

$$\max_Y \left\{\log\left[B_1(Y) - C_1\left(\frac{Y + k}{2}\right) - D_1\right] + \log\left[B_2(Y) - C_2\left(\frac{Y - k}{2}\right) - D_2\right]\right\} \tag{5.1'}$$

where $Y = 2X + k$ is the total reduction of emissions. The first-order condition of the solution to (5.1′) is

$$\frac{B_1'(Y) - (1/2)C_1'((Y+k)/2)}{B_1(Y) - C_1((Y+k)/2) - D_1} + \frac{B_2'(Y) - (1/2)C_2'((Y-k)/2)}{B_2(Y) - C_2((Y-k)/2) - D_2} = 0. \quad (5.2)$$

From the second-order conditions of the maximization problem, Y must change in the same direction as the l.h.s. of (5.2) when k increases. An increase in k will increase C_1 and C_1' and reduce C_2 and C_2'. Both denominators in (5.2) are positive. Assuming that country 1 is the country which has the highest most preferred X-value, i.e., $B_1' > C_1'/2$ and $B_2' < C_2'/2$ at the negotiated X-value, the first numerator in (5.2) is positive, while the second numerator is negative. The reduction in C_2 and C_2' caused by the increase in k makes the second term of the l.h.s of (5.2) larger (i.e., gives this negative term a lower absolute value). The increase in C_1 increases the first term of the l.h.s of (5.2), but the increase in C_1' reduces this term. As long as C_1'' is not too large, the three positive effects on the l.h.s of (5.2) will dominate this last negative effect, implying $dY/dk > 0$. In other words: As long as C_1'' is not too large, an announced commitment from country 1 to overfulfill whatever negotiated agreement one reaches will reduce total emissions.

In practice, the distinction between the unilateral action analyzed in this section and the one analyzed in Sections 2–4 need not be very sharp. The case of reduced CFC emissions mentioned in Section 1 is a good example. As mentioned, most West European countries and the USA have decided to cut back the emissions of CFC in excess of the standards set by the Montreal convention of 1985. To the extent that this was announced in advance and made contingent on the 1987 agreement being reached, this may be seen as the type of unilateral action discussed in the present section. However, the Montreal agreement of 1987 is expected to be renegotiated in 1990, with the aim of reaching stricter standards for emissions of CFC than the present agreement. The unilateral excess reductions of CFC emissions by the abovementioned group of countries is thus a policy of the type discussed in Section 2–4 in relation to these forthcoming negotiations.

6. *n* COUNTRIES

Assume that there are n countries, each with benefit and cost functions $B_i(X_i)$ and $C_i(X_i)$ with $B_i' > 0$, $B_i'' < 0$, $C_i' > 0$, and $C_i'' > 0$. Denote the sum of emission reductions by $X = \Sigma_i X_i$. The Nash equilibrium of the noncooperative simultaneous move game is given by

$$B_1'(X) + h = C_1'(X_1) \quad (6.1)$$

$$B_j'(X) = C_j'(X_j) \qquad j = 2, \ldots, n, \quad (6.2)$$

where $h = 0$ in the standard Nash equilibrium and $h > 0$ if country 1 acts unilaterally by choosing a lower emission level than what follows from its true payoff function $B_1 - C_1$.

From (6.1) and (6.2) it is clear that as h increases, X_1 and X increase, while X_j goes down for $j \neq 1$.[18] As in the 2-country case, we therefore have the following conclusion: If one country acts unilaterally by reducing its emissions, all other countries will increase their emissions. Nevertheless, total emissions will decline. Note that in the limiting case in which $C_i'' = 0$ for one country (other than country 1), total emissions are unaffected by the level of emissions chosen by country 1.[19]

Total welfare is given by $W = \Sigma_i[B_i(X) - C_i(X)]$. Differentiating with respect to h gives

$$\frac{dW}{dh} = \sum_i B_i' \frac{dX}{dh} - \sum_i C_i' \frac{dX_i}{dh}. \tag{6.3}$$

Starting at the Nash equilibrium with $h = 0$, it follows from (6.1) and (6.2) that $C_i' = B_i'$ for all i. It thus follows from (6.3) that

$$\frac{dW}{dh} = \sum_i B_i' \left(\frac{dX}{dh} - \frac{dX_i}{dh} \right). \tag{6.4}$$

In the sum given by (6.4), the first term is negative, since

$$\frac{dX}{dh} - \frac{dX_1}{dh} = \sum_{i \neq 1} \frac{dX_i}{dh} < 0,$$

while all the other terms are positive, since $dX/dh > 0$ and $dX_i/dh < 0$ for $i \neq 1$. The sign of dW/dh is therefore ambiguous. However, as before $B_1' \leq B_i'$ is a sufficient condition for $dW/dh > 0$, since in this case

$$\frac{dW}{dh} \geq B_1' \sum_i \left(\frac{dX}{dh} - \frac{dX_i}{dh} \right) = B_i'(n-1)\frac{dX}{dh} > 0. \tag{6.5}$$

Utilizing $B_i' = C_i'$, we therefore have a similar result as in the 2-country case: Starting in a situation in which all countries follow their self-interest, total welfare will increase if the country which has the lowest marginal cost of reducing its emissions chooses an emission level which is lower than what follows from its self-interest.

While the noncooperative (simultaneous move) game easily extends to n countries, this is not true for cooperative games. The main reason for this that although the Nash bargaining solution is a reasonable outcome in a 2-player bargaining context, it is far from obvious that a generalized Nash bargaining solution is a good prediction for the outcome of negotiations between more than 2 players. Nevertheless, its seems reasonable that also in the n-player case, the bargaining position of the country which unilaterally reduces its emissions is weakened relative to the

[18] *Proof*: Assume $dX \leq 0$. Since $B_i'' < 0$ and $C_i'' > 0$ it follows from (7.1) and (7.2) that $dX_1 > 0$ (since $dh > 0$) and $dX_j \geq 0$ for $j \neq 1$, i.e., $dX > 0$. This is a contradiction; we therefore have $dX > 0$. But from (7.2) this implies $dX_j < 0$ for $j \neq 1$; since $dX = \Sigma_i dX_i$ we therefore also have $dX_1 > 0$. Q.E.D.

[19] This follows from $B_j'(X) = C_j'(X_j)$, which determines X if C_j' is constant.

other countries. We shall therefore consider how the weakening of the bargaining power of country 1 affects total emissions and total welfare.

To find the set of efficient outcomes in the absence of side payments, we maximize $\Sigma_i \alpha_i [B_i(X) - C_i(X_i)]$ where $\alpha_i \geq 0$ and $\Sigma_i \alpha_i = 1$. This gives

$$\sum_i \alpha_i B_i'(X) = \alpha_j C_j'(X_j) \qquad j = 1, \ldots, n. \tag{6.6}$$

For given values of the α-parameters, these n equations determine all X_j. More generally (6.6) gives one equation between the n X_j-values after all α_j have been eliminated. All X_j-combinations satisfying this equation are efficient outcomes.

We want to see how $X = \Sigma_i X_i$ and $W = \Sigma_i (B_i - C_i)$ are affected by a reduction in α_1 and an increase in the remaining α_j-parameters. We shall restrict ourselves to the following simple example:

— $\alpha_1 = \alpha$ and $\alpha_j = (1 - \alpha)/(n - 1)$

— all B_i' are constant and equal; by choice of units we have $B_i' = 1$

— $C_i'(X_i) = c_i X_i$, where c_i are positive constants.

With this example (6.6) may be rewritten as

$$\alpha_j c_j X_j = 1 \tag{6.7}$$

or

$$X_1 = \frac{1}{\alpha c_1}$$

$$X_j = \frac{n-1}{(1-\alpha)c_j} \qquad j = 2, \ldots, n. \tag{6.8}$$

From (6.7) we see that a reduction in α increases X_1 and reduces X_j for $j \neq 1$, as in the 2-country case. To see how total emissions are affected, we differentiate (6.7) for the simple case in which $c_j = c$ for $j \neq 1$:

$$\frac{dX}{d\alpha} = -\frac{1}{c_1 \alpha^2} + \frac{(n-1)^2}{(1-\alpha)^2 c}. \tag{6.9}$$

Total emissions go down or up as country 1's bargaining power α goes down depending on $dX/d\alpha$ negative or positive. From (6.9) we see that

$$\frac{dX}{d\alpha} < 0 \quad \text{iff } \frac{c_1}{c} < \left[\frac{1-\alpha}{\alpha(n-1)}\right]^2. \tag{6.10}$$

Thus, only if country 1 has sufficiently low costs of reducing its emissions will total emissions in the cooperative outcome go down as a consequence of country 1's unilateral emission reductions.

From (6.10) we see that the critical value of c_1/c is lower the higher is α. In particular, consider the case in which $\alpha = 1/n$ initially. In this case it follows from

(6.1) that $dX/d\alpha$ is negative or positive depending on c_1 smaller or larger than c. For $\alpha < 1/n$ the critical value of c_1/c in (6.9) is larger than 1, and conversely for $\alpha > 1/n$.

Total welfare is maximized for $\alpha = 1/n$. If $\alpha < 1/n$, a reduction in α will reduce total welfare, while total welfare goes up if $\alpha > 1/n$. Note that for the special case of equal costs for *all* countries (i.e., $c_1 = c$), $\alpha < 1/n$ implies that a reduction in α reduces total emissions, but also total welfare. If $\alpha > 1/n$ total emissions go up if α is reduced, but total welfare also goes up in this case.

7. CONCLUDING REMARKS

An important lesson from the analysis in the preceding sections is that unilateral emission reductions undertaken by one country need not help to solve global environmental problems. Some policies of this type may even *increase* total emissions of environmentally harmful materials. Such policies may also reduce total global welfare.

In a situation where unilateral reduction of emissions increases total emissions and/or reduces total welfare, one might ask why an altruistic and environmentally concerned country does not *increase* its emissions. The reason why we do not expect this to happen is that a commitment to unilateral emission reductions in many cases is caused by pressure from domestic environmental groups. It is difficult to imagine environmental groups pressing a government to introduce measure which would *increase* emissions. In many cases, pressure from interest groups is not based on a thorough analysis of what the consequences of the policies they argue for might be. The whole point of the present analysis is to show that it might not be particularly sensible for an environmental group in a country to try to force its government to unilaterally reduce the country's emissions.

The analysis has had a rather narrow focus. There are at least three important issues which have been ignored.

In the first place, I have ignored the question of whether unilateral emission reductions by one country may lead to similar behavior by other countries. If this is the case, this type of policy might lead to some kind of tacit cooperative behavior, even in the absence of formal negotiations and agreements. (Guttman [5] gives a formal analysis of how one might reach a Pareto efficient outcome in a noncooperative game of the type I have considered.)

The second issue is that even if unilateral actions by one country might not change the (selfish) behavior of other countries in the absence of a formal international agreement, the unilateral actions might affect the climate in international negotiations, and thus improve the chance of reaching a cooperative agreement. This aspect is lost in my formal modeling of the negotiations, in which an agreement is always immediately reached.

A third issue (related to the fist two issues) is that the present analysis is based on well-defined preferences (given by the B_i- and C_i-functions) for each country. In practice, there will be conflicts of interest within each country. In particular, some interest groups (e.g., producers of products using CFC) may be opposed to large reductions of environmentally harmful residuals. These groups will often argue that the cost of reducing the emissions (which by their nature is uncertain) is high. One effect of a country taking unilateral action and reducing its emissions can be a demonstration that such reductions actually may be made without high costs. Unilateral action by one country may thus weaken the position of interest groups in other countries who are opposed to reduced emissions.

Although the focus of the analysis is rather narrow, the lesson remains: whatever good intentions lie behind a policy of unilateral emission reductions, the consequences may differ from what one hoped and expected. Careful consideration should therefore be given before a country departs from following its own self-interest.

REFERENCES

[1] R. C. d'Arge, Observations on the economics of transational environmental externalities, *in* "Problems in Transfrontier Pollution," pp. 147–174, OECD, Paris, 1974.

[2] R. C. d'Arge, Transfrontier pollution: Some issues on regulation, in "Studies in International Environmental Economics" (I. Walter, Ed.), pp. 257–278, Wiley, New York, 1975.

[3] R. Cornes and T. Sandler, The theory of public goods: Non-Nash behavior, *J. Public Econom.* **23**, 367–379 (1984).

[4] R. Cornes and T. Sandler, Externalities, expectations, and Pigouvian taxes, *J. Environ. Econom. Management* **12**, 1–13 (1985).

[5] J. M. Guttman, Understanding collective action: Matching behavior, *Amer. Econom. Rev.* **68**, 251–255 (1978).

[6] R. F. Kosobud and T. A. Daly, Global conflict or cooperation over the CO_2 climate impact? *Kyklos* **37**, 638–659 (1984).

[3]

Economica (1993) **60**, 281–93

Creating a Good Atmosphere: Minimum Participation for Tackling the 'Greenhouse Effect'

By Jane Black,* Maurice D. Levi*† and David de Meza*

* *University of Exeter*; † *University of British Columbia*

Final version received 14 May 1992.

This paper explores the implications of setting a minimum ratification level on an international agreement to tackle the Greenhouse Effect. Several aspects of the ratification level are considered, including the threshold number of signatories required to effect agreement, the potential number of participating countries, and the distribution of benefits from taking action. The likelihood of reaching agreement on a ratification level is also considered. It is shown, for example, that the optimal ratification level is reasonably robust to variations in circumstances, and that the prospects for effecting a treaty may be improved by there being a large number of countries.

Introduction

With each country standing to enjoy only a small fraction of the global benefit of its own efforts to combat the 'Greenhouse Effect', the potential for sub-optimal spending on atmospheric improvement is disturbingly obvious. If action is not taken and the most pessimistic scientific projections are valid, we may even free-ride this fragile planet into a region in which positive feedbacks send it on an infernal one-way trip.

This paper focuses on the implications of one particular aspect of reaching agreement on tackling the Greenhouse Effect: that concerning the minimum number of countries that are required to commit themselves to participate before action is taken by any.[1] While representing only one dimension of the multi-faceted design of an action plan for overcoming this potentially grave problem, the setting of a required threshold ratification level could be an important element in concluding an agreement.

Several aspects of a minimum ratification level are explored. For example, we consider the consequences of varying the number of participants required to ratify an atmospheric treaty. We also examine how the expected global gain from a treaty depends on the potential number of signatories, and on their costs and benefits of compliance. It is shown, for example, that, within the specific environment of analysis, inclusion of a minimum agreement level, or 'n-rule', is distinctly better than allowing independent action. However, it is also shown that uncertainty over different countries' evaluations of the net benefits of action is a potentially serious difficulty. Specifically, even in a situation in which the threshold number of participants can be optimally set and in which credible threats can be made not to repeat the opportunity to cooperate, the expected benefit of the minimum pre-commitment approach may be well below that which would be achieved if all countries could be forced to cooperate.[2] Nevertheless, it is also shown that the global nature of the problem, specifically the large number of countries involved, has a *positive* influence on what can be achieved by having a ratification threshold, or 'n-rule'. This is a less than intuitive outcome.[3] Furthermore, it is shown that, with sufficient compactness or negative skewness in the distribution of net benefits, the outcome achieved with voluntary commitments to participate is very similar to that achieved by enforced universal participation. Finally, by comparing the different *n*-rules that different countries would prefer, it is argued that agreement on a minimum ratification level may not represent an insurmountable hurdle.

Before proceeding it should be mentioned that, by focusing on the threshold level for treaty ratification, there are numerous aspects of a minimum participation issue that we do not explore. For example, we do not deal with how, *within* countries, the decision to commit is reached. To do so would lead inevitably into public-choice problems that are well beyond the scope of this paper.[4] We also limit consideration to the matter of whether or not a country participates, that is to the binary choice, when in fact there are many issues concerning the *degree* of participation. That is, the negotiations concerning the *amount* of action each country commits to take as part of a treaty, while of great importance, are not investigated. Furthermore, we do not explore *when* action is taken, and how the path of adjustment to an atmospheric treaty could influence the outcome. Nevertheless, while ignoring these clearly relevant matters of treaty design, we believe that the dimension of focus here is an important aspect of this pressing problem. As we shall show, several implications of a minimum ratification level are revealed within the chosen, simplified framework that are relevant for the possible success of an international atmospheric agreement to tackle global warming.

I. Planning with Complete versus Incomplete Information

If the benefit that would be enjoyed by each country from a once-only offered policy to combat the Greenhouse Effect were precisely known, and if the aggregate benefit exceeded the aggregate cost, implementation would be relatively straightforward. Specifically, the aggregate cost would be allocated such that each country benefits, and then a treaty ratification established such that all countries must agree to the programme before it is adopted by any. Assuming that countries really believe that there will be no further opportunities to negotiate, optimality is ensured. With each country standing to benefit, all will participate because were any one country to refrain the whole programme would be scuttled.[5]

The desirability of pursuing a policy requiring unanimity is evidently dependent on being able to ensure that all countries gain.[6] One reason why it is not practicable to design a scheme by which every country is guaranteed to benefit is that there is considerable uncertainty about the consequences of the Greenhouse Effect. Individual countries' policy makers will make their own assessments of the scientific evidence on the impact of global warming on their own environments and of how much weight they attach to the environmental impact, making each country uncertain about the effects of action on its own economy, as well as about the valuations others place on the benefits of action. A second reason why ensuring universal benefits is difficult is that side-payments, which might theoretically achieve this, typically entail significant deadweight costs.[7] This means that a scheme whereby, for example, each country submits a schedule of the compensation it requires to participate as a function of the number of participants may fail because of these costs. Deadweight costs aside, transfers based on a sophisticated revelation mechanism may turn out to be inequitable, with the poor apparently compensating the rich. If instead of well defined rules, some authority is given discretion to evaluate costs and benefits, political manipulation is likely, with the result that again it is possible that side-payments for some countries may be insufficient.[8] Therefore, even if there is a global benefit of action, it is possible that participation may be sub-optimal.

II. Determining the Optimum Participation Level[9]

It seems intuitively reasonable that, if there are countries that might not benefit from a proposed scheme, and if all schemes, current and future, are indeed scuttled if the current proposal fails to meet its approval target, then it may be preferable to settle for less than unanimity; while this may involve fewer countries participating, the increased chance that the programme is adopted could more than compensate. Of course, setting the approval target too low invites free-riding if contribution to the cost of the scheme is contingent on a country's approval. This is because the effect of withholding approval on the expected outcome is smaller the greater is the number of approval withholdals that can occur before the programme is scuttled. That is, with uncertainty about net benefits, it is disadvantageous to set the approval target too high, because this increases the chance that it is not reached, or too low, because this invites free-riding.

To investigate further the issues involved in setting the level of participation required before agreement is reached, we assume that there are N countries that might benefit from a specified action taken to combat the Greenhouse Effect or some other atmospheric threat. We consider a scheme that goes into effect only in the event of approval by a minimum of n of the N countries, and where only those that approve are committed to act.[10] For illustrative purposes the cost of action, c, is assumed to be the same for all countries. Commitment to take action is offered simultaneously, or at least without knowledge of the decisions of others.[11]

In what follows, negotiations over the obligations imposed on signatories are assumed to have been completed and to be enforceable. The problem is how to choose the commitment threshold to maximize global benefits.[12] While actual benefits are unknown, each country is assumed to know the expected value of its own benefit, b, from its own expenditure, c, and to be risk-neutral. It is assumed that $b<c$ so that no country would take independent action. However, each country expects to benefit from the expenditure of all other countries. Over the relevant range, it is assumed that the expected benefits from other countries' actions are the same as from its own action, so that if a total of r other countries participate a country's expected benefit is rb if it does not sign, and $(r+1)b-c$ if it signs and hence incurs expenditure c. Since, by assumption, $b<c$, the country would prefer to free-ride if it could be certain that the agreement would go ahead, but it must take into account the possibility that its own agreement will be pivotal.

If a country believes that the probability that r other countries will sign is $\Pr[r \mid N-1]$ then, given that at least n of the total of N countries must sign for the scheme to come into effect, it will estimate its expected net benefit of signing as

$$(1)\qquad \Delta = b\sum_{n-1}^{N-1}(r+1)\Pr[r\,|\,N-1] - b\sum_{n}^{N-1} r\Pr[r\,|\,N-1] - c\Pr[r\geq n-1\,|\,N-1].$$

The first term in (1) is the expected benefit from the action of those that participate assuming that the country itself participates and the treaty is ratified, while the second term represents the expected benefit if the country does not participate but the treaty is nevertheless ratified. The final term represents the expected cost of action, assuming that a cost is incurred only by those that ratify the treaty. Clearly, Δ is increasing in b, and so there is some critical value, $b=k$, such that if $b\geq k$ the country will sign.

To simplify the numerical simulations, we assume that each country knows that the others' expected valuations are drawn from a common distribution, $f(b)$.[13] Given this assumption of symmetry, the value k will be the same for all countries. The chance that any one country signs is $\Pr[\tilde{b}\geq k]$, and hence each country believes that $\tilde{r}$, the number of other countries that sign, will have a binomial distribution with parameters $N-1$, $\theta=\Pr[\tilde{b}\geq k]$. Since k satisfies the condition that $\Delta=0$, the equilibrium k must satisfy

$$(2)\qquad k=\frac{c\Pr[r\geq n-1\,|\,N-1,\theta]}{b\sum_{n-1}^{N-1}(r+1)\Pr[r\,|\,N-1,\theta]-b\sum_{n}^{N-1}r\Pr[r\,|\,N-1,\theta]},$$

where $\tilde{r}$ has the binomial distribution described above. Equation (2) can be solved numerically to find the value of k given n, N, $f(b)$ and c.

The expected global surplus, if the agreement threshold is that at least n countries must sign, is given by

$$(3)\qquad g=\sum_{n}^{N}[rg_h+(N-r)g_l-rc]\Pr[r\,|\,N,n],$$

where $\Pr[r\,|\,N,n]$ is the probability that r out of the N countries will commit, g_h is the expected gross benefit of those who sign, i.e. those for whom $b\geq k$, and g_l is the expected gain for those who do not sign. This can be compared with the expected benefit if all N countries could be compelled to participate, which is given by

$$(4)\qquad G=N^2E[\tilde{b}]-cN.$$

The expected global surpluses under the voluntary and compulsory schemes given in (3) and (4) exploit the fact that each country's action has as much benefit for itself as for all others. This is the result of the shared nature of the atmosphere, and helps in simplifying the problem. Of course, in reality the assumption of equal country size makes our conclusions only illustrative, although as we shall see the qualitative results are nevertheless potentially valuable for treaty design.

The damage resulting from free-riding can be assessed by comparing g and G assuming that n is chosen optimally. The impact of the voluntary participation constraint will depend upon G, N and the form of the distribution $f(b)$. The optimal n relative to N will also depend upon c and $f(b)$. As n is increased the selected k will decline, because, with a higher benefit from greater participation if the atmospheric clean-up policy is adopted, each country will want to increase its chance of approval. The lower k does not, however, necessarily increase the expected *ex ante* surplus, where this is based on a random drawing of N values of b from the countries' assumed $f(b)$. This is because, with the higher n that accompanies the lower k, there is a reduced probability that the plan will be adopted. The net effect on the surplus that is associated with each n depends on the combination of those two effects.

It is immediately clear from (2) that k is increasing in c so that, *ceteris paribus*, more costly plans are less likely to be adopted at each n. The expected global surplus for the voluntary and compulsory schemes will also be directly reduced by an increase in c; see (3) and (4). What is not so clear from (2) is how the optimal n depends on c. Similarly, the effect of varying N on the voluntary scheme is unclear, not only on the optimal n, but also on the expected surplus. While a higher N offers the potential for a greater surplus, which should increase the chance of approval, the influence of one country's 'vote' is reduced. However, as we shall see, in terms of the expected surplus, the fact that potential benefits grow with the square of the number of countries that might join the plan makes the effect of the greater potential surplus dominate the effect of lower influence.[14] In other words, *ceteris paribus*, the expected surplus increases with N. The effect of N on the optimal n, or at least on n/N, is not so clear even when we make specific assumptions about $f(b)$. The same is true for the effect of c on the optimal n. To investigate these effects further we look at some numerical simulations. These are for illustrative purposes, and are of course conditional on the assumptions that have gone into (2), (3) and (4).

III. Numerical Results

Consider firstly the case where $f(b)$ is a uniform distribution. Because there is substantial probability of there being countries with low b values, at least *vis à vis* a thin-tailed distribution with the same mean, we expect that this could result in the optimum n being below N even though a lower n is associated with a higher cut-off, k. That is, at least during the initial reduction(s) of n below N, the chance of finding n countries with b values above the cut-off k will increase, increasing the expected benefit. Consequently an interior socially optimal n would seem plausible for the uniform distribution. Case A in Table 1 shows that this is indeed the case. Here we show, for $N=10$ and $c=2$ given $f(b)=1$, $0<b<1$, zero elsewhere, what the critical value, k, is for each choice of n.[15] The resulting probability that the plan is adopted is shown, and the expected surplus with the n-rule is compared with G, the expected surplus if universal participation could be enforced. Clearly, without an n-plan or other way of coordinating action, the expected surplus is zero as no country's b could exceed c; and action is not taken.

This example makes it clear that, whichever n is selected, the expected surplus, while above zero and better than no plan, is well below what could be achieved if all countries were forced to spend c, whether they benefited individually or not. Even with the optimum requirement that the plan proceed only if at least seven countries agree, it is possible to achieve only 27·4 per cent of what could be achieved by a body that could compel action by all.

TABLE 1
EXPECTED SURPLUSES AND THEIR DETERMINANTS FOR DIFFERENT n-RULES

n	k	$P[\tilde{r} \geq n \mid N]$	g	$100g/G$ (%)
Case A: $N=10$, $c=2$, $f(b)=1$, $0<b<1$, $G=30$				
10	0·200	0·107	4·295	14·3
9	0·278	0·187	6·905	23·0
8	0·359	0·242	8·087	27·0
7	0·446	0·275	8·226	27·4
6	0·537	0·289	7·572	25·2
5	0·635	0·288	6·380	21·0
4	0·740	0·248	4·440	14·8
3	0·858	0·160	2·129	7·1
Case B: $N=30$, $c=2$, $f(b)=1$, $0<b<1$, $G=390$				
30	0·067	0·126	53·009	13·6
25	0·187	0·442	100·001	41·3
23	0·253	0·497	169·172	43·4
22	0·282	0·518	169·921	43·6
21	0·311	0·535	168·988	43·3
20	0·341	0·550	166·655	42·8
Case C: $N=30$, $c=6$, $f(b)=1$, $0<b<1$, $G=270$				
30	0·200	0·001	0·446	0·2
25	0·352	0·022	6·708	2·5
22	0·447	0·034	9·172	3·4
21	0·479	0·036	9·455	3·5
20	0·511	0·038	9·485	3·5
19	0·544	0·039	9·222	3·4
15	0·678	0·033	6·217	2·3

Case B, in conjunction with case A, shows the effect of increasing N. The same distribution for b and the same value of c are assumed, but N is increased from 10 to 30. Agreement is more likely with a larger N, and the benefits from the scheme with voluntary commitment approach those when all countries can be forced to participate. However, b and c are held constant as N increases, and so it does not follow that the global environmental agency should artificially try to expand N by, for example, asking for approval from individual members of the EC rather than seek collective EC participation: the individual member's b and c values would be correspondingly smaller and the prospect of satisfactory agreements being reached would then be actually lower. The experiment of increasing N, holding all else constant, in effect represents an increase in the extent of spillovers. In order to see this, suppose that the world comprised M islands each partitioned into two countries. If spillovers affected only a country's immediate neighbour, then $N=2$; if all countries were equally affected, then $N=2M$. What we show is that agreement is more likely if externalities are global rather than local.[16] Comparison of case B with case A also shows that the optimal n, as a fraction of the potential number of participants, N, is essentially unaffected by varying N. The extra potential benefits as N increases compensate for the reduced importance of any one country's compliance caused by a higher n.

While inspection of (2) does immediately suggest that, *ceteris paribus*, higher c will increase k and, for a given $f(b)$, will reduce the chance of reaching agreement at any n, the expression for k does not tell us by how much the probability of agreement and expected surplus will be damaged. One example, for $c = 6$, is shown in case C in Table 1. A comparison of case C with case B reveals that a tripling of the cost to which a country commits causes a reduction in the probability of agreement and expected surplus to only about 5 per cent of its earlier values; the temptation to free-ride goes up substantially with c. Of course, our calculations have been made for a given $f(b)$; therefore, we are not comparing different levels of spending which presumably would offer different benefits. However, we again see that the optimum n is very little affected by varying c. The participation rate appears to be remarkably robust given the form of $f(b)$. Cases A, B and C also suggest that, within limits, the benefits of action are reasonably insensitive to the choice of n. For example, where $N = 10$, an n-rule between 5 and 9 offers a global surplus that, while certainly convex *vis à vis n*, does not vary by a substantial amount.

A feature of the uniform distribution is that it has 'fat tails'. To investigate how the optimal n varies with the choice of $f(b)$, simulations for some other distributions are presented.

Case D in Table 2 shows the outcome for $N = 10$, $c = 2$, and $f(b) = 6b(1-b)$, $0 < b < 1$, zero elsewhere. This is a symmetric distribution with the same expectation and support as used earlier, but is more concentrated about its expected value. We see that, as expected, the optimum n is higher than with the comparable situation but a uniform distribution. However, while the expected surplus is higher, as we would expect, the gain over that in case A—that is, g for $n = 7$ in case A versus g for $n = 10$ in case D—is rather small. There remains a substantial probability, approximately 2/3, that the requisite unanimity of commitment would not be reached because at least one country's b is below the $k = 0.2$ they all select.

It would be expected that, if the b values could be assumed to be concentrated in the high end of the possible range, this would imply setting a high

TABLE 2

THE EFFECT OF THE DISTRIBUTION OF BENEFITS: THE BETA DISTRIBUTION

n	k	$P[\tilde{r} \geq n \mid N]$	g	$100g/G$ (%)
Case D: $N = 10$, $c = 2$, $f(b) = 6b(1-b)$, $0 < b < 1$, $G = 30$				
10	0·200	0·333	11·434	38·1
9	0·299	0·333	10·988	36·6
8	0·380	0·322	8·425	28·1
Case E: $N = 10$, $c = 2$, $f(b) = 20b^3(1-b)$, $0 < b < 1$, $G = 46{\cdot}67$				
10	0·200	0·935	43·945	94·2
9	0·410	0·756	34·757	74·5
Case F: $N = 30$, $c = 6$, $f(b) = 12b(1-b)^2$, $0 < b < 1$, $G = 270$				
10	0·200	0·047	0·984	4·9
9	0·257	0·058	1·162	5·8
8	0·310	0·060	1·107	5·5

k, since the chance of having a country with low b scuttle the deal is smaller with high negative skewness. This can be checked by selecting a negative skewness variant of the beta distribution such as $f(b)=20b^3(1-b)$, $0<b<1$. The results for this distribution are shown in case E. We find that the concentration of high b does indeed cause n to be high, in fact requiring that every country commit. However, unlike the previous case, the expected surplus with $n=N$ is extremely close to that which could be achieved with coercion rather than a voluntary agreement to commit.

Not unexpectedly, as case F shows, positive skewness has a very damaging effect on the expected surplus from any n-rule. However, perhaps counter-intuitively, the optimum n-rule remains one of requiring a very high level of commitment before proceeding. This outcome results from the fact that reducing n to increase the chance of the number of signatories exceeding the threshold so increases k that the lower n does not increase the overall chance of agreement; the effect on k of the lower n is, of course, the result of knowing that benefits are small. The fact that all gain from each other is an essential part of this outcome, with this itself being a feature of the shared nature of the atmosphere.

IV. Agreeing on the Agreement Rule

Underlying our analysis is the notion that international society is anarchic. Were it otherwise, a benevolent dictator could institute a Clarke-Groves mechanism (Clarke 1971, Groves 1973, Groves and Ledyard 1977) simultaneously to elicit preferences and make efficient decisions.[17] The problem with such a scheme in the anarchic international arena is that, given the rule allocating costs and knowing their own b, some countries would realize that they could raise their expected utility by opting out of the procedure altogether. It follows that, in the absence of compulsion, the Clarke-Groves mechanism cannot be implemented.[18] In contrast, the mechanism analysed here does obey the constraint that participation is voluntary.

It is well worth considering the procedure by which the number of signatories required to ratify the agreement is determined. We have characterized the globally optimum minimum participation level, call it n^*, which maximizes the expected aggregate surplus. But is it wishful thinking to hope that this rule will emerge in practice? Perhaps nations could agree to hand over the job of setting n to a benevolent bureaucrat, but their willingness to do so surely depends on whether individual countries have much to gain from an n that differs from n^*. Table 3 reports on this the same uniform distribution analysed in case A of Table 1. For selected values of b, the n-rule that would maximize the surplus of a country with that b is recorded in the $\tilde{n}$ column. The final column shows the gain a country obtains from an n^* rule relative to that with an $\tilde{n}$ rule.

In understanding the properties of Table 3 and the similar results obtained from other distributions, it is helpful to plot how a country's expected surplus (conditional on not signing the agreement) varies with n. Consider a country with some particular value of b. Beyond a certain level, the probability that the agreement is activated falls as n is increased. However, the average number signing if agreement is reached increases with n. The net effect is that the

TABLE 3

COUNTRIES' PREFERRED n GIVEN THEIR b WHEN $N=10$, $c=2$, $f(b)=1$, $0<b<1$, $n^*=7$

b	$\tilde{n}$	Signing decision when $n=7$	Signing decision when $n=\tilde{n}$	$g(n^*)/g(\tilde{n})$[a]
0·20	6	no	no	0·95
0·28	6	no	no	0·95
0·36	6	no	no	0·95
0·45	8	indifferent	yes	0·92
0·54	8	yes	yes	0·96
0·63	8	yes	yes	0·96
0·74	8	yes	yes	0·99
0·85	7	yes	yes	1·00

[a] $g(n^*)/g(\tilde{n})$ is the ratio of the country's expected benefit with $n=n^*$ to its expected benefit with $n=\tilde{n}$, where n^* is the n value that maximizes the expected global surplus and $\tilde{n}$ is the country's preferred $\tilde{n}$.

individual country's expected surplus initially rises with n and then decreases. This is sketched by the left-hand solid curve in Figure 1. Consider now the expected gains to the country if it does sign. Agreement is now more likely to be reached for any given n, but the country must bear the cost of taking action. Hence if the country commits to signing it will tend to prefer a higher n than if it does not sign. A move to a lower probability of agreement but with more participants and so larger gains if it should succeed is more attractive to a country committed to pay c if the threshold is reached than it is to a country opting out. This is illustrated by the right-hand solid curve in Figure 1, which is the country's gain conditional on signing.

The broken curves in the figure are for a country with a higher b than is shown by the solid curves. If a country does not sign, the national benefits if an agreement is reached are proportional to its b. Therefore the best n for a non-signer is independent of its b; the broken line for a high b non-signatory

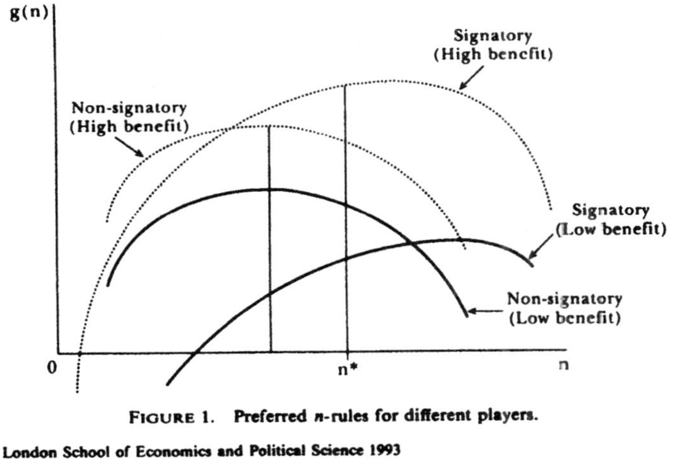

FIGURE 1. Preferred n-rules for different players.

is above the solid line for a low b non-signatory by a constant proportion. On the other hand, if a country signs, its benefit net of participation cost rises more than proportionately with b; $(b-c)$ increases at a faster rate than b, with c, the participation cost, invariant to b. Indeed, the relative increase is greatest when participation is low and net benefits are small. A country with a high b which agrees to sign will therefore be particularly concerned to ensure that agreements succeed, and so (ignoring integer constraints) will favour a lower n than will a country with a lower b.

The qualitative properties of the figure are thus established. As n is increased past some point the low b countries (the non-signers) are worse off even though the high b countries (the signers) are better off. Some countries sign when n is raised and, granted the integer constraint, their welfare may rise or fall. The social planner chooses n as a compromise between the gainers and the losers. At n^* all those who do not sign would prefer the same low n. All the signers would rather that the social planner chose n in excess of n^* or equal to n^*, but, integer constraints aside, the higher a signer's b, the lower is its preferred n. All these properties apply in the example reported in Table 3.

According to the last column of Table 3, even though countries may differ greatly in b, they have little to lose from adopting the n^* rule rather than pressing for the $\tilde{n}$ appropriate to their b. This augurs well for agreement on an n-rule and perhaps for the establishment of a bureaucracy charged with setting n^*. It augurs particularly well for reaching agreement when the bs are high. This is clear in the figure where we see that with high bs, the differences in individually preferred ns are smaller than with low bs. This suggests that, if the global warming problem becomes increasingly threatening, not only does voluntary action become easier to achieve, but the ratification level in drafting the agreement is also easier, shortening the period during which treaty-drafting occurs.

For some other distributions we did find instances where particular countries might obtain a significant gain from a change in n. Does this imply squabbles about the choice of n? If a country has a lot to gain from an n in excess of n^* it may nevertheless hesitate to try to influence the n-setting process. Lobbying for a high n is a sign that the country has a high b. But if this becomes public, other countries are less likely to sign, which is of course bad news for the high b nation. Indeed, if lobbying is the order of the day, countries will tend to press for n below their $\tilde{n}$ so as to convince others they have a low b. Allowing countries to influence the choice of n in publicly observable ways may thus be against the interest even of those with low b values. It therefore seems reasonable that countries might agree *ex ante* to establishing a bureau that impartially computes n^* and incorporates it into the treaty. That is not to say that the present scheme could not be improved on; for example, allowing n to be chosen by some form of secret ballot looks promising. However, our aim here is to explain the properties and feasibility of an n-rule of some sort.

V. LIMITATIONS

By necessity, the numerical results we have generated are only illustrative, and are based on a number of potentially restrictive assumptions. For example, we have assumed that there is only one chance to reach agreement when in fact, if action is assumed to be globally beneficial, participants might realistically expect a further try. With the suspicion of future rounds and for a given n, each country has a lower incentive to ratify in the first round. In the first place, should a refusal to ratify prove pivotal, the opportunity is repeated. Second, it is better for a country that others believe it has a low b, for this increases the subsequent probability that other countries will sign. The motivation to resist ratifying in the first round is, however, tempered by the effect an unratified treaty would have on the assessment of others' assumed benefits, and hence on the n-rule in subsequent rounds; failure on each round of effort would likely reduce n, and hence the benefits to each country with eventual ratification.[19]

We have also assumed that signatories to a treaty do not subsequently abrogate. In reality, it may be necessary to collect a bond from each country on signing, and to redistribute individual contributions to each of the signatories as they take their promised action.[20] This would make abrogation costly. Alternatively, it may be necessary to make continuation conditional on full compliance, before and after ratification, although this runs up against the same credibility arguments concerning once-only ratification: the threat may lack credibility. At the very least, introducing the possibility that any abrogation could trigger abandonment of the entire commitment by others could temper the motive to sign without sincerity concerning follow-through.

Other assumptions we have made, while limiting the practical value of what we have done in selection of an actual n-rule, still leave the results with some potential qualitative value. Let us review what we have determined.

VI. Conclusions

While some of the properties of the n-rule we have described are unsurprising, the relatively high values of n found for the wide variety of postulated circumstances is less intuitive. The same may be said of the finding that free-riding is less of a problem as N increases. Of course, both of these less intuitive outcomes are due to the nature of the Greenhouse Effect. Specifically, they arise from the fact that all countries gain from others' action, so that as the number of countries increases the benefits to each country from an agreement more than offsets the decreased probability of a country being pivotal.

In the presence of uncertainty over net benefits of action, an agreement that stipulates that action is taken only when enough—but not necessarily all—countries commit themselves appears to be preferable to one that comes into force only if there is universal participation. Modelling the emergence of such an n-rule is difficult, given that each country's own preferred n generally differs from that which maximizes the aggregate surplus. But it turns out that countries often have little to lose from adopting the socially maximizing n-rule rather than their individually preferred n, so there is a reasonable prospect of prior agreement to let an international body set the participation level required before action is taken. Our analysis shows that introducing a minimum participation condition into treaties yields considerable benefits, but generally falls well short of perfection.

ACKNOWLEDGEMENTS

This paper was written while Maurice Levi was Nomura Fellow at Exeter University. The authors have benefited greatly from the helpful comments and suggestions of two anonymous referees of this *Journal*, and also Debbie McGurk and seminar participants at Warwick and Strathclyde. However, responsibility for any errors that may remain is solely that of the authors.

NOTES

1. Precommitment before proceeding on a global plan to protect the environment appears to be a feature of the proposed Global Environment Facility of the World Bank. As described by one reporter (Guest 1990), 'Although the bank's officials want voluntary contributions to build up the new facility, some governments want all donors to make a commitment in advance to ensure they are not left carrying the main burden.'
2. In reality, there may not be a known required threshold level of participation before any country takes action, but it may be understood by negotiating countries that insufficient pre-commitment may lead to abandonment of negotiations.
3. This assumes a given amount of action by each country, irrespective of the number of countries that are involved. The analysis of the effect of an *n*-rule distinguishes this work from that of Oakland (1987), Plott (1976) and Sen (1988), and from the work on committees summarized by Peleg (1984).
4. The relative-price and transfer effects within a country make the public-choice problems particularly thorny.
5. This intuitively reasonable proposition has been demonstrated formally by Bagnoli and Lipman (1989).
6. It is also dependent on there being only one chance to reach agreement, and on countries being committed after completion of the ratification process.
7. This conforms with the theoretical analysis of Johnson (1956) and with the observed consequence of the income redistributions following war reparations and the OPEC price rises.
8. This is supported by Nicolaisen and Hoeller (1990), who report that 'the international community has started to take concerted action through international agreements and conventions on general policy goals rather than working out detailed compensation systems' (p. 29).
9. The number of countries that will participate in an international agreement to address ozone depletion or the Greenhouse Effect has also been considered by Barrett (1989). Barrett's purpose is to show that, despite the free-rider problem, some countries will voluntarily accede to a treaty. The reason is that, when a country commits itself to match the actions of the other participants, the countries already committed have an incentive to renegotiate and step up their efforts. Thus, the decision to join has benefits in terms of the activity levels of others, and this affects the direct costs of joining. In this paper the motivation to sign is the contribution that added commitment makes to the likelihood that the treaty is effected. Unlike Barrett's case, here each country can take a single discrete action, and so in the absence of an *n*-rule there would be no agreement. Moreover, as Barrett's case involves complete information, the introduction of an *n*-rule requiring unanimity to the situation he describes would yield a first-best solution rather than the one he analyses.
10. This makes the problem different from that of finding the optimum majority or commitment level where, if reached, all agents are required to contribute whether or not they approved. However, this simpler problem can easily be handled by minor modification to the methodology used below.
11. It is easily seen that self-interested countries would wish others to believe that they will not sign. Consequently, statements of intent will not be credible and no country would actually sign until the last possible moment. Of course, such secrecy does not entirely square with internal democracy. However, the alternative of having a global referendum with nationals of every country voting on the same day on whether to take action conditional on at least $(n-1)$ other countries doing so seems improbable, though attractive.
12. The choice of policy would depend upon the chance that it can be implemented, so the problem we address requires solution before selecting which policy to try to get accepted.
13. The assumptions that $f(b)$ is the same for all countries and that c is common have been made for numerical simplicity. It would be possible to assume different values for c and b values drawn from different distributions, reflecting for example the size and wealth of the countries. This would involve finding different critical k values for each country.
14. This makes the effect of N on the voluntary scheme like that for the compulsory scheme for which the global surplus is given by (4).
15. The choice of a low N and of a uniform distribution, while individually unrealistic, may make sense considered jointly. We might think of the problem as one involving a limited

number of big players with roughly similar benefits, at least after a round of cost allocations. Indeed, it does seem that treaties start with a limited number of large participants. For example, the Montreal Protocol on ozone depletion started with 22 signatories.

16. In Mailath and Postlewaite (1990) the issue is different. Consider a town council soliciting voluntary contributions to pay for a municipal park. Were the town more populous, a correspondingly larger and more expensive park would be needed. As the population size tends to infinity, the probability that the park is provided goes to zero.
17. For an account of this and various other schemes for determining benefits, see Laffont (1987).
18. Nor can the other schemes for allocating costs considered by Moulin (1988).
19. To illustrate that an n-rule may be more beneficial when there are subsequent chances to reach agreement, consider a continuous-time version of the model in which countries vary in their time preferences having different finite horizons beyond which benefits are given no weight. Initially, only one opportunity to reach agreement exists. Assume that countries valuing immediate benefits highly—that is, those with high bs—are also patient, in the sense of having long horizons. In equilibrium let the country on the margin of whether or not to pledge have a time horizon of T^* years. Now suppose it is announced that if the first opportunity to commit fails a second chance will be offered T^* years later. First-time commitment behaviour will be unaffected by this innovation, and in the event of failure an agreement will sometimes be reached at the second attempt. Viewed from time 0, introduction of the second opportunity consequently raises the expected utility of all those with horizons in excess of T^* and no country with a shorter horizon is any worse off.
20. If the bond were set equal to the cost the country's economy would incur from the agreed action, the cost of abrogation would equal the cost of compliance.

REFERENCES

BAGNOLI, M. and LIPMAN, L. (1989). Provision of public goods: fully implementing the core through private contributions. *Review of Economic Studies*, 583–601.

BARRETT, S. (1989). On the nature and significance of international environmental agreements. Mimeo, London Business School.

CLARKE, E. H. (1971). Multipart pricing of public goods. *Public Choice*, **2**, 17–33.

GROVES, T. (1973). Incentives in teams. *Econometrica*, **46**, 617–35.

—— and LEDYARD, J. (1977). Optimal allocation of public goods: a solution to the free-rider problem. *Econometrica*, **45**, 783–809.

GUEST, I. (1990). World bank set to turn green. *The Guardian*, 11 March, p. 11.

JOHNSON, H. G. (1956). The transfer problem and exchange stability. *Journal of Political Economy*, **64**, 212–25.

LAFFONT, J. (1987). Incentives and the allocation of public goods. In A. J. Auerbach and M. Feldstein (eds), *Handbook of Public Economics*, Vol. 2. Amsterdam: North-Holland, pp. 537–69.

MAILATH, J. and POSTLEWAITE, A. (1990). Asymmetric information bargaining problems with many agents'. *Review of Economic Studies*, **57**, 351–67.

MOULIN, H. (1988). *Axioms of Cooperative Decision Making*. Cambridge University Press.

NICOLAISEN, J. and HOELLER, P. (1990). Economics and the environment: a survey of issues and policy options. OECD Working Paper no. 82.

OAKLAND, W. (1987). Theory of public goods. In A. J. Auerbach and M. Feldstein (eds), *Handbook of Public Economics*, Vol. 2. Amsterdam: North-Holland.

PELEG, B. (1984). *Game Theoretic Analysis of Voting in Committees*. Cambridge University Press.

PLOTT, C. R. (1976). Axiomatic social choice theory: an overview and interpretation. *American Journal of Political Science* **20**, 511–96.

SEN, A. K. (1988). 'Social choice theory'. In Kenneth J. Arrow and Michael Intriligator (eds), *Handbook of Mathematical Economics*. Amsterdam: North-Holland.

[4]

Journal of Public Economics 52 (1993) 309–328. North-Holland

Strategies for the international protection of the environment

Carlo Carraro

Department of Economics, University of Udine, Via Tomadini 30, 33 100 Udine, Italy and Fondazione Eni 'Enrico Mattei', Milano, Italy

Domenico Siniscalco*

Faculty of Economics, University of Torino, Pza Albarello 8, 10 122 Torino, Italy and Fondazione Eni 'Enrico Mattei', Milan, Italy

Received July 1991, final version received June 1992

This paper analyses profitability and stability of international agreements to protect the environment in the presence of trans-frontier or global pollution. Each country decides whether or not to coordinate its strategy with other countries. A coalition is formed when conditions of profitability and stability (no free-riding) are satisfied. It is shown that such coalitions exist; that they tend to involve a fraction of negotiating countries; and that the number of signatory countries can be increased by means of self-financed transfers. However, expanding coalitions requires some form of commitment. Such schemes of commitment and transfers can even lead to cooperation by all countries.

1. Introduction

A large amount of pollutants are discharged in the atmosphere and water systems, as a result of human activity in each country. The emissions often affect other countries, as well as the global environment. In economic terms, each polluting country benefits from using the environment as a receptacle for emissions but, at the same time, is also damaged by environmental deterioration. While the benefit is related to domestic emissions only, the damage is related to both domestic and foreign emissions which negatively affect the environment. Hence, a problem of international externalities arises which, in the present institutional setting, can be solved only by voluntary agreements among sovereign countries. Such agreements have been quite common in

Correspondence to: D. Siniscalco, Fondazione Eni Enrico Mattei, Via S. Sofia 27, I-20122 Milano, Italy.

*We are grateful to K.J. Arrow, C. D'Aspremont, M. Hoel, K.G. Maler, P. Michel and two anonymous referees, for helpful comments and suggestions on a previous version of this paper. The usual disclaimers apply.

recent years,[1] and they seem to share some features: they are often characterized by cooperative behaviour among the individual countries involved; they usually have only a sub-group of the negotiating countries as signatories (partial cooperation); and they tend to use various forms of transfers, typically to the developing countries, as a key instrument for increasing the number of signatories.

The existing literature on the protection of the international environment does not sufficiently convey the characteristics of international agreements mentioned above. The traditional contributions on trans-national commons describe countries' environmental interaction as a one-shot Prisoner's Dilemma, where free-riding inevitably leads to the 'tragedy of commons' [for a discussion, see Ostrom (1990)]. In more recent works on the subject, the repetition of the Prisoner's Dilemma, under appropriate assumptions, can enlarge the set of equilibrium outcomes, and characterize situations where all countries cooperate [for a discussion, see Maler (1989), Barrett (1992)]. Partial cooperation and the role of transfers, however, are not usually considered in either approach.

This paper presents a general framework to analyse the profitability and stability of international agreements to protect the environment in the presence of trans-frontier or global pollution. In our analysis, international negotiations are modelled as games in which sovereign countries bargain over emission control. With respect to emission control, countries may choose to act either cooperatively or non-cooperatively. In the former case, cooperative agreements can involve a sub-group of countries, whose number can be expanded by means of 'self-financed' welfare transfers. The framework re-interprets results which were already presented in the recent environmental literature with reference to specific cases [e.g. Maler (1989), Newbery (1991), Barrett (1991, 1992), Hoel (1992), Kaitala et al. (1992)]. More importantly, it provides new results on the emergence of partial cooperation, transfers, and the role of commitment.

The main conclusions of the paper can be summarized as follows:

(i) the strategic interaction among countries in a common environment does not necessarily lead to the 'tragedy of commons', but there is a wide range of possible voluntary agreements to control emissions;

(ii) beyond non-cooperative emission control, there exist partial cooperative agreements among sub-groups of countries (coalitions) which are profitable and stable;

(iii) gains from partial cooperation can be used to expand existing coalitions by inducing other countries to cooperate using self-financed welfare transfers. To sustain broader coalitions by means of transfers, however, a minimum

[1]Experts quote more than 150 international agreements which have been signed to protect the environment in various regions. The protocols on CFC, and the ongoing negotiation on global warming provide examples of agreements at the global level.

degree of commitment must be introduced into the game, thus changing its rules. The various forms of commitment proposed in the paper are less demanding than a commitment of cooperation by all players, since they may involve only a fraction of the cooperating countries. Such schemes of partial commitment and transfers can even lead to cooperation by all countries.

The paper is organized as follows. In section 2, the general framework is introduced and some kinds of agreements which can lead to pollution control are defined. Results on stable coalitions, the role of transfers and commitment are also provided. In section 3, the main results and implications of the proposed framework are discussed. Finally, in section 4, some extensions of the model are proposed, together with the scope for further work.

2. The analytical framework

2.1. Players, payoffs, strategies

Consider n countries ($n \geqq 2$) that interact in a common environment, and bargain over emission control of a specific pollutant. Each country i benefits from using the environment as a factor of production and as a receptable for emissions. The welfare of each country, however, is negatively affected both by its own emissions x_i and by other countries' emissions x_{-i}, where x_{-i} is the vector $(x_1, \ldots, x_{i-1}, x_{i+1}, \ldots, x_n)$.

Country i's benefit and damage can be represented in the welfare function $P_i(x) = B_i(x_i) - D_i(x_i, x_{-i})$, where $B_i(x_i)$ denotes benefits arising from the use of the environment for production and consumption activities; $D_i(x_i, x_{-i})$ denotes damages (welfare losses) resulting from pollution emissions;[2] and $x \equiv (x_1 \ldots x_n) = (x_i, x_{-i})$ is the vector of all countries' emissions.

Let us consider the benefit function $B_i(x_i)$. It is assumed that a reduction in pollution, which can be achieved through domestic environmental policies, is costly and reduces benefits. The benefit function, which depends on abatement costs, is related to the level of technology, the economic structure, the level of development, and the endowment of resources of a country. By technology we mean more than the mechanical process of turning inputs into outputs; we mean useful knowledge and experience, institutions and organizational structures, norms and values that govern the processes of production and exchange.

The damage function $D_i(x_i, x_{-i})$ depends on a country's perception of the effects of emissions of a given pollutant, as well as on the evaluation of such effects. Consequently, the damage function is based on a subjective evaluation of environmental goods. The specific functional form of $D_i(\cdot)$ can be

[2]The parameters of the damage function may include the ith row of the transportation matrix $A = \{\alpha_{ij}\}$, where α_{ij} is the share of the country j's emissions affecting country i.

determined using appropriate models of environmental impact evaluation. In such models, an index usually summarizes both the measurement of the relevant physical damages and their evaluation.

Countries consider one pollutant at a time. Let δ_i be the maximum level of pollution emissions for country i. It is computed by maximizing environmental benefits $B_i(x_i)$ without taking into account the associated costs evaluated through the function $D_i(\cdot)$. Moreover, δ_i can be seen as a measure of a country's size and level of development. The 'emission game' between the n countries is defined by a triple (N, S, P), and by appropriate rules: as usual, $N=\{1\ldots n\}$ is the set of players, $S=S_1\times\cdots\times S_n$, where $S_i=[0,\delta_i]$, is the strategy space, and $P=(P_1(x)\ldots P_n(x))$ is the payoff vector. Complete information is assumed. Problems arising from asymmetric information will briefly be mentioned in section 4.

By taking into account reciprocal externalities, a country may decide whether or not to cooperate with other countries in order to reduce total emissions. At this stage, we assume that cooperative agreements are not binding. The decision regarding whether or not to cooperate is the outcome of a 'metagame' in which each country anticipates the choice (cooperative or non-cooperative) of the other countries, and the relative outcomes in terms of emission levels.[3]

Let us begin by analysing the outcomes of the game under alternative strategic combinations. First, we assume that countries play simultaneously and non-cooperatively. Thus, country i's optimal level of emissions is determined by equating marginal benefits with marginal costs, given the emission levels set by the other countries. The solution of the system of first-order conditions determines the Nash equilibria of the game. For simplicity's sake, we assume the equilibrium to be unique. The Nash equilibrium of the non-cooperative game can also be determined by computing the fixed point of countries' best-reply functions. Let $R_i(x)$, $x=(x_1\ldots x_n)$, the country i's best-reply function, where $R_i(x)=\{x_i\colon P_i(x_i,x_{-i})\geqq P_i(s_i,x_{-i})$, for all $s_i\in S_i\}$. The non-cooperative equilibrium x^0 is defined by $x^0=R(x^0)$, where $R(x)=(R_1(x)\ldots R_n(x))$.

Alternatively, countries can decide to set emissions cooperatively. In this case, we assume that a bargaining process takes place in order to achieve a

[3]We restrict our analysis to one-shot games. In terms of additional equilibrium outcomes, analysing repeated games would be fruitful only if appropriate trigger or stick/carrot strategies could sustain cooperation as an equilibrium outcome. The level of emissions, however, can hardly be conceived as a trigger variable which can be increased strategically in response to other countries' defection. Some reasons are the following: firstly, emission reduction, in cases such as CO_2 or CFC, involves substantial and irreversible investments. Secondly, expanding emissions as a retaliation could generate environmental damage primarily to the triggering country. Finally, an increase in emissions can hardly be used as a selective punishment. Other effective punishments (e.g. trade protectionism) could be even more costly for the triggering country and therefore, not credible. For these reasons, we believe that trigger or stick/carrot strategies are not particularly helpful in sustaining environmental cooperation.

Pareto optimal outcome. The bargaining process may lead to the formation of a coalition among j countries, where j goes from 2 (the smallest feasible coalition) to n (when all countries set emissions by taking into account reciprocal externalities). We define 'full cooperation' as a situation in which a coalition formed by n countries emerges, while a 'partial cooperation' is a coalition formed by $2 \leqq j < n$ countries. In this work, we determine the cooperative outcome of the game by using the Nash bargaining solution.[4] Moreover, we use the non-cooperative equilibrium $x^0 = (x_1^0 \ldots x_n^0)$ as the threat point of the bargaining process.[5] Stated more formally, j countries will act cooperatively when they set emissions maximizing the joint product of the difference between $P_j(x)$ and P_i^0, where P_i^0 denotes the non-cooperative welfare.

Before setting emission levels, each country must therefore decide whether or not to act cooperatively. This decision can be modelled by defining a 'metagame' in which countries choose between the cooperative and the non-cooperative strategy by anticipating the outcomes of the related emission game.[6]

2.2. *Profitability and stability of coalitions*

Let $P_i(j)$ be country i's welfare when it decides to cooperate, and $j-1$ when other countries also cooperate; whereas $Q_i(j)$ is its welfare when country i does not join the coalition formed by j countries. Moreover, let j stand for the set of cooperating countries, and J^0 denote the set of countries that play non-cooperatively. Let us suppose, for simplicity, that all countries are symmetric, i.e. the welfare function is not country specific. We do not therefore index the welfare functions P and Q and their parameters.

A minimum requirement must be met for an environmental coalition to be formed: the welfare of each country signing the cooperative agreement must be larger than the non-cooperative welfare. In other words, country i gains from joining the coalition, with respect to its position when no countries cooperate, if $P(j) > P^0$. This leads to:

Definition 1. A coalition formed by j players is *profitable* if $P(j) > P^0$ for all countries belonging to J.

[4]This assumption is not crucial, because, in the rest of the analysis, all countries will be assumed to have the same benefit and damage functions. As was pointed out by a referee, in this case any bargaining solution in the literature would give the same result.

[5]In a two-player game, this means interpreting Rubinstein's alternating offers model as a model in which players face a risk that, if the agreement is delayed, then the opportunity they hope to exploit it jointly may be lost [see Binmore et al. (1986)].

[6]Most environmental studies model this 'metagame' as a one-shot Prisoner's dilemma, in which non-cooperation is the dominant strategy.

Of course, this only represents a minimum requirement that may not suffice to induce many countries to sign a cooperative agreement. The main problem preventing the formation of any coalition is the possibility of free-riding by some countries. Free-riding can be explained as follows: since one country can profit from the reduction of emissions by cooperating countries, it has an incentive to let other countries to sign the cooperative agreement. If all countries are symmetric, no cooperation takes place. In other words, the 'metagame' in which countries choose between cooperation and non-cooperation is represented as a Prisoner's dilemma. As we will see, however, this representation of countries' strategic choice may not be appropriate.

The problem can also be stated more formally. For each country, the crucial comparison is between $P(j)$, the country's payoff for belonging to the j-coalition, and $Q(j-1)$, the country's payoff when it exists the coalition, and lets other $j-1$ countries sign the cooperative agreement. Let $Q(j-1)-P(j)$ be a country's incentive to defect from a coalition formed by j players, whereas $P(j+1)-Q(j)$ is the incentive for a non-cooperating country to join a j-coalition [which, consequently, becomes a $(j+1)$-coalition]. Thus, a stable coalition can be defined as follows:

Definition 2. A coalition formed by j players is *stable* if there is no incentive to defect, i.e. $Q(j-1)-P(j)<0$, for all countries belonging to J, and there is no incentive to broaden the coalition, i.e. $P(j+1)-Q(j)<0$, for all countries belonging to J^0.

This definition corresponds to that of cartel stability presented in the oligopoly literature [see D'Aspremont and Gabszewicz (1986), a similar definiton is also used in Barrett (1991)].

It has been shown that under fairly general conditions stable coalitions exist [see Donsimoni et al. (1986)]. However, this does not satisfactorily address the problem of protecting international commons because, as has been demonstrated both in the oligopoly and in the environmental literature [see, for example, D'Aspremont et al. (1983), D'Aspremont and Gabszewicz (1986), Carraro and Siniscalco (1991), Hoel (1992)], stable coalitions are generally formed by $j \leqq n$ players, where j is a small number, regardless of n.[7] This leads us to the following question: can the j cooperating countries expand the coalition through self-financed welfare transfers to the remaining players?

Given the previously stated rules of the game, the answer is no. This is demonstrated by the following proposition:

[7]More satisfactory results are presented in Barrett (1991), who shows that, under certain conditions, and given a specific functional form for the welfare function, large stable coalitions exist.

Proposition 1. Suppose no countries can commit to the cooperative strategy. Then, in this case, no self-financed transfer T from the j cooperating countries to the other non-cooperating countries can successfully enlarge the original coalition.

Proof. For the transfer to be self-financed, it cannot be larger than the gain that the j players obtain from moving to a $(j+1)$-coalition. Furthermore, in order to add one player to a j-coalition, the transfer T must be larger than the loss incurred by the $j+1$ player by entering it. These two conditions yield:

$$[P(j+1)-P(j)] \geqq T > Q(j)-P(j+1). \tag{1}$$

This condition makes it possible to self-finance an enlarged coalition. However, is this broadened coalition stable? The $j+1$ player does not defect if the transfer is larger than $Q(j)-P(j+1)$. However, by definition of stable coalition, $P(j+1)<Q(j)$: the j players of the original coalition have therefore an incentive to defect; their incentive being greater because of the transfer made to the $j+1$ player. Hence, the $(j+1)$-coalition is unstable. Q.E.D.

This leads to the following conclusion: welfare transfers from countries belonging to a stable coalition to non-cooperating countries cannot be used to expand the initial coalition, unless the rules of the game are changed. There are various rules that can lead to the formation of larger stable coalitions. We will focus our attention on the role of commitment. If all countries were committed to cooperation, obviously no free-riding would exist. We show, however, that there are several, less demanding forms of commitment which, if associated with appropriate welfare transfers, can lead to large stable coalitions. There are two crucial elements in our analysis: partial commitments (only a subset of the n countries commit to co-operation), and welfare transfers (bribing).

2.3. *Expanding coalitions*

Hereafter, we shall analyse the implications of four types of commitment, that could serve as possible blueprints for environmental cooperation. Of course, other types of institutional mechanisms could be proposed as well. The four types of commitments are:

(i) Only the j countries belonging to the stable coalition commit to cooperation (stable coalition commitment).

(ii) The j countries are committed to cooperation and any new signatory, as soon as it enters the expanded coalition, must commit to cooperation as well (sequential commitment).

(iii) The number of committed countries is such that appropriate transfers can induce all other countries to cooperate (full-cooperation minimum commitment).

(iv) A subset of non-cooperating countries commits to transfer welfare in order to induce the remaining non-signatories to cooperate, and to guarantee the stability of the resulting coalition (external commitment).

As has already been shown, it is necessary to impose constraints on the amount of transfers allowed: if no restriction were imposed, all non-signatories could be bribed. Therefore, we assume:

(i) transfers must be self-financed, i.e. the total transfer T must be lower than the gain that the committed countries obtain from expanding the coalition;

(ii) the move to a larger coalition must be Pareto-improving, i.e. all countries must be better off than in the situation preceeding the coalition expansion, and better off with respect to the case of no-cooperation (the larger coalition must be profitable); and

(iii) committed countries choose the transfer in order to maximize the number of signatories (given the above two constraints).[8]

Given these restrictions, the following question can be asked: Under what conditions can partial commitments and transfers expand the initial j-coalition? Some answers are provided by the following propositions:

Proposition 2 (Stable coalition commitment). *Suppose the j countries belonging to the stable coalition are committed to cooperation. If $P(j+s)>P(j)$ and $Q(j+s)>Q(j)$ for all positive s, $s\leqq n-j-1$, then at most r countries can be induced to join the initial coalition, where r is the largest integer satisfying:*

$$r<j[P(j+r)-P(j)]/[Q(j+r-1)-P(j+r)]. \tag{2}$$

Proof. The initial j countries can use their gains resulting from broadening the coalition in order to finance other countries' cooperation. This gain is equal to $j[P(j+r)-P(j)]$, and it is positive if $P(j+r)>P(j)$. In order for transfers to be self-financed, they must be greater than the incentive to defect for the r countries that have to enter the coalition. This incentive is equal to $r[Q(j+r-1)-P(j+r)]$. Hence:

$$j[P(j+r)-P(j)]>r[Q(j+r-1)-P(j+r)]. \tag{2'}$$

Moreover, the maximum transfer $j[P(j+r)-P(j)]$ must be larger than the

[8]Notice that transfers enter a country's payoff in an additive way. Otherwise, each cooperating country would maximize its payoff with respect to both emissions and transfers. This would be the case if transfers were carried out using policy instruments which interact with other economic variables, and with emissions in particular. Such an extension of the paper is discussed in the concluding section.

total loss suffered by entering countries; this loss is equal to $r[Q(j)-P(j+r)]$. This condition can be expressed as follows:

$$j[P(j+r)-P(j)]>r[Q(j)-Q(j+r-1))+(Q(j+r-1)-P(j+r))]. \quad (3)$$

Notice that $[Q(j)-Q(j+r-1)]\leqq 0$ and $[Q(j+r-1)-P(j+r]>0$. Hence, (2′) implies (3). Since (2) implies (2′), the proposition is proved. The newly entered countries have no incentive to defect, and benefit from joining the coalition; moreover, the initial cooperating countries benefit from expanding the coalition, and are committed to cooperation. Therefore, the new equilibrium constitutes a Pareto improvement. Q.E.D.

The meaning of Proposition 2 is the following: starting from a j-coalition, the commitment of its members induces, through appropriate transfers, other r countries to join the initial coalition; notice that r is larger, the larger the gain attained from expanding the coalition, and the lower the incentive to defect from it.

Proposition 3 (Sequential commitment). *Suppose that a stable coalition formed by j countries exists. If each country, when entering the coalition, commits to cooperation, and if $P(j+s)>P(j+s-1)$ for all $1\leqq s\leqq r$, then at most r countries can be induced to join the initial coalition if*

$$j+s>[Q(j+s-1)-P(j+s-1)]/[(j+s)-P(j+s-1)] \quad (4)$$

for all $1\leqq s\leqq r$, and, when $j+r<n$,

$$j+r<[Q(j+r)-P(j+r+1)]/[P(j+r+1)-P(j+r)]. \quad (4')$$

Proof. Suppose that j countries form a stable coalition, and are committed to cooperation. For one more country to be induced to cooperate, the transfer must be lower than or equal to the total gain derived from moving to a $(j+1)$-coalition, and larger than the loss incurred by the entering country. This gives

$$j[P(j+1)-P(j)]>Q(j)-P(j+1)>0. \quad (5)$$

Suppose this condition is satisfied and that the $(j+1)$th country, when entering the coalition, commits to cooperation. An additional country can be induced to join the coalition if

$$(j+1)[P(j+2)-P(j+1)]>Q(j+1)-P(j+2)>0. \quad (6)$$

By iterating this reasoning, one can say that r countries can be induced to join the initial coalition through appropriate transfers, and the sequential commitment, if

$$(j+s-1)[P(j+s)-P(j+s-1)]>Q(j+s-1)-P(j+s)>0 \tag{7}$$

for all $1 \leqq s \leqq r$. If this condition is satisfied for all s such that $j<s \leqq n-j$, then all countries will join the coalition. Thus, full cooperation can be achieved. Otherwise, the coalition cannot be expanded further if

$$(j+r)[P(j+r+1)-P(j+r)]<Q(j+r)-P(j+r+1). \tag{7'}$$

Full cooperation cannot always be achieved because there may exist values of r for which the gain from further broadening the coalition is lower than the loss incurred by the entering country, i.e. the transfer would not be sufficient to induce one more country to join the coalition.

Eq. (7) can be re-written as

$$j+s>[Q(j+s-1)-P(j+s-1)]/[P(j+s)-P(j+s-1)] \tag{8}$$

for all $1 \leqq s \leqq r$, and

$$j+r<[Q(j+r)-P(j+r+1)]/[P(j+r+1)+P(j+r)]. \tag{8'}$$

It should be noted that, when the $(j+r)$-coalition is formed, all countries gain from broadening the coalition. Moreover, given the assumption regarding commitment, the coalition is stable. Q.E.D.

Proposition 3 has two implications. First, as in the case of stable coalition commitment, the expanded coalition is larger, the larger the gain from moving to a wider coalition, and the lower the incentive to defect from it. Secondly, this form of commitment is more demanding than the previous one, since it eliminates the problem of guaranteeing the coalition stability (by the sequential commitment assumption). Hence, unless (4′) holds for some $r<n-j$, full cooperation can be achieved.

Proposition 4 (Full-cooperation minimum commitment). *If $Q(n-1)>Q(i)$ for all positive $i<n-1$, at least a fraction*

$$i/n>[Q(n-1)-P(n)]/[Q(n-1)-P(i)] \tag{9}$$

of the n countries must be committed to a cooperative strategy for all n countries to cooperate.

Proof. Let us assume that i countries are committed to cooperation regardless of the size of the coalition that is formed. Suppose the i countries offer transfers to induce the other $(n-i)$ countries to join the coalition. The total transfer T must be less than or equal to the gain that the i players achieve from entering the n-coalition. Moreover, this transfer should compensate the $(n-i)$ players for the loss from joining the coalition, and should also offset their incentive to defect from the n-coalition. In order to compensate the $(n-i)$ players for the loss from joining the n-coalition, the following condition must be met:

$$i(P(n)-P(i)) \geqq T > (n-i)(Q(i)-P(n)). \tag{10}$$

This condition ensures that the enlarged coalition is self-financed. It can be re-written as

$$i[Q(i)-P(i)] > n[Q(i)-P(n)]. \tag{10'}$$

In order to offset the incentive to deviate from the n-coalition, the gain $P(n)$ plus the transfer $i(P(n)-P(i))/(n-i)$ must be larger than the defector's welfare $Q(n-1)$, i.e. rearranging the equation

$$i(Q(n-1)-P(i)) > n(Q(n-1)-P(n)), \tag{11}$$

which is equivalent to (9). Notice that both sides of the equation are positive. Eq. (11) can be re-written as

$$i[(Q(n-1)-Q(i))+(Q(i)-P(i))] > n[(Q(n-1)-Q(i))+(Q(i)-P(n))]. \tag{11'}$$

Let us show that (11') implies (10'). Assume that (11') holds as an equality. Thus, we can solve it with respect to $Q(i)-P(i)$. This expression can then be substituted into eq. (10'), yielding $(n-i)[Q(n-1)-Q(i)]>0$, which is satisfied for all positive $i<n-1$. Hence, condition (9) guarantees that both the financing condition (10) and the no-defection condition (11) are satisfied. As a consequence, the $(n-i)$ players that join the initial coalition have no incentive to defect. The initial i players are instead committed to cooperation. Finally, the move to the n-coalition is a Pareto improvement. Q.E.D.

Proposition 4 states that there exists a minimum number of countries that should commit to cooperation for all the remaining countries to be induced to cooperate using appropriate transfers. The minimum number of committed cooperating countries decreases as the gain from moving from the i-coalition to the n-coalition increases, and as the incentive to defect from the latter decreases.

The last case we would like to explore considers how an environmental coalition can be expanded using external commitment. Non-cooperating countries gain when the cooperative agreement is expanded (because they receive less emissions). Consequently, a subset of these countries could find it profitable to induce other non-signatories to enter the coalition, and to secure its stability. Suppose, then, that a fraction of non-cooperating countries commits to finance environmental cooperation (emission reduction in other countries). What is the largest number of countries that can be induced to form a stable coalition?

Proposition 5 (External commitment). *Suppose that j countries cooperate, and that $n-j-r$ non-cooperating countries commit to transfer welfare both to induce r non-signatories to cooperate, and to guarantee the stability of the resulting coalition. If $P(j+s)>P(j)$ and $Q(j+s)>Q(j)$ for all positive $s \leqq n-j-1$, a stable $(j+r)$-coalition can be formed if*

$$(j+r)/n<1/(1+\theta), \tag{12}$$

where $\theta=[Q(j+r-1)-P(j+r)]/[Q(j+r)-Q(j)]$.

Proof. Assume there exists a stable j-coalition. The $(n-j-r)$ countries who do not join the coalition gain from financing, through appropriate transfers, a larger coalition, if $Q(j+r)$, their payoff when the $(j+r)$-coalition is formed, less $(Q(j+r-1)-P(j+r))(j+r)/(n-j-r)$, the transfer to the $(j+r)$ cooperating countries, is larger than $Q(j)$, their payoff before broadening the coalition. This is true if (12) holds. Moreover, $Q(j+r)-(Q(j+r-1)-P(j+r))(j+r)/(n-j-r)$ must be larger than $P(j+r+1)$, i.e. no additional countries want to join the coalition. This is true if

$$(n-j-r)[Q(j+r)-P(j+r+1)]>(j+r)[Q(j+r-1)-P(j+r)], \tag{13}$$

which can be written as

$$n[Q(j+r)-P(j+r+1)]>(j+r)[Q(j+r)-P(j+r)+Q(j+r-1)$$
$$-P(j+r+1)]. \tag{13$'$}$$

Comparing (12) and (13′), it is easy to see that (12) implies (13′) [and therefore (13)].

Finally, we have to prove that the players in the $(j+r)$-coalition have no incentive to defect. This is true if $P(j+r)$, the welfare when the $(j+r)$-coalition is formed, plus $Q(j+r-1)-P(j+r)$, the transfer each cooperating country receives, is not lower than $Q(j+r-1)$, the welfare that each cooperating country would receive by defecting from the coalition. This implies $Q(j+r-1)\geqq Q(j+r-1)$, which obviously holds (we assume that whenever a country is indifferent between cooperation and defection, it cooperates). Moreover, $P(j+r)+[Q(j+r-1)-P(j+r)]$ is larger than $P(j)$, the welfare that countries in the stable coalition received before its expansion, because $P(j+r)>P(j)$ by assumption and $Q(j+r-1)-P(j-r)>0$ by the stability condition; it is also larger than $Q(j)$, the welfare that countries entering the coalition received before, because $Q(j+r-1)>Q(j)$ by assumption.

As a consequence, all players in the $(j+r)$-coalition do not defect, all players outside the coalition do not want to join it, and the move to a $(j+r)$-coalition constitutes a Pareto improvement. Q.E.D.

The conclusion reached is the following: r additional countries can be induced to cooperate, and the $(j+r)$-coalition is stable if the remaining $(n-j-r)$ non-cooperating countries commit to carry on appropriate transfers to the $(j+r)$ cooperating countries. The dimension of the resulting coalition increases as the incentive to defect from a $(j+r)$-coalition decreases, and as the gain that non-cooperators achieve from moving to a $(j+r)$-coalition increases.

3. Results and applications to environmental agreements

3.1. Some general comments

The framework proposed in the previous section aims at explaining the emergence of environmental cooperation without the help of trigger or stick/carrot mechanisms. Our approach was chosen because, to our knowledge, no international negotiation to protect the environment has ever used pollution as a triggering variable, and because partial cooperation and transfers seem to be common features of many recent agreements in this field.

The crucial steps of the analysis are two: we first characterize stable coalitions, and give some formal conditions for their existence (subsection 3.2). We then use such stable coalitions as a starting point for wider coalitions, expanded by means of transfers and commitments (subsection 3.3). The existence of small stable coalitions is a result already obtained in the most recent environmental literature. Subsection 3.3 on expanded coalitions provides some new results.

The whole framework deserves some general comment, at this stage. If stable coalitions exist, the 'metagame' in which countries decide whether or not to cooperate is not a Prisoner's dilemma. Assume that a j-stable coalition is formed: by definition, no incentive to defect exists ($Q(j-1)<P(j)$). All countries, however, have an additional incentive not to cooperate. Since non-cooperating countries gain from the others' cooperative behaviour, each country has an incentive to let other countries form the coalition ($Q(j)>P(j)$). This is not a Prisoner's dilemma because the situation in which

Table 1

		Country h	
		C	N
Country i	C	$P(j+1), P(j+1)$	$P(j), Q(j)$
	N	$Q(j), P(j)$	$Q(j-1), Q(j-1)$

one group of countries cooperates and the others do not is an equilibrium of the 'metagame'. This is shown by the 2×2 example in table 1.

In this table, C and N denote the cooperative and non-cooperative strategies, respectively, and the payoff pairs indicate countries' welfare, as defined in the previous section. Table 1 represents a situation in which $j-1$ countries cooperate. A stable coalition is formed by j countries. Countries i and h are the marginal countries with respect to the stable coalition. Both i and h have an incentive to join the coalition (by definition of stability). Country i's most preferred outcome is the one in which it lets h cooperate. However, if country h does not act cooperatively, country i will choose to do so, in order to belong to the stable coalition (by definition of stability). Formally, this is implied by the following inequalities: $Q(j) > P(j+1) > P(j) > Q(j-1)$. The first and the last inequalities are implied by the stability of the j-coalition; $P(j+1) - P(j)$ holds by assumption (see subsections 2.2 and 2.3). Hence, non-cooperation is not the dominant strategy. This game is known as a *chicken game* (a game belonging to the class of coordination games). There are two equilibria (N, C) and (C, N), but all countries have an incentive to let the others cooperate.[9] The game has no dominant strategy; countries' attempts to choose non-cooperation, in order to let the others cooperate, may lead to the worst possible outcome (N, N). The cooperative outcome (C, C) is not Pareto optimal.

A stable coalition can be expanded by transfers to non-cooperating countries, provided some form of commitment takes place. The intuition behind this result is simple. Welfare transfers to non-cooperating countries decrease by T the payoff of the countries belonging to the j-coalition, preserving profitability (transfers are self-financed), but creating instability. The instability has to be dealt with by some form of commitment. As we

[9]The impasse can be solved by the introduction of asymmetries into the game. If countries have different preferences, technology or environmental endowment, it is possible to determine which countries are likely to form a coalition. For example, in the case of external commitment, countries with higher abatement costs are likely to finance emission reductions in countries with lower abatement costs, who therefore form the coalition. In the case of stable coalition commitment, countries in which environmental policy is part of a package of coordinated policies, or large countries that heavily affect the global environment, are more likely to commit themselves to cooperation, thus attracting other cooperators. If the game were repeated, countries with higher discount rate would be more likely to form a coalition.

anticipated in the introduction, the various forms of commitment we analyse are less demanding than the commitment by all players assumed in cooperative games. In our framework, the commitment of only a fraction of the n countries can ensure the stability of wider coalitions, and can even lead to full cooperation.

Notice, moreover, that welfare transfers are indeed impossible and/or inefficient if they are based only on emission reductions. The simplest instrument to transfer wealth is probably cash. There are, however, other appropriate instruments, such as trade or debt policy and technology transfers.

3.2. Stable coalitions and best-reply functions

Over and above the previous comments, a number of specific questions deserve answers: Under what economic conditions does a stable coalition exist? How many countries belong to the stable coalition? Which form of commitment is likely to increase the number of countries belonging to the stable coalition? What is the size of the largest coalition in each different case?

To answer such questions, it is necessary to specify a particular form for the benefit and damage functions of the different countries. Under such restriction, the environmental literature does provide some helpful insights into stable coalitions: for example, Barrett (1991), Carraro and Siniscalco (1991) and Hoel (1992) show that stable coalitions for the protection of the environment exist under reasonable specifications of the benefit and damage functions. The same conclusion is reached in the cartel stability literature [see D'Aspremont et al. (1983) and Schmalensee (1987), for example]. More general results on the existence of stable coalitions in oligopolistic markets can be found in D'Aspremont and Gabszewicz (1986) and Donsimoni et al. (1986). These results prove that there are cases in which the metagame describing countries' interaction in environmental negotiations is not a Prisoner's dilemma. These works also show that stable coalitions are generally formed by a subset of all players of the game, and that this subset is often small. Only Barrett (1991), using a specific example, provides numerical simulations in which the number of cooperating countries approximates n.

In addition, there is one result which appears in most of the works on the international environment, but is seldom discussed: the pattern of interdependence among countries, as described by the slope of their best-reply function, is crucial for understanding the effectiveness of cooperative and non-cooperative emission control. The reason being that the more negative the slope of the best-reply functions, the larger the incentive to deviate from any coalition [i.e. $Q(j-1)-P(j)$ in the game]. Drawing from results proved in

Carraro and Siniscalco (1991), we would like to clarify the role played by the slope of countries' best-reply function.

Let us first consider non-cooperative emission control. Countries that interact in a common environment with mutual externalities set their emissions by equating their own marginal benefit to marginal damage, given the emissions set by the other countries. In this context, country i's actual emissions are generally lower than emissions δ_i, which maximize its benefit function. Moreover, non-coopeative emissions are increasingly reduced as the slope of the best-reply functions become increasingly negative. The literature shows this is the case when the impact of foreign emissions for country i is high, the perceived damage is high, and the benefit (abatement cost) is low [on this point see Barrett (1991) and Carraro and Siniscalco (1991)].[10]

The reason that lies behind this result is intuitively simple. The best-reply functions reflect, inter alia, the marginal damage produced by foreign countries' emissions. If this marginal damage to country i is relevant, then the best non-cooperative response of country i to an expansion of foreign emission is an emission reduction. This reduction will be greater, the lower the benefit of domestic emissions, and vice versa. The difference between δ_i and the actual non-coopertive emissions of country i is therefore positively related to the slope of country i's best-reply function.

Let us now consider cooperation. In this case, countries bargain over emission levels in order to achieve an optimal aggregate outcome, taking into account reciprocal externalities. As is well known, cooperation among all countries is profitable and optimal, but it is intrinsically undermined by free-riding. However, if the best-reply functions are orthogonal or near orthogonal, there is some scope for partial cooperation in the form of agreements among small groups of countries, which can be profitable and stable. The reason, again, has to do with free-riding behaviour, as reflected by the best-reply function of a country which does not belong to the partial coalition. If this best-reply function is negatively sloped, the non-cooperating country will expand its emissions if the coalition restricts them, offsetting the effort of the cooperating countries. If, on the contrary, the best-reply functions are orthogonal or near orthogonal, the free-rider will simply enjoy the cleaner environment without paying for it, but will not offset the emission reduction by the cooperating countries.

Similarly, with negatively sloped best-reply functions, the number of countries is also crucial for the existence of stable coalitions. If n is large, a stable coalition is unlikely to exist, as a cooperative contraction by few

[10]Notice that high perceived damage, low abatement cost, and high impact of foreign emissions are only necessary conditions for the negative slope of the best-reply functions. Separable damage functions imply orthogonal best-reply functions, whatever the other parameters.

countries is offset by the reactions of many others [see Barrett (1991) and Carraro and Siniscalco (1991)].

The above considerations suggest that, in environmental agreements, there is a sort of trade-off. When the best-reply functions are negatively sloped there is a high degree of interdependence. Likewise, non-cooperative emission control can lead to substantial emission reduction. But if one or more countries unilaterally or cooperatively reduces emissions, this contraction is offset by an expansion by the non-cooperating countries. This kind of interaction undermines all kinds of cooperation, as the free-riding behaviour implies a substantial loss for countries who wish to cooperate. With an orthogonal or near-orthogonal best-reply function the situation is somehow reversed. Non-cooperative emission control leads to small emission reductions, but the scope for cooperation is now greater: if a number of countries cooperatively reduce their emissions, this reduction is not offset by free-riders, who simply enjoy a better environment but do not directly damage countries which cooperate. In this case, then, stable coalitions exist.

3.3. Transfers and commitments

The result that stable coalitions are formed by a subset of the n countries, and that this subset is often small, led us to consider strategies for expanding stable coalitions. Coalition expansions can be achieved through welfare transfers and some form of commitment. How much can a stable coalition be expanded? Which type of commitment leads to full cooperation?

Proposition 1 in section 2 holds for any form of the benefit and damage function: it shows that any attempt to expand a stable coalition by means of transfers is flawed without some form of commitment. This point, which may be relevant to the environmental policy debate, has already been discussed in section 2 and subsection 3.1.

We have attempted, therefore, to explore various forms of commitment in order to sustain expanded coalitions.

The 'stable coalition commitment' (Proposition 2) is the first to be discussed. Let us suppose a stable coalition exists. If all members of the coalition commit to cooperation, they can use the gains resulting from moving to a larger coalition to bribe other countries. How many countries can be induced to enter the coalition using this strategy?

The existing environmental literature is not very helpful in addressing these issues, as they are relatively new. One specific example we provide elsewhere [Carraro and Siniscalco (1991)], assuming symmetric countries and linear-quadratic benefit and damage functions, shows that the answer depends once more on the slope of the best-reply functions. With orthogonal (or near-orthogonal) best-reply functions, a stable coalition of three countries can induce four other countries to cooperate, irrespective of n. When the best-reply functions become negatively sloped, the possibility of bribing other countries gradually decreases to zero.

Besides the example mentioned above, we believe that this type of commitment can be relevant to capture some features of the current negotiation on global warming: why should a group of countries which already cooperate (say EC countries) commit and transfer 'new and additional resources' to other countries (say the LDCs)?

Sequential commitment, discussed in Proposition 3, is possibly less realistic, but shows how it is possible to reach wider coalitions. Countries belonging to a stable coalition commit to cooperation and bribe other countries. As any of the latter countries joins the coalition, it must commit in order to further expand the coalition. In this way, it is easy to show that, with orthogonal (or near-orthogonal) best-reply functions, sequential commitment leads to full cooperation, as the conditions on the stability of the coalition itself are removed by this form of commitment.

Full cooperation can also be achieved if about 60 percent of the n countries commit to cooperation (we are referring here to Proposition 4), while the external commitment of Proposition 5, again with orthogonal or near-orthogonal best-reply functions, can induce about 70 percent of the n countries to cooperate. The latter case can be helpful in understanding the recent proposal by some industrial countries (e.g. the Scandinavian countries) to subsidize environmental programmes in other countries [e.g. Eastern Europe; see Kaitala et al. (1992)].

As the above discussion has already pointed out, if the best-reply functions are negatively sloped, all the results are generally less favourable. In particular, sequential commitment does not lead to full cooperation, and the impact of each type of commitment decreases as the slope of the best-reply functions increases (in absolute value).

As examples can provide only anecdotes and special results, we believe that a better understanding of environmental negotiations can only come from serious applied work. Only empirical work can justify alternative specifications of countries' interdependence. Only empirical work, moreover, can support an intuition we submit: while in the traditional case of common-property goods (fisheries, pastures, forests, etc.) the payoff functions give rise to non-orthogonal best-reply functions, in the case of some global pollutants, e.g. CO_2 or CFC, the best-reply functions are probably orthogonal (or near orthogonal).[11]

[11]Indeed, we can hardly think of any countries that expand their own CO_2 or CFC emissions in response to other countries' reductions. As the above discussion has suggested, this leaves room for cooperative agreements.

4. Conclusions and scope for further work

In the next few years the intenational protection of the environment will increasingly rely on international agreements, although they often involve substantial difficulties. To what extent can the proposed analysis be useful, and how can it be extended?

The analytical framework we proposed is highly simplified and the results obtained must be interpreted with great caution. However, given the difficulties and failures of many attempts to reach global agreements, it shows a promising route for research and policy analysis.

Firstly, the framework and the results show that it is rather sterile to study optimal agreements among all countries, if such agreements are profitable but intrinsically unstable. The structure of such agreements can be useful as a benchmark, but it is very unlikely to be realized in practice. Secondly, they show that there is a full range of possible agreements among sovereign countries to protect the international environment. There are cases in which an effective protection can be obtained non-cooperatively. In other cases, an effective environmental protection can be reached through partial co-operation and transfers.

Coming to the scope for further work, a number of relevant issues have still to be addressed. First, it would be useful to provide a sort of taxonomy relating the various pollutants to appropriate damage functions. Only then would it be possible to contextualize policy analysis, obtaining meaningful results for each case. Secondly, it would be useful to re-appraise the instruments to implement cooperation. Emissions, in many cases, are very difficult to monitor. The various economic instruments needed to implement an agreement, therefore, must be designed in a way that prevents cheating. So far, the literature has compared the various agreements in terms of efficiency, i.e. maximum profitability. Our analysis proposes another criterion: an instrument must be efficient, but it must also be effective in preventing or discouraging free-riding. In other words, it must also be designed to promote the stability of the agreements.

Finally, three extensions should be attempted:

(i) Asymmetric information should be introduced. Countries' preferences can hardly be observed. If we remove the assumption of complete information, each country that is induced to enter a coalition would be tempted to overstate the damage and claim for greater incentives. The solution to this problem is to embody an appropriate information or self-selection premium in the transfer to each country that enters the coalition.

(ii) It would be relevant to introduce some asymmetries into the game (by assuming for example different damage and abatement costs across countries), in order to evaluate coalition profitability and stability when countries have different incentives to join it.

(iii) The benefit function should account for the interaction between environmental variables and the policy instruments designed to carry on transfers. This prevents the analysis of environmental policy as such, but implies its integration into a wider analysis which accounts for other economic variables in each country's payoff.

A last point concerns institutions. In the present setting there is not an institution that has the authority to impose supernational regulations on countries and regions. Stable and expanded coalitions can be seen as a first step towards such institutions, as the member countries would find it costly to individually perform the transfer, the monitoring, and the enforcement activities which are usually associated with the management of a cooperative agreement.

References

Barrett, S., 1991, The paradox of international environmental agreements, Mimeo. (London Business School).

Barrett, S., 1992, International environmental agreements as games, in: R. Pethig, ed., Conflicts and cooperation in managing environmental resources (Springer-Verlag, Berlin) 18–33.

Binmore, K., A. Rubinstein and A. Wolinski, 1986, The Nash bargaining solution in economic modelling, Rand Journal of Economics 17, 176–188.

Bohm, P., 1990, Efficiency aspects of imperfect treaties on global public bads: Lessons from the Montreal protocol, Mimeo.

Carraro, C. and D. Siniscalco, 1991, Transfers and commitments in international negotiations, paper prepared for the ESF task force 3 on environmental economics, in: K.G. Maler, ed., International environmental problems: An economic perspective (Kluwer Academic Publishers, Dordrecht) forthcoming.

D'Aspremont, C.A. and J.J. Gabszewicz, 1986, On the stability of collusion, in: G.F. Matthewson and J.E. Stiglitz, eds., New developments in the analysis of market structure (Macmillan, New York) 243–264.

D'Aspremont, C.A., A. Jacquemin, J.J. Gabszewicz and J. Weymark, 1983, On the stability of collusive price leadership, Canadian Journal of Economics 16, 17–25.

Donsimoni, M.P., N.S. Economides and H.M. Polemarchakis, 1986, Stable cartels, International Economic Review 27, 317–327.

Hardin, G., 1968, The tragedy of commons, Science 162, 1243–1248.

Hardin, G. and J. Baden, 1977, Managing the commons (Freeman and Co., New York) 294.

Hoel, M., 1992, International environment conventions: The case of uniform reductions of emissions, Environmental and Resource Economics 2, 141–160.

Kaitala, V., M. Pojola and O. Tahvonen, 1992, Trans-boundary air pollution and soil acidification: A dynamic analysis of acid rain game between Finland and the USSR, Environmental Resource Economic 2, 161–182.

Maler, K.G., 1989, The acid rain game, in: H. Folmer and E. Ireland, eds., Valuation methods and policy making in environmental economics (Elsevier, New York) 188–205.

Newbery, D.M., 1991, Acid rains, Economic Policy 1, 42–88.

Nitze, W.A., 1990, The greenhouse effect: Formulating a convention (The Royal Institute of International Affairs, London) 66.

Ostrom, E., 1990, Governing the commons (Cambridge University Press, Cambridge).

Schmalensee, R., 1987, Competitive advantage and collusive optima, International Journal of Industrial Organisation 5, 351–367.

[5]

Oxford Economic Papers 46 (1994), 878–894

SELF-ENFORCING INTERNATIONAL ENVIRONMENTAL AGREEMENTS

By SCOTT BARRETT

Faculty of Economics, London Business School, Sussex Place, Regent's Park, London, NW1 4SA

Centre for Social and Economic Research on the Global Environment

1. Introduction

IT IS WELL-KNOWN that collective well-being can be increased if all countries cooperate in managing shared environmental resources like the climate and ozone layer, but that if this improved situation is attained, every country will earn even higher returns by free-riding on the virtuous behavior of the remaining cooperators. However, the fact that countries can do better if cooperation can be sustained suggests that countries have incentives to develop institutions which can punish free riding. Such institutions do in fact exist in the form of international environmental agreements (IEAs). Indeed, more than 100 IEAs are currently in force, the most recent of which include the Montreal Protocol on Substances that Deplete the Ozone Layer and the Framework Convention on Climate Change. The essential feature of IEAs is that they must be self-enforcing. No country can be forced to sign an IEA, and signatories to an IEA can always withdraw from the agreement. If IEAs can improve the management of shared environmental resources, they must make it attractive for countries to want to sign, and to want to carry out the terms of the agreement. This paper employs some concepts from game theory to explore the properties of self-enforcing IEAs.

Two different approaches are considered. The first is a model in which the number of signatories, the terms of the agreement, and the actions of non-signatories are all determined endogenously. This model assumes that signatories maximize their collective net benefits, recognizing how their choice of treaty obligations affects the actions of nonsignatories, while nonsignatories each choose their actions on the assumption that other countries will not respond. The mechanism that sustains the IEA is as follows. When a country joins the IEA, the other signatories increase their abatement levels, and hence reward the country for acceding to the agreement; when a country withdraws, the remaining signatories reduce their abatement levels, and hence punish the country for withdrawing from the agreement. These punishments and rewards are credible, because the signatories always maximize their collective net benefits. However, the magnitude of the punishments and rewards may not be sufficiently large to sustain a self-enforcing IEA consisting of many countries. Depending on the functional specification, Section 2 of this paper shows that the self-enforcing IEA may not exist, or it may consist of no more than two or three countries, or it may support up to as many countries as share the resource (depending in this last case on parameter values).

The other approach is to model the IEA as an infinitely repeated game. This approach has the attraction of increasing credible punishments compared with the other model, but it has the drawback of not solving endogenously for the number of signatories, the terms of the agreement, and the actions of non-signatories. Instead, this model can be employed to calculate the maximum number of countries that could support the full cooperative outcome. While the folk theorem guarantees that the full cooperative outcome can be sustained by any number of countries provided the rate of discount is sufficiently small, we shall see in Section 3 that this result may not hold for a self-enforcing IEA.[1] The reason is that the punishments that sustain the full cooperative outcome may be vulnerable to renegotiation, and a self-enforcing IEA must clearly be renegotiation-proof. As with the previous model, the ability of the infinitely-repeated game to sustain the full cooperative outcome depends on the functional specification and parameter values.

These different models yield one consistent and striking result. The first model shows that for global environmental problems, an IEA may achieve a high degree of cooperation, but only when the difference between global net benefits under the noncooperative and full cooperative outcomes is small. When this difference is large, a self-enforcing IEA cannot support a large number of signatory countries.[2] The second model shows that the maximum number of countries that can sustain the full cooperative outcome may be large, but only when the difference between global net benefits under the noncooperative and full cooperative outcomes is small. When this difference is large, the full cooperative outcome cannot be sustained by a self-enforcing IEA.

By necessity, the analysis imposes a number of restrictive assumptions, and the above result must be seen in the light of these. The most important assumptions are: (i) that all countries are identical; (ii) that each country's net benefit function is known by all countries, and known to be known by all countries; (iii) that the choice instrument is restricted to pollution abatement; (iv) that abatement levels are instantly and costlessly observable; (v) that the pollutant does not accumulate in the environment; and (iv) that the cost functions are independent. Further research is needed to learn whether the basic conclusion of this paper would be upset by changes in these assumptions.[3]

[1] Of course, the folk theorem only asserts that any feasible individually rational payoffs can be supported as a Nash equilibrium if the game is repeated infinitely often and players are sufficiently patient. Hence, the full cooperative outcome is only one among many supergame equilibria.

[2] Unless, of course, the agreement merely codifies the noncooperative outcome.

[3] A number of studies have considered these issues, but not within the context of the models presented in this paper. Black *et al.* (1993) consider information asymmetries in a model where the agreement specifies the minimum number of countries that must sign the agreement for it to come into force. With complete information, the solution to their model would trivially require that all countries sign the agreement. Such an agreement would not, however, be (*ex post*) self-enforcing. Barrett (1992) considers the implications for reaching a negotiated agreement when countries are different and may select different policy instruments (abatement levels, pollution taxes, and tradeable emission entitlements), but this study does not require that the agreement that is reached

2. The model of an IEA

2.1. *Linear marginal abatement benefits and costs*

Consider a world of $i = 1, \ldots, N$ identical countries, each of which emits a pollutant that damages a shared environmental resource. i's current abatement benefits are assumed to depend on current total abatement as follows

$$B_i(Q) = b(aQ - Q^2/2)N \tag{1}$$

where $B_i(Q)$ is i's abatement benefit, a and b are positive parameters, and Q is global abatement. According to (1), the marginal benefit of the first unit of abatement for i is ab/N, and that of the ath is zero.[4] The parameter b is the slope of the global marginal benefit function (found by summing (1) over all N countries, and differentiating with respect to Q).

Each country's abatement costs are assumed to depend on its own abatement level and no one else's. For country i, the abatement cost function is assumed to be given by

$$C_i(q_i) = cq_i^2/2 \tag{2}$$

where $C_i(q_i)$ is i's abatement cost and q_i is i's abatement (in eq. (1), $Q = \Sigma_i q_i$). The parameter c represents the slope of each country's marginal abatement cost curve.

2.1.1. *The gains to full cooperation.* Denote i's net benefits by π_i (i.e., $\pi_i = B_i(Q) - C_i(q_i)$), and denote global net benefits by Π (i.e., $\Pi = \Sigma_i \pi_i$). The full cooperative outcome is found by choosing Q to maximize Π. The solution requires setting each country's marginal cost of abatement (MC_i) equal to the global marginal benefit of abatement (MB), and is illustrated in Fig. 1. The full cooperative abatement levels are

$$Q_c = aN/(N + \gamma), \qquad q_c = a/(N + \gamma) \tag{3}$$

where Q_c is global abatement and q_c is an individual country's abatement under the full cooperative outcome, and $\gamma \equiv c/b$.

The noncooperative or open access outcome can be computed by invoking the usual Cournot conjecture that every country chooses its abatement level

be sustainable by a self-enforcing IEA. Carraro and Siniscalco (1991) consider a model in which signatories to an IEA may choose side payments to induce nonsignatories to accede to the IEA, but for signatories to want to make such side payments, it is essential that these countries commit to certain abatement levels, and such a commitment is inconsistent with the notion of self-enforcement. Mäler (1989) and Hoel (1990) analyze cooperative solutions to the control of persistent pollutants, but which are not subject to a self-enforcement constraint. Finally, Heal (1992) considers the case where each country's abatement costs depend on the abatement actions of other countries, as well as its own, but evaluates only the Nash noncooperative equilibrium.

[4] The problem specified here does not impose an upper bound on each country's abatement effort. Clearly, emissions must be at least as great as a units, since the marginal benefit of abating a units is zero. To solve the problem we can assume that emissions exceed a by a sufficient margin so that the maximal abatement constraint is never binding.

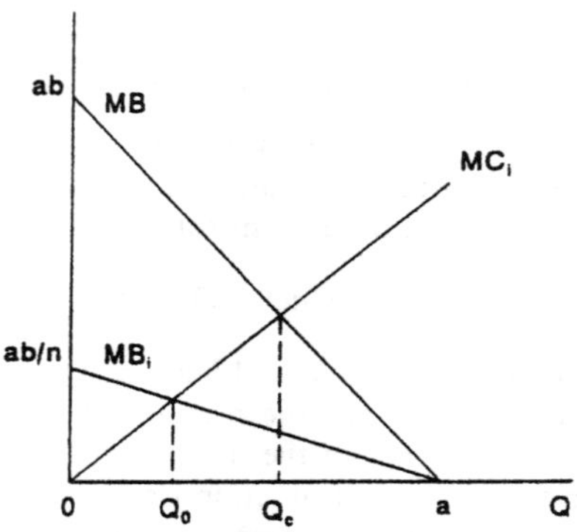

FIG. 1. The non-cooperative and full-cooperative outcomes

on the belief that the abatement levels of all other countries are given. That is, each country chooses q_i to maximize π_i, taking all $q_j, j \neq i$, as fixed. The solution requires setting each country's own marginal benefit of abatement (denoted MB_i in Fig. 1) equal to its own marginal cost of abatement. Denoting Q_o global abatement and q_o any individual country's abatement under the noncooperative or open access outcome, we find

$$Q_o = a/(1 + \gamma), \qquad q_o = a/N(1 + \gamma) \tag{4}$$

We see immediately that $Q_c > Q_o$.[5] Each country is better off at the full cooperative solution, but none has an incentive to choose q_c unilaterally.

It is clear from Fig. 1 that the difference between global net benefits under the full cooperative and non-cooperative outcomes depends on the slopes of the marginal abatement cost and benefit curves. Let Π_c and Π_o denote global net benefits under full cooperation and open access, respectively. Then we have:

Lemma 1 Let $\theta(N) = [\sqrt{(N^2 + 8N)} - N]/4$. Then (i) $\Pi_c - \Pi_o$ increases in b when $\gamma > \theta(N)$ and decreases in b when $\gamma < \theta(N)$ for c given; (ii) $\Pi_c - \Pi_o$ increases in c for γ fixed; and (iii) θ is monotonic and approaches a value of 1 as N becomes very large.

Proof See Appendix.

Lemma 1 tells us that the gains to cooperation ($\Pi_c - \Pi_o$) are larger the closer γ is to $\theta(N)$ and the larger is c. For global environmental problems, N exceeds 100 and $\theta \approx 1$. When c is small and b is large, unilateral abatement is substantial, and the gains to cooperation are relatively small. When c is large and b is small, countries will not abate their emissions by much, even if cooperation is full. When $c \approx b$ and both parameter values are small, $Q_c - Q_o$ will be large, but the gains to cooperation will be small. When $c \approx b$ and both

[5] This is a well known result. See, for example, chapter 2 of Dasgupta (1982).

parameters are large, both $Q_c - Q_o$ and $\Pi_c - \Pi_o$ will be large. Clearly, IEAs can achieve the most when these last conditions hold.

2.1.2. *The self-enforcing IEA.* Suppose that a number of countries negotiate an IEA. Clearly, the number of signatories, the terms of the IEA, and the abatement levels of nonsignatories must be determined jointly. It seems reasonable to suppose that nonsignatories will choose their abatement levels taking as given the abatement decisions of all other countries. Let α denote the proportion of countries that sign the IEA. There are then αN signatories and $(1 - \alpha)N$ nonsignatories. Let Q_n denote the abatement of all nonsignatories, and let q_n denote the abatement of any individual nonsignatory. Since all nonsignatories are identical, $Q_n = (1 - \alpha)Nq_n$. The reaction functions of nonsignatories are given by

$$Q_n(\alpha, Q_s) = (1 - \alpha)(a - Q_s)/(\gamma + 1 - \alpha) \tag{5}$$

Signatories are assumed to choose Q_s to maximize their collective net benefits, with q_s being identical for all signatory countries, subject to (5).[6] The solution is

$$Q_s^*(\alpha) = a\alpha^2 N\gamma/[(\gamma + 1 - \alpha)^2 + \alpha^2 N\gamma] \tag{6}$$

Substituting (6) into (5) yields

$$Q_n^*(\alpha) = a(1 - \alpha)(\gamma + 1 - \alpha)\ [(\gamma + 1 - \alpha)^2 + \alpha^2 N\gamma] \tag{7}$$

It is easily verified that the full cooperative ($\alpha = 1$) and noncooperative ($\alpha = 0$) solutions, given by eqs (3) and (4) respectively, are special cases of (6) and (7).

The remaining problem is to determine $\alpha^* N$, or the number of signatories to the self-enforcing IEA. In determining α^*, it will prove helpful to invoke a concept of stability developed for the analysis of cartels (d'Aspremont *et al.* 1983). Let π_s be the net benefit of every signatory and π_n that of every nonsignatory.

Definition An IEA consisting of αN signatories is self-enforcing if

$$\pi_n(\alpha - 1/N) \leqslant \pi_s(\alpha) \quad \text{and} \quad \pi_n(\alpha) \geqslant \pi_s(\alpha + 1/N) \tag{8}$$

If (8) holds, no signatory will want to withdraw unilaterally from the agreement; such a withdrawal would reduce the signatory's abatement level, and hence its costs, but its defection from the IEA would weaken the agreement, and the resulting loss in benefits would more than offset the reduction in costs gained by the withdrawal. Similarly, no nonsignatory, acting alone, would want

[6] The assumption that the q_s are identical is easily justified. If the problem of signatories agreeing on individual country obligations is modelled as a cooperative game, then it can be shown that if all signatories are identical, the Nash bargaining solution will require that each country undertake the same level of abatement.

TABLE 1
Stability analysis for hypothetical example

α	q_s	q_n	π_s	π_n	Q	Π
0.0	—	8.0	—	472.0	80.0	4,720.0
0.1	1.9	8.5	476.8	468.1	78.7	4,690.0
0.2	4.2	8.7	474.0	466.6	78.2	4,681.2
0.3	6.7	8.4	472.3	468.9	78.9	4,699.4
0.4*	8.9*	7.6*	472.2*	474.9*	81.1*	4,738.1*
0.5	10.5	6.3	473.7	482.5	84.2	4,781.2
0.6	11.3	4.9	476.4	489.4	87.7	4,816.0
0.7	11.5	3.6	479.5	494.3	91.0	4,839.8
0.8	11.1	2.5	482.7	497.3	93.8	4,855.9
0.9	10.5	1.6	485.4	498.8	95.9	4,867.8
1.0	9.8	—	487.8	—	97.6	4,878.0

to accede to the IEA; although the recruit's benefits would rise, its abatement costs would rise even more.[7]

The concept is best understood by considering an example. Let $N = 10$, $a = 100$, $b = 1$, and $c = 0.25$; and denote global net benefits by $\Pi(\alpha)$; i.e. $\Pi(\alpha) = \alpha N\pi_s + (1-\alpha)N\pi_n$. Table 1 shows the net benefit and abatement levels corresponding to each possible α, and Fig. 2 illustrates the example. To solve for α^*, start at $\alpha = 0$ and compare $\pi_n(0)$ with $\pi_s(0.1)$. Clearly, $476.8 > 472.0$, and hence it will play a nonsignatory to accede to the agreement. Now compare $\pi_n(0.1)$ with $\pi_s(0.2)$. Again, $474.0 > 468.1$, and it will pay a nonsignatory to cooperate. Continuing in this way one finds that nonsignatories always do better by acceding when $\alpha < 0.4$. Likewise, starting at $\alpha = 1.0$, one finds that signatories always do better by withdrawing from the agreement whenever $\alpha > 0.4$. Hence, an IEA consisting of four signatories is the only self-enforcing IEA for this problem.[8]

[7] The concept of self-enforcement defined by (8) was first employed by Barrett (1989), but has also been used by Carraro and Siniscalco (1991) and Hoel (1992). The essential feature of (8) is that it does not consider whether coalitions of two or more countries would want to accede to or withdraw from the IEA. Heal (1992) defines a related concept which he calls the minimum critical coalition. This is a group of countries S, which (i) adopts an abatement policy yielding each member of S positive net benefits, and (ii) does not contain a proper subset of countries which yields its members positive net benefits.

[8] Notice that $\pi_s(\alpha^* + 1/N) - \pi_s(\alpha^*) > \pi_n(\alpha^*) - \pi_s(\alpha^* + 1/N)$ in this example. This implies that signatories to a self-enforcing IEA have an incentive to offer a side payment to nonsignatories to join the agreement. The difficulty is that the agreement to offer a side payment is not self-enforcing. While the signatories to the self-enforcing IEA have a collective incentive to offer a side payment to a nonsignatory, each of the original signatories would do better still by withdrawing from the agreement since $\pi_n(\alpha^*) > \pi_s(\alpha^* + 1/N)$ (by definition).

Carraro and Siniscalco (1991) propose a way out of this dilemma. They show that if the signatories to the self-enforcing IEA can commit themselves to cooperate whatever the magnitude of α, then the total number of signatories can be increased (although the full cooperative outcome may still be unattainable). The snag in this proposal, as noted in footnote 2, is that the commitment is not credible; the expanded agreement is not self-enforcing. If commitment could be made credible, then the full cooperative outcome would be easy to sustain: every country would simply commit to choose the full cooperative abatement level q_c.

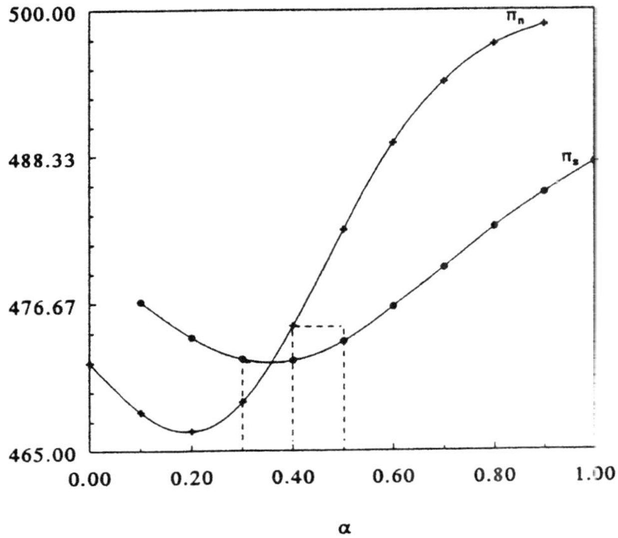

FIG. 2. Graphical analysis of self-enforcing IEA

Unfortunately, a full characterization of the solution cannot be obtained analytically for this functional specification. However, simulations reveal a very simple and compelling relationship between γ and α^*, and between γ and the ability of an IEA to close the gap between the full cooperative and non-cooperative outcomes.

2.1.3. *Simulations.* Table 2 presents solutions to α^*N for various values of b and c when $N = 100$.[9] It is clear from the simulations that the number of signatories to the self-enforcing IEA increases as γ decreases. It is encouraging to find that a self-enforcing IEA can consist of many signatories, if only when γ is small. However, Lemma 1 demonstrated that if γ is small, then the difference between global net benefits under the full cooperative and noncooperative outcomes will also be small. Hence, IEAs signed by many countries do not increase global net benefits by very much compared with the non-cooperative outcome. Indeed, Tables 3 and 4, which give the total abatement and net benefit figures corresponding to a selection of nine cells from Table 2, confirm that the self-enforcing IEA increases global abatement and global net benefits by very little when γ is small. These results suggest that IEAs signed by a large number of countries have very little effect.

Table 2 shows that when γ is large, few countries will sign the self-enforcing

[9] The value taken by the parameter a does not affect the results in Table 2.

TABLE 2
Number of signatories out of 100 for various values of c and b

	c										
	0.01	*0.05*	*0.10*	*0.25*	*0.50*	*1.00*	*2.00*	*5.00*	*10.00*	*20.00*	*100.00*
0.01	3	3	3	2	2	2	2	2	2	2	2
0.05	6	3	3	3	3	2	2	2	2	2	2
0.10	11	4	3	3	3	3	2	2	2	2	2
0.25	21	6	4	3	3	3	3	2	2	2	2
0.50	35	11	6	4	3	3	3	3	2	2	2
1.00	51	18	11	5	4	3	3	3	3	2	2
2.00	68	30	18	9	5	4	3	3	3	3	2
5.00	84	51	35	18	11	6	4	3	3	3	2
10.00	92	68	51	30	18	11	6	4	3	3	3
20.00	96	81	68	46	30	18	11	5	4	3	3
100.00	100	96	92	81	68	51	35	18	11	6	3

TABLE 3
*Global abatement under the noncooperative, IEA, and full co-operative outcomes**

		c		
		0.01	*1*	*100*
	0.01	500.0	9.9	0.1
		503.9	10.1	0.1
		990.1	500.0	9.9
b	1	990.1	500.0	90.9
		990.2	503.9	95.2
		999.9	990.1	909.1
	100	999.9	990.1	500.0
		1,000.0	990.2	503.9
		1,000.0	999.9	990.1

* Assumes $N = 100$ and $a = 1{,}000$. The top number in each cell is Q_o, the middle $Q(\alpha^*)$, and the bottom Q_c.

IEA. Since IEAs typically specify a minimum number of signatories,[10] this means that an agreement is unlikely to be reached when γ is large. But Tables 3 and 4 indicate that the difference in global abatement and global net benefits under the full cooperative and noncooperative outcomes is trivial in absolute terms when γ is large. Hence, failure to reach agreement is of no great consequence when γ is large.

[10] For example, the Framework Convention on Climate Change will not come into force until 50 countries have ratified the agreement. See Black *et al.* (1993) for an analysis showing why countries might want to specify a minimum number of signatories.

TABLE 4
*Global net benefits under the noncooperative, IEA, and full cooperative outcomes**

		c		
		0.01	*1*	*100*
	0.01	3,738 3,757 4,950	98 100 2,500	1 1 50
b	1	499,902 499,903 499,950	373,750 375,659 495,050	9,803 9,990 250,000
	100	49,999,949 49,999,950 49,999,950	49,990,197 49,990,293 49,995,000	37,375,000 37,565,851 49,504,950

* Assumes $N = 100$ and $a = 1{,}000$. The top number in each cell is Π_0, the middle $\Pi(x^*)$, and the bottom Π_c.

The situation is very different where c and b are both large. As Lemma 1 showed, it is here that the difference between global net benefits under the noncooperative and full cooperative outcomes is large. Table 4 confirms this. But from Table 2 we see that few countries are likely to sign an IEA for such a pollutant.

Proposition 1 For global environmental problems characterized by eqs (1) and (2), the self-enforcing IEA will be signed by a lot of countries, each undertaking substantial abatement, when γ is small, but under these circumstances the IEA increases global net benefits by very little compared with the noncooperative outcome. Cooperation would increase net benefits substantially when c and b are both large, but under these circumstances the self-enforcing IEA cannot sustain a large number of signatories.

Table 5 shows the magnitude of free riding for these simulations. Signatories abate more than they would in the absence of an IEA, while nonsignatories abate less. When $\gamma = 1$, only three countries cooperate. Every signatory abates significantly more than under the noncooperative outcome, and every nonsignatory just a little less. But because there are so many more nonsignatories in this case, the free-rider effect is huge in total and the IEA has little overall impact. When $\gamma = 0.01$, there are 51 signatories. In this case the free-rider effect is small—but so too is the additional abatement of signatories. Again, the self-enforcing IEA has little overall impact. Finally, Table 6 shows the net benefit levels corresponding to the abatement levels in Table 5. All countries receive higher net benefits when there exists a self-enforcing IEA compared with the noncooperative outcome, but nonsignatories take a free ride on signatories.

It must be emphasized that Proposition 1 applies to environmental problems

TABLE 5
*Country abatement under the noncooperative, IEA, and full cooperative outcomes**

		c 0.01	1	100
	0.01	5.00	0.10	—
		7.55	0.20	—
		4.96	0.10	—
		9.90	5.00	0.10
b	1	9.90	5.00	0.10
		10.00	7.55	0.20
		9.80	4.96	0.10
		10.00	9.90	5.00
	100	10.00	9.90	5.00
		10.00	10.00	7.55
		—	9.80	4.96
		10.00	10.00	9.90

* Assumes $N = 100$ and $a = 1{,}000$. The top number in each cell is q_o, the second $q_s(\alpha^*)$, the third $q_n(\alpha^*)$, and the bottom q_c.

TABLE 6
*Country net benefits under the noncooperative, IEA, and full cooperative outcomes**

		c 0.01	1	100
	0.01	37.38	0.98	0.01
		37.41	0.99	0.01
		37.57	1·00	0.01
		49.50	25.00	0.50
b	1	4,999.02	3,737.50	98.03
		4,999.02	3,740.84	98.50
		4,999.04	3,757.07	99.93
		4,999.50	4,950.50	2,500.00
	100	499,999.50	499,901.97	373,750.00
		499,999.50	499,901.98	374,083.96
		—	499,903.92	375,707.21
		499,999.50	499,950.00	495,049.50

* Assumes $N = 100$ and $a = 1{,}000$. The top number of each cell is π_o, the second $\pi_s(\alpha)$, the third $\pi_n(\alpha^*)$, and the bottom π_c.

for which N is large. As N becomes small, the effect of withdrawal or accession by any country on the abatement level of the other cooperators increases, and hence free riding can be punished more effectively. To take an example, suppose $N = 5$, $a = 100$ and $c = b = 1$. Then the self-enforcing IEA consists of three countries with $Q_o = 50$, $Q(\alpha^*) = 63$ and $Q_c = 83$; and with $\Pi_0 = 3{,}500$, $\Pi(\alpha^*) = 3{,}869$, and $\Pi_c = 4{,}162$. In this case, the self-enforcing IEA is able to close the gap between the noncooperative outcomes quite substantially.

2.2. *Constant marginal benefits and linear marginal costs*

Suppose that maginal benefits are constant; i.e.

$$B_i(Q) = \omega Q \tag{9}$$

Then, if the abatement cost function is given by e.g. (2), the self-enforcing IEA can be solved analytically.

Proposition 2 For the model specification given by eqs (2) and (9), the self-enforcing IEA consists of 2 countries when $N = 2$ and 3 countries when $N \geqslant 3$.

Proof See Appendix.

2.3. *Constant marginal benefits and logarithmic marginal costs*

Suppose now that abatement benefits continue to be given by eq. (9) but that total abatement costs for country i are now given by

$$C_i(q_i) = x\sigma[(1 - q_i/x)\ln(1 - q_i/x) + q_i/x] \tag{10}$$

The marginal abatement cost function is then

$$MC_i(q_i) = -\sigma \ln(1 - q_i/x) \tag{11}$$

If the parameter x is taken to equal emissions in the absence of any abatement effort, q_i/x is percentage abatement. In that case, the marginal abatement cost function (11) is the same form as was estimated by Nordhaus (1990) for US carbon dioxide emissions.[11] Since Nordhaus's model also assumes constant marginal benefits, eqs (9) and (10) describe Nordhaus's model of the greenhouse effect. However, Nordhaus does not disaggregate to the individual country level. Here it is assumed that all countries are identical and have the same cost and benefit functions.[12] The solution to this problem, like the previous one, can be derived analytically.

[11] The cost function specification is described in footnote 10 of Nordhaus (1990), p. 19.

[12] Since Nordhaus (1990) calculates a global marginal benefit, the parameter ω in eq. (9) can be taken to equal each country's (identical) share of the global marginal benefit.

Lemma 2 For the model specification given by eqs (9) and (10),

(i) $\pi_n(0) = \pi_s(1/N) = \pi_n(1/N)$
(ii) $\pi_s(2/N) > \pi_n(1/N)$
(iii) $\pi_n(\alpha) > \pi_s(\alpha + 1/N)\,\forall\,\alpha \geqslant 2/N$

Proof See Appendix.

Lemma 2 implies:

Proposition 3 For the model specification given by eqs (9) and (10), the self-enforcing IEA consists of 2 countries for $N \geqslant 2$.

2.4. *Linear marginal benefits and constant marginal costs*

Suppose now that country i's benefit function is given by (1) and its cost function by

$$C_i(q_i) = dq_i \tag{12}$$

Then the self-enforcing IEA may be solved easily.

Proposition 4 For the model specification given by eqs (1) and (12), a self-enforcing IEA consisting of 2 or more countries does not exist.

Proof See Appendix.

With this specification, any increase in Q_s is entirely offset by a reduction in Q_n. There is therefore nothing to be gained by cooperating.

Clearly, the results obtained using the specification given by eqs (1) and (2) are not generally robust. According to the specifications examined in this section, the number of signatories may be limited to just a few whatever parameter values characterise the problem being investigated.[13] However, the results of all specifications considered here are consistent in one respect: when N is large, an agreement achieving substantial emission reductions over and above the non-cooperative levels is not self-enforcing.

3. IEAs as repeated games

The preceding model is unable to sustain the full cooperative outcome in general because its punishments, though credible, are small. It is well known that the full cooperative outcome of the one-shot game can be sustained as a sub-game perfect equilibrium of the infinitely repeated game if the rate of discount is sufficiently small. However, this section will show that repetition may not allow IEAs to sustain the full cooperative outcome, even for arbitrarily small discount rates, because the punishments that sustain cooperation in infinitely repeated games may be vulnerable to renegotiation, and such punishments could not be supported by a self-enforcing IEA.

[13] d'Aspremont *et al.* (1983), Hoel (1992), and Carraro and Siniscalco (1991) also solve for models yielding two or three cooperators.

Let π_i now denote country i's average payoff in the infinitely repeated game, and consider the following functional specification

$$\pi_i = b(aQ - Q^2/2)/N - dq_i - (ab - dN)^2/2bN \tag{13}$$

where the constant term ensures that each country is guaranteed a payoff of at least zero. Proposition 4 tells us that specification (13) will not allow a stable IEA to improve on the noncooperative outcome. We shall see that this is not necessarily so when the game is infinitely repeated.

The full cooperative outcome yields a global payoff of $d(N-1) \times (2ab - d(N+1))/2b$. Hence, the set of feasible, individually rational payoffs is

$$V^* = \{v \mid v_i \geqslant 0, \textstyle\sum v_i \leqslant d(N-1)(2ab - d(N+1))/2b\}$$

Following Farrell and Maskin (1989), a payoff vector v may be said to be (weakly) renegotiation proof (for discount rates near zero) if abatement levels q_j^j, q_k^j can be chosen to punish j for cheating, such that

$$\max_{q_j} \{(b/N)[a(q_j + (N-1)q_k^j) - (q_j + (N-1)q_k^j)^2/2] - dq_j - (ab - dN)^2/2bN\} \leqslant v_j \tag{14}$$

$$(b/N)[a(q_j^j + (N-1)q_k^j) - (q_j^j + (N-1)q_k^j)^2/2] - dq_k^j - (ab - dN)^2/2bN \geqslant v_k \tag{15}$$

Condition (14) ensures that any one country cannot gain by cheating on the agreement.[14] Condition (15) ensures that countries have no incentive to renegotiate. For this problem, it also makes sense to require that the payoff vector v be Pareto efficient in the punishment phase.[15] If we further assume that j chooses for q_j^j its minimax abatement level, $q_j^j = (ab - dN)/b$, then $q_k^j = \mathrm{d}/b$. Substituting, we require for every country i

$$\mathrm{d}[2abN - \mathrm{d}(N+1)^2]/2bN \geqslant v_i \geqslant \mathrm{d}^2(N-1)/b \tag{16}$$

Under the full cooperative outcome, every country receives a payoff of $\mathrm{d}(N-1)(2ab - \mathrm{d}(N+1))/2bN$. Substituting this value into (16), we find:

Proposition 5 For the specification given by eq. (13), the full cooperative outcome can be sustained as a self-enforcing IEA for a common discount rate close to zero if the number of countries N does not exceed

$$\bar{N} = \min\,(ab/d - 1, 2ab/3d - \tfrac{1}{3})$$

It is easy to see that $\bar{N}$ is increasing in a and b, and decreasing in d. $\bar{N}$ is calculated for various values of b and d in Table 7.[16] The number of countries that can sustain the full cooperative outcome varies substantially, depending

[14] As elsewhere in the paper, I am assuming that countries do not form coalitions.

[15] Farrell and Maskin (1989) refer to such an equilibrium as being strongly perfect.

[16] The table considers parameter values which yield only interior solutions.

TABLE 7

*Illustration of maximum number of countries that can sustain the full cooperative outcome**

a	b	d	$\bar{N}$	$(\Pi_c - \Pi_o)/(N^* - 1)^2$
100	1	0.99	67	0.49
100	1	0.75	88	0.28
100	1	0.65	102	0.21
100	2	1.98	67	0.98
100	2	1.50	88	0.56
100	2	1.30	102	0.42
1,000	1	9.9	67	49
1,000	1	7.5	88	28
1,000	1	6.5	102	21
1,000	2	19.8	67	98
1,000	2	15.0	88	56
1,000	2	13.0	102	42

* Assumes $N = 100$, to ensure interior solutions.

on the parameter values, and is higher the larger is b and the smaller is d. It can be shown that $\Pi_c - \Pi_o = d^2(N-1)^2/2b$ for specification (13): The last column in Table 7 indicates that when $\bar{N}$ is large, the difference $\Pi_c - \Pi_o$ is small, and that when $\bar{N}$ is small, the difference $\Pi_c - \Pi_o$ may be very large. These results are reminiscent of those obtained in Section 2.1. Clearly, even infinite repetition may not allow the IEA to sustain the full cooperative outcome when IEAs must be self-enforcing.[17]

4. Conclusions

This paper has shown that self-enforcing international environmental agreements (IEAs), which establish rules for managing shared environmental resources, may not be able to improve substantially upon the noncooperative outcome. Two different modelling approaches support this conclusion. The model of a self-enforcing IEA, which solves jointly for the number of signatories, the terms of the IEA, and the actions of nonsignatories, shows that, depending on the functional specification, a self-enforcing IEA may not exist, or it may not be able to sustain more than two or three signatory countries, in which case the IEA cannot increase global net benefits substantially when the number of countries that share the resource is very large. For one functional specification, the self-enforcing IEA can sustain a large number of signatories—up to as many as share the resource—but only when the difference in net benefits between the noncooperative and full cooperative outcomes is very small. When this difference is very large, the self-enforcing IEA can sustain only a small number of signatories, and hence can only marginally improve upon the noncooperative

[17] Barrett (1994) carries out a similar analysis for the conservation of biological diversity, a global public good, but using a different functional form. Though this model can only be evaluted using simulation, the analysis arrives at a similar conclusion.

outcome when the environmental resource is shared globally. The other model, which takes the IEA to be an equilibrium to an infinitely repeated game, but one which is renegotiation-proof, shows that the full cooperative outcome can be sustained by a large number of countries, but only when the difference in global net benefits between the noncooperative and full cooperative outcomes is small. When this difference is large, the full cooperative outcome can be sustained by only a few countries, or possibly by none at all.

Despite the arguably harsh assumptions that underpin these models, it is tempting to consider an actual IEA in the light of this analysis. The Montreal Protocol on Substances that Deplete the Ozone Layer, originally negotiated in 1987, has now been signed by about 80 countries, and in its original form committed each signatory to cut its production and consumption of the so-called hard CFCs by 50%.[18] This agreement is understandably considered to be a substantial achievement of international cooperation.[19] However, when seen in the context of this paper, an analysis of ozone depletion by the US Environmental Protection Agency (1988) suggests that the Montreal Protocol may not have increased global net benefits substantially compared with the noncooperative outcome. Assuming 'substantial levels of participation by other nations', the EPA estimates that the US would receive a benefit, primarily in the form of a reduction in the incidence of skin cancers, of $3,575bn, and incur a cost of $21bn, if it acceded to the treaty. If the US cut its production and consumption of CFCs by 50% unilaterally, the cost to the US would remain unchanged, but the benefit to the US would fall to only $1,373bn. While one would ideally like to know the marginal costs and benefits, these total benefit and cost figures strongly suggest that the US had an incentive to carry out the terms of the Montreal Protocol unilaterally. There is no compelling reason to believe that these benefit and cost estimates would be wildly different for most other countries in relative terms, and so, if the EPA's figures are broadly correct and consistent with the beliefs of the Montreal Protocol negotiators, it seems that this agreement may not have achieved as much as is commonly claimed. That conclusion is consistent with the analysis presented in this paper.

[18] The agreement has since been amended, and strengthened in a number of respects.
[19] But see the analysis by Bohm (1990).

REFERENCES

D'ASPREMONT, C. A., JACQUEMIN, J., GABSZEWEIZ, J., and WEYMARK, J. A. (1983). 'On the Stability of Collusive Price Leadership', *Canadian Journal of Economics*, **16**, 17–25.

BARRETT, S. (1989). 'On the Nature and Significance of International Environmental Agreements', mimeo, London Business School.

BARRETT, S. (1992). 'International Environmental Agreements as Games', in R. Pethig (ed.), *Conflict and Cooperation in Managing Environmental Resources*, Springer-Verlag, Berlin.

BARRETT, S. (1994). 'The Biodiversity Supergame', *Environmental and Resource Economics*, **4**, 111–22.

BLACK, J., LEVI, M. D., and DE MEZA, D. (1992). 'Creating a Good Atmosphere: Minimum Participation for Tackling the "Greenhouse Effect"', *Economica*, **60**, 281–93.

BOHM, P. (1990). 'Efficiency Aspects of Imperfect Treaties on Global Public Bads: Lessons from the Montreal Protocol', mimeo, Department of Economics, University of Stockholm.

CARRARO, C. and SINISCALCO, D. (1991). 'Strategies for the International Protection of the Environment', mimeo, Fondazione E.N.I. 'Enrico Mattei'.

DASGUPTA, P. (1982). *Control of Resources*, Harvard University Press, Cambridge, MA.

FARRELL, J. and MASKIN, E. (1989). 'Renegotiation in Repeated Games', *Games and Economic Behaviour*, **1**, 327–60.

HEAL, G. (1992). 'International Negotiations on Emission Control', *Structural Change and Economic Dynamics*, forthcoming.

HOEL, M. (1990). 'CO_2 and the Greenhouse Effect: A Game Theoretic Exploration', mimeo, Department of Economics, University of Oslo.

HOEL, M. (1992). 'International Environment Conventions: The Case of Uniform Reductions of Emissions', *Environmental and Resource Economics*, **2**, 141–59.

MÄLER, K.-G. (1989). 'The Acid Rain Game, 2', mimeo, Department of Economics, Stockholm School of Economics.

NORDHAUS, W. D. (1990). 'To Slow or Not to Slow: The Economics of the Greenhouse Effect', mimeo, Department of Economics, Yale University.

US ENVIRONMENTAL PROTECTION AGENCY (1988). *Regulatory Impact Analysis: Protection of Stratospheric Ozone*, Washington, D.C.

APPENDIX

Proof of Lemma 1 (i) The potential gains to cooperation are

$$\Pi_c - \Pi_o = a^2 c\gamma(N-1)^2/2N(N+\gamma)(\gamma+1)^2 \tag{A.1}$$

Differentiating with respect to γ while holding c constant gives

$$\partial(\Pi_c - \Pi_o)/\partial\gamma \gtreqless 0 \quad \text{if} \quad (2\gamma^2 + \gamma N - N) \gtreqless 0 \tag{A.2}$$

This quadratic equation has one positive solution, $\gamma = \theta(N)$.

(ii) From (A.1) we see immediately that $\partial(\Pi_c - \Pi_o)/\partial c|_{\gamma=\bar\gamma} > 0$.

(iii) Notice that $\theta(N) = [\sqrt{(N^2 + 8N)} - N]/4$ can be rewritten

$$(1-\theta)/(2\theta^2) = 1/N \tag{A.3}$$

As $N \to \infty$, $1/N \to 0$, and hence $\theta \to 1$. □

Proof of Proposition 2 The solutions to the appropriate optimization problems are

$$q_n = \omega/c, \qquad q_s = \omega\alpha N/c$$

Substituting, we obtain

$$\pi_n(\alpha) = \omega^2 N(1 - \alpha + \alpha^2 N - 1/2N)/c \tag{A.4a}$$

$$\pi_s(\alpha) = \omega^2 N(1 - \alpha + \alpha^2 N/2)/c \tag{A.4b}$$

$$\pi_n(\alpha - 1/N) = \omega^2 N(1 - 3\alpha + 3/2N + \alpha^2 N)/c \tag{A.46c}$$

$$\pi_s(\alpha + 1/N) = \omega^2 N(1 - 1/2N + \alpha^2 N/2)/c \tag{A.4d}$$

Substituting (A.4a) and (A.4d) into (8) yields $\alpha \geq 2/N$. Substituting (A.4b) and (A.4c) into (8) and solving for the resulting quadratic equation yields $3/N \geq \alpha \geq 1/N$. Since we require that both of these conditions hold, the self-enforcing IEA consists of $3 \geq \alpha N \geq 2$ countries. Clearly, if $N = 2$, then both countries will sign the IEA. Upon substitution, it is easy to show that $\pi_s(3/N) = \pi_n(2/N)$. If it is assumed that an additional country will joint the IEA when $\pi_s(\alpha + 1/N) = \pi_n(\alpha)$, then the self-enforcing IEA will consist of three countries whenever $N \geqslant 3$. □

Proof of Lemma 2 (i) The solutions to the appropriate optimization problems are

$$q_n = a(1 - e^{-\omega/\sigma}), \qquad q_s = a(1 - e^{-\omega\alpha N/\sigma})$$

Substituting , we obtain

$$\pi_n(\alpha) = [\omega N - \sigma - \alpha\omega N\, e^{-\omega\alpha N/\sigma} + e^{-\omega/\sigma}(\alpha\omega N - \omega N + \sigma + \omega)] \tag{A.5a}$$

$$\pi_s(\alpha) = a[\omega N - \sigma - \omega N(1 - \alpha)\, e^{-\omega/\sigma} + \sigma\, e^{-\omega\alpha N/\sigma}] \tag{A.5b}$$

Part (i) of Lemma 2 can be proved by substituting the appropriate values for α into eqs (A.5a) and (A.5b).

(ii) Setting $\alpha = 2/N$ in (A.5b) and $\alpha = 1/N$ in (A.5a), and substituting, the inequality in (ii) implies

$$\omega/\sigma > 1 - e^{-\omega/\sigma} \tag{A.6}$$

Let $z = \omega/\sigma$. When $z = 0$, both sides of inequality (A.6) equal zero (and hence the inequality does not hold at $z = 0$). The LHS of inequality (A.6) rises with z at rate 1, while the RHS rises at rate e^{-z}. The LHS of (A.6) therefore rises more rapidly with z than the RHS. Since both sides of (A.6) equal zero when $z = 0$, the inquality holds $\forall z > 0$.

(iii) Upon substitution, the inequality in (ii) implies

$$-\alpha\omega N\, e^{-\omega\alpha N/\sigma} + \sigma\, e^{-\omega/\sigma} > \sigma\, e^{-\omega/\sigma}\, e^{-\omega\alpha N/\sigma} \tag{A.7}$$

$\forall\alpha \geqslant 2/N$.

First determine that (A.7) holds for $\alpha = 2/N$. Upon substituting, one obtains

$$1 - e^{-2\omega/\sigma} > 2w\, e^{-\omega/\sigma}/\sigma \tag{A.8}$$

Again, let $z = \omega/\sigma$. When $z = 0$, both sides of (A.8) equal zero. The derivative of the LHS is $2\,e^{-2z}$, while that of the RHS is $2\,e^{-z}(1 - x)$. When $\alpha = 2/N$, the derivative of the LHS of (A.8) exceeds that of the RHS provided $z > 1 - e^{-z}$. But this condition is the same as (A.6), which has already been shown to hold. Hence (iii) holds for $\alpha = 2/N$. Now take the derivative of both sides of (A.7) with respect to α. The derivative of the LHS of (A.7) exceeds the derivative of the RHS if

$$\alpha\omega N/\sigma > 1 - e^{-\omega/\sigma} \tag{A.9}$$

We know (A.9) holds for $\alpha = 1/N$. Hence, it must hold for $\alpha > 1/N$. Since (A.7) holds for $\alpha = 2/N$, it must therefore also hold for all $\alpha \geqslant 2N$. □

Proof of Proposition 4 Each non-signatory will equate its own marginal benefit with its own constant marginal cost, yielding the non-signatory reaction function

$$Q_n = a - dN/b - Q_s \tag{A.10}$$

Signatories will equate their combined marginal benefit with their individual marginal costs, yielding the reaction function

$$Q_s = a - d/\alpha b - Q_n \tag{A.11}$$

Solving (A.10) and (A.11) yields $\alpha N = 1$. From (A.10) we see that $Q_n + Q_s = a - dN/b$, which is the same abatement level achieved when $Q_s = 0$.

[6]

ELSEVIER Journal of Public Economics 60 (1996) 95–110

JOURNAL OF PUBLIC ECONOMICS

Environmental consciousness and moral hazard in international agreements to protect the environment

Emmanuel Petrakis[a], Anastasios Xepapadeas[b,*]

[a]*Universidad Carlos III de Madrid, Madrid, Spain*

[b]*Department of Economics, University of Crete, Perivolia 74100 Rethymnon, Crete, Greece*

Received October 1993; final version received January 1995

Abstract

A group of countries that can potentially commit to cooperation to protect the environment are identified as environmentally conscious countries. Conditions are examined under which they can provide self-financing side payments too a second group of less environmentally conscious countries, so that the two groups form a global or partial stable coalition that agrees to reduce emissions. A mechanism that detects cheating is also developed in order to induce the desired emissions even when the emissions level of an individual country cannot be observed by the rest of the participating countries.

Keywords: Transboundary pollution; International agreements; Coalitions; Stability; Moral hazard

JEL classification: C72; F42; Q25

1. Introduction

The international dimension of environmental policy arises from the fact that pollutants generated as an inevitable byproduct of production in any country can cross national borders, carried by physical media like water or air. As a result, it is the total amount of accumulated pollutants that affects a country and not just the country's own emissions. These international

* Corresponding author.

SSDI 0047-2727(95)01518-3

environmental problems vary in nature from truly global problems, such as depletion of the ozone layer or global warming associated with the greenhouse effect, to more localized problems, such as pollution of the Mediterranean or the acid rain problem in Europe. In practice, attempts to form a policy capable of dealing with international problems have focused on international agreements (e.g. the Helsinki Protocol or the Montreal Protocol). In the recent literature on environmental economics, the focus has been on the emergence of international cooperation and underlying incentives (Carraro and Siniscalco, 1992). International cooperation among countries is necessary in the case of global pollution, since outcomes related to laissez-faire equilibria are inefficient, because each country chooses its pollution behavior ignoring the cost imposed on other countries as a result of its behavior.[1]

The basic question in the case of cooperation is whether sovereign countries can voluntarily (since there is no authority to force their cooperation) reach an agreement to protect the international commons. In the environmental literature, voluntary cooperation among sovereign countries has been analyzed both in terms of cooperative games with externalities (Chander and Tulkens, 1992, 1994) where conditions for the full cooperation of all countries are examined, as well as in terms of agreement of subgroups of countries which seek to expand the agreement by self-financing welfare transfers (Barrett, 1990, 1991; Carraro and Siniscalco, 1991, 1993; Hoel, 1992). When this last type of cooperation is examined, there is a major difficulty because each county has an incentive to defect from the agreement when everybody else cooperates, since, by doing so, a country can reduce the cost of abating pollution and enjoy the benefits from the overall reduced pollution brought about by the cooperation of the rest of the countries. Furthermore, as has been shown by Carraro and Siniscalco (1993), a small number of cooperating countries cannot enlarge the coalition with self-financed utility transfers to countries that have no incentive to join it, unless the cooperating countries are committed to signing the agreement and then providing incentives for the enlargement of the cooperating group. This paper follows that argument. It builds upon and extends the existing literature by considering coalition enlargement with non-identical countries, and then introducing, for the first time to our knowledge, asymmetries in information among countries, in the sense that countries entering into agreements know their own emissions but cannot observe the emissions of the remaining participating countries.

A group of countries that can potentially commit to cooperation are identified as environmentally conscious countries (ENCCs). By assuming

[1] For an analysis of specific environmental problems in such a framework, see, for example, Mäler (1989), Barrett (1992), Hoel (1992), and Xepapadeas (1995).

that the ENCCs are committed to an agreement to protect the environment, conditions are examined under which these countries can provide side payments, which are self-financing, to a second group of less environmentally conscious countries (LENCCs). Under the proposed side payments scheme, all countries form a stable coalition that agrees to adjust emissions so that a first-best global welfare optimum is achieved. A process for arriving at a side payment scheme capable of securing a stable partial coalition of ENCCs with a subset of LENCCs is also discussed.

Having determined the system of side payments, the second problem examined relates to the difficulties in enforcing the agreement, due to moral hazard. In particular, the case is considered in which the level of global pollution can be measured at a relatively low cost, whereas the cost of measuring each individual country's contribution to global pollution is prohibitively costly for an external observe. The country itself, on the other hand, can measure and report its contribution to global pollution at a relatively low cost. The inability to measure each country's emissions creates problems in the enforcement of the agreement, since countries have an incentive to cheat by emitting more than the agreement dictates. This is, therefore, a type of non-point-source pollution case with an international dimension. Although a non-point-source problem arising within a country can be handled by the imposition of collective penalty schemes (Segerson, 1988; Xepapadeas, 1991), the same formula does not apply here, since there is no supranational authority to impose collective penalty schemes on sovereign countries. Thus, in a second stage, a mechanism is developed which must be incorporated into the agreement between the ENCCs and the LENCCs, and which will induce the latter countries to emit at the desired level, even when global pollution has non-point-source characteristics. The advantage of the proposed mechanism is that it detects cheating, while keeping the potential costs low for the countries that respect the agreement.

The rest of the paper is organized as follows. Section 2 analyzes the conditions for the achievement of stable coalitions; Section 3 presents the mechanism that secures the enforcement of the agreement when the monitoring of individual countries' emissions is not possible; and Section 4 provides some concluding remarks.

2. First-best optimum, transfer payments and stable coalitions

We consider a group of $i = 1, \ldots, N$ countries. Production activities in each country generate pollution. Pollution crosses boundaries and its total concentration in the environment affects the whole group. Let e_i be the emissions of country i. The ambient concentration of the pollution, defined as $X = \sum_i e_i$, causes damages to all N countries. We assume that the damage function in each country takes the simple linear form m_iX, where $m_i \geq 0$ measures marginal damage in country i. Following Hoel (1992), we assume that $m_1 \geq m_2 \geq \cdots \geq m_N$, $M = \Sigma_i m_i > 0$. Therefore, countries with a low index, or high m, are considered to suffer the most damage from environmental pollution. If $m = 0$ for some country, then this country does not suffer any damage from global pollution. On the benefit side, we consider a more general case where benefit functions are not identical. The benefit of each country is a strictly concave function of its emissions, e_i, defined as $B_i(e_i)$, $B_i(0) = 0$, $B_i' > 0$, $B_i'' < 0$, where e_i belongs to some compact and convex subset of R_+. Thus the net benefit function for country i is defined as a function of all other countries' emissions levels, $b_i(e_i, e_{-i}) = B_i(e_i) - m_iX$, where $e_{-i} \equiv (e_1, \ldots, e_{i-1}, e_{i+1}, \ldots, e_N)$.

If there is no international cooperation, each country's emissions are determined as the Nash equilibrium of the non-cooperative game where countries choose emissions simultaneously to maximize their net benefits.[2] Thus the Nash equilibrium emissions level for each country is defined as[3]

$$\hat{e}_i : B_i'(\hat{e}_i) - m_i = 0\,, \quad i = 1, \ldots, N\,. \tag{1}$$

The non-cooperative emissions levels can be compared with the emissions levels corresponding to the first-best optimum which is obtained by maximizing global welfare, defined as the sum of individual countries' net benefit functions, $V(e_1, \ldots, e_N) = \Sigma_i b_i(e_i, e_{-i})$. A solution to the maximization of global welfare can be regarded as the case where a supranational authority, if it existed, would set the emissions levels for each country at the first-best optimum. This first-best emissions level for each country is defined as

$$\bar{e}_i : B_i'(\bar{e}_i) - M = 0\,, \quad i = 1, \ldots, N\,. \tag{2}$$

Assuming that at least two m's are non-zero, then from (1) and (2) we have that $\bar{e}_i < \hat{e}_i$, $\forall i$, $\bar{X} < \hat{X}$. This is a well-established result in the analysis of the international aspects of pollution (e.g. van der Ploeg and de Zeeuw, 1992). However, not all countries are better off at the first-best optimum as com-

[2] Although the international pollution game is not inherently one-shot, we choose this approach, because of the conceptual difficulties associated with the use of emission levels as trigger strategies in a repeated game. For example, countries committed to reducing emissions undertake irreversible investment expenses to introduce new technologies. Therefore, expanding their emissions in response to other countries' increased emissions could prove more harmful to themselves.

[3] It should be noted that in this simplified context the separability of the damage function implies that the best reply functions of countries are orthogonal. For the effect of the slope of the countries' best reply functions under noncooperative behavior cooperation, see, for example, Barrett (1991) and Carraro and Siniscalco (1993).

pared with the Nash equilibrium (Hoel, 1992). Some countries for which

$$m_i < \frac{B_i(\bar{e}_i) - B_i(\hat{e}_i)}{\bar{X} - \hat{X}} \tag{3}$$

will be better off at the first-best optimum. On the other hand, countries for which the reverse holds will be worse off at the first-best optimum in comparison with the Nash equilibrium. These countries will be characterized by low m in the case where the benefit functions of all countries are fairly similar. It is clear that in the presence of winners and losers from moving to the first best, there will be no voluntary cooperation by all N countries to achieve the first best. There is, however, the possibility of improving upon the inefficient laissez-faire outcome. There are alternative ways of approaching potential improvements and this essentially depends on how the countries that might agree to cooperation are determined and how their corresponding emissions levels are chosen.

Let us identify countries for which (3) holds as environmentally conscious (ENCCs), and countries for which the reverse holds as less environmentally conscious (LENCCs). We index the ENCCs by $j \in J$ and the LENCCs by $k \in K$. The sets J and K are assumed to be non-empty in order to make the problem interesting. They partition the set $I = \{1, \ldots, N\}$, i.e.,

$$J \cup K = I, \; J \cap K = \emptyset .$$

Assume that the ENCCs consider forming a coalition under which each country agrees to emit at the first best and then try to expand the coalition by inducing, through welfare transfers, some or all of the LENCCs to reduce their emissions too. Different assumptions can be made about the choice of the emissions levels by the countries considering cooperation. The ENCCs can choose to emit at the first best and then try to induce the LENCCs to reduce their emissions too, to the first-best level. Alternatively, the ENCCs can choose emissions levels for themselves and the LENCCs that maximize their own welfare, subject to the constraints of paying transfer payments to the LENCCs for moving from the Nash emissions.[4] The way of choosing the emissions levels by the cooperating countries is not, however, crucial to the development of a mechanism that induces truth-telling by the LENCCs when the emissions cannot be observed, and therefore it is not possible to verify whether they are following the agreement or not. The mechanism needs only knowledge of the required transfers to the LENCCs, independent of the way in which these transfers have been determined. In our approach, we analyze the case in which the

[4] This approach gives a cost-effective outcome, that is, equal marginal benefits for all countries, but with higher emissions as compared with the first bet (Hoel, 1994; Kverndokk, 1994).

ENCCs agree to emit at the first best and then try to induce the LENCCs to join the agreement by welfare transfers. Apart from being a simplified way to define the transfers to be used in our mechanism, the approach can also be justified by the results of Chander and Tulkens (1994), indicating that full cooperation at the first best is possible. Since the spirit of our results is valid under any reasonable assumption about which countries are cooperating and what emissions levels they are choosing for themselves and the rest of the countries, we will proceed with our simplified assumption.

The coalition of ENCCs will be stable if none of the ENCCs has an incentive to defect from the agreement while the other countries are participating.[5] As is known, the size of a stable coalition when problems of climate are analyzed is likely to be small (Barrett, 1992; Hoel, 1992). This type of stability requirement, which might be satisfied for a small – but not the whole – group of ENCCs, can however be regarded as too restrictive in reality.[6] With respect to CO_2 emissions, for example, a coalition of countries from the European Union (EU) (considered as ENCCs), can be regarded as a stable coalition since breaking the agreement by one country will not only entail costs in terms of the EU's legal apparatus but also costs in terms of breaking social norms (e.g. Hoel, 1994).[7] Thus, although in strict economic terms an EU country might have an incentive to defect from the agreement, the above more general types of cost could ensure stability of the coalition. It seems natural, therefore, to consider the ENCCs as a prime candidates for forming a stable coalition of countries agreeing to emit to the first best and to seek ways to expand the coalition to the LENCCs. This coalition cannot be expanded, however, with self-financed transfers, unless the ENCCs additionally commit to cooperation (Carraro and Siniscalco, 1993). Therefore, assuming *stable coalition commitment*. the following proposition can be stated.

Proposition 1. (i) *If all J countries commit to cooperation, and* (ii) *if*

$$\Big[\sum_i B_i\bar{e}_i) - M\bar{X}\Big] - \Big[\sum_i B_i(\hat{e}_i) - M\hat{X}\Big] \geq \sum_k m_k[(\hat{X} - \bar{X}) - (\hat{e}_k - \bar{e}_k)]\,, \tag{4}$$

then there exists a system of self-financed side payments t_k, $k \in K$, such that

[5] Formally, the stability of a coalition requires both internal and external stability in the sense of cartel stability (e.g. D'Aspremont et al., 1983; Barrett. 1991).

[6] Bauer (1993) indicates that if the decision of one country as to whether or not to cooperate affects the cooperation decisions of other countries – that is, the countries sequentially decide whether or not to cooperate – then the stable coalition could be large.

[7] Fankhauser and Kverndokk (1992) have also suggested that the OECD countries can be regarded as a group of countries committed to internal cooperation for CO_2 reductions.

all LENCCs enter the coalition and emit at the first-best level of emissions. The coalition of all N countries is stable.

Proof. The kth country from the LENCCs will be no worse off under the first best if it receives a side payment,

$$\hat{t}_k = B_k(\hat{e}_k) - B_k(\bar{e}_k) - m_k(\hat{X} - \bar{X}) ,$$

which is equal to its losses for moving to the first best. This transfer might not, however, be enough to ensure stability of the coalition, since country k will have an incentive to defect once all other countries have entered the coalition. The gains from defection are defined as

$$d_k = \left[B_k(\hat{e}_k) - m_k\left(\hat{e}_k + \sum_{i \neq k} \bar{e}_i\right)\right] - \left[B_k(\bar{e}_k) - m_k \sum_i \bar{e}_i\right]$$

or (5)

$$d_k = B_k(\hat{e}_k) - B_k(\bar{e}_k) - m_k(\hat{e}_k - \bar{e}_k) .$$

If the actual transfer is such that $t_k \geqslant d_k$, then there will be no incentive for country k to defect. If the benefits of the ENCCs from moving to the first best are sufficiently large, either because there is a large number of them or because the individual benefits of a small number of ENCCs are sufficiently large, then the sum of benefits of the ENCCs exceeds the sum of the potential gains from defection of the LENCCs. This is, however, satisfied if (ii) holds, since (4) can be equivalently written as

$$\sum_j [B_j(\bar{e}_j) - B_j(\hat{e}_j) - m_j(\bar{X} - \hat{X})]$$
$$\geqslant \sum_k [B_k(\hat{e}_k) - B_k(\bar{e}_k) - m_k(\hat{e}_k - \bar{e}_k)] = \sum_k d_k , \quad (4')$$

which implies that the system of side payments is self-financed. Thus the coalition is internally stable since by (i) the J countries are committed to cooperation and also by (ii) the side payments are self-financed. Q.E.D.

This proposition, in a sense, extends the results of Carraro and Siniscalco (1993) to the case in which the participating countries are not identical. It implies, by using (4′), that if the benefits from moving to the first best are large for the ENCCs, then these countries can offer sufficient inducement for the LENCCs to form a stable coalition wherein all countries will emit at the first best. On the other hand, it can be seen – by using (4) – that a stable coalition can always be achieved if the marginal pollution damage of the LENCCs is sufficiently small. This follows directly from (4) which represents the welfare gains from the international agreement. Its left-hand side is always positive, since it represents the difference in total benefits between the first best and the non-cooperative Nash equilibrium. Thus (4) will be satisfied if m_k are sufficiently small.

The approach used to derive conditions that ensure the stability of the coalition of all countries can be used to examine partial expansions. The partial expansion of the coalition will be successful if the benefits from moving away from the Nash equilibrium of a subset of countries, which will now represent the ENCCs, are sufficient to compensate another subset of countries, which will now represent the LENCCs, for entering the agreement. It should be noted, however, that in this case the benchmark of the ENCCs for comparisons with the Nash equilibrium is not the first-best emission level, $\bar{e}_i$. This is because when the countries which in the end do not participate in the coalition choose the Nash equilibrium emissions, $\hat{e}_i$, the emissions $\bar{e}_i$ do not maximize either global welfare or the welfare of the ENCCs. The new emissions level can be chosen by maximizing the welfare of different subgroups of countries. One of these subgroups will eventually form the partially expanded coalition.[8]

The achievement of the desired emissions levels by the coalition of ENCCs requires, however, that the emissions of each individual country can be observed. If this is not possible, either because it is too costly or because it is technically impossible, then the LENCCs will have an incentive to cheat. An additional mechanism is required to ensure the enforcement of the agreement so that the first best or a partial enlargement of the initial coalition of ENCCs is achieved. This is the problem addressed in the next section.

[8] A possible starting point for determining a stable, partially expanded coalition could be to exclude the country that requires the largest compensation to participate in the all-country coalition, and given that this country emits at the Nash equilibrium, to redefine the groups of ENCCs and LENCCs. One way to redefine the groups would be to use as a benchmark the emission levels that correspond to the cooperative equilibrium of the $N-1$ countries. If the benefits of the newly defined ENCCs from moving to the new cooperative optimum are sufficient to compensate the newly-defined LENCCs so that they will not defect, the partial coalition will be stable. If not, another country from the newly defined group of LENCCs can be excluded (alternatively, a second country from the initial LENCCs could be excluded) and proceed in the same way. The way that the new ENCCs and LENCCs are defined does not alter the validity of our results.

3. Enforcing the agreement under moral hazard

If monitoring of the emissions level of an individual country is prohibitively costly, then the ENCCs – which in what follows are assumed to act as a single agent because they are committed to cooperation – cannot observe the contribution to global pollution by each LENCC. On the other hand, an individual country is able to measure its own emissions at some cost. This asymmetry between the costs of monitoring and own measurement can easily be justified. An external observer sent by the ENCCs to measure the emissions levels of an LENCC will spend a lot of money collecting the required information, while the same information could be collected at a much lower cost by the country itself. In particular, we assume that a LENCC k asked to 'verify' its emissions levels will incur a small fixed cost $0<f_k<t_k$, $k \in K$, to measure and report its emissions. The latter includes the cost of setting up a formal committee, collecting the adequate information, preparing the text of the report and so forth, a procedure which is demanding both in terms of time and resources. Those expenses will be incurred even if LENCC k chooses to misreport its emissions level when asked to 'verify' it. Such costs would probably be much smaller than the agreed transfer t_k to LENCC k. We further assume that an LENCC asked for further evidence to support its initial report can provide it at no cost.[9] If monitoring from outside is impossible, it is also reasonable to assume that an LENCC's reported measurements of its emissions cannot be verified by the ENCCs. We finally assume that the cost of measuring global pollution is zero and that there are no measurement errors.

The question addressed in this section is whether the global optimum (or the optimal level of pollution in the case of a partial agreement) can still be achieved in the presence of *moral hazard*; that is, when each LENCC has an incentive to first sign the agreement and then over-emit. If a supranational authority existed, it could impose collective penalty schemes to eliminate any incentives for an LENCC to cheat, but this is not possible in an international set-up. To deal with moral hazard in the international com-

[9] Our results hold in the more general case where the $(n+1)$th supplement to the initial report costs less than the nth supplement. This is a reasonable assumption given that any new addition to the existing evidence most probably costs less in terms of time and resources than the last addition. This assumption is satisfied, for example, if the costs of the supplements decline geometrically. That is, the first supplement costs λf_k, the second $\lambda^2 f_k$, etc., with $0<\lambda<1$. What turns out to be an important assumption is that the total cost (of the infinite sequence) of the initial report and its supplements incurred by an LENCC k is finite and sufficiently small so that it does not exceed the amount of transfer which it expects to receive from the ENCC. With geometrically declining costs, the latter is satisfied only if $f_k<(1-\lambda)t_k$.

mons, we set up a mechanism that detects cheating.[10] Furthermore, we require that this mechanism keeps to a minimum level any penalties and costs imposed on an LENCC which respects the agreement in the case when one or more LENCC has over-emitted. Often over-emission is the result of an accident or a technical omission; it might also occur because the central government sometimes fails to control its private sector. It is then reasonable that, in order to sign the agreement, an LENCC would require that the mechanism not only detects cheating, but also that it imposes the least possible costs on the countries that respect the agreement. Note that a collective penalty scheme lacks this property, since it dictates very severe punishments to all 'innocent' LENCCs: it cancels all transfers – even if only one LENCC cheats.

We proceed next to a formal description of the game. The players are the LENCCs, each acting in its own interest, and the group of ENCCs acting as a single agent. The game is played in *three stages*. The first is the *negotiation* stage. In this stage all parties involved sign a binding agreement which specifies (i) each individual country's level of emissions x_i^*, $i = 1, \ldots, N$; (ii) a vector of lump-sum transfers from the ENCCs to the LENCCs, t_k, $k \in K$, with $T = \Sigma_k t_k$, to be paid if the measured global pollution, X_m, is less than or equal to the agreed $X^* = \Sigma x_i^*$; and (iii) a total amount of transfers, $T_c = T - \min_k t_k$, in the case when $X_m > X^*$, to be distributed among the LENCCs through mechanism M^* described below. The second is the *actual pollution* stage. Each country decides independently its emissions level x_i, $i = 1, \ldots, N$. Given that by assumption $x_j = x_j^*$ for all $j \in J$, if $X_m \leq X^*$ each LENCC receives t_k and the game ends. If, however, $X_m > X^*$, that is, if one or more of the LENCCs have over-emitted, we proceed to the last stage of the game, the *implementation of mechanism* M^* stage. The clearing and actual transfer payments are then left for the end of the procedure dictated by mechanism M^*.

[10] The initial idea for the set-up of a mechanism that deals with the international commons comes from a modification of a procedure which constitutes an integral part of the Civil Code of many countries (see, for example, section IV, chapter III, book IV of the Spanish Civil Code) and has been applied repeatedly in the courts. This procedure mandates that if a debtor A owes a given amount of money to a group of agents, without knowing how much he/she owes to each one of them, he/she has the right to choose one agent arbitrarily (say, his/her creditor 1) and transfer the whole amount of debt to him/her. Creditor 1 then becomes a debtor towards the rest of the group. Creditor 1, in turn, may arbitrarily choose one of the other creditors and transfer the whole amount of debt to him/her, minus the part he/she claims A owes to him/her. This procedure continues up to the point where only one creditor is left, who then receives the residual. If the last creditor is not satisfied with the residual, then he/she may appeal to the courts, asking for more money from his/her predecessor. If the last creditor proves his/her claim to be valid, then he/she may in turn appeal to the courts, accusing the previous creditor in the chain of a false claim, and so on.

Note that whenever the measured pollution level is higher than the agreed one, by no matter how much, the *same* total amount of transfers is available for distribution among the LENCCs. This amount is equal to the sum of the transfers minus its smallest component, if all parties respect the agreement. This implies that there is always enough money for transfers to those LENCCs that respect the agreement. Put otherwise, given that an LENCC which cheats has no right to receive any side payments, the ENCCs 'owe' at most T_c to the group of LENCCs if $X_m > X^*$.

Mechanism M^*, which deals with moral hazard, works as follows.[11] First, the LENCCs are ordered randomly. The *announcement procedure* then follows. LENCC 1 in the chain first announces a claim s_1 on the funds available for transfers T_c. If it claims anything but t_1 – thus revealing it has over-emitted – it will actually receive zero at the clearing while T_c will be automatically reduced by t_1. LENCC 2 then announces its claim s_2 on the remaining funds $T_c - t_1$, and so on. Given that $T_c = T - \min_k t_k$, the funds available for transfers never suffice for the last LENCC (say ℓ) to make its agreed claim t_ℓ. Then a costly and binding *measurement procedure* starts. It is binding because an LENCC asked to measure and report its emissions is obliged to do so. LENCC ℓ with the unsatisfied claim gets the initiative to carry out the measurement procedure. LENCC ℓ has the right to pass the initiative to its first predecessor with an outstanding claim – thus revealing it has over-emitted. If so, it will actually get zero at the clearing and T_c will be automatically reduced by t_ℓ

The LENCC with the initiative (say i) first asks all the LENCCs who have admitted cheating to measure and report their emissions. If the sum of their reported over-emissions equals $X_m - X^*$, the game ends and the ENCCs satisfy all the outstanding claims (including a transfer t_ℓ to LENCC ℓ whenever the latter has the initiative). If not, LENCC i asks sequentially, starting from the nearest and going backwards in the chain, all its predecessors with outstanding claims to measure and report their emissions. If at the end of this first round the reported over-emissions are not equal to $X_m - X^*$, LENCC i is obliged first to measure and report its own emissions, and then it starts a second round of sequential requests for supplementary reports from all its predecessors which still have outstanding claims; and so on ad infinitum. An LENCC who reports over-emissions during this procedure will receive zero at the clearing. The measurement procedure stops as soon as the sum of the reported over-emissions turns out to be

[11] We wish to thank an anonymous referee for suggesting a simplified version of the mechanism on which our current version of M^* is based. The simpler measurement procedure described in footnote 12 leads to the same results but at the cost of imposing unnecessary penalties on the LENCCs that respect the agreement in the case – for example – of an accidental over-emission by one LENCC.

equal to $X_m - X^*$. Then the game ends and all the remaining claims are satisfied by the ENCC.[12]

The intuition is as follows. Whenever there is cheating, the available funds T_c cannot cover all the agreed transfers T, and whenever a cheating LENCC k attempts to get its agreed transfer t_k in the announcement procedure, the measurement procedure is triggered. If the cheater is the last LENCC ℓ and does not renounce the initiative, it will eventually be obliged to measure and report its emissions. Because measurement is perfect, the stopping rule of the measurement procedure guarantees that all cheaters will be exposed. A cheater has nothing to gain by misreporting its emissions, because it will never receive any transfer. This is because (i) actual transfer payments will be made only when the reported over-emissions account exactly for the gap between the measured and the agreed global pollution, and (ii) an LENCC that respects the agreements always reports its true emissions. Furthermore, because measurement is costly, no cheater has the incentive to provoke it by attempting to get its agreed transfer during the announcement procedure. Thus cheaters never claim their agreed transfer, thus receiving zero transfer at the clearing. If the transfers are properly chosen, then no LENCC will ever have an incentive to cheat.

Note that mechanism M^* penalizes least the LENCC that respects the agreement. First, if some LENCCs have cheated – say by accident – it is best for them to claim 0 during the announcements. Then no cost is imposed on the 'innocent'; only the cheaters measure and report their emissions. If, in addition, the cheater – say by mistake – attempts to get its agreed-upon transfer, it is optimal for it to report its emissions truthfully.[12] Then, on average, the 'innocent' LENCCs bear the least cost of measurements.

To show that the global optimum can be achieved, suppose that $t_k = d_k$ with d_k defined in (5). An LENCC receives a transfer equal to its gains from defection from the first best whenever it emits at the first-best level, or over-emits but is not caught. Then if condition (4) is satisfied and ENCCs are committed to cooperation, all countries will be better off at the global

[12] In a simpler mechanism, the LENCC ℓ with the unsatisfied claim starts a measurement procedure by which each LENCC, starting with itself and working backward from $\ell - 1$ to 1, measures and reports its own emission. If at the end of the first round the reported over-emissions are not equal to $X_m - X^*$, LENCC ℓ starts a second round requesting supplementary evidence. This simpler mechanism M' detects cheating, but imposes higher costs on the LENCCs that respect the agreement once – for some reason – the mechanism is triggered. If, for example, LENCC 1 has accepted its over-emissions, M' will unnecessarily impose costs of measuring on all LENCC.

[13] Accidental over-emissions by the ENCC will not impose any cost on the LENCCs. We assume that the stable coalition commitment implies that any accidental emissions by the ENCC will be reported before the implementation of the mechanism, and that the ENCCs will bear the cost of these over-emissions.

optimum, provided that no LENCC has an incentive to cheat by over-emitting. Hence, if the above mechanism detects cheating, all countries have an incentive to sign the proposed scheme in the negotiation stage. The above are given formally in Propositions 2 and 3.

Proposition 2. Given that $x_j = \bar{e}_j$ *for* $j \in J$, $x_k = \bar{e}_k$, $k \in K$, *is a perfect equilibrium for the sub-game starting from the actual pollution stage. Equivalently, each LENCC will independently choose its emissions level according to the first best.*

Proof. See the appendix.

Note that in equilibrium no country will ever be asked to measure and reports its emissions level, thus no cost f_k will ever be incurred. Notice further that there might be cases out of equilibrium where the system of transfers is not self-financed. However, it could be assumed that the ENCCs are committed not only to cooperation, but also to incurring some additional costs if something goes wrong. Proposition 2 allows us to extend Proposition 1 in the presence of moral hazard.

Proposition 3. If (i) *all J ENCCs commit to cooperation, and* (ii) *condition* (4) *holds, there exists a system of self-financed side payments* t_k, $k \in K$, *and a mechanism* M^* *such that each LENCC has an incentive to emit at its first-best emissions level even if individual monitoring is not possible.*

Similar results can be obtained if the required side payments are not sufficient to obtain the cooperation of all countries involved, but instead are enough for a partial augmentation of the initial coalition of the ENCCs.

4. Summary

When each country is affected not just by its own emissions but by the total amount of global pollution, then an international environment policy should be developed. In this paper, conditions under which sovereign countries can voluntarily achieve an agreement to protect the international commons are examined. A problem that arises in the case of international commons is that each country has an incentive to defect from the agreement when all other countries cooperate, since by doing so a country can reduce the cost of abating pollution and enjoy the benefits from the overall reduced pollution brought about by the cooperation of the rest of the countries.

It is shown, by extending recent results to the case of non-identical countries, that if there exists a group of ENCCs – identified as countries gaining from moving from the non-cooperative equilibrium to the first best – which are committed to protecting the environment, these countries can induce larger stable coalitions to reduce emissions by a system of self-financed side payments if either of the following conditions holds: (i) the number of ENCCs is large enough, and/or their benefits from achieving the global first best are sufficiently high, or (ii) the marginal disutility of each of the LENCCs is sufficiently small. The implicit assumption here is that ENCCs act as a single agent, which therefore has an incentive to stick to its first best emissions level and pay the total amount of transfers.

In the second part of the paper we show that observability of the emissions level of each LENCC is not crucial to achieve reduced emissions. Even if individual monitoring is not possible, the optimal level of emissions can be achieved under the same conditions as previously. Given that global pollution can be measured costlessly, and that an LENCC is able to measure and report its emissions level if ever asked to do so, by incurring a fixed cost, a mechanism is developed that guarantees that each LENCC has an incentive to report its emissions level truthfully. The proposed mechanism has the advantage that it does not impose high costs on countries that respect the agreement. In a way, the mechanism developed in this paper can be regarded as a step in the direction of designing regulatory mechanisms under asymmetric information, when there is no regulator in the usual sense of an authority (e.g. government) which can interfere with agents' activities (see, for example, Laffont, 1994). In our framework the regulatory mechanism is agreed upon by the sovereign members of the international team pursuing global emissions reductions under asymmetric information. The possibility of errors in measurement of the global or individual levels of emissions has not been examined in this paper. It remains for further research to answer whether a global first best can be achieved if errors exist in measuring pollution and/or uncertainty on the part of certain countries in controlling their pollution level.

Acknowledgments

Earlier versions of this paper were presented at the 1993 Econometric Society European Meeting, Uppsala, Sweden, and at the Eighth Annual Congress of the European Economic Association, Helsinki, Finland, 1993. Special thanks to Sofia Katsulaki for bringing to our attention the article of the Civil Code on which the construction of our mechanism is based. Finally, we are grateful to Carlo Carraro and two anonymous referees for their comments on an earlier draft of this paper.

Appendix

Proof of Proposition 2. We first prove that mechanism M^* detects all cheaters. Note that whenever there is cheating, $T_c < T$, and the measurement procedure is initiated at the end of the announcement procedure. Suppose that LENCC i, which receives the initiative, starts the measurement procedure. First, it is a dominant strategy for an LENCC which emitted at the agreed level to report its emissions truthfully, because the total cost of the initial measurement and the supplementary reports is strictly less than its agreed transfer. Furthermore, an LENCC k which accepted over-emissions, either by claiming $s_k \neq t_k$ during the announcement procedure or by renouncing the initiative, has nothing to gain by misreporting its emissions. It will receive zero in any case at the clearing, and is obliged to bear the fixed cost f_k of measuring emissions even if the report is fake. Moreover, a cheater LENCC k which claimed its agreed transfer during the announcement procedure, or did not renounce the initiative, has nothing to gain by misreporting its emissions. It is obliged to measure its emissions at a cost f_k, as well as to provide as many additional reports as are asked for. An infinitely misreporting cheater LENCC k bears the cost f_k while never receiving any transfer, because the measurement procedure stops, and actual transfers are paid, only when the reported over-emissions turn out to be equal to $X_m - X^*$. Of course, if LENCC k reports truthfully at some round, it will receive zero at the clearing, while always bearing the cost f_k. Note that even though there are many subgame perfect equilibria (SPE) in the measurement game, there is a unique subgame perfect payoff for any cheater LENCC k which is equal to $-f_k$.

A cheater LENCC k has nothing to gain by claiming $s_k = t_k$ in the announcement procedure, or by not renouncing the initiative, because the measurement game follows. It will end up paying the fixed cost of measuring its emissions and receiving zero transfer in any SPE of the measurement game. On the other hand, a LENCC which emitted at the agreed level has a dominant strategy to claim its agreed transfer during the announcement game. Hence in an SPE of the announcement game each cheater claims zero, or, if last in the chain, renounces the initiative. Thus our mechanism detects all cheaters in an SPE of the implementation of the M^* game. Furthermore, in all SPE a cheater k ends up paying the fixed cost of measuring its emissions f_k, while receiving zero transfer.

It remains to prove that $x_k = \bar{e}_k$, $k \in K$, is a Nash equilibrium of the actual pollution game. Given that M^* is implemented whenever one or more LENCC chooses $x_k > \bar{e}_k$ and that a cheater LENCC k ends up paying f_k in an SPE of an implementation of the M^* game, it follows by the construction of the transfers that an LENCC has no incentive to over-emit. It is also obvious that it has no incentive to under-emit. This proves that $x_k = \bar{e}_k$, $k \in K$, is an SPE of the game starting from the actual pollution stage. Q.E.D.

References

Barrett, S., 1990, The problem of global environmental protection, Oxford Review of Economic Policy 6, no. 1, 168–179.

Barrett, S., 1991, The paradox of international environmental agreements, mimeo, London Business School.

Barrett, S., 1992, International environmental agreements as games, in: R. Pethig, ed., Conflicts and cooperation in managing environmental resources (Springer-Verlag, Berlin) 18–33.

Bauer, A., 1993, International cooperation over environmental goods, mimeo., University of Munich.

Carraro, C. and D. Siniscalco, 1991, The international protection of the environment: Voluntary agreements among sovereign countries, in: P. Dasgupta, K.G. Mäler and A. Vercelli, eds., The protection of trans-national commons (Clarendon, Oxford).

Carraro, C. and D. Siniscalco, 1992, The international dimension of environmental policy, European Economic Review 36, 379–387.

Carraro, C. and D. Siniscalco, 1993, Strategies for the international protection of the environment, Journal of Public Economics 52, 309–328.

Chander, P. and H. Tulkens, 1992, Theoretical foundations of negotiations and cost sharing in transfrontier pollution problems, European Economic Review 36, 288–299.

Chander, P. and H. Tulkens, 1994, The core of an economy with multilateral environmental externalities, mimeo, CORE and Indian Statistical Institute.

D'Aspremont, C., A. Jacquemin, J. Gabszewicz and J. Weymark, 1983, On the stability of collusive price leadership, Canadian Journal of Economics 16, 17–25.

Fankhauser, S. and S. Kverndokk, 1992, The global warming game – simulation of a CO_2 reduction agreement, Memo No. 13, Dept. of Economics, University of Oslo.

Hoel, M., 1992, International environment conventions: The case of uniform reductions of emissions, Environmental and Resource Economics 2, 141–160.

Hoel, M., 1994, Efficient climate policy in the presence of free riders, Journal of Environmental Economics and Management 27, 259–274.

Kverndokk, S., 1994, Coalition and side payments in international CO_2 treaties, in: E.C. van Ireland, ed., International environmental economics: Themes and applications to climatic change acidification and international trade (Elsevier Science Publishers).

Laffont, J.-J., 1994, The new economics of regulation ten years after, Econometrica 62, 507–537.

Mäler, K.G., 1989, The acid rain game, in: H. Folmer and E. Ireland, eds., Valuation methods and policy making in environmental economics (Elsevier, New York) 188–205.

Segerson, K., 1988, Uncertainty and incentives in nonpoint pollution control, Journal of Environmental Economics and Management 15, 87–98.

van der Ploeg, F. and A. de Zeeuw, 1992, International aspects of pollution control, Environmental and Resource Economics 2, 117–139.

Xepapadeas, A., 1991, Environmental policy under imperfect information: Incentives and moral hazard, Journal of Environmental Economics and Management 20, 113–126.

Xepapadeas, A., 1995, Induced technical change and international agreements under greenhouse warming, Resource and Energy Economics 16, in press.

[7]

JOURNAL OF ENVIRONMENTAL ECONOMICS AND MANAGEMENT **32**, 170–188 (1997)
ARTICLE NO. EE960959

Negotiating an Agreement on Global Warming: A Theoretical Analysis

ZHIQI CHEN*

Department of Economics, Carleton University, Ottawa K1S 5B6, Canada

Received June 29, 1994; revised January 11, 1996

The outcome of international negotiation on combatting global warming is derived and analyzed using a two-country bargaining model. It is shown that while side payments between countries will generally be part of an agreement, some of these payments are made purely as a result of asymmetry in bargaining power and have nothing to do with the polluter pays principle or the victim pays principle. Factors affecting the outcome of negotiation include a country's size of population, the welfare level at the disagreement point, and the order of making offers. The enforcement issue is also discussed. © 1997 Academic Press

1. INTRODUCTION

The issue of global warming has attracted a great deal of attention in recent years. It has been the subject of heated debates and has become an important policy issue in many countries. Indeed, a major item on the agenda of the 1992 Earth Summit in Rio de Janeiro was the global warming problem. More recently, another United Nations summit on global warming, attended by environment ministers, was held in Berlin in April 1995.

It is widely recognized that the key to solving the global warming problem is international cooperation (see, e.g., [1–3]). However, while governments of most countries pay lip service to the importance of international cooperation, so far they have not yet signed any binding international agreement on global warming that would commit them to a firm course of action. Given that global warming is such an important issue and that international agreement is crucial to solving this problem, a theoretical investigation into the process of negotiating an international agreement is warranted.

In this paper we present a theoretical analysis on the process and outcome of international negotiation on global warming. Using a two-country model we study how the responsibilities for combatting global warming can be allocated through negotiation. We approach the problem from the perspective of non-cooperative bargaining theory and study the outcome of a two-country bargaining game. We demonstrate that, in a world of perfect information, Pareto efficiency can be achieved through a negotiated agreement. Furthermore, the agreement can be implemented in decentralized economies through a system of taxes and interna-

*This paper is based on a chapter of my Ph.D. thesis. I am grateful to Glenn MacDonald and Ignatius Horstmann for their encouragement and helpful suggestions. I also benefitted from comments by Randy Wigle, Quan Wen, Lutz Busch, and participants of the second annual meeting of the Canadian Resource and Environmental Economics Study Group. Constructive comments from three referees of this *Journal* have led to significant improvement of the paper.

0095-0696/97 $25.00

tional transfers. Compliance with the terms of the agreement can be ensured by the threat that, should one country cheat on the agreement, all countries will suspend the implementation of the agreement and revert to the state of laissez faire for a fixed amount of time.

One important issue most frequently discussed in the literature on global environmental problems is the side payments between countries (see, e.g., [1, 10]). In the existing analysis side payments are made either for compensating the victim of pollution for damages (the polluter pays principle) or for compensating the polluter for not polluting (the victim pays principle). The results from our model show that in general international transfers from one country to the other will be observed as part of the agreement. Not all of these transfers, however, are made by the heavy-polluting country for compensating the damages in the other country. Parts of these transfers are made purely as a result of asymmetry in bargaining power. Therefore, while we expect that a future agreement on global warming will involve international transfers, the reasons for which these transfers are made may be very different from what most economists have in mind.

The results from this model also shed light on the effects of various factors on the outcome of international negotiation. It is shown that a country may gain from being able to make the first move in negotiation. However, being the first mover does not guarantee the country a higher per capita welfare than the other country because of the effects of other factors such as the relative population sizes of the two countries and the welfare levels at the status quo.

It is shown that, other things being equal, a country with a small population gains more from the international agreement than a country with a large population. This is because in the negotiation process what is considered a small concession by a large country could mean a substantial gain for a small country. Suppose, for example, country A in terms of population is 10 times as large as country B. Then a donation of $1 per capita by the citizens of country A to country B will translate into $10 for every citizen of B. On the other hand, a donation of $1 from every citizen of B will mean a mere 10 cents per capita for A. Hence it is easier for a large country to "bribe" a small country into an agreement than for a small country to "bribe" a large country. As a result, the small country can credibly take a less compromising stand in the negotiation process than the large country.

It is demonstrated that an increase in the welfare level at the status quo raises (respectively, reduces) the per capita welfare of the country whose gain from the agreement is smaller (respectively, larger). Since in equilibrium a large country gains less from the agreement than a small country does, an increase in the welfare level at the status quo benefits the large country but hurts the small country.

The paper is organized as follows. In Section 2 we describe the economic and natural environment of a world economy, and in Section 3 we derive the world welfare possibility frontier that will be used in the analysis of the bargaining game. In Section 4 we specify the bargaining game and derive the equilibrium of the game. The effects of various factors on the outcome of negotiation are examined in Section 5. It is shown in Section 6 that the agreement can be implemented in decentralized economies by a system of taxes and international transfers. In Section 7 we discuss the punishment mechanism that can be used to enforce the agreement. Section 8 contains concluding remarks.

2. ECONOMIC AND NATURAL ENVIRONMENT

In this section the production, consumption, and climatic aspects of a world economy are specified. Roughly speaking, we shall consider a world that consists of two countries. Two goods are produced, one of which is an agricultural good and the other a manufactured good. The productivity of the agricultural sector is affected by the global temperature. The manufacturing activities, on the other hand, affect temperature.

The formal specification of the model follows. Time, denoted by t, is discrete and the horizon is infinite: $t \in \{0, 1 \dots\}$. The world consists of two countries: H and F. Population in each country is constant over time. Let the size of world population be normalized to one. Country H has a population of size α, whereas country F, $1 - \alpha$.

The two countries are assumed to have identical production technologies, identical preferences, and identical climate. In what follows the production and consumption sides of the model are specified for country H. The variables of country F, which will be denoted by attaching a superscript *, can be specified in the same way.

On the production side of the world, two non-storable goods are produced, an agricultural good and a manufactured good, with quantities being denoted by X_1 and X_2. Goods can be transported at zero cost.

There is a fixed continuum of firms in each industry. Hence both industries are perfectly competitive. Labor is the only input of production. At each date a representative firm in industry i ($i = 1, 2$) chooses the level of employment in the industry, l_{it}.

The production technology of both goods exhibits constant returns to scale. The productivity of labor in the manufacturing sector does not depend on climate and is denoted by b. Output of the manufacturing sector at date t can then be written as $X_{2t} = bl_{2t}$. In the agricultural sector, however, the productivity of labor depends on one aspect of the climate, namely, the global temperature. Let $a(\tau_t)$ denote the productivity coefficient of the agricultural sector, i.e., $X_{1t} = a(\tau_t)l_{1t}$, where τ_t is the world average temperature level in period t.

The variable $a(\tau_t)$ captures the effects of global warming on agriculture. It is assumed that $a(\tau_n) > 0$; $a(\tau_u) = 0$; and $a'(\tau_t) < 0$ for all $\tau_t \in [\tau_n, \tau_u]$. The temperature level τ_n denotes the "natural" temperature level, i.e., the level at which the global temperature would stay in the absence of any manufacturing activities, while τ_u ($> \tau_n$) is the temperature level at which the agriculture productivity equals zero.[1] Therefore, by assumption the agriculture productivity is positive when there have been no manufacturing activities. A higher level of temperature reduces the agriculture productivity.[2] The agriculture productivity eventually approaches zero as temperature level reaches τ_u.

[1] According to Cline [7], crop yields collapse to zero at 45°C.

[2] Readers should note this is a hypothesis that is still subject to scientific investigation. "[T]here is presently no firm evidence for believing that the net effects of higher CO_2 and climatic change on agriculture in any specific region of the world will be adverse rather than beneficial. But it is certain that some will gain and others will lose, although we know neither where they will be found nor the magnitude of the impacts" [4, p. 24]. In a recent paper, Mendelsohn *et al.* [11] estimate that the impact of global warming on farmland values in the United States is negative if observations are weighted by the percentage of cropland, but is positive if they are weighted by the value of crop revenue.

On the consumption side of the economy there is a fixed continuum of identical consumers. A representative consumer is endowed with one unit of labor which is supplied inelastically. He has no initial wealth. His preferences over consumptions of the agricultural good and the manufactured good, denoted by C_{1t} and C_{2t}, are represented by the utility function $\Sigma_{t=0}^{\infty} \beta^t U(C_{1t}, C_{2t})$, where $U(C_{1t}, C_{2t})$ is concave and homogenous of degree γ.

The law of motion of the global average temperature is represented by a variation of the zero-dimensional climate system model presented in Dickinson [8],

$$\tau_{t+1} = (1-c)(\tau_t - \tau_n) + \tau_n + g(X_{2t} + X_{2t}^*), \tag{1}$$

where $c \in (0,1)$, $g(0) = 0$, $g'(\cdot) > 0$, and $g''(\cdot) \leq 0$.

Equation (1) states that manufacturing activities raise temperature. When temperature is above its natural level, τ_n, nature has the ability of absorbing a percentage of excess greenhouse gases and cooling down the climate toward its natural level at a rate c. Without loss of generality the unit of temperature is chosen in such a way that $\tau_n = 0$.

3. WELFARE POSSIBILITY FRONTIER

Suppose there is a world central planner whose objective is to maximize the weighted sum of per capita utility of the two countries over an infinite time horizon. Let $\psi \in (0,1)$ denote the weight attached to H's per capita welfare and $1-\psi$, the weight attached to F's per capita welfare. Let L_{it} $(i = 1,2)$ be the labor input allocated to sector i worldwide (i.e.,$L_{it} = l_{it} + l_{it}^*$). The world planner's problem is to

$$\max_{\{C_{1t}, C_{2t}, C_{1t}^*, C_{2t}^*, L_{1t}, L_{2t}, \tau_{t+1}\}_{t=0}^{\infty}} \sum_{t=0}^{\infty} \beta^t[\psi U(C_{1t}, C_{2t}) + (1-\psi) U(C_{1t}^*, C_{2t}^*)] \tag{2}$$

subject to

$$\alpha C_{1t} + (1-\alpha) C_{1t}^* = a(\tau_t) L_{1t} = X_{1t} + X^*_{1t}, \tag{3}$$

$$\alpha C_{2t} + (1-\alpha) C_{2t}^* = b L_{2t} = X_{2t} + X^*_{2t}, \tag{4}$$

$$L_{1t} + L_{2t} = 1, \tag{5}$$

$$\tau_{t+1} = (1-c)\tau_t + g(X_{2t} + X_{2t}^*), \tag{6}$$

and $\tau_0 \in (0, \tau_u)$ given.

In the above problem, given the sequences of the world outputs

$$\{X_{1t} + X_{1t}^*, X_{2t} + X_{2t}^*\}_{t=0}^{\infty},$$

the allocation of the consumption goods between the two countries is a static problem and is governed by the first-order condition

$$\psi U_i(C_{1t}, C_{2t}) = (1-\psi) \frac{\alpha}{1-\alpha} U_i(C_{1t}^*, C_{2t}^*), \tag{7}$$

where $U_i(\cdot,\cdot)$ denotes the partial derivative of $U(\cdot,\cdot)$ with respect to its ith argument $(i = 1,2)$.

Define $\omega = (1-\psi)\alpha/[\psi(1-\alpha)]$. Note that $\omega = 1$ if $\psi = \alpha$. The assumption of homogeneity on $U(\cdot)$ and Eqs. (3), (4), and (7) imply that for $i = 1, 2$,

$$C_{it} = \frac{X_{it} + X_{it}^*}{\alpha + (1-\alpha)\omega^{1/(1-\gamma)}}, \tag{8}$$

$$C_{it}^* = \frac{\omega^{1/(1-\gamma)}(X_{it} + X_{it}^*)}{\alpha + (1-\alpha)\omega^{1/(1-\gamma)}}. \tag{9}$$

Since $g(\cdot)$ is monotonically increasing in its argument, we can define its inverse function $G(\cdot) \equiv g^{-1}(\cdot)$. Equation (6) can then be written as

$$X_{2t} + X_{2t}^* = G(\tau_{t+1} - (1-c)\tau_t). \tag{10}$$

The assumptions on $g(\cdot)$ imply that $G(0) = 0, G'(\cdot) > 0$, and $G''(\cdot) \geq 0$.

Using (3)–(5) and (8)–(10) and the homogeneity property of $U(\cdot)$, we can rewrite (2) as

$$W(\tau_0; \psi) = \max_{\{\tau_{t-1}\}_{t=0}^{\infty}} \left[\psi\left(\frac{1}{\alpha + (1-\alpha)\omega^{1/(1-\gamma)}}\right)^{\gamma} + (1-\psi)\left(\frac{\omega^{1/(1-\gamma)}}{\alpha + (1-\alpha)\omega^{1/(1-\gamma)}}\right)^{\gamma}\right] \sum_{t=0}^{\infty} \beta^t \times U\left[a(\tau_t)\left(1 - \frac{1}{b} G(\tau_{t+1} - (1-c)\tau_t)\right), G(\tau_{t+1} - (1-c)\tau_t)\right]. \tag{11}$$

Note that if $\psi = \alpha$, $W(\tau_0; \psi)$ is independent of ψ and α. Hence we can define $W(\tau_0) \equiv W(\tau_0; \alpha)$. Note that the solution to (11) is the same as the solution to

$$W(\tau_0) = \max_{\{\tau_{t+1}\}_{t=0}^{\infty}} \sum_{t=0}^{\infty} \beta^t \times U\left[a(\tau_t)\left(1 - \frac{1}{b} G(\tau_{t+1} - (1-c)\tau_t)\right), G(\tau_{t+1} - (1-c)\tau_t)\right]. \tag{12}$$

In other words, the sequence of optimal temperatures $\{\tau_t\}_{t=1}^{\infty}$ is independent of ψ. Since the sequences of optimal outputs $\{X_{1t} + X_{1t}^*, X_{2t} + X_{2t}^*\}_{t=0}^{\infty}$ depend only on the sequence of optimal temperatures [see Eq. (10)], they are independent of ψ as well. Hence the sequence of optimal temperatures can be solved from (12). Define

$$V(\tau_t, \tau_{t+1}) \equiv U\left[a(\tau_t)\left(1 - \frac{1}{b}(\tau_{t+1} - (1-c)\tau_t)\right), G(\tau_{t+1} - (1-c)\tau_t)\right] \tag{13}$$

as the value function describing H's per capita welfare in period t. The first-order condition to solve (12) is[3]

$$-\frac{\partial V(\tau_t, \tau_{t+1})}{\partial \tau_{t+1}} = \beta \frac{\partial V(\tau_{t+1}, \tau_{t+2})}{\partial \tau_{t+1}}. \tag{14}$$

[3] Chen [5] contains a rigorous treatment of the dynamic programming problem.

Equation (14) can be used to derive the value of $W(\tau_0)$. Note that given $\tau_0, W(\tau_o)$ is a constant. Therefore, we can derive the world welfare possibility frontier taking $W(\tau_0)$ as given.

Define $\pi \equiv \sum_{t=0}^{\infty} \beta^t U(C_{1t}, C_{2t})$ and $\pi^* \equiv \sum_{t=0}^{\infty} \beta^t U(C_{1t}^*, C_{2t}^*)$. It is clear that π and π^* are discounted sums of the per capita utility for H and F. Using (8) and (9) and homogeneity of $U(\cdot)$, we obtain

$$\pi = \left(\frac{1}{\alpha + (1-\alpha)\omega^{1/(1-\gamma)}} \right)^{\gamma} W(\tau_0), \tag{15}$$

$$\pi^* = \left(\frac{\omega^{1/(1-\gamma)}}{\alpha + (1-\alpha)\omega^{1/(1-\gamma)}} \right)^{\gamma} W(\tau_0), \tag{16}$$

It is easy to verify that as ω increases, π decreases but π^* increases. Denote the world welfare possibility frontier by $\pi^* = v(\pi)$. We can obtain $v(\pi)$ by eliminating ω from (15) and (16):

$$\pi^* = v(\pi) = \frac{\left([W(\tau_0)]^{1/\gamma} - \alpha \pi^{1/\gamma} \right)^{\gamma}}{(1-\alpha)^{\gamma}}. \tag{17}$$

It is clear that π^* is decreasing in π. If $\gamma = 1$, (17) is a linear function:

$$\alpha\pi + (1-\alpha)\pi^* = W(\tau_0). \tag{18}$$

Note that for each $\psi \in (0,1)$, there is a unique ω and hence a unique pair (π, π^*) that satisfies (15) and (16). Thus, there is a one-to-one relationship between a value of ψ and a feasible utility pair (π, π^*) that satisfies (17).

4. NEGOTIATION

This section and next are devoted to the analysis of a bargaining game between the two countries. In these two sections the assumption of competitive economies is abandoned temporarily and is replaced with the assumption that there is a central planner in each country. The two central planners can negotiate a binding agreement on future production and consumption plans. The outcome of this bargaining game is derived in this section, while the properties of the outcome are analyzed in Section 5.

Consider a world where competitive equilibrium has been prevailing in the past. To simplify analysis, assume that the world has reached a steady state in the competitive equilibrium.[4] Let τ_c denote the steady-state temperature. Then $\tau_0 = \tau_c$ by assumption. Now suppose that in each country there is a central planner who

[4] The assumption that the status quo is a competitive steady state is somewhat arbitrary. In reality, this will not necessarily be the case. It is quite possible that the global temperature will not be in a steady state when international negotiation on global warming begins (see Chen [6]). Alternatively, it is also likely that countries will have adopted measures to control global warming non-cooperatively before they sit down to negotiate a cooperative plan. The assumption serves to make the analysis on the bargaining game tractable.

has the authority to choose consumption and production plans for the citizens in her country. The objective function of the central planner is to maximize the per capita utility of her citizens over an infinite time horizon. The central planner is identified by the country she represents, i.e., H or F.

We assume that the central planners have perfect information about the economic and natural environment. Recognizing the inefficiencies caused by the global externalities of manufacturing activities, the two planners want to negotiate an agreement on future production and consumption plans for the two countries in an effort to correct the problem. The negotiation procedure is similar to that of the Rubinstein bargaining game (Rubinstein [14]). At the beginning of period 0, H proposes a sequence of consumption and production plans over an infinite time horizon for both countries, to which F immediately replies "yes" or "no." If F says "yes," an agreement is reached and the two planners will implement the agreement from period 0 on. If F replies "no," the planners will continue to allow the competitive equilibrium to prevail in period 0 and wait until period 1 when the second round of negotiation begins. At the beginning of period 1, the same process is repeated except that now F makes a proposal to which H immediately replies, and so on.

We focus on the subgame perfect equilibrium of this game. Define $\pi_s \equiv \sum_{t=s}^{\infty} \beta^t U(C_{1t}, C_{2t})$ and $\pi_s^* \equiv \sum_{t=s}^{\infty} \beta^t U(C_{1t}^*, C_{2t}^*)$ as the payoffs received by the two countries in a subgame starting from period s ($s = 0, 1, 2, \dots$). In any subgame starting from an even period s (i.e., $s = 0, 2, 4, \dots$), the problem faced by H is

$$\max \pi_s \tag{19}$$

subject to (3)–(6) and

$$\pi_s^* \geq \bar{\pi}^*, \tag{20}$$

where $\bar{\pi}^*$ is the minimum payoff that H believes F must obtain in a subgame perfect equilibrium.[5] The problem faced by F in any subgame starting from an odd period ($s = 1, 3, \dots$) is symmetric to the problem (19)–(20) faced by H.

PROPOSITION 1. *A subgame perfect equilibrium in this game is pareto efficient.*

Proof. It can be verified that the problem (19)–(20) generates the same set of first-order conditions as the world planner's problem (2) with appropriately chosen π. Thus the proposal made by H or F in any subgame is Pareto efficient. Q.E.D.

Therefore, a subgame perfect equilibrium must be a point on the world welfare possibility frontier (17). In other words, a subgame perfect equilibrium will generate the sequences of optimal world outputs, denoted by $\{\hat{X}_{1t} + \hat{X}_{1t}^*, \hat{X}_{2t} + \hat{X}_{2t}^*\}_{t=0}^{\infty}$.

Let $\hat{\pi}$ and $\hat{\pi}^*$ be the subgame perfect equilibrium payoff to H and F, respectively. Suppose the sequences $\{\hat{C}_{1t}, \hat{C}_{2t}, \hat{C}_{1t}^*, \hat{C}_{2t}^*\}_{t=0}^{\infty}$ yield a payoff $\hat{\pi}$ to H and $\hat{\pi}^*$ to F. Equations (8) and (9) and Proposition 1 imply that $\hat{C}_{it}, \hat{C}_{it}^*$ ($i = 1, 2$) are proportional to the world output of good i. Define λ as the share of country H's

[5] Here $\bar{\pi}^*$ is treated as a parameter in this maximization problem. As shown below, in equilibrium $\bar{\pi}^* = \hat{\pi}^*$ whose value is determined by Eqs. (26) and (17). (See the discussion at the end of this section.)

consumption of good i in the world total output of good i, i.e.,

$$\alpha \hat{C}_{it} = \lambda\left(\hat{X}_{it} + \hat{X}^*_{it}\right). \tag{21}$$

Then,

$$(1-\alpha)\hat{C}^*_{it} = (1-\lambda)\left(\hat{X}_{it} + \hat{X}^*_{it}\right). \tag{22}$$

Using (21) and (22) and the homogeneity assumption of utility function, we obtain

$$\frac{\hat{\pi}}{\hat{\pi}^*} \equiv \frac{\Sigma\, \beta^t U\left(\hat{C}_{1t}, \hat{C}_{2t}\right)}{\Sigma\, \beta^t U\left(\hat{C}^*_{1t}, \hat{C}^*_{2t}\right)} = \frac{(1-\alpha)^\gamma \lambda^\gamma}{\alpha^\gamma (1-\lambda)^\gamma}, \tag{23}$$

which implies that

$$\lambda = \frac{\alpha \hat{\pi}^{1/\gamma}}{\alpha \hat{\pi}^{1/\gamma} + (1-\alpha)(\hat{\pi}^*)^{1/\gamma}}. \tag{24}$$

Therefore, if we are given a pair of equilibrium payoffs $(\hat{\pi}, \hat{\pi}^*)$, we can uncover the sequences of consumptions that are implied by these payoffs. Hence we can characterize the outcome of the game by the equilibrium payoffs $(\hat{\pi}, \hat{\pi}^*)$.

It is convenient for later analysis to note that the equilibrium can also be expressed in terms of ψ, the welfare weight in the world planner's problem. Equations (15) and (16) imply that there is a one-to-one relationship between the value of ψ and a feasible utility pair (π, π^*). Thus, there is a unique $\hat{\psi}$ that corresponds to the equilibrium payoff pair $(\hat{\pi}, \hat{\pi}^*)$. The bargaining game can be viewed as a process of determining the welfare weight ψ of the world planner's problem.

The subgame perfect equilibrium in this game can be derived by using arguments similar to those in Sutton [15]. Let $\bar{u}$ (> 0) be the per period utility a consumer will obtain at the competitive steady state. The value of $\bar{u}$ is the same for both countries since the two countries have the same per capita consumption level in the competitive equilibrium. If the world stayed in the competitive equilibrium forever, the payoff received by each country would be $\Sigma_{t=0}^{\infty} \beta^t \bar{u} = \bar{u}/(1-\beta)$. From the definition of $W(\tau_c)$ we know that $W(\tau_c) > \bar{u}/(1-\beta)$. To simplify notation, we define $W \equiv W(\tau_c)$.

Let π_m be the maximum payoff H will obtain in any subgame perfect equilibrium. Therefore, π_m is also the maximum payoff H will obtain in the subgame perfect equilibrium that starts from period 2. It is obvious that π_m must be greater than the payoff received from staying in competitive equilibrium. In other words, $\pi_m > \bar{u}/(1-\beta)$.

Now consider period 1. If H rejects a proposal made by F, she obtains $\bar{u}$ in period 1, plus $\beta\pi_m$ at maximum in the future. Hence, any proposal that gives H a payoff higher than $\bar{u} + \beta\pi_m$ will certainly be accepted, which implies that the minimum payoff F will obtain in period 1 is $v(\bar{u} + \beta\pi_m)$.

In period 0, F will reject any proposal that offers her a payoff smaller than $\bar{u} + \beta v(\bar{u} + \beta\pi_m)$, which means that the maximum payoff H will obtain is $v^{-1}[\bar{u} + \beta v(\bar{u} + \beta\pi_m)]$. By the definition of π_m, we have $\pi_m = v^{-1}[\bar{u} + \beta v(\bar{u} + \beta\pi_m)]$, or

$$v(\pi_m) = \bar{u} + \beta v(\bar{u} + \beta\pi_m). \tag{25}$$

It can be shown that (25) holds when π_m is defined instead as the minimum payoff H receives in a subgame perfect equilibrium. Therefore, (25) characterizes the subgame perfect equilibrium in this game.[6]

PROPOSITION 2. *The unique subgame perfect equilibrium in this game is characterized by*

$$(W^{1/\gamma} - \alpha\hat{\pi}^{1/\gamma})^{\gamma} - \beta\left[W^{1/\gamma} - \alpha(\bar{u} + \beta\hat{\pi})^{1/\gamma}\right]^{\gamma} = (1-\alpha)^{\gamma}\bar{u} \tag{26}$$

and $\hat{\pi} > \bar{u}/(1-\beta)$.

Proof. Equation (26) is obtained by rewriting (25) using (17). Define the left-hand side of (26) as $h(\pi)$. For $\pi \geq \bar{u}/(1-\beta)$,

$$h'(\pi) = -\frac{\alpha\pi^{(1-\gamma)/\gamma}}{(W^{1/\gamma} - \alpha\pi^{1/\gamma})^{1-\gamma}} + \frac{\alpha\beta^2(\bar{u} + \beta\pi)^{(1-\gamma)/\gamma}}{\left[W^{1/\gamma} - \alpha(\bar{u} + \beta\pi)^{1/\gamma}\right]^{1-\gamma}} < 0. \tag{27}$$

Since

$$\begin{aligned} h\left(\frac{\bar{u}}{1-\beta}\right) &= (1-\beta)\left(W^{1/\gamma} - \alpha\left(\frac{\bar{u}}{1-\beta}\right)^{1/\gamma}\right)^{\gamma} \\ &> (1-\beta)\left[\left(\frac{\bar{u}}{1-\beta}\right)^{1/\gamma} - \alpha\left(\frac{\bar{u}}{1-\beta}\right)^{1/\gamma}\right]^{\gamma} = (1-\alpha)^{\gamma}\bar{u} \end{aligned} \tag{28}$$

and

$$h\left(\frac{W}{\alpha^{\gamma}}\right) = -\beta W\left[1 - \left(\frac{\alpha^{\gamma}\bar{u}}{W} + \beta\right)^{1/\gamma}\right]^{\gamma} < 0 < (1-\alpha)^{\gamma}\bar{u}, \tag{29}$$

there exists a unique $\hat{\pi} \in [\bar{u}/(1-\beta), \infty)$ that satisfies (26).[7] Q.E.D.

Therefore, the unique subgame perfect equilibrium of this game is such that in period 0, H proposes a sequence of consumption and production plans that yields a payoff $\hat{\pi}$ as defined by (26) and F says "yes." The equilibrium payoff to F, $\hat{\pi}^*$, is obtained by substituting $\hat{\pi}$ into (17).

5. COMPARATIVE STATICS

In this section we investigate how the equilibrium of the bargaining game is affected by various parameters of this model. To simplify presentation, we focus

[6] It may be of interest to readers familiar with the Nash bargaining game that the subgame perfect equilibrium in the Rubinstein bargaining game converges to the Nash bargaining solution as the length of a period converges to 0 (see [13, Proposition 4.5].

[7] We are unable to rule out the possibility that (26) has a solution for π in the interval $(0, \bar{u}/(1-\beta))$ in the case where $\gamma < 1$. Such a solution, if it exists, is obviously not a subgame perfect equilibrium.

our analysis on the special case where the function $U(C_{1t}, C_{2t})$ is homogenous of degree 1 ($\gamma = 1$). The extension of these results to the general case $\gamma \in (0, 1]$ is presented in Chen [5].

When $\gamma = 1$, the subgame perfect equilibrium can be solved explicitly from (26), together with (18):

$$\hat{\pi} = \frac{W}{\alpha(1+\beta)} + \frac{\alpha(1+\beta)-1}{\alpha(1-\beta^2)}\bar{u}, \tag{30}$$

$$\hat{\pi}^* = \frac{\beta W}{(1-\alpha)(1+\beta)} - \frac{\alpha(1+\beta)-1}{(1-\alpha)(1-\beta^2)}\bar{u}. \tag{31}$$

It is obvious from the above equations that the equilibrium per capita welfare of a country depends on its relative population size. In fact,

$$\frac{d\hat{\pi}}{d\alpha} = -\frac{1}{\alpha^2(1+\beta)}\left(W - \frac{\bar{u}}{1-\beta}\right) < 0, \tag{32}$$

$$\frac{d\hat{\pi}^*}{d\alpha} = \frac{\beta}{(1-\alpha)^2(1+\beta)}\left(W - \frac{\bar{u}}{1-\beta}\right) > 0. \tag{33}$$

In other words, the per capita welfare of a country is decreasing in its relative population size.

Note that $\alpha\hat{\pi}$ and $(1-\alpha)\hat{\pi}^*$ measure the aggregate welfare of country H and country F. Since

$$\frac{d(\alpha\hat{\pi})}{d\alpha} = \frac{\bar{u}}{1-\beta} > 0, \tag{34}$$

$$\frac{d((1-\alpha)\hat{\pi}^*)}{d\alpha} = -\frac{\bar{u}}{1-\beta} < 0, \tag{35}$$

the aggregate welfare of a country is increasing in its relative population size.

The above results are illustrated in Figs. 1–3.[8] When drawing the diagrams, we multiply all payoff terms by $(1-\beta)$ to convert them into average per period payoffs. Hence, $(1-\beta)\pi$ and $(1-\beta)\pi^*$ are average per period per capita welfare, while $(1-\beta)\alpha\pi$ and $(1-\beta)(1-\alpha)\pi^*$ are average per period aggregate welfare of H and F. In Fig. 1 *PP* is the welfare possibility frontier. Point *D* is the status quo or the disagreement point. Point *R* is the bargaining solution. The slope of *DR* is $\alpha\beta/(1-\alpha)$. In Fig. 1 *DR* is below the 45° line, which corresponds to the case $\alpha < 1/(1+\beta)$. If $\alpha > 1/(1+\beta)$, *DR* will be above the 45° line. Figure 2 demonstrates the comparative statics of an increase in the value of α. As the value of α is increased, the bargaining frontier rotates from *PP* to *P'P'*. The slope of *DR* becomes steeper as well. As a result, $(1-\beta)\hat{\pi}$ decreases while $(1-\beta)\hat{\pi}^*$ increases. Figure 3 illustrates the same comparative statics in the space of ((1 –

[8] I benefitted from the comments and suggestions by Ignatius Horstmann on the construction of Figs. 1–4.

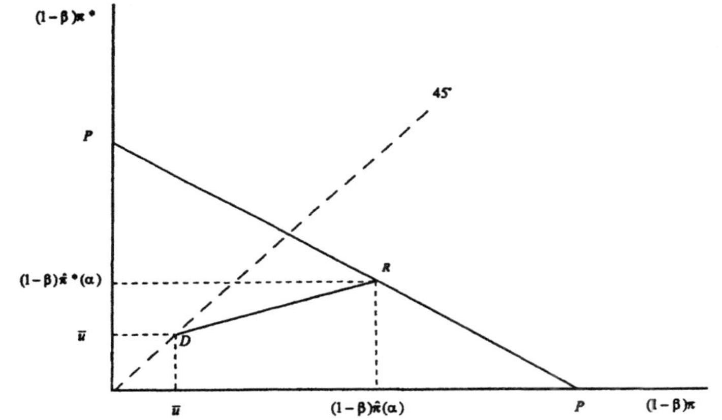

FIG. 1. Negotiation outcome for the case $\alpha < 1/(1+\beta)$.

$\beta)\alpha\pi, (1-\beta)(1-\alpha)\pi^*)$, the space of per period aggregate welfare of the two countries. As α changes, the welfare possibility frontier does not shift but the disagreement point moves from D to D'. We can see from the diagram that $(1-\beta)\alpha\hat{\pi}$ increases while $(1-\beta)(1-\alpha)\hat{\pi}^*$ decreases in response to an increase in α.

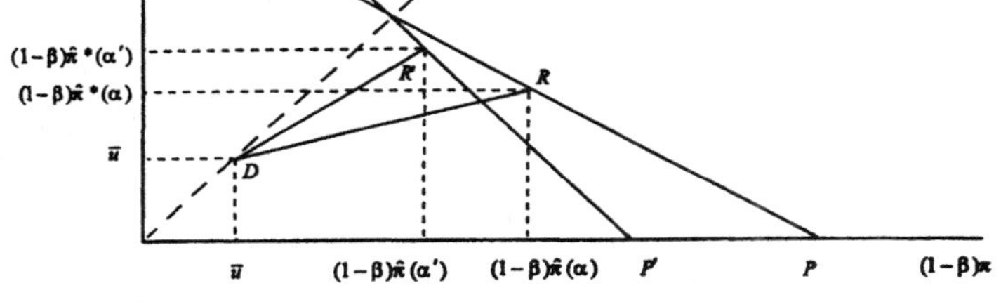

FIG. 2. Per capita welfare and the value of α ($\alpha < \alpha'$).

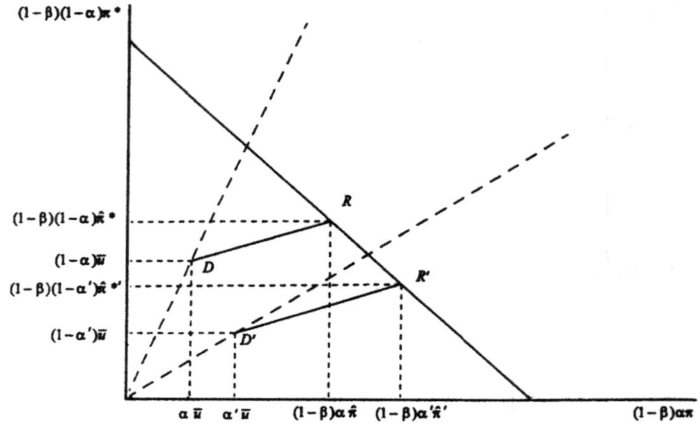

FIG. 3. Aggregate welfare and the value of α ($\alpha < \alpha'$).

Therefore, other things being equal, a country with a small population gains more from the international agreement than a country with a large population.[9] Intuitively, this is because in the negotiation process, what is considered to be a small concession by a large country could mean a substantial gain to a small country. Suppose, for example, country F in terms of population is 10 times as large as country H. Then a donation of $1 per capita by the citizens of country F to country H will translate into $10 for every citizen of country H. On the other hand, a donation of $1 from every citizen of H will mean a mere 10 cents per capita for country F. Hence it is easier for a large country to "bribe" a small country into an agreement than for a small country to "bribe" a large country. As a result, the small country can credibly take a less compromising stand in the negotiation process than the large country.

In the standard Rubinstein bargaining game with identical time discount factors, the player who moves first obtains a higher pay-off than the other player (the first mover's advantage). In this model, the first mover's advantage still exists in the sense that if the two countries have the same size population (i.e., $\alpha = 1/2$), country H, the first mover in the negotiation game, obtains a higher per capita welfare than F (i.e., $\hat{\pi} > \hat{\pi}^*$).[10] One can verify this by setting $\alpha = 1/2$ in (30) and

[9] Note that this result is different from the result in Olson and Zeckhauser [12] that a large country bears a disproportionately larger share of the total cost of providing an alliance good (public good) than a small country. In Olson and Zeckhauser, a large country is defined as a country that "places the higher absolute value on the alliance good" [12, p. 169], whereas in this model the size of a country is measured by the size of its population. Furthermore, Olson and Zeckhauser's result is derived from a model in which two countries take actions non-cooperatively, which is completely different from this model in which two countries attempt to reach a cooperative agreement on actions to be taken.

[10] Given the existence of the first mover's advantage, it is natural to ask what makes country H the first mover. We can consider the order of making moves in the negotiation process as the outcome of some political processes in the two countries. For example, we can suppose that country H is the initiator and hence the first mover of the negotiation process because voters in country H are more environment conscious and apply more political pressure on their government than voters in country F.

(31) and using the fact $W > \bar{u}/(1-\beta)$ to show that $\hat{\pi} > W$ and $\hat{\pi}^* < W$. However, if H has a larger population than F ($\alpha > 1/2$), the first mover's advantage of H may be offset by the effects of its larger population. Indeed, from (30) and (31) one can verify that $\hat{\pi} > W > \hat{\pi}^*$ if $\alpha < 1/(1+\beta)$ (see Fig. 1); $\hat{\pi} < W < \hat{\pi}^*$ if $\alpha > 1/(1+\beta)$; and $\hat{\pi} = \hat{\pi}^* = W$ if $\alpha = 1/(1+\beta)$.

Note that the critical value of $\alpha, 1/(1+\beta)$, depends on the value of β. The smaller the value of β, the larger the relative size of population needed to offset the first mover's advantage. In other words, the more the countries discount their future welfare, the larger is the first mover's advantage.

Intuitively, the discounting of future welfare is the source of the first mover's advantage. Both countries gain from international cooperation on combatting global warming. But this gain is not realized until the two countries reach an agreement. Because of discounting, a delay in reaching the agreement will lead to, in present value terms, a smaller gain from the agreement. Consequently, delay is costly to both countries. This cost of delay gives country H, the first mover, an advantage because in period 0, F is willing to sacrifice some of her payoff for an immediate agreement as long as the sacrifice in payoff is smaller than the cost of a one-period delay. The more the countries discount the future (smaller β), the larger is the cost of delay and the larger is the first mover's advantage.

Equations (30) and (31) show that the equilibrium per capita welfare of a country depends also on the value of $\bar{u}$. While $\bar{u}$ is calculated endogenously from the competitive equilibrium of the model, it is exogenous to the bargaining game. Therefore, we can perform comparative statics on (30) and (31) to find out how $\bar{u}$ affects the bargaining outcome.

$$\frac{d\hat{\pi}}{d\bar{u}} = \frac{\alpha(1+\beta)-1}{\alpha(1-\beta^2)} \begin{cases} > 0, & \text{if}\,\alpha > 1/(1+\beta); \\ = 0, & \text{if}\,\alpha = 1/(1+\beta); \\ < 0, & \text{if}\,\alpha < 1/(1+\beta). \end{cases} \tag{36}$$

That is, country H's payoff is increasing in $\bar{u}$ if $\alpha > 1/(1+\beta)$ and is decreasing in $\bar{u}$ if $\alpha < 1/(1+\beta)$. The reverse is true for country F.

Figure 4 demonstrates the comparative statics with respect to $\bar{u}$. As the value of $\bar{u}$ is increased, the disagreement point moves from D to D'. As a consequence the bargaining solution moves from R to R'. Figure 4 is drawn under the condition $\alpha < 1/(1+\beta)$, in which case an increase in $\bar{u}$ reduces $(1-\beta)\hat{\pi}$ but raises $(1-\beta)\hat{\pi}^*$. If $\alpha > 1/(1+\beta)$, the lines DR and $D'R'$ will be above the 45° line, in which case the reverse will be true.

Recall that $\hat{\pi} < \hat{\pi}^*$ when $\alpha > 1/(1+\beta)$ and $\hat{\pi} > \hat{\pi}^*$ when $\alpha < 1/(1+\beta)$. Equation (36) then implies that an increase in $\bar{u}$ benefits the country whose payoff from the agreement is smaller. Intuitively, the gain from the agreement for both countries decreases as $\bar{u}$ increases, in which case countries have less to lose if an agreement is delayed. But relatively speaking, the country that stands to gain less from the agreement also has less to lose from a delay than the other country does. Consequently, an increase in $\bar{u}$ strengthens its bargaining position.

6. DECENTRALIZATION

In Section 4 the negotiation outcome is derived under the assumption that the two planners have the authority to choose consumption and production plans for

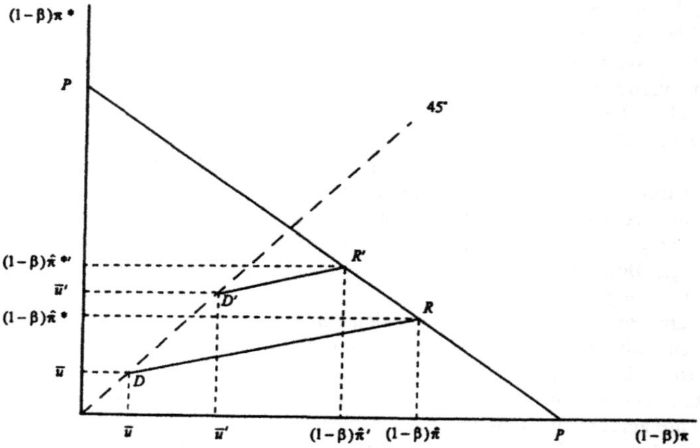

FIG. 4. Per capita welfare and the value of $\bar{u}$ ($\bar{u} < \bar{u}'$).

their countries. The purpose of this section is to demonstrate that the agreement negotiated by the two planners can be implemented in decentralized economies.

The agreement specifies sequences of consumption and production plans

$$\left\{\hat{C}_{1t}, \hat{C}_{2t}, \hat{C}^*_{1t}, \hat{C}^*_{2t}, \hat{L}_{1t}, \hat{L}_{2t}, \hat{X}_{1t} + \hat{X}^*_{1t}, \hat{X}_{2t} + \hat{X}^*_{2t}\right\}_{t=0}^{\infty}.$$

Since the two countries have identical production technologies and identical climate, the location of production can be determined arbitrarily as long as the resource constraints are satisfied. The implementation of the agreement in competitive economies is to devise a system of tax and international transfers so that the competitive equilibrium generates the same sequences of output and consumption for the two countries as required by the agreement.

Consider a tax/transfer system where there is a worldwide pollution tax on the unit cost of the manufacturing production and a country-specific lump-sum tax (transfer) on (to) consumers. The total revenue from the pollution tax is distributed equally among the world residents in a lump-sum fashion. The lump-sum transfer to the consumers of one country is financed by the lump-sum tax on the consumers in the other country.

To be more specific, let η_t be the period t world pollution tax rate. Set

$$\eta_t = \frac{b\beta(1-c)G'(t+1)}{a(\tau_t)G'(t)}\,\frac{U_1(t+1)}{U_1(t)}\left[\frac{U_2(t+1)}{U_1(t+1)} - \frac{a(\tau_{t+1})}{b}\right] - \frac{\beta U_1(t+1)}{U_1(t)}\,a'(\tau_{t+1})\left(1-\hat{L}_{2t+1}\right)\frac{b}{a(\tau_t)G'(t)}, \tag{37}$$

in which the arguments of $U_i(s)$ $(i = 1, 2)$ are $\hat{X}_{1s} + \hat{X}^*_{1s}$ and $\hat{X}_{2s} + \hat{X}^*_{2s}$ and $G'(s) \equiv G'(\tau_{s+1} - (1 - c)\tau_s)$ with $s = t, t + 1$. Let ω_t denote the wage rate in period t. Zero profits condition in competitive equilibrium implies that the total revenue of the manufacturing industry in period t is equal to total cost $(1 + \eta_t)\omega_t(l_{2t} + l^*_{2t}) = (1 + \eta_t)\omega_t L_{2t}$. Hence the worldwide pollution tax revenue is $\eta_t \omega_t L_{2t}$. Since the tax revenue is distributed equally among the world residents, the share of tax rebate received by country H is $\alpha\eta_t \omega_t L_{2t}$.

Let ρ_t and ρ^*_t denote the per capita lump-sum tax (transfer) in country H and country F, respectively:

$$\rho_t = \left(\hat{X}_{1t} + \hat{X}^*_{1t} - \hat{C}_{1t}\right) + \frac{U_2\left(\hat{C}_{1t}, \hat{C}_{2t}\right)}{U_1\left(\hat{C}_{1t}, \hat{C}_{2t}\right)}\left(\hat{X}_{2t} + \hat{X}^*_{2t} - \hat{C}_{2t}\right), \quad (38)$$

$$\rho^*_t = \left(\hat{X}_{1t} + \hat{X}^*_{1t} - \hat{C}^*_{1t}\right) + \frac{U_2\left(\hat{C}^*_{1t}, \hat{C}^*_{2t}\right)}{U_1\left(\hat{C}^*_{1t}, \hat{C}^*_{2t}\right)}\left(\hat{X}_{2t} + \hat{X}^*_{2t} - \hat{C}^*_{2t}\right). \quad (39)$$

The sequences of η_t, ρ_t, and ρ^*_t can be calculated using the consumption and production sequences specified by the agreement. The value of η_t is the same in both countries so that the pollution tax will not cause price disparities across countries. It is easy to verify that

$$\alpha\rho_t + (1 - \alpha)\rho^*_t = 0. \quad (40)$$

PROPOSITION 3. *The agreement by the two central planners can be implemented in competitive economies by the tax/transfer system specified above.*

This proposition can be proved by showing that given the tax/transfer system, the competitive equilibrium yields the same sequences of output and consumption as specified by the agreement. Chen [5] contains the details of the proof.

Proposition 3 implies that, instead of negotiating consumption and production plans for the two countries, the two governments can negotiate a tax/transfer system that generates exactly the same outcome.

In the tax/transfer system discussed above, the pollution tax revenue from the two countries is pooled and is distributed equally among the world residents. In this process, some transfers of the tax revenue from one country to the other may occur. To see this consider country H's government budget of the pollution tax. The pollution tax revenue is equal to $\eta_t \omega_t l_{2t}$ while the rebate to its citizens is equal to $\alpha\eta_t \omega_t L_{2t}$. Therefore, if country H's share of the output of the manufactured good is larger than its share in the world population, i.e., $l_{2t}/L_{2t} > \alpha$, part of the pollution tax revenue will be transferred to country F to finance the payment to residents in F.

In addition to the distribution of pollution tax revenue, there are also transfers from the consumers in one country to the consumers in the other country, as captured by ρ_t and ρ^*_t. The direction of transfers is determined by the negotiation.

PROPOSITION 4. $\rho_t > 0 > \rho^*_t$ *if* $\hat{\pi} < W < \hat{\pi}^*$, *and* $\rho_t < 0 < \rho^*_t$ *if* $\hat{\pi} > W > \hat{\pi}^*$.

Proof. Equations (8) and (9) and the definitions of π, π^*, and W imply

$$\hat{C}_{it} < \hat{X}_{it} + \hat{X}^*_{it} < \hat{C}^*_{it}, \qquad (i = 1, 2) \quad (41)$$

if $\hat{\pi} < W < \hat{\pi}^*$; and the reverse is true if $\hat{\pi} > W > \hat{\pi}^*$. The result follows from (38) and (39). Q.E.D.

Therefore, in equilibrium, we will observe two kinds of international transfers. First, the rebates of pollution tax revenue are the transfers that are made because of disproportional distribution of the manufacturing productions. We will observe that the country that produces more than its share of manufacturing output and hence emits more than its share of pollution transfers part of its pollution tax revenue to finance the compensation in the other country. Second, ρ_t and ρ_t^* represent the transfers that are made due to the asymmetry in bargaining power. The gain from international cooperation is not shared equally between the two countries as a result of asymmetry in the bargaining procedure and in relative population sizes. Depending on the direction and the relative magnitudes of these two kinds of transfers, the net transfer may move in either direction.

In the literature, the issue of side payments between countries is frequently discussed in terms of either the polluter pays principle (PPP) or the victim pays principle (VPP). The above results suggest that while side payments from one country to another will indeed be observed as part of an international agreement, the reason behind these payments may have nothing to do with the PPP or VPP. The asymmetry in bargaining power, rather than any pre-conceived principle, may be the main force in determining the identity of the contributors and the receivers of these side payments.

Underlying the PPP and VPP are two completely different ethics for the settlement of transboundary pollution problems. To declare that side payments should be made according to, say, the PPP is in effect to impose an ethic on the settlement. The analysis here shows that the actual outcome of a negotiation process may defy any declared ethic. In some sense, a negotiation process will generate an ethic of its own. Therefore, if we believe that the PPP should govern any international agreement on global warming, a mere declaration of the principle by the United Nations will not be enough. Care has to be taken in the design of negotiation process to ensure that the actual agreement that emerges from the process will indeed be consistent with the declared ethic.

7. ENFORCEMENT

An important assumption maintained throughout the analysis in the previous sections is that the agreement negotiated by the two countries is binding on both governments. This assumption would be justified if there were a third party, say a supranational court, that had the power to enforce the agreement. In reality, however, there is no such supranational court. It is doubtful that on the issue of global warming, governments will ever agree to subject themselves to binding rulings from a supranational court. Indeed, a major difficulty in international cooperation is how to enforce an agreement when the signatories are sovereign nations.

In this model, it is clear that countries have incentives to cheat on the agreement. It is a standard free-rider problem. Both countries benefit when a country takes measures to combat global warming. But combatting global warming is costly. As a consequence, after signing an agreement to fight global warming, a country has incentives to cheat and to free-ride on the efforts of the other country.

To solve this free-rider problem, a country that cheats on the agreement must be punished. In the absence of a supranational court empowered to enforce the agreement, the agreement itself has to include a "punishment clause" whose purpose is to deter cheating. Therefore, when the two countries negotiate an agreement on global warming in period 0, they also have to decide on a mechanism that would ensure that countries comply with this agreement.

With the help of non-cooperative game theory, we can devise a variety of punishment strategies that can be used to ensure compliance with the agreement. Here we describe one of these punishment strategies. Roughly speaking, it works as follows.[11] The international agreement on global warming specifies a cooperative plan of production and consumption (or, equivalently, a tax/transfer system). Each country will implement the cooperative plan as long as no country has cheated on the agreement. However, if a cheat occurs in period t, then starting from period $t + 1$, both countries suspend the implementation of the cooperative plan for T periods, during which the state of laissez faire prevails. After both countries implement this T-period punishment strategy, they will go back to the implementation of a cooperative plan in period $t + T + 1$. If either country does not follow the punishment strategy in any of the punishment periods (say in period $t + s$ with $1 \leq s \leq T$), then starting from the next period both countries will have to play the punishment strategy for another T periods (i.e., from period $t + s + 1$ to period $t + s + T$), after which they implement a cooperative plan.

The above strategy will ensure that both countries will comply with the agreement provided that countries care enough about the future (i.e., the discount factor β is large enough). Intuitively, when a country cheats, it gains in the short run. But under this punishment mechanism, cheating will trigger a T-period suspension of the cooperative plan. This causes the global temperature to deviate from its optimal path, which causes long-term welfare losses to both countries. As long as countries care enough about the future, the long-term losses from a T-period suspension of the cooperative plan will outweigh the short-term gain. Hence a country does not have any incentives to cheat on the agreement.

To make the punishment mechanism work, the punishment strategy itself must be credible; in other words, the countries should have incentives to implement the punishment strategy should cheating occur. This is accomplished by the stipulation that if a country does not implement the T-period punishment strategy, it will be punished by a further T-period suspension of the cooperative plan. The longer the time of suspension, the larger the losses that the countries have to incur. As a result, once cheating has occurred, it is in the interest of both countries to comply with the T-period punishment strategy so that they can move to the cooperative time path at the earliest possible date.

Note that after one round of cheating and punishment, the cooperative plan to be implemented by the two countries is different from the original cooperative plan if cheating had not occurred. This is because cheating and subsequent punishment cause the global temperature to deviate from its optimal path. Without any government control over the manufacturing activities during the punishment periods, the level of temperature in each period is higher than its optimal level. Consequently, at the end of the punishment periods, the level of temperature is

[11] This punishment strategy is similar to the one used by Fudenberg and Maskin [9] in the proof of their Theorem 1.

higher than it would be if there had been no cheating. The cooperative plan that will be implemented after the punishment periods, therefore, begins with this higher temperature level.

This post-punishment cooperative plan is derived from the world planner's dynamic programming problem presented in Section 3 and the bargaining solution presented in Section 4. Recall from Section 3 that the optimal production plan depends only on the initial temperature level τ_0. Let $\bar{\tau}$ be the temperature level at the end of the punishment periods. The post-punishment production plan then is the solution to the dynamic programming problem with $\tau_0 = \bar{\tau}$. Recall from Section 4 that the outcome of negotiation can be characterized by the welfare weight $\hat{\psi}$ of the planner. The post-punishment consumption plan, therefore, is calculated using this welfare weight $\hat{\psi}$.

Finally, it is worth noting that the enforcement mechanism presented here is a fairly sensible one. In contrast to the well-known trigger strategy with which a deviation is punished for an infinite number of periods, this enforcement mechanism requires that punishment last only a finite number of periods. Furthermore, the punishment clause itself represents a plausible reaction of a country to another country's failure to honor an agreement. Under the tax/transfer system discussed in Section 6. taxes are collected and revenue is distributed among consumers in the two countries. When a country, say H, reneges on its promise by not collecting the taxes or not making the necessary transfers, the tax/transfer system as specified by the agreement can no longer be implemented even if the other country (F) wanted to. Given that H is not honoring the agreement, it is unlikely that F will continue to carry out its obligations under the agreement. In fact, a more likely response of F is to stop implementing the agreement as well. The acrimony and distrust that follow the collapse of the tax/transfer system will likely last for some time before the countries can make any attempt at re-starting the tax/transfer system. Therefore, the punishment clause simply formalizes and legitimizes these reactions as part of the agreement. Indeed, one might expect this kind of reaction even if the agreement did not explicitly contain such a punishment clause.

8. CONCLUDING REMARKS

This paper demonstrates that the disagreement over the allocation of responsibility of combatting global warming can be resolved through negotiation. The governments can negotiate a tax/transfer system that will lead to Pareto efficient production and consumption. The agreement can be enforced by a punishment mechanism under which the threat of suspension of the agreement deters signatories from cheating on the agreement. The terms of the agreement are affected by various factors such as the order of making offers in the negotiation process, the relative size of population, and the welfare level at the status quo. In particular, it is shown that, ceteris paribus, a country with a small population will gain more from the agreement than a country with a large population. It is also shown that while side payments between countries will generally be part of the agreement, some of these payments are made purely as a result of asymmetry in bargaining power and have nothing to do with the polluter pays principle or the victim pays principle. This implies that if the international community accepts that the polluter pays principle should govern any agreement on transboundary pollution, a mere declaration of this principle will not do the job. Care has to be taken in the design of the negotiation process to ensure that the actual outcome of this process will be consistent with the declared principle.

To simplify analysis, we have made many assumptions in this paper. For example, we have assumed that there are only two countries and hence the international negotiation is bilateral. In reality, there are more than 100 countries in the world, and the negotiation on global warming is multilateral. Two other assumptions in this model are that there is no capital accumulation and there is no technological progress. Clearly, capital accumulation and technological progress in the agricultural sector can offset the loss of labor productivity caused by the greenhouse effect. Finally, perhaps the most unrealistic assumption of this paper is that governments have complete information about the climate system and the world economy. In reality, our understanding of the climate system, while improving, is still very limited. There are still debates in the scientific community on whether global warming is indeed happening. Because of these restrictive assumptions, this paper should be viewed as one modest step in the direction of applying bargaining theory to explore theoretical issues related to international cooperation on global warming. More research on this subject is clearly needed.

REFERENCES

1. S. Barrett, The problem of global environmental protection, *Oxford Rev. Econom. Policy* **6**, 68–79 (1990).
2. S. Barrett, International environmental agreement as games, *in* "Conflicts and Cooperation in Managing Environmental Resources" (R. Pethig, Ed.), Springer-Verlag, Berlin (1992).
3. R. Blackhurst and A. Subramanian, Promoting multilateral cooperation on the environment, *in* "The Greening of World Trade Issues" (K. Anderson and R. Blackhurst, Ed.), Harvester Wheatsheaf, New York (1992).
4. B. Bolin, J. Jäger, and B. R. Döös, The greenhouse effect, climatic change, and ecosy tems: A synthesis of present knowledge, *in* "The Greenhouse Effect, Climatic Change and Ecosystems" (B. Bolin, Ed.), Wiley, New York (1986).
5. Z. Chen, "Economic Growth: Dynamic Interactions with International Trade and Global Environment," Ph.D. thesis, University of Western Ontario, London, Canada (1991).
6. Z. Chen, Can economic activities lead to climatic chaos: An economic analysis on global warming, *Can. J. Econom.* (forthcoming).
7. W. R. Cline, Cooperative approaches to global warming: comments, *in* "Global Warming: Economic Policy Responses" (R. Dornbusch and J. M. Poterba, Ed.), MIT Press, Cambridge, MA (1991).
8. R. E. Dickinson, How will climate change? The climate system and modelling of future climate, *in* "The Greenhouse Effect, Climate Change and Ecosystems" (B. Bolin, Ed.), Wiley, New York (1986).
9. D. Fudenberg and E. Maskin, The Folk Theorem in repeated games with discounting or with incomplete information, *Econometrica*, **54**, 533–554 (1986).
10. K. Mäler, International environmental problems, *Oxford Rev. Econom. Policy* **6**. 80–108 (1990).
11. R. Mendelsohn, W. D. Nordhaus, and D. Shaw, The impact of global warming on agriculture: A Ricardian analysis, *Am. Econom. Rev.* **84**, 753–771 (1994).
12. M. Olson and R. Zeckhauser, An economic theory of alliances, *Rev. Econom. Statistics* **48**, 266–279 (1966).
13. M. J. Osborne and A. Rubinstein, "Bargaining and Markets," Academic Press. New York (1990).
14. A. Rubinstein, Perfect equilibrium in a bargaining model, *Econometrica* **50**, 97–109 (1982).
15. J. Sutton, Non-cooperative bargaining theory: An introduction, *Rev. Econom. Stud.* **53**, 709–724 (1986).

[8]

THE EFFECTS OF COLLUSION AND LIMITED LIABILITY ON THE DESIGN OF INTERNATIONAL ENVIRONMENTAL AGREEMENTS FOR DEVELOPING COUNTRIES[1]

by

AMITRAJEET A. BATABYAL
Department of Economics
Utah State University
3530 Old Main Hill
Logan, UT 84322-3530
USA
Phone (435) 797-2314
Fax (435) 797-2701
Internet batabyal@b202.usu.edu

[1] I acknowledge financial support from the Utah Agricultural Experiment Station, Utah State University, Logan, UT 84322-4810, by way of project UTA 024. This paper has benefitted from the comments of seminar participants at the College of William and Mary and at the University of California, Berkeley. The usual disclaimer applies.

The Effects of Collusion and Limited Liability on the Design of International Environmental Agreements for Developing Countries

Abstract

I analyze the problem faced by an imperfectly informed supra-national governmental authority (SNGA) with limited financial resources that wishes to design an International Environmental Agreement (IEA). The SNGA cannot contract directly with polluting firms in the various developing countries (DCs). Instead, it must deal with such firms through their governments. I study this tripartite hierarchical interaction and focus on the properties of the optimal *limited liability* IEA that can be implemented by the SNGA when governments and firms in the individual DCs collude. I show that obtaining voluntary participation and preventing *ex post* breach of contract is costly for the SNGA. Further, because the optimal IEA satisfies budget balance, the level and the pattern of pollution abatement will generally not be ideal. My analysis suggests that IEAs are not inherently doomed due to a basic monitoring and enforcement problem arising from national sovereignty. However, the success of IEAs is fundamentally contingent on the funds available for environmental protection.
JEL Classification: D82, H77, Q25

Keywords: Developing Country, International Environmental Agreement, Limited Liability

1. Introduction

With the passage of time, it has increasingly been recognized that environmental protection is an international issue. As noted by Bernauer (1995, p. 354), the scope and significance of this issue have been amply demonstrated by the events of the 1992 Earth Summit in Rio. At this Summit, it became clear that if the developed countries of the world wanted "the environment to be secured for future generations, [then they would] have to radically assist the South in choosing a different road to development than the one they [had] been [traveling] on." (Rogers, 1993, p. 27). Indeed, to combat the twin evils of poverty and environmental degradation, developing countries (DCs) have demanded the transfer of resources and technology from developed countries. In such a contentious setting, the success or failure to protect the environment will depend crucially on the ability of international institutions to craft effective international environmental agreements (IEAs).[2] Given this, a key question becomes "How can international institutions, which necessarily respect the principle of state sovereignty, contribute to the solution of difficult global problems?" (Keohane *et al.*, 1993, p. 6). This is the central question that I propose to analyze in this paper.

On the academic front, researchers have begun to study issues related to global environmental protection in a systematic manner only very recently.[3] As a result, many specific questions remain unanswered. What kinds of pollution abatement patterns can one expect to observe in economic environments in which an imperfectly informed supra-national governmental authority (SNGA) contracts with governments and polluting firms in individual DCs? What kinds of monetary transfers will be needed to get sovereign nations to voluntarily participate in an IEA? What can the SNGA do to prevent sovereign nations from breaching contracts they had agreed to *ex ante*?[4] How does the SNGA's inability to monitor pollution abatement in the individual countries affect the contract design question? Finally, how does the limited

2 In this paper, I use the terms IEA and contract interchangeably.

3 See Bernauer (1995) and Keohane *et al.* (1993) for a more detailed corroboration of this claim.

4 By *ex ante* I mean contracting that takes place with all the parties holding symmetric but imperfect information about the quality of the pollution abatement technology of firms. By *ex post* I mean contracting that takes place with the players holding asymmetric information about the quality of the pollution abatement technology of the same firms.

availability of funds affect the SNGA's IEA design question? These are the specific questions that I answer in this paper.

Although my analysis is in principle applicable to any country, the hierarchical interaction that I analyze is particularly relevant to DCs; consequently, the reader should note that it is these countries that I have in mind in all the subsequent analysis.[5] I now discuss the nascent literature on IEAs and then move on to discuss my model in detail.

2. International Environmental Agreements: A Brief Synopsis

Barrett (1992, 1994) has modeled IEAs as games between different countries. While Barrett's analyses are not in the design framework, Barrett makes the important point that for IEAs to work, they must be self-enforcing. However, the thrust of this point is weakened by Barrett's focus on identical countries, with no uncertainty. As a result, this line of research is unable to address fundamental questions arising from imperfectly held information and the heterogeneity of the contracting countries.

Hoel (1991, 1992) addresses the implications of, in turn, unilateral emissions reduction by countries, and uniform emissions reduction by all the countries. Hoel (1991, p. 69) shows that unilateral actions "may...reduce global welfare..." by increasing the total emission of pollutants. Hoel (1992) argues against the institution of uniform emissions reduction policies in international agreements, showing that other policies yield higher levels of global welfare.

Shogren, Baik, and Crocker (1992, SBC), Black, Levi, and de Meza (BLD), and Sandler and Sargent (1995, SS) have all addressed the question of the minimal number of countries needed to sustain an IEA. In a multi-player strategic setting, SBC show that countries will sometimes join IEAs because the expected gains from such an action outweigh the gains from not joining. However, beyond a critical threshold value, some countries will prefer to free ride and not join the IEA, whereas the IEA members will want non-participants

[5] The countries I have in mind are those that would be eligible to receive monetary transfers under the Global Environmental Facility's (GEF) standard of per capita income of $4000 or less. For more details, see Rogers (1993, p. 155).

to join. BLD have explored this notion of a threshold value, which they call "the optimal ratification level." BLD show that this level is reasonably robust to variations in contractual circumstances; more significantly, BLD argue that the prospects for effecting an IEA are not necessarily diminished by there being a large number of countries. SS (1995, p. 152) show that the attainment of international coordination by a "minimal-sized group" is fundamentally dependent on "how individual pollution activities add to the total pollutants experienced...[by nations]." While these papers have certainly advanced our understanding of some aspects of "the multi-faceted design...problem," (BLD, p. 281), many other important questions—which I discussed in section 1—remain unanswered. Consequently, I now discuss my modeling approach to the IEA design question.

Recall that my principal objective is to study the efficacy of international institutions in solving global environmental problems. To this end, I model the international environment as a multi-forked, three tiered hierarchy. Occupying the top most tier of the hierarchy is the relevant international institution or SNGA. This SNGA could be an organization like the World Bank,[6] or the Commission on Sustainable Development created in Agenda 21 at the Rio Earth Summit. The second and the third tiers of the hierarchy consist of the government and a representative polluting firm in each DC. Each fork of the hierarchy represents a single DC, and there are N such forks (countries).[7]

Three tiered hierarchies have been studied by Tirole (1986, 1988), by Kofman and Lawarree (1993), and by Batabyal (1996, 1997, 1998a, 1998b). These researchers have studied the contractual effects of collusion between the various players in their three tiered hierarchies. However, to the best of my

6 Specifically in its role as an administrator of the Global Environmental Facility (GEF).

7 The reader will note that in this modeling scheme, I have conferred on the SNGA, the role of principal. Consequently, there is a distinct asymmetry in the assumed power of the SNGA as opposed to that of governments and firms. Given that I am interested in DCs which typically have limited bargaining power in their dealings with international organizations owing to the fact that their monetary contributions to the budgets of such organizations are minimal, this hierarchical modeling scheme appears to be apposite. For more on the power of SNGAs over DCs, see Mosley *et al.* (1991).

knowledge, the problem of designing budget balanced, *limited liability contracts* in a hierarchical international setting has not been studied to date.

As such, I shall build on and apply the theories of hierarchy to study *ex ante*, limited liability contracting between the SNGA, national governments and polluting firms in the various DCs. By limited liability, I mean contracts which impose limits on the maximum *ex post* loss that governments and firms in the individual DCs can be forced to bear as a result of pollution abatement in adverse states of nature. This feature of the IEA that I study would appear to be relevant because international institutions generally cannot guarantee that there will be no *ex post* breach of contract by nations. The rationale for the actual contracting stems from issues including, but not limited to, the harmful atmospheric effects of sulphur and/or nitrogen emissions. The incidence of pollution may be domestic or transboundary.[8] The key element of uncertainty stems from the SNGA's lack of knowledge about the *quality* of the pollution abatement technology available in each country. Whereas the firm in the DC always knows the quality of its technology and the government does too in some states of nature, the SNGA is never privy to this information. The random variable denoting the private information about pollution abatement technology quality is uncorrelated across countries. This rules out the possibility of the SNGA engaging in relative performance evaluation. Because most DCs are heterogeneous, and because there are many circumstances in which a SNGA would not want to design contracts involving relative performance evaluation, this assumption of uncorrelatedness appears not to be restrictive.[9] Put differently, the analysis of this paper holds for any finite set of countries, with the SNGA/government/firm interaction in one country being independent of the SNGA's dealings with some other country. Consequently, without loss of generality, I shall focus on an arbitrary country, say country j, in the finite set of N countries. The SNGA's task is to design a limited liability IEA that is incentive compatible, collusion-proof, and that will lead to optimal pollution abatement in the jth DC.

The rest of this paper is organized as follows: In section 3, I describe the model in detail and then I study the properties of the first best optimum. In

8 See Crane (1993) and Paarlberg (1993) for a discussion of the relevance of international institutions when the incidence of an environmental externality is domestic.

9 Batabyal (1998b) has analyzed contracting with relative performance evaluation.

section 4, I study the above described three tiered hierarchy with possible collusion by the government and the polluting firm in the DC. In particular, I analyze an *ex ante*, limited liability contract that can be implemented by the SNGA in a Bayes-Nash equilibrium. Finally, in section 5, I summarize the salient findings of this paper.

The reasons for wanting to study collusion between the polluting firm and the DC government are threefold. First, while the DC government participates in the IEA because it recognizes the value of such international participation, this government also acts as the polluting firm's advocate. This aspect of the problem will give rise to scenarios in which government/firm collusion becomes a desirable option.[10] Second, the government and the firm receive monetary transfers from the SNGA for their roles in abating pollution.[11] Further, both these players know that the SNGA cannot monitor their activities owing to sovereignty. Consequently, there will be circumstances in which there are incentives for the government and the firm in each DC to collude to maximize the transfers received from the SNGA. Third, as Mookherjee and Png (1995) have noted, corruption is an endemic part of public life in many DCs. This suggests a need for explicitly modeling the activities of potentially corruptible players. Due to these three reasons, an important part of this paper will consist of analyzing a collusion-proof IEA.

3. The Theoretical Framework

3.1. Description of the Model

Subscript $i = 1,2,3,4$ will refer to the state of nature, and superscript $j = 1,\ldots,N$ will refer to the country. Let θ denote the uncertainty about the quality of the pollution abatement technology that is currently available; θ has binary support $[\theta^L, \theta^H]$, where $0 < \theta^L < \theta^H$, and $\Delta\theta \equiv \theta^H - \theta^L$. I shall refer to θ^L as the low abatement quality parameter and to θ^H as the high abatement

[10] See Peterson (1993) for a discussion of some practical instances of possible government/firm collusion in an international setting.

[11] The exact nature of these roles is described in section 3.1.

quality parameter.

The risk averse firm produces clean air, whose output and value are denoted by $x = a+\theta, x \geq 0.$ The firm chooses pollution abatement $a > 0,$ and the firm's cost of abatement is $g(a),$ where $g' > 0, g'' > 0,$ and $g(0) = 0.$ This firm has a differentiable payoff from abatement function $B[T_i - g(a_i)]$ with $0 < B' < \infty, \forall i.$ $T_i \geq 0$ is the state i monetary transfer made by the SNGA to the firm for abating pollution. The firm's reservation payoff is $B_r = B[T_r],$ and T_r is the reservation transfer. B_r and T_r are common knowledge.

The DC government is risk averse. It has a strictly concave and differentiable utility function $V(G_i),$ where $G_i \geq 0$ is the state i monetary transfer made by the SNGA to the government for its role in participating in the IEA. The government's reservation utility is $V_r = V(G_r),$ where $G_r \geq 0$ is the reservation transfer, and $V' \in (0, \infty), \forall G_i.$ By employing a monitoring device, the government receives a signal $s,$ from the firm regarding its private information and then it sends a report r to the SNGA indicating what it observed about the firm's pollution abatement technology quality parameter. In some states of nature, this monitoring device malfunctions and hence in these states, the government is unable to provide the SNGA with a useful report. Upon receiving $r,$ the SNGA offers the government a transfer $G_i \geq 0.$ The reader should note that making reporting a key government function is consistent with the government/SNGA interaction proposed for one specific SNGA, namely, the Commission on Sustainable Development. As noted by Rogers (1993, p. 310), a key aspect of this interaction involves the "Commission's...considering information provided by governments..."

The SNGA is risk neutral and it has a welfare function defined over clean air which takes the form $U = \Sigma_j(a^j + \theta^j - G^j - T^j), j = 1,..., N,$ where the index j runs over $N,$ the total number of DCs. As indicated earlier, the quantity of clean air produced by the firm in country j is $x^j = a^j + \theta^j.$ As stated, the SNGA's welfare is the difference between total clean air production and the sum of the government and the firm transfers. In what follows, when there is no cause for confusion, I shall suppress the country superscript; the analysis will focus on country $j.$ The SNGA designs the IEA which it offers to the government and the firm. Clearly, the contract can only be conditioned on what the SNGA actually observes, i.e., the government's report r and the firm's production of clean air x.[12]

There are four states of nature, each occurring with probability $p_i > 0$, where $\Sigma_{\forall i}\, p_i = 1$. The SNGA, the government, and the firm sign the IEA holding symmetric but imperfect information about θ. The firm always observes θ before choosing its abatement level. The government on the other hand may or may not observe the firm's private information. This depends on whether the government's monitoring device functions or malfunctions. In other words, the government's signal s, may or may not be informative. I can now characterize the four states of nature:

⇒ State 1: The firm and the government both observe θ^L.

⇒ State 2: The firm observes θ^L and the government observes nothing.

⇒ State 3: The firm observes θ^H and the government observes nothing.

⇒ State 4: The firm and the government both observe θ^H.

In state 1, the firm and the government both observe the low abatement technology quality parameter. The government's monitoring device works and hence yields useful information. In state 2, the firm observes the low abatement technology quality parameter but the government observes nothing. In this state, the government's monitoring device malfunctions. In state 3, the firm observes the high abatement technology quality parameter and once again, the government's monitoring device malfunctions. Finally, in state 4, the firm and the government both observe the high abatement technology quality parameter.

The timing of the game between the SNGA, the government, and the firm is as follows: First, the SNGA offers the contract to the government and the firm. Second, the firm observes the actual realization of θ and the government receives its signal s. Third, the firm chooses a. Fourth, clean air x is produced by the firm and the government sends its report r to the SNGA indicating what it observed. Fifth, the SNGA compensates the government and

[12] I do not discuss the manner in which the SNGA raises revenue. One possibility would be to conform to the text of Agenda 21. According to this document, developed countries are supposed to contribute 0.7% of their GNP for the purpose of environmental protection. For more details, see Rogers (1993, pp. 151-160).

the firm with transfers $G(x,r)$ and $T(x,r)$.

In this paper, I shall analyze a zero liability contract. In such a contract, the SNGA must compensate the government and the firm with transfers equal in magnitude to, respectively, the government reservation utility V_r and the firm reservation payoff B_r. Put differently, in such a contract, the government and the firm have the right to disassociate themselves from their *ex ante* contractual obligations without any penalty, once they have acquired their private information. For most practical situations, this zero liability restriction is without loss of generality. Indeed, my subsequent analysis will remain unaltered qualitatively as long as the magnitudes of the government and the firm liabilities—L_G and L_F respectively—are less than the government reservation utility V_r and the firm reservation payoff B_r.[13]

In the remainder of this paper I shall assume that the SNGA can verify the veracity of the government's report r. In other words, if the government's signal s is noninformative, then the corresponding report r reflects this fact and the SNGA can verify that the true facts are indeed as they have been reported. In symbols, $s = 0 \Rightarrow r = 0$. On the other hand, to keep the SNGA's

[13] In a two tiered hierarchy, Sappington (1983, pp. 15-17) discusses how zero liability contracts would be altered by restrictions in which a player's liability exceeds his reservation utility.

design problem interesting and to allow for the possibility of government/firm collusion, I permit the government to lie and report that its signal is non-informative when in fact such is not the case.[14] That is, $s = \theta \Rightarrow r \in \{\theta, 0\}$. This completes the description of my model. I now consider the benchmark case in which perfect information is acquired by the SNGA.

3.2. The First Best Optimum

In this case, the SNGA observes θ *and* the firm's pollution abatement choice. When this happens, the SNGA bypasses the government and contracts with the firm directly. The government receives its reservation transfer $G_r = V^{-1}(L_G)$, and hence its reservation utility V_r, in all states. The SNGA maximizes $\Sigma_{\forall j}(a_i^j + \theta_i^j - G_i^j - T_i^j)$, subject to the firm participation constraint (A1) $\Sigma_{\forall i}\, p_i B[T_i - g(a_i)] \geq B_r$, the firm liability constraints (A2) $B[T_i - g(a_i)] \geq L_F, \forall i$, and the budget constraint (A3*) $\hat{M} \geq \Sigma_{\forall j}\{T_i^j + G_r^j\}$. This maximization problem can be simplified in two ways. First, note that because $B_r = L_F$, (A1) is redundant. Second, the liability constraints in (A2) hold with equality. Using these two facts, the SNGA's problem becomes

$$\max_{a_i^j} \Sigma_{\forall j}\{ a_i^j + \theta_i^j - g^j(a_i^j) - \{T_r^j = (B^j)^{-1}[L_F]\} - G_r^j\}, \qquad \text{(A)}$$

subject to (A3) $\hat{M} \geq \Sigma_{\forall j}\{\{T_r^j = (B^j)^{-1}[L_F]\} + g^j(a_i^j) + G_r^j\}$. The first order

---

14 The reader will note that I have restricted the government's message space in certain states. Specifically, the government can lie only in states 1 and 4. The government can also announce the wrong state, but in my setup, this is equivalent to obtaining a noninformative signal. While in principle this restriction can be relaxed by allowing for an expanded range of reporting options, from a practical standpoint, such an action would make it exceedingly difficult to obtain concrete results. This is because relaxing the above restriction would lead to an increased number of states and hence to more constraints on the SNGA's overall optimization problem.

necessary conditions to this problem are $dg^j(a_*)/da_i^j = 1/(1+\gamma), \forall i, j,$ where γ is the multiplier on the budget constraint (A3) and a_* is the first best level of pollution abatement. We see that in the first best optimum, the marginal cost of pollution abatement in DC j is set equal to the reciprocal of one plus the marginal welfare of the SNGA's funds. The optimal level of abatement a_* is independent of the state; consequently, the firm's transfer for abating pollution is also independent of the state. This transfer equals $\{T_r = B^{-1}[L_F]\} + g_*$ where T_r is the reservation transfer and $g_* \equiv g(a_*)$.

Note that it is not possible to determine whether the SNGA's budget constraint binds in equilibrium. To see this, note the following: The SNGA's welfare function exhibits constant marginal welfare in the authority's own funds. As opposed to this, the funds spent making transfers do not exhibit constant marginal welfare. As a result, it is possible that in equilibrium, the SNGA will disburse only a part of $\hat{M}$ because the effect of such disbursement drops below one before the SNGA exhausts $\hat{M}$. The second case in which the SNGA exhausts $\hat{M}$ before the effect on clean air production drops below one is also possible. Which case will prevail depends on the curvature of the $g^j(\bullet)$ function. In the rest of this paper I assume that the curvature of this function is such that the budget constraints bind in equilibrium. From a practical standpoint, this is the relevant case. I now discuss the more interesting case in which the DC government and the firm may collude, and the SNGA cannot observe θ or the actual abatement undertaken by the firm.

4. IEA Design in the Presence of Collusion and Limited Liability

Recall that because countries are sovereign, the SNGA is unable to either monitor the actions of the government and the firm or enforce the terms of the IEA in the event of a contractual breach. Because the SNGA can never acquire the firm's private information and must rely on the government's report to design the optimal contract, an efficient zero liability contract must not only be individually rational and incentive compatible, but it must be collusion-proof as well.[15]

I model collusion between the government and the firm as follows: Before the resolution of the uncertainty regarding abatement technology quality and at the time of signing the main contract, i.e., the SNGA/government/firm contract, the firm and the government sign a secondary contract which entails the offer and acceptance of a bribe from the firm to its government. Naturally, this secondary contract is unobservable by the SNGA. The bribe $b(\bullet,\bullet)$ is a function of what the firm and the government both observe, i.e., the government's report r and clean air x. With the offer and acceptance of this bribe, the firm's total transfer becomes $\{T(\bullet)-b(r,x)\}$ and the government's total transfer becomes $\{G(\bullet)+b(r,x)\}$. I shall not be concerned with the question of how the surplus from the bribe is divided. For my purpose, it is only necessary to stipulate that the bribe is actually paid by the firm to its government. To see why the firm might want to bribe its government in my four state world, consider state 4. In state 4, the government is indifferent between reporting that it has observed θ^H and reporting that it has observed 0. However, the firm would prefer that the government report 0. This is one instance in which a clear rationale exists for the firm to bribe its government.[16]

In order to formulate and solve the SNGA's problem when there is collusion, I shall follow Tirole (1986, 1988) and Batabyal (1997). This method involves imposing constraints in addition to the usual participation and incentive compatibility constraints. These additional constraints are designed to preclude government/firm collusion and hence make the main contract collusion-proof.

Denote the collusion proof transfers to the government and the firm by $\overline{G}$ and $\overline{T}$ respectively. The SNGA solves

$$\max_{\{\overline{G}_i,\overline{T}_i,a_i\}} \Sigma_{\forall i}\, p_i(a_i+\theta_i-\overline{G}_i-\overline{T}_i) \qquad \text{(B)}$$

subject to (A1)-(A2) with T_i and G_i replaced with $\overline{T}_i$ and $\overline{G}_i$,

[15] See footnote 10 as well.

[16] Also see the discussion in the last paragraph of section 2.

(B1) $\Sigma_{\forall i}\, p_i V(\overline{G}_i) \geq V_r$,

(B2) $V(\overline{G}_i) \geq L_G, \forall i$,

(B3) $\overline{T}_3 - g(a_3) \geq \overline{T}_2 - g(a_2 - \Delta\theta)$,

(B4) $\overline{T}_2 - g(a_2) \geq \overline{T}_3 - g(a_3 + \Delta\theta)$,

(B5) $\overline{G}_1 + \overline{T}_1 - g(a_1) \geq \overline{G}_2 + \overline{T}_2 - g(a_2)$,

(B6) $\overline{G}_4 + \overline{T}_4 - g(a_4) \geq \overline{G}_3 + \overline{T}_3 - g(a_3)$,

(B7) $\overline{G}_3 + \overline{T}_3 - g(a_3) \geq \overline{G}_2 + \overline{T}_2 - g(a_2 - \Delta\theta)$,

(B8) $\overline{G}_2 + \overline{T}_2 - g(a_2) \geq \overline{G}_3 + \overline{T}_3 - g(a_3 + \Delta\theta)$, and

(B9) $\hat{M} \geq \Sigma_{\forall j} \{\overline{G}_i^j + \overline{T}_i^j\}, \forall i$.

The constraint (B1) is the government's *ex ante* participation constraint. The four constraints in (B2) denote the government's zero liability constraints. These constraints can be interpreted as the maximum penalty that can be imposed on the government by the SNGA in the event that *ex post*, the government chooses to disassociate itself from its contractual obligations. Because I am studying zero liability contracts, $V_r = L_G$ and $B_r = L_F$. Constraints (B3) and (B4) are the firm's incentive compatibility constraints. Constraint (B3) says that in state 3, the firm should not claim that the state is actually 2. Similarly, (B4) tells us that in state 2, the firm should not claim that the state is actually 3. Note that these are also the two states in which the government's signal s is noninformative. Constraints (B5) and (B6) are the collusion constraints. Recall that in states 1 and 4 the government's signal s is informative. Consequently, in these two states, the government can hide this fact. Given this, constraints (B5) and (B6) tell us that should the firm bribe its government, then the total sum of the transfers less the cost of pollution abatement in states 1 and 4 cannot be less than the corresponding totals in states 2 and 3, respectively. Constraint (B7) tells us that the government should not be able to bribe the firm in state 3 to abate at the level that is appropriate for state 2. Similarly, (B8) says that the government should not be able to bribe the firm to claim that the state is 3 when it is 2. Finally, (B9) denotes the

SNGA's budget constraints. These constraints tell us that irrespective of state, the total sum of transfers paid to the government and the firm in the various countries cannot exceed the SNGA's available budget $\hat{M}$ for environmental protection. Solving the SNGA's problem (B) subject to (A1)-(A2) and (B1)-(B9), I get

THEOREM 1: The optimal zero liability contract when there is government/firm collusion has the following properties:

(i) $a_i = (g')^{-1}\{p_i/(p_i+\gamma_i)\}, i \neq 2, a_2 = (g')^{-1}[(p_2 - D)/(p_2+\gamma_2)],$

(ii) $\tilde{A}_1 g'(a_1) = \tilde{A}_3 g'(a_3) = \tilde{A}_4 g'(a_4) > \tilde{A}_2 g'(a_2),$

(iii) $\overline{G}_4 > \overline{G}_1 = \overline{G}_2 = \overline{G}_3,$

(iv) $\overline{T}_3 - g(a_3) > \overline{T}_4 - g(a_4) > \overline{T}_1 - g(a_1) = \overline{T}_2 - g(a_2)$, and

(v) at the optimum all the constraints except (A1), (A2, $i = 3,4$), (B1), (B2, $i = 4$), (B4) and (B8) bind.[17]

PROOF: See the Appendix.

In order to intuitively verify that the above contract is collusion-proof, I have to show that constraints (A1)-(A2) and constraints (B1)-(B9) are satisfied. First, note that because I am studying a zero liability contract, constraints (A1) and (B1) are redundant. Second, by part (v) of Theorem 1, constraints (A2, $i = 1,2$), (B2, $i = 1,2,3$), (B3), (B5), (B6), (B7) and (B9) are satisfied. Third, the proof of Theorem 1 tells us that constraints (A2, $i = 3,4$), (B2, $i = 4$), (B4) and (B8) are slack at the optimum. Thus the equilibrium contract is indeed collusion-proof. Let us now analyze this collusion-proof contract in greater detail.

---

[17] For an exact representation of $\tilde{A}_i$ and D, see the proof of Theorem 1 in the Appendix.

First, part (i) of Theorem 1 tells us that the actual level of pollution abatement in any state is a function of the state probability p_i, and the multiplier on the budget constraint γ_i. Part (ii) tells us that the optimal contract equalizes the weighted marginal cost of pollution abatement in states 1, 3, and 4. That is, $\tilde{A}_1 g'(a_1) = \tilde{A}_3 g'(a_3) = \tilde{A}_4 g'(a_4) > \tilde{A}_2 g'(a_2)$ holds, where $\tilde{A}_1, \ldots, \tilde{A}_4$ are weights.[18] Because the budget constraints bind in equilibrium, the contractually specified levels of pollution abatement will generally not be ideal. In this connection, the reader should note that because the equation specifying the first best level of abatement a_* in section 3.2 involves the multiplier γ that is specific to the first best problem, no direct comparison of the optimal abatement levels across the two modeling scenarios can be made.

Second, part (ii) of Theorem 1 tells us that the transfers to the DC government reflect the usefulness of the government's report to the SNGA. In particular, because the government's report is noninformative to the SNGA in states 2 and 3, $\overline{G}_2 = \overline{G}_3$ holds. Further, in order to prevent collusion and to encourage the government to tell the truth in the high abatement technology quality state 4, the SNGA offers $\overline{G}_4 > \overline{G}_1 = \overline{G}_2 = \overline{G}_3$. The government earns no informational rents in the low abatement technology quality state 1 because the SNGA is successful in inducing the government to reveal its private information truthfully at least cost.

Third, parts (iv) and (v) of Theorem 1 tell us that at the optimum, the firm and the government liability constraints bind more often than not. This means that the optimal contract offered by the SNGA must respect the fact that *ex post*, the firm and the government may choose to disassociate themselves from their contractual obligations in several states of nature. To see why these liability constraints do not bind in every state of nature, consider the firm liability constraints for states 3 and 4. The state 3 liability constraint is slack because the incentive compatibility constraint for this state binds at the optimum. This reflects the fact that in this high abatement technology quality state, the incentive compatibility constraint (B3) is always more restrictive than the liability constraint. Similarly in state 4, as compared to the liability

[18] See Step 13 in the proof of Theorem 1 for an exact representation of these weights.

constraint, the collusion incentive compatibility constraint (B6) is more pressing to the SNGA. In particular, in order to ensure that no collusion takes place in this high abatement technology quality state, the SNGA has to pay a premium to the firm. This is why the state 4 firm liability constraint is slack at the optimum.

Note that as compared to the case in which the government and the firm do not collude, the SNGA is clearly worse off in this collusion case. This is because the possibility of government/firm collusion necessitates the inclusion of constraints (B5)-(B8). In other words, the number of binding constraints in the collusion case exceeds the number of binding constraints in the no collusion case. However, if the SNGA does indeed offer the contract with the characteristics described in Theorem 1, then its monetary obligations will be as described in the Theorem. The reader should note that the SNGA offers the best contract possible from the set of feasible, zero liability contracts that are constrained to be budget balancing and collusion-proof.

5. Conclusions

In this paper I analyzed the question of environmental protection for developing countries within the framework of the directives set forth in the various agreements reached at the 1992 Rio Earth Summit. I modeled the institutional setting for the underlying problem as a three tiered hierarchy with N forks and then I studied the effects of collusion and limited liability on the SNGA's IEA design problem. Four significant policy conclusions emerge.

First, the liability constraints for the government and the firm generally bind at the optimum. This means that from the perspective of the SNGA, obtaining voluntary participation by individual DCs and preventing *ex post* breach of contract are costly. Barrett (1994) has argued that for IEAs to work, they must be self-enforcing. Along the same lines, Rogers (1993, p. 236) has worried that many of the Earth Summit directives "offer a back door option by which signatories can excuse themselves at a later date if the going gets too tough." The implementability of limited liability contracts of the sort analyzed in this paper should allay such concerns because a limited liability contract is self-enforcing. Put differently, as compared to an *ex ante* contract, a limited liability contract is more likely to be renegotiation-proof.

Second, money matters. Although one cannot be certain that budgetary considerations will have a qualitative impact on the contractually specified pollution abatement levels, it seems reasonable to suppose that in any practical setting, such considerations will influence actual pollution abatement patterns by limiting the magnitude of the transfers that a SNGA can make to governments and to polluting firms in DCs.

Third, the SNGA will prefer *ex ante* contracting to contracting with limited liability constraints. Because *ex ante* contracting involves optimization with fewer constraints, the SNGA's expected welfare with *ex ante* contracting will generally be higher than its expected welfare with limited liability contracting. However, in the context of DCs, unless a SNGA can limit the *ex post* liability of the players, nations are unlikely to participate in *ex ante* contracting schemes. Further, *ex ante* contracting schemes will generally not be self-enforcing.

Fourth, the SNGA can indeed circumvent the monitoring and enforcement problem stemming from national sovereignty by designing collusion-proof contracts. This tells us that the concerns of scholars such as Krasner (1983) who have worried about the deleterious effects of sovereignty, are somewhat misplaced. At least in the realm of international environmental affairs, the main impediments to the design of efficient IEAs appear to involve funds and informational imperfections.

With talk of rising disparity between the South and the North and the increasingly acrimonious nature of international discussions regarding the use of environmental resources, the IEA design question studied in this paper takes on particular significance. This is in no small measure due to the fact that the implementation of such agreements will do more to engender and maintain international security than will most strategic or unilateral policy measures.

Appendix

PROOF OF THEOREM 1: I proceed in 14 steps. Because $B_r = L_F$ and $V_r = L_G$, (A1) and (B1) are redundant and can be ignored. Omitting (B4) and (B8) temporarily,[19] the Lagrangian is

$$\zeta = \Sigma_i p_i(x_i - \overline{G}_i - \overline{T}_i) + \Sigma_i \alpha_i\{B[\bullet] - L_F\} + \Sigma_i \upsilon_i\{V(\bullet) - L_G\} +$$

$$\beta\{\overline{T}_3 - g(a_3) - \overline{T}_2 + g(\bullet)\} + \varepsilon_1\{\overline{G}_1 + \overline{T}_1 - g(\bullet) -$$

$$\overline{G}_2 - \overline{T}_2 + g(\bullet)\} + \varepsilon_2\{\overline{G}_4 + \overline{T}_4 - g(\bullet) - \overline{G}_3 - \overline{T}_3 + g(\bullet)\} +$$

$$\kappa\{\overline{G}_3 + \overline{T}_3 - g(\bullet) - \overline{G}_2 - \overline{T}_2 + g(\bullet)\} + \Sigma_i \gamma_i[\hat{M} - \Sigma_j\{\overline{G}_i^j + \overline{T}_i^j\}],$$ where

$\alpha_i, \upsilon_i, \beta, \varepsilon_l, \kappa, \gamma_i, i = 1,2,3,4, l = 1,2,$ are the multipliers associated with (A2), (B2), (B3), (B5), (B6), (B7), and (B9). The first order necessary conditions are

(b1) $\upsilon_1 V'(\overline{G}_1) = p_1 - \varepsilon_1 + \gamma_1,$

(b2) $\upsilon_2 V'(\overline{G}_2) = p_2 + \varepsilon_1 + \kappa + \gamma_2,$

(b3) $\upsilon_3 V'(\overline{G}_3) = p_3 + \varepsilon_2 - \kappa + \gamma_3,$

(b4) $\upsilon_4 V'(\overline{G}_4) = p_4 - \varepsilon_2 + \gamma_4,$

(b5) $\alpha_1 B'[\bullet] = p_1 - \varepsilon_1 + \gamma_1,$

(b6) $\alpha_2 B'[\bullet] = p_2 + \beta + \varepsilon_1 + \kappa + \gamma_2,$

(b7) $\alpha_3 B'[\bullet] = p_3 + \varepsilon_2 - \beta - \kappa + \gamma_3,$

(b8) $\alpha_4 B'[\bullet] = p_4 - \varepsilon_2 + \gamma_4,$

(b9) $\{\alpha_1 B'[\bullet] + \varepsilon_1\} g'(a_1) = p_1,$

[19] Step 14 of the proof shows that these two constraints are slack at the optimum.

(b10) $\{\alpha_2 B'[\bullet] - \varepsilon_1\}g'(a_2) = p_2 + \{\beta + \kappa\}g'(a_2 - \Delta\theta)$,

(b11) $\{\alpha_3 B'[\bullet] + \beta - \varepsilon_2 + \kappa\}g'(a_3) = p_3$, and

(b12) $\{\alpha_4 B'[\bullet] + \varepsilon_2\}g'(a_4) = p_4$.

Step 1: The budget constraints bind at the optimum.

Proof: This follows by assumption. Also see the related discussion in section 3.2.

Step 2: The state 2 firm and government liability constraints bind at the optimum.

Proof: Suppose $\alpha_2 = 0$.
Then (b6) tells us that $p_2 = -(\beta + \varepsilon_1 + \kappa + \gamma_2)$, which is impossible irrespective of whether $\beta \geq 0, \varepsilon_1 \geq 0$, and $\kappa \geq 0$.
Thus $\alpha_2 > 0$.
Similarly, (b2) says that $\upsilon_2 = 0 \Rightarrow p_2 = -(\varepsilon_1 + \kappa + \gamma_2)$, which is impossible irrespective of whether $\varepsilon_1 \geq 0$ and $\kappa \geq 0$.
Thus $\upsilon_2 > 0$.

Step 3: The state 1 firm and government liability constraints bind at the optimum.

Proof: (b1) tells us that $\upsilon_1 = \varepsilon_1 = 0$ is impossible. (b1) and (b5) tell us that either (i) $\alpha_1 = \upsilon_1 = 0$ or (ii) $\alpha_1 > 0$ and $\upsilon_1 > 0$.
If (i) holds, then (B5) is slack and $\varepsilon_1 = 0$. But this is impossible.
Thus $\alpha_1 > 0$ and $\upsilon_1 > 0$.

Step 4: The state 3 government liability constraint binds at the optimum.

Proof: $\upsilon_3 = 0 \Rightarrow \kappa = p_3 + \varepsilon_2 + \gamma_3$.
Substituting this into (b7) I get $\alpha_3 B'[\bullet] + \beta = 0$.
This equality holds iff $\alpha_3 = \beta = 0$. If the state 3 liability and the incentive compatibility constraints are slack, then the SNGA can raise

its welfare by lowering $\overline{T}_3$.
But this violates $\gamma_3 > 0$.
Thus $\upsilon_3 > 0$.

Step 5: (B3) binds at the optimum.

Proof: Suppose $\beta = 0$.
Then (b3) and (b7) give $\alpha_3 > 0$.
Using this in (B3) yields $g(a_2 - \Delta\theta) > g(a_2)$.
This is impossible. Thus $\beta > 0$.

Step 6: The state 3 firm liability constraint is slack at the optimum.

Proof: Clearly, $\alpha_3 = \beta = 0$ and $\alpha_3 > 0, \beta > 0$ are impossible.
Suppose $\alpha_3 > 0$ and $\beta = 0$.
Then
$\overline{T}_3 - g(a_3) = T_r > T_r + g(a_2) - g(a_2 - \Delta\theta) \Rightarrow 0 > g(a_2) - g(a_2 - \Delta\theta)$.
This is impossible because $\Delta\theta > 0$. I conclude that $\alpha_3 = 0, \beta > 0$.

Step 7: The state 4 firm and the government liability constraints are slack at the optimum.

Proof: (b4) and (b8) tell us that either
(i) $\alpha_4 > 0$ and $\upsilon_4 > 0$ or
(ii) $\alpha_4 = \upsilon_4 = 0$.
If (i) holds, then (B6) is violated.
Thus $\alpha_4 = \upsilon_4 = 0$.

Step 8: $\overline{G}_4 > \overline{G}_1 = \overline{G}_2 = \overline{G}_3$.

Proof: This follows because $\upsilon_1 > 0, \upsilon_2 > 0, \upsilon_3 > 0$, and $\upsilon_4 = 0$.

Step 9: (B5) and (B6) bind at the optimum.

Proof: $\alpha_1 > 0, \alpha_2 > 0, \upsilon_1 > 0, \upsilon_2 > 0$ tell us that $\varepsilon_1 > 0$. (b4) and $\upsilon_4 = 0$ tell us that $\varepsilon_2 > 0$.

Step 10: $\overline{T}_3 - g(a_3) > \overline{T}_4 - g(a_4) > \overline{T}_1 - g(a_1) = \overline{T}_2 - g(a_2)$.

Proof: $\alpha_1 > 0, \alpha_2 > 0, \alpha_4 = 0 \Rightarrow \overline{T}_4 - g(a_4) > \overline{T}_1 - g(a_1) = \overline{T}_2 - g(a_2)$.
$\varepsilon_2 > 0, \upsilon_3 > 0, \upsilon_4 = 0 \Rightarrow \overline{T}_3 - g(a_3) > \overline{T}_4 - g(a_4)$.
Hence the claim follows.

Step 11: (B7) binds at the optimum.

Proof: This follows because $\beta > 0$ and $\overline{G_2} = \overline{G_3}$.

Step 12: For $i \neq 2, a_i = (g')^{-1}\{p_i/(p_i + \gamma_i)\}$ and
$a_2 = (g')^{-1}[(p_2 - D)/(p_2 + \gamma_2)]$,
where $D = (\beta + \kappa)\{g'(a_2) - g'(a_2 - \Delta\theta)\}$.

Proof: From (b5) and (b9) I get $a_1 = (g')^{-1}\{p_1/(p_1 + \gamma_1)\}$.
From (b6) and (b10) I get $a_2 = (g')^{-1}[(p_2 - D)/(p_2 + \gamma_2)]$.
From (b7) and (b11) I get $a_3 = (g')^{-1}\{p_3/(p_3 + \gamma_3)\}$.
Finally, from (b8) and (b12) I get $a_4 = (g')^{-1}\{p_4/(p_4 + \gamma_4)\}$.

Step13: $\tilde{A}_1 g'(a_1) = \tilde{A}_3 g'(a_3) = \tilde{A}_4 g'(a_4) > \tilde{A}_2 g'(a_2)$, where
$\tilde{A}_i = (p_i + \gamma_i)/p_i, i = 1,...,4$.

Proof: From the proof to Step 12, it follows that
$\tilde{A}_2 g'(a_2) < 1 = \tilde{A}_1 g'(a_1) = \tilde{A}_3 g'(a_3) = \tilde{A}_4 g'(a_4)$.

Step 14: (B4) and (B8) are slack at the optimum.

Proof: Suppose (B4) binds at the optimum. Then $\overline{T}_2 - g(a_2) = \overline{T}_3 - g(a_3 + \Delta\theta)$. Because $\beta > 0$, this means that $g(a_3 + \Delta\theta) - g(a_3) = g(a_2) - g(a_2 - \Delta\theta)$. Because $\Delta\theta > 0$ and $g'' > 0$, this last equality holds iff $a_2 > a_3$. However, a contract which requires that relative to state 3, there be more abatement in the low abatement technology quality state 2, cannot be optimal. Hence (B4) is slack at the optimum. Intuitively, we know that for $i = 2,3$, either the incentive compatibility constraint binds or the liability constraint binds, but not both. For state 3, the high abatement technology quality state, the incentive compatibility constraint binds; hence the liability constraint is slack. As contrasted to this, in the low abatement technology quality state 2, the liability constraint binds; hence the incentive compatibility constraint is slack. Having shown that (B4) is satisfied, to verify that (B8) is satisfied, it suffices to note that $\overline{G}_2 = \overline{G}_3$. This completes the proof of Theorem 1.

References

Barrett, S. 1992. International Environmental Agreements as Games, in R. Pethig, (ed.), *Conflicts and Cooperation in Managing Environmental Resources*. Springer-Verlag, Berlin.

Barrett, S. 1994. Self-Enforcing International Environmental Agreements, *Oxford Economic Papers*, 46, 878-894.

Batabyal, A.A. 1996. An Agenda for the Design and Study of International Environmental Agreements, *Ecological Economics*, 19, 3-9.

Batabyal, A.A. 1997. Developing Countries and Environmental Protection: The Effects of Budget Balance and Pollution Ceiling Constraints, *Journal of Development Economics*, 54, 285-305.

Batabyal, A.A. 1998a. Developing Countries and Environmental Protection: The Effects of *Ex Ante* versus *Ex Post* Contracting, *Journal of Regional Science*, 38, 253-271.

Batabyal, A.A. 1998b. Developing Countries and International Environmental Agreements: The Case of Perfect Correlation, *International Review of Economics and Finance*, 7, 85-102.

Bernauer, T. 1995. The Effect of International Environmental Institutions: How We Might Learn More, *International Organization*, 49, 351-377.

Black, J., Levi, M., and de Meza, D. 1993. Creating a Good Atmosphere: Minimum Participation for Tackling the 'Greenhouse Effect', *Economica*, 60, 281-293.

Crane, B.B. 1993. International Population Institutions: Adapting to a Changing World Order, in R. Keohane, P. Haas, and M. Levy, (eds), *Institutions for the Earth*. MIT Press, Cambridge, MA.

Hoel, M. 1991. Global Environmental Problems: The Effects of Unilateral Actions Taken by One Country, *Journal of Environmental Economics and Management*, 20, 55-70.

Hoel, M. 1992. International Environmental Conventions: The Case of Uniform Reductions of Emissions, *Environmental and Resource Economics*, 2, 141-159.

Keohane, R., Haas, P., and Levy, M. 1993. The Effectiveness of International Environmental Institutions, in R. Keohane, P. Haas, and M. Levy, (eds), *Institutions for the Earth*, MIT Press, Cambridge, MA.

Kofman, F., and Lawarree, J. 1993. Collusion in Hierarchical Agency, *Econometrica*, 61, 629-656.

Krasner, S. 1983. Regimes and the Limits of Realism: Regimes as Autonomous Variables, in S. Krasner, (ed.), *International Regimes*. Cornell University Press, Ithaca, NY.

Mookherjee, D., and Png, I. 1995. Corruptible Law Enforcers: How Should They Be Compensated? *Economic Journal*, 105, 145-159.

Mosley, P., Harrigan, J., and Toye, J. 1991. *Aid and Power: The World Bank and Policy-Based Lending in the 1980s*. Routledge, London.

Paarlberg, R. 1993. Managing Pesticide Use in Developing Countries, in R. Keohane, P. Haas, and M. Levy, (eds), *Institutions for the Earth*. MIT Press, Cambridge, MA.

Peterson, M.J. 1993. International Fisheries Management, in R. Keohane, P. Haas, and M. Levy, (eds), *Institutions for the Earth*. MIT Press, Cambridge, MA.

Rogers, A. 1993. *The Earth Summit*. Global View Press, Los Angeles, CA.

Sandler, T., and Sargent, K. 1995. Management of Transnational Commons: Coordination, Publicness, and Treaty Formation, *Land Economics*, 71, 145-162.

Sappington, D. 1983. Limited Liability Contracts between Principal and Agent, *Journal of Economic Theory*, 29, 1-21.

Shogren, J., Baik, K., and Crocker, T. 1992. Environmental Conflicts and Strategic Commitment, in R. Pethig, (ed.), *Conflicts and Cooperation in Managing Environmental Resources*. Springer-Verlag, Berlin.

Tirole, J. 1986. Hierarchies and Bureaucracies: On the Role of Collusion in Organizations, *Journal of Law, Economics, and Organization*, 2, 181-214.

Tirole, J. 1988. The Multicontract Organization, *Canadian Journal of Economics*, 21, 459-466.

Part II
International Environmental Agreements: Applications

[9]

POLITICAL INSTITUTIONS AND POLLUTION CONTROL

Roger D. Congleton*

Abstract—This paper models the selection of environmental policies under authoritarian and democratic regimes, and tests the hypothesis that political institutions systematically affect the enactment of environmental regulations. The results support the contention that political institutional arrangements, rather than resource endowments, largely determine policies concerning environmental regulation.

I. Introduction

THE essential economics of pollution are fairly straightforward. Pollution is largely an undesired byproduct of production and transport. Consequently, countries that engage in more production and/or more transport will, *ceteris paribus*, generate more pollution. A country's output of pollution, thus, is evidence of its material prosperity, and is to a large extent a consequence of purely economic considerations: the pool and distribution of natural resources available to it, the productivity of its people, the nature of available production technologies and market structure.[1]

However, clearly *more* than economic considerations are involved. Political institutions affect the extent of a nation's output of effluents insofar as they directly affect environmental policies, or indirectly encourage or discourage economic development. Grier and Tullock (1989) demonstrate that economic growth rates in nations with liberal democratic institutions are higher than those with less liberal political arrangements, other things being equal. Ignoring direct regulation, democratic regimes would tend to exhibit higher growth rates of pollutants than less liberal regimes. Democratic political institutions will moderate these economic tendencies if they are systematically more likely to adopt policies that encourage firms and/or consumers to use less polluting technologies.

Domestic political institutions also affect attempts to negotiate international environmental standards insofar as decisions to sign and abide by multilateral agreements are ultimately decisions of distinct policies. In most cases, states that find a particular proposed regulation or convention to be against "their interests" can opt out of the negotiations and ignore any conventions signed by those that remain at little cost; as there are, at best, only weak international legislative and enforcement institutions. Inasmuch as domestic political institutions effectively determine the range of interests that are accounted for in policy decisions, regimes that enact stringent domestic environmental standards are likely to find international agreements along similar lines to be in their interest.[2]

The purpose of this paper is to explore the effect of political institutions on the willingness of governments to control outputs of domestic effluents. To this end, models of democratic and authoritarian environmental policy making are developed in section II. The analysis demonstrates that an authoritarian confronts a higher relative price for pollution abatement than a median voter does. In cases where this relative price effect dominates, authoritarian regimes will adopt less stringent domestic environmental standards than democratic regimes, and by extension, be less willing to sign international conventions on environmental matters.

Empirical evidence on the latter proposition is developed in section III of the paper. Generally,

Received for publication October 16, 1990. Revision accepted for publication August 5, 1991.

* George Mason University.

Financial support from the International Institute is gratefully acknowledged. The paper has benefited from discussions with John Moore, the data assistance of Nicole Verrier, and the comments of three anonymous referees.

[1] See Baumol and Oates (1975) for an overview of economic aspects of pollution. Tobey (1990) and Leonard (1988) discuss trade aspects of environmental policies. However, Tobey was unable to find a relationship between domestic environmental policies and patterns of international trade. For recent overviews of the economics of air pollution, see Firor (1990). Drysek (1987) discusses the effects of political institutions on environmental policy. The analysis developed here supports Drysek's contention that liberal democracies are more responsive to environmental concerns than authoritarian or bureaucratic regimes.

[2] Economic aspects of domestic and international environmental protection differ somewhat for import and export industries. For example, export industries restricted by environmental domestic standards would be inclined to oppose cost increasing domestic standards. However, once domestic standards are enacted, affected domestic industries would tend to support similar strictures for their international competitors.

the results support the contention that liberal democracies are both relatively high sources of air pollution (because of their higher income) and more likely to sign international conventions on the environment. Section IV summarizes the results and suggests possible extensions.

II. Environmental Politics

The essential difference between authoritarian regimes and democracies is their decision-making procedure. Democracies make policy by counting the votes of ordinary citizens or their elected representatives. Authoritarian regimes only take account of the "votes" of an unelected elite, in the limit the "vote" of a single ruler. While many secondary features of authoritarian and democratic regimes indirectly influence public policies insofar as they affect public debate or planning horizon, they are initially neglected to focus attention on similarities in decision-making procedures. With this in mind, global markets in technology and capital are assumed to be sufficiently competitive that technological aspects of environmental policy are the same for authoritarian and democratic regimes.[3] Voters and dictators are assumed to face the same technological tradeoff between environmental quality and non-environmental income.

At this level of abstraction, both authoritarian and democratic decision-making procedures are fundamentally similar in that they yield environmental policies that maximize the welfare of a single individual given various political and economic constraints. Under a democratic regime, the pivotal voter is the mean or median voter.[4] Under an authoritarian regime, the pivotal decision maker is the dictator (or the pivotal member of the ruling group). Any systematic difference between policies adopted by these regimes must be ascribed to differences in the parameters of their decision problems.

A. *Utility Maximizing Pollution Standards*

For purposes of analysis, individuals are assumed to maximize a two-dimensional utility function defined over measured real income (or consumption) as per GNP accounting practices and environmental quality. Measured real income is a pure private good measured as an index of goods purchased in markets. Environmental quality is a public good measured as an index of the average density of undesired (often toxic) chemicals in the voter's environment. These two areas of choice, while technologically linked, are disjoint since environmental quality is not normally included in measured real income.

The relationship between measured (real) national income and the measured (real) income of a typical individual is assumed to be a monotone increasing function of national income. This is a fairly severe assumption since environmental regulations often have quite different effects on different industries or regions within a country. However, the voter of most interest for the purposes of this paper is the median voter, who, because of his position at the midpoint of the distribution of voter ideal pollution standards, is unlikely to be one of the most (or least) affected individuals. Authoritarians also have incomes that

[3] Nations will face different costs for capital in perfectly competitive markets if they are more or less stable and/or have different regulatory environments. However, such differences are fundamentally political in nature inasmuch as they reflect political uncertainties, and/or import-export restrictions. Kormendi and Meguire (1985) report that political regimes provide the strongest explanation of international investment flows. Costs will also vary if there are important non-transportable natural resources that affect local relative prices of alternative production techniques. Cost differences due to differences in tax policies, infrastructure, land use restrictions and so forth can be modelled in a manner similar to that used for economic standards developed above.

The paper models the enactment of environmental standards rather than pollution taxes or land use regulations to simplify analysis. Buchanan and Tullock (1975) argue that political considerations tend to make standards more attractive than appropriate Pigovian taxes.

[4] Stochastic models of voter choice generally imply an equilibrium at the average voter's ideal point. See Enelow and Hinich (1984) or Coughlin (1990) for an overview of such models. In the case where voter ideal points are symmetrically distributed, the mean and median voter positions are the same and the policy predictions of both models are identical. The median voter model is used in this paper because of its more conventional representation of voter decision making and because median voter models are more widely used in the public policy literature. Sufficient conditions are met in the model for the existence of a median voter equilibrium. The policy domain is single dimensioned and the concavity of equation (2) implies that objective functions are single peaked in this domain.

The political effects of economic interest groups are ignored in this paper. As a first approximation, the efforts of economic interest groups are assumed to offset each other as in the symmetric case characterized by Congleton (1989), leaving the median voter or authoritarian decisive.

are linked to the national economy insofar as their income is based on tax revenues and gratuities. Initially, each individual is assumed to receive a constant share of GNP. Given national income Y and an individual's income share v, personal income is $C = vY$.

National income is a function of environmental regulations, E^*, market institutions, M, and resource base, R, in the country of interest. National income increases as economic resources increase, and as market arrangements become less centrally managed. National income initially rises as environmental standards become more stringent, peaks at standard E^y, and falls thereafter. Over the initial range, more stringent environmental standards increase national output by improving the health and productivity of labor and/or by freeing resources previously devoted by individuals to reduce exposure to the local environment, air conditioners and the like, for more valuable uses. Over the latter range, more stringent environmental standards reduce ordinary national output as less productive technologies are mandated and inputs are diverted from ordinary economic production to environmental improvement without offsetting productivity increases.[5] In this range, more stringent regulations improve average environmental quality but increase the cost of consumer goods relative to income, reducing measured national income and thereby the measured income of individuals.

Economic regulations affect the size of a voter's opportunity set through relative and absolute price effects that affect the size of national GNP. In this respect, environmental standards (and other regulations) are unlike ordinary public expenditure programs for which tax revenues are raised to finance provision of a publicly produced service. The cost of environmental quality is not reflected by changes in ordinary tax burden, but rather by indirect effects that environmental standards have on personal income.

The link between environmental standard E^* and environmental quality is assumed to be probabilistic. This reflects stochastic elements of the underlying natural processes and scientific uncertainty about the physical and social mechanisms involved. An individual's assessment of the probability of environmental deterioration, $P = p(E|E^*, Y)$, falls as the environmental standard, E^*, becomes more stringent and increases as national output, Y, increases. Environmental standards are a form of social insurance which reduce downside environmental risk.

Each individual prefers the environmental standard that maximizes life-time expected utility given various personal constraints. Given our characterization of the choice at issue and a finite time horizon, T,[6] an individual's preferred standard can be modelled as that which maximizes:

$$U^e = \int_0^T \left[U^o P^o + \int u(C, E, t) P(E|E^*, Y, t)\, dE \right] dt \tag{1a}$$

where

$$U^o \equiv U(Y, E^o, t)$$

and

$$P^o \equiv 1 - \int P(E|E^*, Y, t)\, dE$$

with

$$U_C > 0,\ U_E > 0,\ U_t < 0,$$
$$U_{CC} < 0,\ U_{CE} > 0,\ U_{EE} < 0$$
$$U_{tC} < 0,\ U_{tE} < 0,\ U_{tt} > 0,$$
$$P \geq 0,\ P_{E^*} < 0,\ P_{Y/A} > 0$$

[5] For those skeptical of the initial range where GNP increases with increases in environmental controls, recall that resources have been invested in waste management (dumps, latrines and so forth) by even prehistoric human communities. These investments tend to improve the health and longevity of community members with a consequent increase in the effective labor supply of the community. This suggests that over some range environmental standards increase productivity and thereby personal income. Ridgeway (1970) reports that such arguments played an important role in promoting sanitation efforts by western democracies during the last century.

To see that a similar upward sloping range exists for air quality, imagine the problem faced by a mine owner. If he fails to maintain some minimal level of environmental controls within the mine, his labor force will be less productive as air quality and temperature take their toll. A suitable investment in ventilation and cooling equipment can increase productivity.

[6] Congleton and Shughart (1990) provide evidence that median years to retirement and expected longevity affect policy decisions regarding social security benefit streams. Their results suggest that the median voter has a finite planning horizon in excess of thirty years.

subject to

$$C = \upsilon Y \tag{1b}$$

$$Y = y(E^*, M, R, t) \tag{1c}$$

with

$$Y_R > 0, Y_{E^*} > 0$$

and

$$Y_{E^*E^*} > 0 \text{ for } E^* < E^{y'},$$
$$Y_{E^*} = 0 \quad \text{for } E^* = E^y,$$

and

$$Y_{E^*} < 0 \text{ for } E^* > E^y.$$

Subscripted variables represent partial derivatives with respect to the variable subscripted. U^o is utility generated by the original (or maximum) level of environmental quality with a measured income determined by the implied public policy. Conditional probability function P represents the probability distribution of environmental qualities below E^o in period t. Thus, the integral of P represents the probability that environmental quality falls below E^o. Utility increases as measured income, C, and/or environmental quality, E, increase and declines with postponement, t.

Substituting the constraints into the objective function, in order to specify the choice in terms of the environmental standard, E^*, yields:

$$U^e = \int_0^T \Big[U(\upsilon Y, E^o, t) P^o + \Big[\int u(\upsilon Y, E, t) P(E|E^*, y(E^*), t) \Big] dE \Big] dt. \tag{2}$$

Differentiating with respect to environmental standard E^*, and setting the result equal to zero yields a single first order condition for a typical individual's ideal environmental standard:

$$\int_0^T \upsilon U_C^o Y_{E^*} P^o + U^o(P_{E^*}^o + P_Y^o Y_{E^*}) + \Big[\int \upsilon U_C Y_{E^*} P + U(P_{E^*} + P_Y Y_{E^*})\, dE \Big] dt = 0 \tag{3a}$$

or

$$\int_0^T \upsilon U_C^o Y_{E^*} P^o - \Big[\int \upsilon U_C Y_{E^*} P\, dE \Big] dt = \int_0^T - U^o(P_{E^*}^o + P_Y^o Y_{E^*}) + \int U(P_{E^*} + P_Y Y_{E^*})\, dE \Big] dt. \tag{3b}$$

FIGURE 1.—UTILITY MAXIMIZING ENVIRONMENTAL REGULATIONS

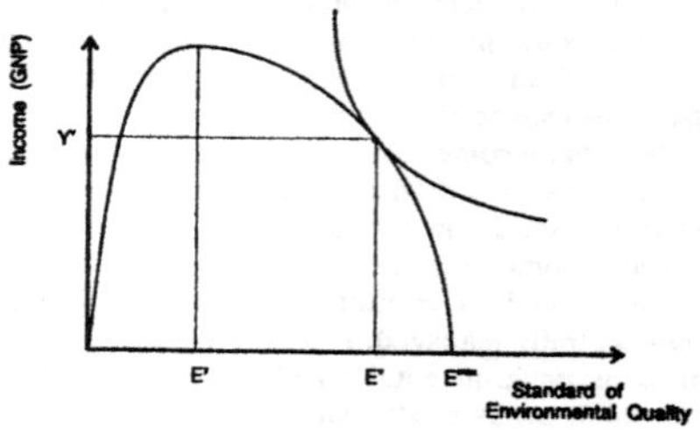

Equation (3b) demonstrates that the effect of environmental regulation on utility occurs through its effects on personal income and the probability distribution of environmental quality. Each individual prefers the environmental standard that sets the expected present value of his subjective marginal cost for the standard in terms of reduced measured income (consumption) equal to the present discounted value of the time stream of marginal utility from greater environmental quality.

Such environmental standards have the geometry of the curves in figure 1. The tradeoff between economic output and environmental quality is the envelope of the opportunity set. It represents the steady-state tradeoff between measured (or pecuniary) income and environmental quality. The indifference curves represent constant levels of expected lifetime utility over the time horizon of interest. Note that the relevant part of the constraint is from E^y to E^{max}. A rational decision maker who regards neither economic income nor environmental quality as "bads" would never intentionally adopt a standard below E^y. An individual who values income but cares nothing for the environment, *per se*, prefers the standard which maximizes measured income, E^y. The median voter is by definition in the middle of the distribution voter ideal points, and therefore opts for an intermediate solution similar to that depicted. The situation of a dictator is not similarly constrained, and thus more extreme environmental policies are possible. Yet the general shape of the opportunity set implies that both sorts of regimes tend to have some environmental regulation.

The implicit function theorem implies the existence of an equation, based on (3a), which represents an individual's preferred environmental standard as a function of variables beyond his control.

$$E^{**} = e(v, T, R, M). \quad (4)$$

Ultimately, the level of environmental regulation preferred depends upon the individual's share of national income, v, his time horizon, T, the resource base of the country, R, and its market institutions, M. The implicit function differentiation rule allows the effect of changes in these parametric variables on environmental standards to be calculated.

Define the left-hand side of equation (3a) to be H, then

$$E_v^{**} = H_v / - H_E \quad (5a)$$

$$E_T^{**} = H_T / - H_E \quad (5b)$$

$$E_R^{**} = H_R / - H_E \quad (5c)$$

$$E_M^{**} = H_M / - H_E. \quad (5d)$$

H_E is the second derivative of equation (2) with respect to environmental quality, which must be negative at the expected utility maximum. Consequently, the signs of equations (5a) through (5d) are determined by the numerators. Somewhat surprisingly, given the simplicity of the model used, none of these are unambiguously determined. An increase in the share of national income going to the individual, an increase in his time horizon, or an increase in national resources or geographical area can lead to stronger or weaker environmental standards according to the relative sizes of various interaction terms.

An increase in the fraction of national income going to the individual of interest increases the marginal cost of environmental standards faced by him, since he will now bear a larger fraction of associated reductions in national income. On the other hand, his income is higher for any given standard and thus would, except for the relative price effect, opt for greater expected environmental quality. In the case where the relative price effect dominates, $E_v^{**} < 0$, the utility maximizing environmental standard becomes less stringent as the individual's share of national income increases.

The effect of an increased planning horizon depends on the incremental costs and benefits from higher environmental standards at the end of the period evaluated. It is often argued that the time stream of benefits from environmental standards is such that the costs of environmental standards are concentrated in the early periods while the benefits are concentrated in later time periods. See, for example, Nordhaus (1989). Consequently, it is likely that at the end of the planning horizon the marginal benefits of environmental standards exceed their marginal costs, which implies that $E_T^{**} > 0$. In this case, the longer the time horizon used, the more stringent an individual's ideal environmental standards tend to be.

The effect of changes in a nation's resource base or market institutions is more complex. A larger resource base or more efficient collection of market institutions implies a larger national income for any environmental standard, which increases the probability of environmental deterioration and makes more stringent environmental standards more attractive. However, greater national income also implies that each voter is wealthier and inclined to "purchase" both more measured income and more environmental quality. On the other hand, greater personal wealth may increase the marginal cost of environmental regulation to the voter. In the case where increased environmental downside risk and income effects more than offset any increase in the marginal cost of environmental standards, equations (5c) and (5d) will exceed zero. Here, the stringency of environmental standards would increase as the resource base and/or quality of market institutions increase, $E_R^{**} > 0$ and $E_M^{**} > 0$.

B. Differences Among Utility Maximizing Political Regimes

The above analysis implies that utility maximizing decision makers will disagree about the optimal environmental standard, even if their utility functions are fundamentally similar, if their position in the national economy, planning horizon, or national endowments differ. To demonstrate that political regimes affect environmental policies, it is sufficient to show that the circumstances of policy makers under these two systems tend to be systematically different.

FIGURE 2.—UTILITY MAXIMIZING ENVIRONMENTAL REGULATIONS FOR DICTATOR AND MEDIAN VOTER

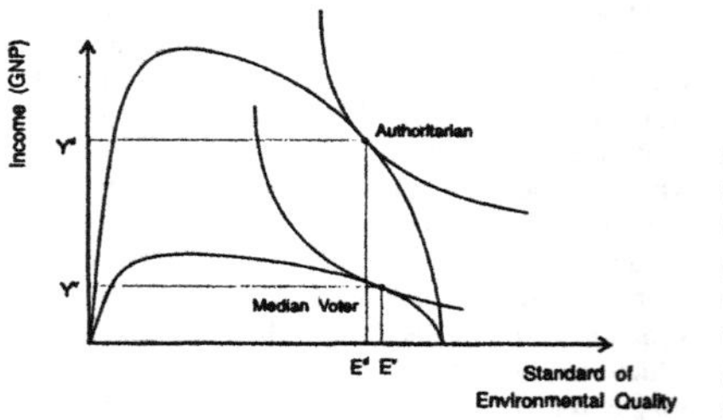

The effect of a change in regime on environmental policy can be analyzed with reference to equations (5a) and (5b). Recall that the median voter is approximately the voter with the median income share and time horizon. Authoritarians have greater than the median income share, and probably tend to have a shorter than average time horizon given the high turnover of authoritarian regimes.[7] Under the restricted circumstances previously discussed, a larger national income *share* and shorter time horizon tends to reduce the stringency of the desired environmental standard. Consequently, authoritarians tend to prefer a lower environmental standard than a median voter does.

The essential geometry of such median voter and authoritarian choices is depicted in figure 2. The effect of a change from authoritarian regimes to democratic regimes in a given economy is analogous to a rise in the price of environmental quality. The higher marginal cost faced by a dictator is evidenced by the more steeply downward sloping portion of his income/environmental-standard constraint. In the case depicted, the marginal rate of substitution between income and environmental quality is independent of measured income, and consequently differences in marginal cost are decisive. Here, the authoritarian opts for more pecuniary income and less stringent environmental standards than the median voter does.

III. Empirical Evidence

The above analysis makes a fairly good case for democratic regimes to be inclined to adopt more stringent environmental regulations than authoritarian regimes, although the results are not completely general. The model provides a framework for testing this and other hypotheses generated in the course of analysis. Equation (4) is the reduced form equation for environmental policy formulation. Under both authoritarian and democratic regimes, pollution standards are functions of national endowments and characteristics of the decisive voter. If democratic regimes are more inclined to enact strict environmental standards than authoritarian regimes, then estimates of equation (4) should have positive coefficients for democratic variables. Reduced form equations for other endogenous variables are similarly functions of policy-maker characteristics, national resources and market institutions. The model also characterizes several structural equations. The estimates reported below are broadly consistent with the model, although a variety of data problems had to be circumvented in order to generate the estimates.

(1) Data on domestic environmental regulations tend to be sparse and the regulations themselves different enough to make a cross section analysis problematic. On the other hand, there have been several recent international agreements on environmental concerns. So while it is not possible to test hypotheses with respect to domestic policies, it is possible to test whether a country's political regime affects its international environmental policies. To the extent that domestic considerations dictate whether a nation signs on to a particular covenant or protocol, these international agreements also indirectly cast light on domestic policies.

In 1985, a global convention was negotiated under United Nations auspices at Vienna which committed signatories to coordinate research efforts and to enact domestic legislation for reducing emissions of ozone depleting substances, chiefly chlorofluorocarbons (CFCs). In 1987, a protocol was developed in Montreal which obliged developed countries to reduce their CFC production and consumption levels to half their 1986

[7] The median term of office for African authoritarians reported by Bienen and van de Walle (1989) is about 4 years. Differences in utility functions are also very likely. The highly uncertain career path to the top of an authoritarian regime, and the relatively low typical term of office suggest that authoritarians tend to be relatively less risk averse than median voters tend to be. The relatively risky nature of the ascent to power suggests that authoritarians will be less inclined to purchase insurance of any kind, including environmental insurance.

levels by June 1999 and developing nations to limit their future consumption of CFCs.[8] In both agreements, countries could exempt themselves from the negotiated targets by not signing the final document. As of 1989, 27 countries had signed the 1985 conventions or enacted national legislation which accomplished the same end. Twenty-nine countries signed or enacted national legislation supporting the Montreal protocol, *World Resources 1989–90*, table 24.1. Nineteen countries supported both agreements. To the extent that domestic politics determine whether a particular country agrees to sign a particular covenant or protocol, the above analysis suggests that democratic regimes will be more likely to participate in these international agreements than other regimes, other things being equal.

(2) Data on the personal characteristics of median voters and dictators are largely unavailable. However, if these characteristics vary systematically with the type of regime, one can use regime-type as a proxy for the personal characteristics of decision makers under the two regimes. Unfortunately, (3) classification of countries into democratic and authoritarian regimes is also somewhat problematic. Many authoritarian regimes have formal institutional structures that superficially parallel those of democratic regimes. For example, according to the *CIA Fact Book*, 1988, both Zaire and Syria have political parties and elections, although most would consider these governments to be authoritarian. Gastil (1987, p. 40–41) classifies countries into seven categories according to their political liberties. Although Gastil's classification scheme yields a plausible ranking of countries, only the extremal values are used here to distinguish democratic from non-democratic government types. Countries that receive the highest values for political liberties (categories 1 and 2, table 3) are essentially well-functioning democracies whose citizens have broad political rights of participation. Differences in time horizon and share of national income relevant for policy makers are proxied by the resulting 0-1 dichotomous variable labeled "Democratic Country" in the tables below. Gastil also constructed a nine-fold classification of countries according to market structure (p. 74, table 8). The two most market-oriented categories are countries with relatively unregulated open markets. A 0-1 dichotomous variable constructed from these two categories, denoted capitalist country in the tables below, is used as a proxy for the efficacy of a country's market institutions.

(4) The model implies that a country's resource base plays a role in determining national standards insofar as resources affect personal income and the marginal cost of environmental regulation. However, reliable data on a nation's mineral reserves and labor force are available for relatively few countries. For example, complete data on recoverable fossil fuel reserves are available for only 46 countries from the World Petroleum Institute. However, resource endowments are largely the result of geological accidents more or less uniformly distributed about resource base. Consequently, resource endowment is proxied using area. (Area is highly correlated with proven fossil fuel reserves.) Labor force numbers are similarly problematic, and are proxied by national population. Data for population and area are from the *World Fact Book* (CIA, 1988). Data on real gross national product in U.S. dollars (1987) are from the World Petroleum Institute (1990/91).

Linear estimates of equation (4) are reported in the first 4 columns of table 1. Columns 1 and 2 report logit estimates of the probability that a particular country would have agreed to the 1985 Vienna Convention or the 1987 Montreal Protocol, using proven reserves of fossil fuels as a proxy for national resource endowment. Columns 3 and 4 report similar estimates based on the full

[8] Paragraph 4 of Article 2 of the Protocol specifies that "each party shall ensure that for the period 1 July 1998 to 30 June 1999, and in each twelve month period thereafter, its calculated level of consumption on the controlled substances in Group I of Annex A (chiefly CFCs) does not exceed, annually, fifty percent of its calculated level of consumption in 1986." Paragraph 1 of Article 5 exempts developing countries with "consumption of controlled substances . . . less than 0.3 kilograms per capita" from reductions in their current consumption levels, but restricts them to "either the average of its annual calculated level of consumption for the period 1995 to 1997 inclusive or a calculated level of consumption of 0.3 kilograms per capita, which ever is lower." CFC levels ranged from 0 to 0.91 kilogram per capita in 1986 within the 118 countries used above. A typical western democracy had levels of 0.75 kilograms per capita.

Signatories or contracting parties to the Montreal Protocol, as of 1989, include: Egypt, Ghana, Kenya, Morocco, Senegal, Togo, Canada, Mexico, Panama, United States, Venezuela, Israel, Japan, Belgium, Denmark, Finland, France, W. Germany, Greece, Italy, Luxembourg, Netherlands, Norway, Portugal, Sweden, Switzerland, United Kingdom, USSR, and New Zealand (*World Resources* 1988–90, table 24.1).

TABLE 1.—SIGNATORIES OF INTERNATIONAL CFC AGREEMENTS

Variable Name	$CFC85_{89}$ Logit	$CFC87_{89}$ Logit	$CFC85_{89}$ Logit	$CFC87_{89}$ Logit	$CFC85_{89}$ Logit	$CFC87_{89}$ Logit
C	−0.437 (0.642)	−1.869 (2.330)[a]	−2.254 (5.516)[c]	−2.114 (5.37)[c]	−2.448 (5.586)[c]	−2.286 (5.474)[c]
Democratic Country	2.228 (2.863)[b]	3.033 (3.422)[c]	2.596 (4.836)[c]	2.836 (5.151)[c]	2.227 (3.832)[c]	2.506 (4.261)[c]
Capitalist Country	−0.896 (1.049)	−0.755 (0.836)	−0.267 (0.458)	−0.726 (1.194)	−0.251 (0.415)	−0.748 (1.193)
GNP per capita					0.064 (1.817)[a]	0.058 (1.675)[a]
Oil Reserves	−6.05 E-7 (0.050)	−1.040 E-5 (0.556)				
Coal Reserves	2.252 E-5 (1.706)[a]	1.403 E-6 (0.157)				
Gas Reserves	1.490 E-8 (0.628)	2.423 E-6 (0.963)				
Area			2.356 E-4 (1.857)[a]	1.102 E-4 (1.266)	2.356 E-4 (1.672)[a]	9.672 E-5 (1.097)
Population	−0.017 (1.868)[a]	−0.00202 (0.355)	−3.624 E-3 (0.784)	−8.270 E-4 (0.324)	−0.004 (0.671)	−0.0007 (0.251)
Sample Size	46	46	118	118	118	118
Log Likelihood	−22.671	−20.830	−46.377	−47.264	−44.632	−45.814

[a]Significant at the 10% level.
[b]Significant at the 1% level.
[c]Significant at the 0.1% level.

118 country sample using national area as a proxy for national resources. Columns 5 and 6 augment the model by adding real per capita gross national product to the list of dependent variables. This creates some risk of simultaneous equation bias, but demonstrates that the results of the reduced form estimates of the model are not an artifact of the higher income levels of democratic governments. (The simple correlation coefficient for democracy and real per capita gross national product is 0.46 which is well outside the range where multicollinearity is considered to be a problem.)

Note that, consistent with the main thesis of this paper, the coefficient for the democratic country variable is significantly different from zero at the one thousandth level of significance for each of the six estimates of international environmental policy although the economic endowment and market structure variables are not. This suggests that environmental policy decisions are largely determined by a nation's political institutions rather than by its economic resource endowments. Moreover, these results are robust in the sense that small changes in data set or specification do not change the signs or significance of the coefficient estimates.

Table 2 reports estimates of other structural and reduced form equations from the model. Columns 1–4 focus on two pollutants of current interest because of their roles as greenhouse gases: net methane and CFC output as reported in *World Resources 1989–1990*. Column 5 reports a reduced form estimate of real gross national product. Column 1 reports a two stage estimate of methane output. This is an estimate of the probability function of environmental quality characterized used in equation (1) of the model. Recall that observed environmental quality is a probabilistic function of *RGNP* and environmental standards. A country's participation in the Montreal Protocol is used as a proxy for its

TABLE 2.—NATIONAL EFFLUENT OUTPUT AND ECONOMIC PRODUCTION

Variable Name	Methane 2-Stage LS	Methane/GNP OLS	Methane OLS	CFC OLS	GNP OLS
C	235.204 (2.079)[a]	12.363 (6.553)[c]	−86.239 (1.367)	−2.105 (0.849)	−73.640 (1.421)
GNP_{1987} (in US dollars)	2.481 (8.145)[c]				
Montreal Signatory or Contracting Party	−1011.481 (2.506)[b]				
Democratic Country		−9.501 (2.980)[b]	236.868 (2.904)[b]	12.285 (2.934)[b]	254.147 (2.904)[b]
Capitalist Country		0.128 (0.042)	122.570 (1.483)	4.103 (1.038)	122.570 (1.483)
Area		−0.0028 (0.478)	0.1004 (6.234)[c]	0.0043 (5.601)[c]	0.1004 (6.234)[c]
Population		0.00885 (0.720)	0.161 (0.478)	0.008 (0.499)	0.1612 (0.477)
Sample Size	118	118	118	118	118
R^2	0.219	0.082	0.748	0.321	0.386
Log Likelihood	−964.424	−483.430	−897.538	−515.596	−874.302
F-Statistic	16.092	2.522	84.087	14.829	17.747

[a]Significant at the 10% level.
[b]Significant at the 1% level.
[c]Significant at the 0.1% level.

regulatory environment. Both coefficient estimates are statistically distinguishable from zero. An increase in a country's GNP increases its Methane output while the domestic propensity to regulate reduces it. Column 2 provides indirect evidence of the effects of domestic regulation on national outputs of methane per unit of GNP. Democratic regimes produce more methane in total but significantly less per unit of national output. Together with the other results, this suggests that liberal democracies are more inclined to regulate environmental outputs than other regimes are.

Columns 3 and 4 are reduced form estimates of net outputs of methane and CFCs. A country's area again serves as a proxy for its natural resource base. The coefficients all have positive signs consistent with our previous discussion. However, again, only the coefficient estimates for the effects of liberal democratic regimes and national area are statistically significant. Democratic regimes produce more methane and more CFCs than their less liberal and/or authoritarian counterparts. This apparently reflects the higher national incomes associated with liberal democracies and the consequent production of more refuse of all sorts.

Both series of estimates are broadly similar. They suggest that liberal democracies are significantly more likely than other regimes to have supported global efforts at environmental regulation. While the signs of other coefficients are plausible, for example, capitalist countries are less inclined to regulate than other regimes, the estimates cannot rule out the possibility that the other variables had no effect on the probability of supporting the Vienna Convention or the Montreal Protocol. In contrast, the coefficients for democratic regime are statistically significant in every case.[9]

[9] Similar results for domestic policies can be obtained using indexes from Gastil (1987), and Walter and Ugelow (1979). Walter and Ugelow constructed a seven value index of the severity of environmental regulations for 25 countries. Regressing this environmental index (E) on the seven value Gastil index (adjusted to make higher numbers imply greater political liberty) of the liberalness of a country's political institutions (D) yields:

$$E = 2.135 + 0.390D \qquad F = 4.391$$
$$(1.86)^{a} \quad (2.07)^{a}$$

[a] Significant at the 10% level.

IV. Conclusion

This paper has argued that environmental policies are affected by political institutions. Analysis of incentives faced by authoritarian regimes and democratic policy makers implies that relevant decision makers in democracies have a smaller marginal cost for pollution control than authoritarians do. Moreover, the highly uncertain career path to the top of an authoritarian regime, and their relatively short term of office suggest that authoritarians tend to have a relatively shorter time horizon and be relatively less risk averse than median voters tend to be. Together these differences imply that authoritarian regimes are inclined to enact less stringent environmental standards than democratic regimes.

Empirical evidence supports the contention that political institutions affect domestic and international environmental policies. Cross-sectional analysis of both pollution outputs and willingness to take part in international conventions on the environment strongly suggests that liberal democracies are more willing to regulate environmental effluents than less liberal regimes. The empirical results support the contention that political institutions largely determine environmental regulation, rather than technological aspects of pollution control or market structure.

The results also suggest that international agreements on environmental matters of global concern will attract more signatories as the number of democratic regimes increases. Seen in this light, the recent increase in the number of countries with democratic political institutions implies that global environmental agreements will be more broadly supported in the future.

In this quite restricted sample, the more liberal (democratic) a political regime is, the more severe its environmental regulations tend to be.

REFERENCES

Baumol, W., and W. Oates, *The Theory of Environmental Policy*, second edition (New York: Cambridge University Press, 1975).

Bienen, H., and N. van de Walle, "Time and Power in Africa," *American Political Science Review* 83 (1989), 19–34.

Buchanan, J. M., and G. Tullock, "Polluters' Profits and Political Response: Direct Controls Versus Taxes," *American Economic Review* 65 (1975), 139–147.

Congleton, R. D., "Campaign Finances and Political Platforms: The Economics of Political Controversy," *Public Choice* 62 (1989), 101–118.

Congleton, R. D., and W. F. Shughart, "The Growth of Social Security: Electoral Push or Political Pull?," *Economic Inquiry* 28 (1990), 109–132.

Coughlin, P., "Majority Rule and Elections Models," *Journal of Economic Surveys* (1990).

Dryzek, J. S., *Rational Ecology: Environment and Political Economy* (New York: Basil Blackwell, 1987).

Enelow, J. M., and M. J. Hinich, *The Spatial Theory of Voting* (New York: Cambridge University Press, 1984).

Firor, J., "The Straight Story about the Green House Effect," *Contemporary Policy Issues* 8 (1990), 3–15.

Gastil, R. D., *Freedom in the World: Political Rights and Liberties 1986–1987* (New York: Greenwood Press, 1987).

Grier, K. B., and G. Tullock, "An Empirical Analysis of Cross-National Economic Growth, 1951–80," *Journal of Monetary Economics* 24 (1989), 259–276.

Kormendi, R. C., and Meguire, "Macroeconomic Determinants of Growth: Cross Country Evidence," *Journal of Monetary Economics* 16 (1985), 141–163.

Leonard, H. J., *Pollution and the Struggle for World Product* (New York: Cambridge University Press, 1988).

Nordhaus, W. D., "The Economics of the Green House Effect," mimeograph Yale University (1989).

Ridgeway, J., *The Politics of Pollution* (New York: Dutton, 1970).

Tobey, J. A., "The Effects of Domestic Environmental Policies on Patterns of World Trade," *Kyklos* 43 (1990), 191–208.

Walter, I., and J. Ugelow, "Environmental Policies in Developing Countries," *Ambio* 8 (1979), 102–109.

World Resources Institute, *World Resources 1989–90* (New York: Oxford University Press, 1989).

———, *World Resources 1990–91* (New York: Oxford University Press, 1990).

[10]

KYKLOS, Vol. 46 – 1993 – Fasc. 3, 363 - 397

Efficiency and Distribution in Greenhouse Negotiations

JOHAN EYCKMANS, STEF PROOST and ERIK SCHOKKAERT*

I. INTRODUCTION

In recent years the concern about the possibility of an enhanced greenhouse effect as a consequence of the emission of so-called greenhouse gases (GHGs) is rapidly growing[1]. Under a business-as-usual scenario the IPCC Scientific Assessment [1990] expects that global mean temperature will rise by 3°C ± 1.5°C before the end of next century. This would cause the sea level to rise by approximately 0.6 meter, and precipitation patterns would change, resulting in shifts of agricultural production zones. If one wants to reduce the risk of this enhanced greenhouse effect, emissions of GHGs must be curbed significantly. According to the IPCC [1990], the most important of the anthropogenetic GHGs is carbon dioxide (CO_2), which is produced mainly by burning fossil fuels like coal, oil and natural gas.

The greenhouse effect is a typical example of a global commons problem. Many fossil fuel users emit CO_2 which dissipates into the atmosphere and is mixed uniformly. The ensuing greenhouse effect affects all individuals in all countries of the world. It is well known that in this case the noncooperative Nash-equilibrium resulting from the individual abatement efforts will not be Pareto efficient. In order to reach a Pareto efficient solution, international

*Katholik University of Leuven, Centre for Economic Studies and Centre for Economics and Ethics, Van Euvenstraat 2 B, B-3000 Leuven.

1. An excellent introduction to the scientific background of the greenhouse effect is given by CLINE [1991].

coordination to gear the CO_2 abatement efforts of the individual countries for one another will be needed[2].

However, observation of reality immediately shows that the quest for Pareto efficiency is not the only driving force in international negotiations on the coordination of greenhouse policies. Arguments related to the international income distribution are likely to play an important role. Leaders of developing countries emphasize that their economic situation justifies a lower abatement effort, the more so since the industrial world has been responsible for the large bulk of CO_2-emissions in the past. The problem is further complicated by the asymmetries related to costs and benefits of greenhouse policies. The negative effects of global warming are spread unevenly over the various parts of the globe and it is even possible that some regions might gain from a moderate temperature increase, at least in the beginning. More important for the present discussions are the huge international differences in the cost of abating emissions. An efficient worldwide abatement effort will require abatement levels wich differ between countries. Moreover, in most cases such cost-efficient allocation will require greater efforts from the poorer countries. In that case there is a direct conflict between equity and efficiency considerations.

The relationship between efficiency and international distribution will be the main focus of this paper. The bargaining literature does not give a generally accepted solution for the highly asymmetrical problem of international greenhouse negotiations. Different (and sometimes contradictory) approaches have been followed in papers by (among others) BARRETT [1991a, 1991b, 1992a, 1992b, 1992c, 1992d], BOHM [1990], HOEL [1991a, 1991b, 1992a, 1992b], KOSOBUD and DALY [1984], MÄLER [1989], WELSCH [1991] and ROSE [1992]. Some of these authors agree with us that distributional considerations are crucial and propose a set of equity principles. However, given the huge variety in approaches available and the extremely fragile basis to choose between them, we prefer a more agnostic approach and we will specify the problem as the maximization of a social welfare function. This does *not* mean that we have to assume the existence of an omniscient international social planner. We will discuss a set of different ethical and bargaining interpretations of our approach

2. To achieve in an efficient way a substantial level of CO_2-abatement, decisions at the international level have to be supplemented by decisions at the level of the individual countries. At the international level one needs to agree on the way to share the CO_2-abatement efforts between countries. At the national level each government chooses its own set of policy instruments in order to achieve the internationally agreed upon objectives. In this paper we will only consider the policy problem at the international level.

and we will show how it can be used to compute the power weights *implicit* in a given proposal.

To concentrate on the conflict between equity and efficiency in its pure form, two important simplifying assumptions are made. In the first place, we neglect all problems of implementation and we assume that the international negotiations relate directly to the vector of individual abatement levels and (possibly) to a vector of side payments. A more realistic setting would include an analysis of different tax and/or tradeable quotas-arrangements (see, e.g., HOEL [1992a]). We analyse some of these instruments in a companion paper (EYCKMANS, PROOST and SCHOKKAERT [1992]). In the second place, we are well aware of the essentially dynamic and uncertain character of the greenhouse problem. Because the oceans act as thermal buffers, the climate responds slowly to increases in the stock of GHGs in the atmosphere. Emissions now will only have consequences with a time delay of about 50 years. Moreover, at present one can only guess at the magnitude and the economic evaluation of these consequences. However, to keep our focus on the relationship between efficiency and international income distribution we have chosen to neglect the problem of uncertainty and to make the dynamic structure as simple as possible[3].

Because it is difficult to derive definite analytical results, we try to get a better insight into the real world-aspects of the problem by supplementing the theoretical analysis with some empirical illustrations, calculated within a model incorporating the best available information. For this exercise, we represent the world by 12 homogeneous blocks of countries. Since the information on benefits is extremely scarce, we assume constant marginal benefits. Cost information is based upon NORDHAUS [1991a, 1991b] and upon simulations performed with the OECD GREEN-model, reported in BURNIAUX et al. [1992].

In section II we present our model and discuss the different interpretations which can be given to our maximization of social welfare-approach. We also show that the international income distribution plays a crucial role in the allocation of abatement efforts over the different countries if side payments are not available. Of course, this relates to the traditional distinction between first-best and second-best analysis. In section III we describe the empirical information used to illustrate the theoretical analysis. Two applications are discussed in section IV, using the Nash-Cournot noncooperative solution as a

3. Authors working in a dynamic setting have until now concentrated on the case of *symmetric* players or show at most some simulation with *two* asymmetric players (HOEL [1992a], MARTIN, PATRICK and TOLWINSKI [1991], VAN DER PLOEG and DE ZEEUW [1992]).

benchmark for comparison. In the first we give an ethical interpretation to the social welfare function and we illustrate how the optimal solution depends upon the degree of inequality aversion and on the availability of side payments. In the second one we follow an inverse optimum approach and we compute the power weights implicit in actual agreements. Section V concludes.

II. PARETO EFFICIENCY AND DISTRIBUTION IN GREENHOUSE NEGOTIATIONS: THE MAXIMIZATION APPROACH

1. The Model for Individual Countries

Assume a set of regions $N=\{1,2,\ldots,n\}$. Each region/country has to decide now on the level of CO_2 emission abatement and will incur the known effects of climate change afterwards. To concentrate on the international differences we want to make the dynamic structure of the model as simple as possible but at the same time allow for differences in intertemporal preferences. Let us therefore represent the preferences of each country by a simple two-period utility function (the same for all countries):

$$U\{y_i^0, y_i^1\} = U\left\{\frac{Y_i^0}{n_i^0}, \frac{Y_i^1}{n_i^1}\right\} \qquad \forall i \in N \tag{1}$$

with y_i^0 and y_i^1 the per capita income, Y_i^0 and Y_i^1 the income level and n_i^0 and n_i^1 the population of country i in period 0 and 1, respectively. Income is defined as:

$$Y_i^0 = \overline{Y}_i^0 - C_i(R_i) \qquad \forall i \in N$$
$$Y_i^1 = \overline{Y}_i^1 - B_i(R) \qquad \forall i \in N$$

where $\overline{Y}_i^0$ and $\overline{Y}_i^1$ are the base line income levels (without any emission restrictions) in periods 0 and 1, respectively. The amount of emission abatement by country i is denoted $R_i (0 < R_i < E_i^0)$ where E_i^0 is the initial level of emissions. Curbing emissions involves costs of fuel substitution, research on alternative energy sources and forgone output. This cost of abatement is given by the twice continuously differentiable cost function $C_i(R_i)$. We assume that this cost function is increasing, bounded and convex. Let R denote the sum of all individual abatement levels: $R = \Sigma_i R_i$. The benefits to country i of the reduction of emissions are given by the bounded and twice continuously differentiable function $B_i (R)$ which is increasing and concave in the global level of abatement R[4]. Each country bears the cost of abatement in the first period, but the benefits of that abatement are realised in the second period.

We assume that, in the absence of international cooperation, each country will follow its own noncooperative Nash-Cournot strategy. This behaviour will result in a noncooperative Nash-equilibrium[5]. Maximizing (1) with respect to R_i (for a given level of the abatement efforts by other countries) yields immediately:

$$-\frac{\partial U}{\partial y_i^0}\frac{1}{n_i^0}MC_i + \frac{\partial U}{\partial y_i^1}\frac{1}{n_i^1}MB_i = 0 \qquad \forall i \in N$$

or

$$MC_i^{NC} - \theta_i^{NC} MB_i^{NC} = 0 \qquad \forall i \in N \tag{2}$$

$$\text{with} \quad \theta_i^{NC} = \frac{\partial U / \partial Y_i^1}{\partial U / \partial Y_i^0}$$

where MC^{NC} and MB^{NC} are marginal cost and marginal benefit, respectively, and θ_i^{NC} is the intertemporal marginal rate of substitution, evaluated in the Nash-Cournot equilibrium. In this equilibrium each country undertakes emission abatement up to the point where its own marginal cost of reducing emissions by one additional unit equals its own marginal benefit of such an

4. We specify environmental damage as a function of emission flows and not as a function of the *stock* of greenhouse gases. This is no problem in our static model because there is a one-to-one relationship between the once and for all emission abatement decisions and the stock of pollutants.

5. Since the strategy space $[0, E_i^0]$ are compact and convex and since the payoff functions U(.) are assumed to be continuous, bounded and concave in R_i for all i, the sufficient conditions for the existence of at least one Nash-Cournot equilibrium point in this noncooperative game are fulfilled (theorem 2.4, FRIEDMAN [1986]).

additional unit of abatement. This individual willingness to pay is influenced by the intertemporal marginal rate of substitution. Let us define for later reference the utility V_i^{NC} obtained by country i in the Nash-Cournot equilibrium:

$$V_i^{NC} = U\left\{\frac{\overline{Y}_i^0 - C_i(R_i^{NC})}{n_i^0}, \frac{\overline{Y}_i^1 + B_i(R^{NC})}{n_i^1}\right\} \qquad \forall i \in N \tag{3}$$

Eq. (2) implicitly defines the best reaction curve of each country i, which can be shown to be downward sloping. It is well known that under these conditions the Nash-Cournot equilibrium will *not* be a Pareto efficient point. This is the basic reason for international coordination of environmental policies. Of course, a necessary but not sufficient condition for a country i to participate in an agreement is that the utility it can get from it is higher than V_i^{NC} as defined in (3).

2. The Maximization Approach to International Bargaining Issues

There exist different approaches to model the international bargaining process on the greenhouse problem. Most bargaining game models are characterized by linear utility functions (in monetary payoff terms)[6]. Concerning the cooperative social optimum, it is often assumed that income can be redistributed in a lump sum way. This assumption makes it possible to seperate equity from efficiency arguments. HOEL [1991a] treats the problem of how efficient outcomes should look like in the absence of lump sum side payments. Some models take into account the possibility of coalition formation (e.g., BARRETT [1991a, 1992a, 1992b, 1992c], HOEL [1992b]), but others assume full cooperation. Almost all authors stress the importance of equity and income distribution considerations, but mostly one sticks to rather ad hoc equity concepts (BARRETT [1992d], ROSE [1992]). WELSCH [1991] on the other hand illustrates some axiomatic equity concepts.

In the present state of our knowledge, it seems worthwhile to take an agnostic stance and work within a framework, which is sufficiently flexible to accomodate different approaches. One possibility is to look for the maximum of an objective function, which is increasing in the individual (here: national) utility

6. For an exception, see HOEL [1992b].

functions. This implies that we model the international bargaining process as a maximization exercise:

$$\max_{R_1,\ldots,R_n} \quad W[\ U\{y_1^0, y_1^1\}, \ldots, U\{y_n^0, y_n^1\}\ ] \tag{4}$$

It is obvious that this approach does not yield a description of the actual bargaining process. However, it would be quite wrong to state that problem (4) only makes sense if there exists an ethically inspired social planner at the international level. Indeed, many other interpretations can be given to the maximization exercise (4)[7]:

1. The first interpretation is the most traditional one, in which we see $W(.)$ as an (ethically inspired) strictly concave *social welfare function*, where the degree of concavity captures our ideas about income distribution. Interpreted in this way, the predictive power of the maximization exercise may be minimal. Indeed, there is no international social planner which could implement the results. However, the exercise has an obvious *normative* appeal, because it yields the optimal solution for an ethical observer with a given set of value judgements. And we can do sensitivity analysis with respect to the degree of inequality aversion. Moreover, as ethical considerations are likely to play a role in negotiations of this kind, the results of similar optimization exercises may (perhaps unconsciously) influence the participants in the negotiations.
2. An interesting special case is the choice of a linear (and, hence, not strictly) concave specification, in which

$$W = \sum_{j=1}^{N} \lambda_j U\{y_j^0, y_j^1\} \qquad \lambda_j > 0 \qquad \sum_{j=1}^{N} \lambda_j = 1 \tag{5}$$

It is well known that in a model with a strictly convex utility possibility frontier, the full set of Pareto efficient points can be found as the solution to the maximization of (5) by varying the λ-vector. This is interesting, since

7. We agree with STERN [1987, p. 47], who writes: 'It should be clear that the approach cannot sensibly be criticized on the grounds that it presupposes a benevolent and monolithic government. A little careful thought makes plain several different and useful interpretations of the approach. It therefore seems rather odd that this last criticism should surface from time to time.'

rational and well-informed negotiators will reach a point on the *Pareto-frontier* as the result of their negotiations. Of course, additional assumptions will be needed to choose between the different points on the frontier. But the maximization of (5) with different values for λ gives us an insight into the characteristics of the bargaining space. Note that (5) does not need to have any ethical connotation: it is not at all necessary to give a greater weight to poorer countries. As a matter of fact, to describe the full set of Pareto efficient points, also solutions with a greater weight for richer countries will have to be calculated.

3. By choosing $\lambda_i = 1$ and $\lambda_j = 0 \quad \forall j \neq i$, we get corner solutions, giving the '*ideal*' negotiation results *for individual country i.*
4. Finally, eq. (4) can be seen as a shortcut to compute many traditional *game-theoretic solutions* to the bargaining process. All cooperative and noncooperative solutions leading to a Pareto efficient result are special cases of (5) (and hence, (4)) and will be recovered in our framework for a specific choice of the λ-vector. Some solution concepts lead directly to a maximization exercise: this is true, for instance, for the Nash-bargaining solution, which basically boils down to one specific choice for the function W in (4) if the threat points are treated parametrically. In general the specification of W may reflect the differential power positions of the different countries. This interpretation readily suggests itself for specification (5), which has already been derived as the outcome of a bargaining game (on taxation), e.g. by AUMANN and KURZ [1977]. The λ-vector then immediately gives the weights in a social power function.

There may be a problem with the latter interpretation. The maximization of W guarantees that we reach a Pareto efficient point, but *not* that we realise a Pareto-improvement with respect to a predetermined threat point (e.g., the Nash-Cournot solution). This can be solved by introducing additional constraints in the problem, stating that no country should become worse off as a result of the agreement. In this paper, we want to concentrate on the ethical and power aspects of the trade-off between efficiency and distribution and our formal treatment will neglect these so-called participation constraints. We will come back to them in our empirical illustrations and explore some theoretical consequences in EYCKMANS, PROOST and SCHOKKAERT [1992].

The interpretation of the maximization process as a result of bargaining leads to an interesting analytical possibility. Instead of solving problem (4) for a given W (i.e., given power weights), we can start from an actual solution and determine the function W (parameterized in one form or another) which is *implicitly* maximized by this actual solution. This gives us an idea about the power weights to be attached to the different countries, if we are willing to interpret their agreement as a maximization exercise. Or, in the linear framework (5): the set of λ_i's which has guided the choice of a specific point on the Pareto-frontier. We will illustrate this so-called *inverse optimum approach* in section 4[8].

3. The Importance of Side Payments

Pareto efficiency can only be defined with respect to a *feasible* set: in our context of public good-provision this implies that the set of Pareto efficient points will be dependent on the *instruments* which are available during the negotiations. The description of the problem therefore has to be completed by a specification of the set of available instruments. Because we want to concentrate in this paper on the equity/efficiency trade-off in its pure form, we will neglect the problem of implementation and assume that the set of instruments to be considered during the negotiations consists of the vector of individual abatement levels R_i, $i = 1,...,n$. Moreover, to illustrate the importance of side payments, we will first assume that these are *not* available[9].

The first-order conditions of problem (4) can then be written as

$$-\frac{\partial W}{\partial U_i}\frac{\partial U}{\partial Y_i^0}MC_i + \sum_{j=1}^{N}\frac{\partial W}{\partial U_j}\frac{\partial U}{\partial Y_j^1}MB_j = 0 \qquad \forall i \in N \tag{6}$$

where the partial derivatives of the W-function boil down to the constants λ in the linear specification (5). Let us now introduce the notation:

$$\tilde{\lambda}_i = \frac{\partial W}{\partial U_i}\frac{\partial U}{\partial Y_i^0} \qquad \forall i \in N \tag{7}$$

It is obvious that $\tilde{\lambda}_i$ gives the marginal weight or the 'social value' attached by the negotiation process to one additional unit of period 0 income in country i. This weight can be interpreted in ethical or in power terms. For the linear case,

8. Interesting examples of the inverse optimum approach in the context of taxation can be found in CHRISTIANSEN and JANSEN [1978] and AHMAD and STERN [1984].

9. This implies the absence of instruments like marketable emission permits for an international carbon tax with lump sum-redistribution of the proceeds.

where $\lambda_i = 1, \forall i$, corresponding to a utilitarian social welfare function or a bargaining process with equal power weights, the social value coincides with the marginal utility of income. Using (7) in (6) we obtain

$$\tilde{\lambda}_i^{SB} MC_i^{SB} = \sum_{j=1}^{N} \tilde{\lambda}_j^{SB} \theta_j^{SB} MB_j^{SB} \qquad \forall i \in N \tag{8}$$

where the superscript '*SB*' refers to the fact that this is only a second-best solution, due to the inavailability of side payments.

The interpretation of eq. (8) is more instructive when we compare it with the solution of the full cooperative (first-best) problem, i.e. the case where the group of negotiating countries dispose of the additional (strong) instrument of lump sum-side payments. The maximization problem can then be formulated as:

$$\max_{R_1,\ldots,R_n,T_1,\ldots,T_n} W\left[\, U\{y_1^0, y_1^1\}, \ldots, U\{y_n^0, y_n^1\} \,\right] \tag{9}$$

$$\text{s.t.} \qquad \sum_{j=1}^{N} T_j = 0 \qquad [\mu]$$

$$\text{with} \quad Y_i^0 = \overline{Y}_i^0 - C_i(R_i) + T_i \quad \text{and} \quad Y_i^1 = \overline{Y}_i^1 + B_i(R) \qquad \forall i \in N$$

The first-order conditions with respect to the abatement levels are the same as in eq. (6). However, now we have in addition the condition with respect to the transfers T_i:

$$\tilde{\lambda}_i = \mu \qquad \forall i \in N \tag{10}$$

where μ is the Lagrange multiplier attached to the constraint in (9). The interpretation of (10) is very straightforward: the lump sum-transfers are used to equalize the marginal social value of income for all countries[10]. As long as the marginal power weights differ, the marginally more powerful country will increase the payment it obtains in the agreement. (Alternatively: as long as the ethical social values differ, social welfare can be increased by a further redistribution of income).

Using (10) in (6) and rewriting, we get the well known first-best-Samuelson condition for the optimal provision of the public good 'emission abatement' (indicated by the superscript '*FB*' for first-best):

$$MC_i^{FB} - \sum_{j=1}^{N} \theta_j^{FB} MB_j^{FB} = 0 \qquad \forall i \in N \tag{11}$$

We now see that there are two important differences between the solutions with and without side payments (equations (11) and (8), respectively). In the first place, the first-best solution is cost-efficient: equation (11) shows that the marginal cost of abatement is the same for all countries. This is not true in (8). In the solution without side payments, what is the same for all countries is $MC_i^{FB}\,\tilde{\lambda}_i^{SB}$. Hence, countries with a high marginal social value of income (poor countries with a high marginal utility of income or countries with a strong power position) will have to abate less. The reason is intuitively obvious: because the international community has no lump sum redistribution instrument at its disposal, differences in abatement costs are used to influence the distribution of welfare. Note that, although this is not cost-efficient in the traditional sense of the world, it *is* a Pareto efficient solution in the sense that it leads to an efficient result in *utility* terms. In the second place, the right-hand-side of (8) indicates that in this pseudo-Samuelson-condition the simple sum of the willingness to pay of the different countries (appearing in the first-best condition (11)) has to be replaced by a weighted sum, where the weights are given by the λ's. Both these results are well known from the second-best-literature.

10. Note that lump sum-payments are used here as (unconstrained) instruments for the maximization of W and, more specifically, play the role of a powerful redistributive instrument. This is not realistic as a description of actual negotiations. Yet, from an ethical point of view it is useful to formalize the necessity of an international redistribution. From a descriptive point of view, we only use the first-best-solution as a point of comparison for the (more realistic) situation where unconstrained side payments are not available. In the literature, it is often stated that side payments are necessary to induce countries to participate in the agreement: this is of course a much more limited objective and not relevant for our treatment, in which we neglect participation constraints. These issues are dealt with in EYCKMANS, PROOST and SCHOKKAERT [1992].

III. COST AND BENEFIT OF EMISSION REDUCTION: AN EMPIRICAL APPROXIMATION

For our empirical application we divide the world into 12 homogeneous blocks of countries. Each of these regions will be interpreted as one player in the game. In *Table 1* we summarize the definition of the regions and some relevant information on their percentage shares in world emissions of CO_2, world GDP and world population. The fourth column reports the carbon emission intensity of production (kg C per $ unit GDP) and the last one gives 1990 per capita GDP ($ per capita) for all regions. As was to be expected, the differences between the regions are immense and even a casual look at the data immediately confronts us with the problem of the international distribution of income.

Table 1

Description of the Regions[11]

	E^0_i emissions %	$\overline{Y}^0_i$ GDP %	n^0_i population %	$E^0_i/\overline{Y}^0_i$ emissions/ GDP	$\overline{Y}^0_i/n^0_i$ GDP/capita
North America	26.446	23.096	5.317	0.278	20391
EC	14.589	17.825	6.589	0.199	12689
other Europe	1.845	2.933	1.711	0.153	8046
Pacific	6.627	8.654	2.861	0.186	14200
former USSR	16.346	8.107	5.534	0.490	6876
Eastern Europe	4.749	2.682	2.327	0.430	5412
Middle East	2.975	2.318	2.305	0.312	4721
China	11.070	12.039	21.441	0.223	2636
Africa	2.991	3.732	12.265	0.195	1428
Latin America	4.717	8.046	8.350	0.142	4523
Developing Asia	3.370	5.329	7.465	0.154	3350
rest Asia	4.274	5.237	23.835	0.198	1031

11. E_i^0 emissions of carbon for 1990 were calculated using fossil fuel consumption data from BP [1991] and emission coefficients form GRUBB [1989]. GDP, population and GDP per capita (in 1988 US $) data for 1990 are based on SUMMERS and HESTON [1991] and take into account the concept of Purchasing Power Parity.

To compute the solutions described in (2), (8) and (11), we tried to use as well as possible the limited information, which is presently available about the benefits and costs of emission reduction for different countries. To incorporate this (monetary) information in a consistent way, we have to reinterpret our two-period-model with nonlinear utility functions. We explain this reinterpretation in section III.1. The information introduced on costs and benefits is then further described in sections III.2 and III.3, respectively.

1. Reinterpretation of the Model

In all our examples the discrete changes (ΔR_i, ΔR) considered amount to relatively limited changes in GDP per capita. We therefore can reasonably assume that the marginal utility of income and the marginal intertemporal rate of substitution remain constant *within that interval*[12]. If we measure emission reduction with respect to the actual level of emissions (i.e., the starting values of R_i,R are zero), we then can write:

$$\Delta U = \frac{\partial U}{\partial Y_i^0}\left\{ \theta_i \int_0^{\Delta R} MB_i dR - \int_0^{\Delta R_i} MC_i dR_i \right\} \tag{12}$$

or, simplified,

$$\Delta U = \frac{\partial U}{\partial Y_i^0}\{\theta_i \Delta B_i - \Delta C_i\} \tag{13}$$

The expression between brackets in (12) and (13) gives a *monetary* evaluation of present costs and (discounted) future benefits. It can be evaluated on the basis of available information, as will become clear in the following subsections. Note that this information is sufficient to calculate the Nash-Cournot and first-best-levels of emission reduction (given by equations (2) and (11)). When lump sum-transfers are not freely available, however, we also need an evaluation of the distributional weights. Specification (13) allows us to combine the marginal utility term (about which there is no 'objective' information) directly

12. This local approximation obviously does not imply that the utility functions are linear over the whole range.

with the (ethical or power) weights λ, so that we can parameterize immediately the vector $\tilde{\lambda}$, defined in (7). This will be explained further when we come to our concrete applications.

2. *Marginal Cost of Carbon Abatement*

A major part of the literature concerning abatement costs consists of simulations of the effects of some particular emission reduction with applied general equilibrium models (see, e.g., WHALLEY and WIGLE [1991], or BURNIAUX et al. [1992]). Hence, these estimates give only a snapshot of reduction costs. However, to evaluate the cost term in (12) or (13), we need a general functional form for the cost of CO_2 emission abatement and this for the 12 regions we distinguish[13].

An attempt to specify such a complete functional form on the basis of empirical information from different studies about abatement costs is presented by NORDHAUS [1991a][14]. He proposes the function:

$$\ln(1 - r_i) = \alpha + \beta MC_i \tag{14}$$

where r_i stands for the percentage emission reduction ($= R_i/E_i^0$) and MC is the associated marginal cost of an additional unit of carbon abatement[15]. For the world as a whole, NORDHAUS estimated α= -0.0223 and β= -0.0054. In this specification, zero reduction implies a slightly negative marginal cost: since there is at present a zero market price for emissions, this implies irrational behaviour by the users of energy. To avoid this complication, we impose the restriction that α=0. The total cost of abating r_i percent of carbon can then easily be shown to be:

$$C_i(R_i) = \left(-\frac{E_i^0}{\beta_i}\right)\{(1 - r_i)\ln(1 - r_i) + r_i\} \tag{15}$$

13. We concentrate on the reduction of CO_2 emissions, because the cheapest greenhouse gases to be abated (the CFC's) have already been the subject of an international agreement to phase them out.

14. The same specification is also used in the empirical work of BARRETT [1992a].

15. All emission figures are expressed in carbon (C) weight. One ton of carbon corresponds to 3.66 tons of carbon dioxide (CO_2).

We used the Nordhaus-functional form for our 12 regions and calibrated the parameters β_i to the simulation results obtained with the OECD-GREEN-model (BURNIAUX et al. [1992]). The advantage of the GREEN-results is their regional disaggregation and the incorporation of general equilibrium effects. We selected as benchmark the results for the year 2010[16]. GREEN aggregates the European Community and the Rest of (OECD-)Europe and also the (former) Soviet Union and Eastern Europe. We disaggregated the marginal costs in function of the carbon emission intensity of production ψ_i, defined as $\psi_i = E_i^0/Y_i^0$ by specifying:

$$\beta_i = \beta \frac{\psi_i}{\overline{\psi}} \tag{16}$$

where β is the aggregate coefficient and $\overline{\psi}$ is a weighted average of the individual ψ_i's (where the weights are the shares in the total emission by the group). For Africa, Latin-America, Developing Asia and the Rest of Asia GREEN does not give cost estimates. For this group of countries we used therefore the aggregate cost estimate by NORDHAUS [1991a] for the world as a whole, and disaggregated the cost functions as described above.

The resulting cost functions are presented in *Figure 1*. They are reported in US$ for 1989 per ton of carbon to make them comparable to the results reported in the literature. The huge differences in these cost functions are as expected. They are strongly correlated with the differences in energy efficiency (internal energy pricing) and with the differences in the carbon intensity of the energy mix. The Pacific region is characterized by the highest marginal cost, mainly because Japan invested heavily in energy efficiency after the oil shock in the seventies. On the other hand, most energy experts agree that both China and the former Soviet Union can abate their carbon emissions at relatively low cost.

16. In fact, the GREEN-results are too rich for our simple static model, because they cover different periods and different types of agreements and policy instruments of emission abatement. Incorporation of these features would require the specification of a much more complex cost function. We selected the data from what they consider to be the central case.

Figure 1

Cost Functions for Reduction of Emissions

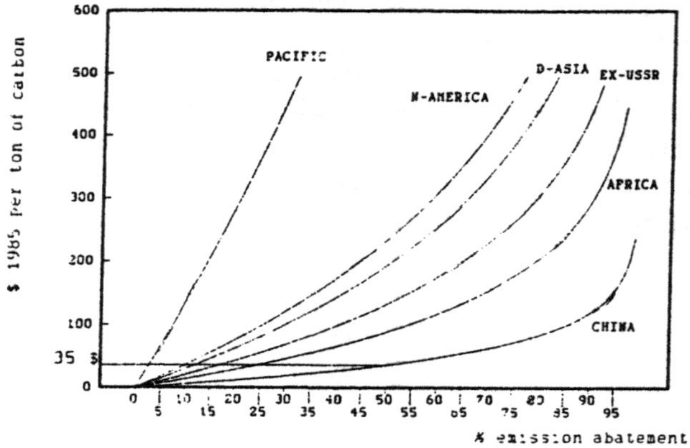

3. Marginal Benefit of Carbon Abatement

To evaluate (12) or (13) we also need a specification for the benefit function of carbon emission reduction for our 12 zones. There is much less information available about benefits (avoided future damage or adaptation costs) than about abatement costs. Benefits are concentrated in the uncertain future. Atmospheric concentrations of greenhouse gases are linked to climatic changes through a complex physical process, the parameters of which are not yet fully known. Moreover, to use NORDHAUS' [1991b] terminology, in addition to the *terra infirma* of climate change there is the *terra incognita* of the social and economic impacts of this climate change. Nothing is known about the functional form of the benefit of emission reduction function. We will adhere to the current practice (see, e.g., MÄLER [1989], BARRETT [1992a]) of taking the simplest possible form, in which country *i*'s benefits are linearly related to world emission reduction *R*:

$$\theta_i B_i(R) = \delta_i . w_i . MB . R \qquad (17)$$

We first describe the estimates of the damages (and, hence, of the marginal benefits, *MB*) related to a doubling of the CO_2 concentration[17]. We then discuss

17. A doubling of the concentration of CO_2 is generally accepted as benchmark case in climate studies and damage estimates.

the problem of disaggregating this world benefit over the various regions by means of the weights w_i in (17). In a third step, we specify a modified discount factor δ_i which is used to push the complex dynamic processes of the real world into our primitive two-period-model.

a. It is almost generally accepted that a doubling of the CO_2 concentration in the atmosphere will, in equilibrium, lead to a temperature increase of, on average 3C (with a range from 1 to 5C) and a rise in the sea level in the range of 3060 cm. NORDHAUS [1991b] has tried to estimate the economic damage from these effects on the basis of data for the United States. He argues that the bulk of US economic activity is only negligibly sensitive to climate change and that even the consequences for agriculture are ambiguous, because the fertilization effect of higher CO_2 levels may compensate the negative effects of the increase in temperature. He estimates these costs to be about 0.25% of US GNP. While he is well aware that there are some remaining and unquantifiable factors, he nevertheless formulates 'a hunch that the overall impact upon human activity is unlikely to be larger than 2% of total output' (NORDHAUS [1991b, p. 933]).
Many other authors argue that these figures underestimate the true damages from global warming (see, e.g., DALY et al. [1991] and PEARCE [1991]). Using a methodology similar to the one of NORDHAUS, but with different land prices and vulnerability coefficients, AYRES and WALTER [1991] obtain figures which are about ten times higher than NORDHAUS' central estimate (and slightly above its upper limit) and they argue that even in their calculations important aspects (e.g., the problem of environmental refugees) are not treated adequately. For our own empirical exercise, we will take their central estimate of approximately 35 $ per ton of carbon abated as our benchmark case for *MB* in (17).
b. A main problem with the NORDHAUS approach (and one which he mentions himself quite explicitly) is the extrapolation of the US situation to the rest of the world, where the structure of GNP (and more specifically also of the energy sector) and the expected climatic changes may be quite different. According to climatologists, the temperature increase (always as a consequence of doubling the CO_2 concentration in the atmosphere) can vary regionally between -3 and +10C. But they are far from unanimous in their prediction of the actual interregional distribution. This implies that *a fortiori* there will be no unanimity about the economic evaluation of the disaggregated benefits. For our empirical work we assumed that the share of country i in global abatement benefits is a function of vulnerability variables z_i. We started, like BARRETT [1992a], from the assumption that $w(z_i)$, the share of

country i in total damage due to climate change, is given by $w_i = GDP_i / GDP_{world}$[18].

c. Until now, we only concentrated on the damage associated with a doubling of CO_2 concentrations in the atmosphere. The question remains how to link the evaluation of a (stock) situation far in the future to the complex dynamic process following the actual (reduction in the) emission flow of one unit of CO_2. Future benefits of such a reduction are dependent on physical parameters, relating to the time delay in the reaction of the climate to changing atmospheric concentrations (as a consequence of the thermal inertia of the oceans) and to the natural rate of carbon decay (determining the residence time of CO_2 in the atmosphere). An emission reduction now will, given an average time lag of 50 years and a residence time for CO_2 of 200 years, generate benefits in the years 2050-2250. To get an estimate of the benefits of reducing the emissions of CO_2 by one unit, we need to aggregate the (discounted) future damages for all the years a unit of CO_2 is active in the atmosphere.

It is difficult to capture all these considerations adequately in our primitive two-period model but an interesting way out is suggested by NORDHAUS [1991b]. He formulates a dynamic emission model, incorporating the main physical features of the greenhouse problem. Assuming that the economy is in a resource steady-state, i.e. that all physical flows in the global economy are constant, he derives an expression for a general discount factor δ_i which aggregates the damage in all future years caused by the current emission of one unit of carbon. The factor δ_i contains both economic and physical parameters.

Concerning the *physical* parameters, the discount rate δ_i depends upon (1) the time lag between carbon emissions and the induced temperature change, (2) the atmospheric residence time of CO_2, (3) the airborne fraction of carbon dioxide emissions, and (4) the linearized equilibrium increase in global mean temperature in response to increasing CO_2 concentrations. The discount rate δ_i is lower for a long time lag, for a high natural rate of carbon decay in the atmosphere, for a low airborne fraction or low equilibrium temperature increase (see NORDHAUS [1991b]).

Important economic variables in δ_i are (1) the growth rate of per capita income h, (2) the real discount rate on goods d, and (3) the pure rate of society's time preference. Nordhaus shows that the discount factor δ_i is determined by physical parameters and by the difference between d and h. In *Table 2* (inspired by table 3 in NORDHAUS [1991b, p. 927]) we illustrate this relationship. The

18. The results of sensitivity analysis w.r.t. $w(z_i)$ can be obtained from the authors.

second column shows values of the discount factor δ_i for different values of d-h. The other columns represent discounted marginal benefit of CO_2 emission abatement for different estimates of climate damage. Damage is assumed to range from 0.25% to 5% of GDP.

Table 2

Discount Rates and Marginal Benefit of Abatement

		damage as % of GDP						
d-h	δ	0.25	0.50	1.00	2.00	3.00	4.00	5.00
0	0.500	8.25	16.50	33.00	66.00	99.00	132.00	165.00
1	0.111	1.83	3.67	7.33	14.67	22.00	29.33	36.67
2	0.050	0.83	1.65	3.30	6.60	9.90	13.20	16.50
3	0.029	0.47	0.94	1.89	3.77	5.66	7.54	9.43
4	0.019	0.31	0.61	1.22	2.44	3.67	4.89	6.11

While NORDHAUS proposes this approach for the world as a whole, we will also apply it to each of our regions separately. It can be shown that δ_i will be larger if $(d$-$h)$ is smaller. This implies that countries will value the future benefits of actual abatement more if their pure rate of time preference is smaller[19] or if their expected growth rate is lower.

IV. SOME EMPIRICAL APPLICATIONS

In this section we show some numerical results for 'realistic' values of the parameters[20]. To get a better feeling for the model we first present the Nash-Cournot solution for our benchmark case in section IV.1. We then illustrate our maximization framework with two applications. In the first one we follow the traditional welfare economic approach in which the objective function W is interpreted as a social welfare function. By varying the distributive values

19. It can be argued that society's pure rate of time preference should be equal to zero in an intergenerational context.

20. If one accepts the specifications (14) and (23) it is not difficult to derive the different solutions analytically. This is illustrated in the appendix.

embodied in W, we get a better insight into the equity/efficiency-trade-off from an ethical point of view. The differences between first-best and second-best solutions will turn out to be crucial. The second application is in line with a bargaining approach, where W is interpreted as a social power function. We will compute the implicit power weights leading to a cost-efficient solution without side payments and to a Toronto-type agreement.

1. The Benchmark: Nash-Cournot Equilibrium

For our benchmark case we choose what we consider to be the most 'realistic' approximations. For the cost functions we use the ones calibrated on the GREEN-model and illustrated in *Figure 1*. The overall discounted marginal benefit of emission reduction is taken to be 35 $ per ton of carbon (taken from AYRES and WALTER [1991])[21]. This benefit is distributed over the various regions in proportion to their share in world GDP[22].

The results for the Nash-Cournot solution are given in *Table 3*. The first column shows the emission reduction (in percentage of the initial emissions); the second column shows the marginal cost of abatement in $ per ton of carbon, and the third column is the net payoff (discounted benefits minus costs of abatement) per capita. It is not exaggerated to say that there is almost *no* reduction of emissions in this case and that (as a logical consequence) there is hardly any change in the base line growth of GNP[23]. The differences in emission reduction efforts are determined by the shares of the regions in global abatement benefits (i.e., their shares in world GDP in our approximation), and by the convexity of their cost functions. The lack of efficiency is illustrated in the second column, showing the marginal costs of emission reduction for the different countries, as evaluated in the Nash-Cournot equilibrium. The results suggest that there is a clear rationale for international coordination of abatement policies. The same global emission reduction could be attained at a lower total cost.

21. If we take the discount rates δ_i to be the same for all countries and equal to the average value of 0.111, this amounts to a damage of doubling the CO_2 concentration of about 5% of GNP. (But if δ_i would be equal to 0.5, implying $(d\text{-}h)$ to be equal to zero, the same result is obtained by a damage of only slightly more than 1% of GNP.)

22. Of course, we have performed a sensitivity analysis with respect to the cost and benefit parameters and the international distribution of benefits. The results are in line with what could be expected. They are available from the authors on request.

23. Notice that the Nash-Cournot solution would yield even smaller reductions if we considered all countries individually instead of aggregating some of them in artificial coalitions.

Table 3

Noncooperative Nash-Cournot Solution

	R_i^{NC} %	MC_i^{NC}	net payoff per capita
North America	2.364	8.084	3.287
EC	1.634	6.239	2.255
other Europe	0.203	1.027	1.509
Pacific	0.236	3.029	2.656
former USSR	1.933	2.837	1.198
Eastern Europe	0.564	0.939	1.009
Middle East	0.482	0.811	0.833
China	7.846	4.214	0.399
Africa	0.476	1.306	0.267
Latin America	0.752	2.816	0.842
Developing Asia	0.536	1.865	0.626
rest Asia	0.701	1.833	0.192
World	2.206		0.816

2. *Application 1: Varying the Degree of Inequality Aversion*

As a first application of our maximization approach, we will compute the optimal results for a given specification of W, interpreted as a social welfare function. As noted before, this could be the optimal policy to be implemented by a (hypothetical) international social planner, *or* it gives us a first insight into the ethical aspects of the trade-off between efficiency and distribution in international greenhouse negotiations. All cost and benefit functions are specified as in the benchmark Nash-Cournot-case.

Combining (13) and (7) it is immediately obvious that the changes in monetary costs and benefits for the different countries are to be weighted by their 'social value' in the calculation of the optimal solutions. This social value is a combination of the social welfare evaluation of marginal increases in the utility of country i ($\partial W/\partial U_i$ or, in the linear case, λ_i) and the marginal utility of income. Both are unobservable values, of course, and different combinations will lead to the same set of $\tilde{\lambda}_i$'s. We therefore follow a procedure which is quite common in the second-best literature and parameterize $\tilde{\lambda}_i$ directly by the general form:

$$\tilde{\lambda}_i = \left\{\frac{\overline{y}_i^0}{\overline{y}_p^0}\right\}^{-\varepsilon} = \left\{\frac{\overline{Y}_i^0 / n_i^0}{\overline{Y}_p^0 / n_p^0}\right\}^{-\varepsilon} \qquad \forall i \in N \tag{18}$$

where $\overline{y}_i^0$ is the base line GDP per capita in period 0 for country i and the subscript p refers to the poorest country (which thus gets a weight equal to one for all values of ε[24]). Specification (18) may result from the assumption of constant elasticity of marginal utility (with this elasticity given by ε) for the utility function and the restriction that $\lambda_i = 1\ \forall i$. But it could as well follow from the combination of linear utility functions with a concave parameterization of social welfare W as a function of GDP per capita.

Table 4

Distributional Weights

	$\varepsilon = 0.00$	$\varepsilon = 0.10$	$\varepsilon = 0.25$	$\varepsilon = 0.50$	$\varepsilon = 1.00$	$\varepsilon = 1.50$	$\varepsilon = 2.00$
North America	1.000	0.742	0.474	0.225	0.051	0.011	0.003
EC	1.000	0.778	0.534	0.285	0.081	0.023	0.007
other Europe	1.000	0.814	0.598	0.358	0.128	0.046	0.016
Pacific	1.000	0.769	0.519	0.270	0.073	0.020	0.005
former USSR	1.000	0.827	0.622	0.387	0.150	0.058	0.022
Eastern Europe	1.000	0.847	0.661	0.437	0.191	0.083	0.036
Middle East	1.000	0.859	0.684	0.467	0.219	0.102	0.048
China	1.000	0.910	0.791	0.626	0.392	0.245	0.153
Africa	1.000	0.968	0.922	0.850	0.722	0.614	0.521
Latin America	1.000	0.863	0.691	0.478	0.228	0.109	0.052
Developing Asia	1.000	0.889	0.745	0.555	0.308	0.171	0.095
rest Asia	1.000	1.000	1.000	1.000	1.000	1.000	1.000

24. This is a simple normalization rule.

The parameter ε is often called the degree of inequality aversion. Although the theoretical framework allows for any (positive or negative) relationship between $\tilde{\lambda}_i$ and GDP per capita, we will restrict ourselves in this first (social welfare) application to the case where $\varepsilon \geq 0$. If $\varepsilon = 0$, all countries get an equal weight (= 1). For increasing ε, a smaller and smaller weight will be attached to the richer countries. In *Table 4* we show the pattern of weights for different values of ε. It has sometimes been argued that $\varepsilon \approx 1.5$ is a reasonable value for the degree of inequality aversion (see, e.g., STERN [1976]). Note that within this context of huge international income differences, this would imply that one considers almost exclusively the welfare position of the poorest countries.

Table 5

First-Best Solution (Before Side Payments)

	R_i^{FB} %	MC_i^{FB}	net payoff per capita
North America	9.841	35.000	18.581
EC	8.826	35.000	13.710
other Europe	6.695	35.000	9.697
Pacific	2.693	35.000	18.387
former USSR	21.500	35.000	-2.609
Eastern Europe	19.027	35.000	-0.001
Middle East	18.800	35.000	1.849
China	49.270	35.000	-0.865
Africa	11.993	35.000	1.403
Latin America	8.954	35.000	5.258
Developing Asia	9.589	35.000	3.782
rest Asia	12.576	35.000	0.985
World	16.249		3.424

Let us now first look at the first-best solution, as given in *Table 5*. As we will discuss later on, the per capita payoff levels in this table have to be interpreted carefully. The results for the optimal (percentage) reduction of emissions are given in the first column. There is a striking difference with the Nash-Cournot solution: the overall level of emission reduction for the world should be almost

17%[25]. The efforts required from China and Eastern Europe are especially large: this follows immediately from their low marginal costs. Cost considerations also lead to the almost complete freedom left for the Pacific. As shown in the second column, marginal abatement costs are equalized in this first-best solution. Note that there is a huge discrepancy between the solution in *Table 5* and the often proposed 'equal percentage reduction'-rule. It is well known that the latter rule is cost-inefficient if abatement costs differ between countries.

The third column in *Table 5* gives the net payoffs in the first-best case. This column has to be interpreted carefully. The implementation of the full set of first-best 'optimal' lump sum transfers, as given by condition (10), would require a huge international income redistribution. To give an extreme example: in the linear case for $\lambda_i = \lambda \ \ \forall i$ the world income distribution should become completely equal. This is an extremely unrealistic solution (the big losers would never be willing to participate in that agreement)[26]. Moreover, our linear approximation, as described in section III.1, can no longer be assumed to hold for such large income changes. Therefore, *Table 5* gives the payoffs, following from the abatement policy itself, and *without* implementing the optimal lump sum transfer scheme. One observes immediately that this solution (without side payments) is not individually rational for the former Soviet Union, Eastern Europe and China, who all have a per capita payoff below the Nash-Cournot level. Even disregarding all equity considerations they will only be willing to participate in the world agreement if they are adequately compensated for their effort.

If the lump sum instrument is not available we will have to resort to the second-best solution (8). It is immediately obvious from (8) that in the special case where ε is equal to zero and, hence, $\tilde{\lambda}_i = 1 \ \ \forall i$, this second-best solution coincides with the first-best solution without side payments, as shown in *Table 5*. Indeed, this is the situation where distributional considerations do not matter in the social welfare function (which then boils down to the maximization of world income). In general, however, distributional considerations will play a crucial role in the determination of individual abatement efforts. *Table 6* shows the results for increasing values of ε, i.e., an increasing degree of inequality aversion.

25. This figure can be compared with the reductions proposed in the Toronto-agreement. These are in general much larger, which means that the (implicit) evaluation of marginal benefits also must be larger. This has been for us an additional argument to work with larger benefit estimates than the ones proposed by NORDHAUS [1991b].

26. This is perhaps not so big a disadvantage in an *ethical* interpretation of our results. It nicely illustrates that the present world income is completely inacceptable if one is inequality averse.

Table 6

Second-Best Solutions

	$\varepsilon = 0.25$			$\varepsilon = 0.50$			$\varepsilon = 1.00$			$\varepsilon = 1.50$			$\varepsilon = 2.00$		
	R_i	MCi	payoff	R_i	MC_i	payoff	R_i	MC_i	payoff	R_i	MC_i	payoff	R_i	MCi	payoff
North America	12.83	46.38	11.29	17.51	65.04	-1.65	36.24	152.05	-102.37	72.49	436.00	-637.83	98.64	1451.65	-1673.60
EC	10.31	41.20	12.04	12.67	51.32	10.42	22.12	94.68	0.99	43.20	214.25	-61.60	77.37	562.90	-353.01
other Europe	7.02	36.76	9.40	7.77	40.85	9.76	11.20	60.00	12.63	19.26	108.08	15.73	36.08	226.04	-4.90
Pacific	3.25	42.37	17.54	4.15	54.27	17.68	7.93	105.88	18.51	17.93	253.37	-8.50	42.25	703.94	-283.94
former USSR	21.58	35.35	-2.96	22.88	37.77	-3.94	29.73	51.27	-9.91	44.42	85.38	-33.69	67.88	165.07	-118.30
Eastern Europe	18.19	33.29	0.56	18.29	33.50	0.97	22.00	40.35	1.49	30.19	59.61	-0.81	46.02	102.24	-21.25
Middle East	17.42	32.18	2.44	16.99	31.29	3.07	18.90	35.20	5.06	25.10	48.57	7.93	37.06	77.81	4.77
China	41.68	27.81	0.48	36.45	23.38	1.51	31.69	19.65	3.75	32.49	20.26	7.39	37.52	24.25	11.14
Africa	8.34	23.86	1.67	6.09	17.21	1.93	3.81	10.65	2.91	2.91	8.08	4.95	2.57	7.12	7.35
Latin America	8.18	31.83	5.34	7.88	30.63	5.80	8.64	33.73	8.45	11.49	45.55	14.14	17.42	71.42	19.47
Dev. Asia	8.15	29.53	3.96	7.31	26.36	4.38	6.94	24.99	6.51	8.03	29.05	11.11	10.68	39.20	16.24
rest Asia	8.10	22.00	1.23	5.46	14.63	1.42	2.91	7.69	2.12	1.89	4.96	3.59	1.42	3.71	5.32
World	16.02		3.30	17.08		2.86	24.38		-2.17	41.04		-34.59	60.70		-119.98

The pattern is clear for the richest and the poorest countries. North-America, the European Community, Other Europe and the Pacific have to make a greater and greater abatement effort if they get a smaller and smaller weight in the overall objective function. At the other extreme we see a lower and lower effort for Africa and Rest of Asia. For values of ε below 1.00 the emission reduction of China and Developing Asia are decreasing, for higher values of inequality aversion, however, they have to abate more. The effort of the other regions first remains about constant (or increases a little bit) but they have to make greater effort if ε grows above 0.5. The intuition is obvious, when one looks at the distributional weights in *Table 4*. For large values of ε, the objective function gets completely dominated by the poorest regions only (Africa and the Rest of Asia, including Bangla Desh and India).

Table 6 shows the huge differences in marginal abatement costs in the 'optimal' second-best solution. For small values of ε, the overall abatement effort does not differ very much from the firstbest optimum. Only the distribution changes. When ε starts growing above 0.5, however, the total abatement level increases sharply. The reason was already hinted at in section 2. Given the unavailability of direct income transfers, the poor countries use the greenhouse agreement to redistribute purchasing power. Indeed they make almost no abatement efforts but still receive the benefits of reduced climate change. From a first-best perspective, this policy is extremely inefficient. In a second-best world with a very unequal international income distribution, however, it is quite understandable.

The results for the net monetary payoffs are in line with the 'optimal' abatement efforts. The payoffs of the richer countries decrease and for North-America it soon becomes negative. On the other hand, the net monetary payoff for China becomes positive for increasing ε. The results for the former Soviet Union and Eastern Europe remain negative throughout. The second-best solution tends to penalize the countries which have a low ratio of energy efficiency over GDP. Note that the change in world GDP as a consequence of the greenhouse policies decreases as compared to the first-best solution and for large ε even becomes negative: this is a measure of the cost to be paid for a more equal world distribution.

It is worthwhile emphasizing that there is not one solution in *Tables 5* and *6* which gives a positive net payoff for *all* countries involved. This means that it will not be possible for sovereign nations to reach an international agreement over any of these solutions. To find a more realistic blueprint for an agreement, we will have to add participation constraints (see EYCKMANS, PROOST and SCHOKKAERT [1992]). Again, for the social welfare interpretation in this section, this is not much of a problem. Moreover, our application gives a better insight into the bargaining space for these negotiations.

3. Application 2: the Inverse Optimum Approach

Rather than using our approach to prescribe or predict a distribution of efforts, we can also start from a given international agreement and then determine the objective function which could rationalize (or: underlies implicitly) that agreement. We therefore assume that the negotiators used the same commonly available information on cost functions and the same benefit distribution as we do (namely proportional to GDP). The given vector of emission reductions is then used to compute the relevant marginal costs for the different countries: inserting this information in (8) (for an agreement without side payments) allows us to calculate the set of implicit relative welfare weights $\tilde{\lambda}_i$, $i = 1,...,n$ (subject to a normalization) and the implicit estimate of the overall marginal benefit level.

We can go somewhat further with this interpretation. As emphasized before, the marginal social value of one unit of income for country i $(\bar{\lambda})_i$ is the product of the weight in the social welfare function and the marginal utility of income. If we accept for convenience the linear specification (5), this gives:

$$\tilde{\lambda} = \lambda_i \frac{\partial U}{\partial Y_i^0} \qquad \forall i \in N \tag{19}$$

Disentangling the power weight and the marginal utility of income requires the specification of the utility function. As an illustration, let us assume that all countries are in a steady state with respect to income and that their social welfare can be specified (in line with eq. (18)) with a constant elasticity of marginal utility function[27]:

$$\text{for } \varepsilon \neq 1: \quad U_i = \frac{k}{1-\varepsilon}\left[\frac{Y_i^0 - C_i(R_i) + \delta_i w_i MB}{n_i^0}\right]^{1-\varepsilon} \qquad \forall i \in N \tag{20a}$$

27. For this specification of the utility function the marginal rate of intertemporal substitution θ_i, is constant and independent of per capita income.

$$\text{for } \varepsilon = 1: \qquad U_i = k \ln\left[\frac{\overline{Y}_i^0 - C_i(R_i) + \delta_i w_i MB}{n_i^0}\right] \qquad \forall i \in N \tag{20b}$$

where the constant k is used for normalization. For this specification of the utility function the first-order condition (10) becomes:

$$\tilde{\lambda}_i = \lambda_i \left[\frac{\overline{Y}_i^0 - C_i(R_i) + \delta_i w_i MB}{n_i^0}\right]^{-\varepsilon} \left[\frac{1}{n_i^0}\right] = \mu \qquad \forall i \in N \tag{21}$$

The use of this procedure allows us to derive information about the λ-vector, i.e., about the relative distribution of power leading to the agreement[28].

We give two examples. The first is representative for the type of Toronto-like international agreements that we have seen in recent years. We consider an (hypothetical) international carbon protocol, requiring the industrial countries to make much larger abatement efforts (25% carbon emission reduction to be reached in 2010 w.r.t. 1990 emission levels) than the developing countries (1% emission reduction). The implied marginal costs and λ are given in the first part of *Table 7*. The results of this exercise are straightforward: we get very low welfare weights for the OECD countries and certainly for those with higher abatement costs. The overall abatement level is 18% which is comparable in size with our base case and the implicit marginal benefit of carbon abatement equals 28 $/ton, lower than our benchmark of 35 $.

As a second example we consider the cost-efficient solution, maximizing world income: in the previous subsection, we have called this the first-best solution without side payments, and we have argued that it is only optimal for a function W, leading to an identical $\tilde{\lambda}_i$ for all countries. Equation (19) shows why equal $\tilde{\lambda}_i$'s for all countries are difficult to accept from an ethical point of view: this indeed implies that the power weights λ_i are inversely proportional to the marginal utility of income, i.e., that the richer countries get a proportionally larger power weight.

This is illustrated in *Table 7* for different values of ε. The figures show that the cost-efficient agreement implies large differences in power weights. Recalling (21) it is obvious that for ε = 0.00 the implied welfare weights λ_i are equal

28. Instead of calculating the welfare weights $\tilde{\lambda}_i$, one could also determine the individual valuation of abatement benefits $w_i\theta_i MB$ which is implied by a given carbon agreement

Table 7

Inverse Optimum Solutions

			$\varepsilon = 0.00$	$\varepsilon = 0.50$	$\varepsilon = 1.00$	$\varepsilon = 1.50$			$\varepsilon = 0.00$	$\varepsilon = 0.50$	$\varepsilon = 1.00$	$\varepsilon = 1.50$
	R_i	MC_i	λ_i	λ_i	λ_i	λ_i	R_i	MC_i	λ_i	λ_i	λ_i	λ_i
North America	25.00	97.19	0.006	0.027	0.118	0.524	9.841	35.00	0.223	0.992	4.410	19.607
EC	25.00	108.97	0.007	0.023	0.082	0.286	8.826	35.00	0.276	0.970	3.404	11.944
other Europe	25.00	145.29	0.001	0.004	0.010	0.028	6.695	35.00	0.072	0.201	0.560	1.565
Pacific	25.00	368.82	0.001	0.003	0.012	0.043	2.693	35.00	0.120	0.445	1.653	6.134
former USSR	25.00	41.81	0.015	0.037	0.097	0.249	21.400	35.00	0.232	0.599	1.546	3.989
Eastern Europe	25.00	47.71	0.005	0.012	0.028	0.064	19.027	35.00	0.098	0.223	0.512	1.172
Middle East	25.00	48.35	0.005	0.011	0.024	0.051	18.800	35.00	0.097	0.207	0.442	0.946
China	0.01	0.52	4.542	7.261	11.607	18.555	49.270	35.00	0.900	1.437	2.296	3.668
Africa	0.01	2.75	0.489	0.576	0.677	0.797	11.993	35.00	0.515	0.606	0.713	0.839
Latin America	0.01	3.75	0.245	0.512	1.072	2.245	8.954	35.00	0.350	0.734	1.537	3.218
Developing Asia	0.01	3.49	0.235	0.423	0.763	1.376	9.589	35.00	0.313	0.565	1.018	1.834
rest Asia	0.01	2.62	1.000	1.000	1.000	1.000	12.576	35.00	1.000	1.000	1.000	1.000
World	18.66						16.249					

to the shares of the regions in world population (the values reported in *Table 7* are normalized such that the weight of R-Asia equals 1).

V. CONCLUSION

Starting point for this paper was the observation that arguments concerning equity and the international distribution of income are likely to play an important role in multilateral negotiations on a carbon treaty. We used a welfare maximization framework to illustrate differences between the benchmark noncooperative outcome and the first- and second-best solutions in an international carbon emission game. This maximization framework allows for ethical or bargaining power interpretations, and can be used to solve the inverse optimum solution, i.e., compute the social welfare weights implied by a given carbon emission abatement agreement. If lump sum redistribution of income is impossible at world scale, the traditional cost-efficient abatement agreement need not be optimal. The Samuelson rule for the optimal provision of greenhouse gas abatement is replaced by the condition that weighted marginal abatement costs should be equalized across all countries. Weighted marginal costs should equal the weighted sum of discounted marginal benefits.

A highly stylized two-period simulation model with 12 aggregate regions was used to illustrate the different solution concepts and interpretations of the welfare maximizing framework for the case of an international carbon emission game. In the noncooperative Nash-Cournot outcome, emissions of carbon were reduced by only 2% whereas the first-best optimal reduction amounts almost 17%. If side payments are not available distributional considerations start to play. For a high degree of inequality aversion the poorest regions (India, Bangladesh, Africa,...) have to abate less than in the first-best reference case and the carbon agreement is used to redistribute income. No emission reduction scheme was found which made all regions better off compared to the Nash-Cournot situation. The inverse optimum solution for a Toronto-type of agreement yields a high bargaining power weight for China and a cost-efficient emission reduction agreement would imply high weights for OECD countries if one is inequality averse.

We are well aware of the theoretical and empirical limitations of the approach. As hinted in section IV participation constraints are to be taken into account if one wants to propose an acceptable carbon agreement. Also the assumption that negotiations relate directly to emission abatement efforts is questionable. Rather a carbon tax or tradable permit system is likely to be negotiated.

EFFICIENCY AND DISTRIBUTION IN GREENHOUSE NEGOTIATIONS

REFERENCES

AYRES, R.U. and WALTER, J.: 'The Greenhouse Effect: Damages, Costs and Abatement', *Environmental and Resource Economics*, Vol. 1 (1991), pp. 237-270.

AHMAD, E. and STERN, N.: 'The Theory of Tax Reform and Indian Indirect Taxes', *Journal of Public Economics*, Vol. 25 (1984), pp. 259-298.

AUMANN, RJ and KURZ, M.: 'Power and Taxes', *Econometrica*, Vol. 45 (1977), pp. 1137-1162.

BARRETT, S.: 'The Paradox of International Environmental Agreements', mimeo, London Business School, 1991a.

BARRETT, S.: 'Economic Analysis of International Environmental Agreements: Lessons for a Global Warming Treaty', in: OECD (ed.), *Responding to Climate Change, Selected Economic Issues*, Paris: OECD, 1991b.

BARRETT, S.: 'Reaching a CO_2 Emission Limitation Agreement for the Community: Implications for Equity and Cost-effectiveness' *European Economy, Special Edition No. 1*, (1992a).

BARRETT, S.: 'Convention on Climate Change: Economic Aspects of Negotiations', in: OECD (ed.), *Negotiating a Framework Convention on Climate Change: Economic Considerations*, Paris: OECD, 1992b.

BARRETT, S.: 'International Environmental Agreements as Games', in: PETHIG, R. (ed.), *Conflicts and Cooperation in Managing Environmental Resources*, Berlin: Springer Verlag, 1992c.

BARRETT, S.: 'Acceptable' Allocations of Tradeable Carbon Emission Entitlements in a Global Warming Treaty', in: UNCTAD (ed.), *Combating Global Warming: Study on a Global System of Tradeable Carbon Emission Entitlements*, New York: UNCTAD, 1992d.

BOHM, P.: 'Efficiency Issues and the Montreal Protocol on CFC's', Environment Working Paper, No. 40, World Bank, 1990.

BP: *BP Statistical Review of World Energy*, London: BP, 1991.

BURNIAUX, J.M. et al.: 'The Costs of Reducing CO_2 Emissions: Evidence from GREEN', OECD Working Paper, No. 115, 1992.

CHRISTIANSEN, V. and JANSEN, E.S.: 'Implicit Social Preferences in the Norwegian System of Indirect Taxation', *Journal of Public Economics*, Vol. 10 (1978), pp. 217-245.

CLINE, W.R.: 'Scientific Basis for the Greenhouse Effect', *Economic Journal*, Vol. 101 (1991), pp. 904-919.

DALY, G.; EHRLICH, P.R.; MOONEY, H.A. and EHRLICH, A.H.: 'Greenhouse Economics: Learn Before You Leap', *Ecological Economics*, Vol. 4 (1991), pp. 1-10.

EYCKMANS, J.; PROOST, S. and SCHOKKAERT, E.: 'Tax Instruments and Participation Constraints in Greenhouse Negotiations', Discussion paper, Center for Economic Studies, K.U. Leuven, 1992.

FRIEDMAN, J.: *Game Theory with Applications to Economics*, Oxford: Oxford University Press, 1986.

GRUBB, M.: 'The Greenhouse Effect: Negotiation Targets', mimeo, London: Royal Institute for International Affairs, 1989.

HOEL, M.: 'Global Environmental Problems: the Effects of Unilateral Action Taken by One Country', *Journal of Environmental Economics and Management*, Vol. 20 (1991a), pp. 55-70.

HOEL, M.: 'Efficient International Agreements for Reducing Emissions of CO_2', *Energy Journal*, Vol. 12 (1991b), pp. 93-107.

HOEL, M.: 'Emission Taxes in a Dynamic Game of CO_2 emissions', in: PETHIG, R. (ed.), *Conflicts and Cooperation in Managing Environmental Resources*, Berlin: Springer Verlag, 1992a.

HOEL, M.: 'International Environment Conventions: the Case of Uniform Reductions of Emissions', *Environmental and Resource Economics*, Vol. 2 (1992b), pp. 141-159.

IPCC: *Climate Change: the IPCC Scientific Assessment*, Cambridge: Cambridge University Press, 1990.

KOSOBUD, R.F. and DALY, T.: 'Global Conflict or Cooperation over the CO_2 Climate Impact?', *Kyklos*, Vol. 37 (1984), pp. 638-659.

MÄLER, K.G.: 'The Acid Rain Game', in: FOLMER, H. and VAN IERLAND, E. (eds.), *Valuation Methods and Policy Making in Environmental Economics*, Amsterdam: Elsevier, 1989.

MARTIN, W.E.; PATRICK, R.H. and TOLWINSKI, B.: 'A Dynamic Game of CO_2 Emissions with Asymmetric Players', paper presented at the Meeting of the European Association of Environmental and Resource Economists, Stockholm, 1991.

NORDHAUS, W.D.: 'The Cost of Slowing Climate Change: A Survey', *Energy Journal*, Vol. 12 (1991a), pp. 37-65.

NORDHAUS, W.D.: 'To Slow or Not to Slow: the Economics of the Greenhouse Effect', *Economic Journal*, Vol. 101 (1991b), pp. 920-937.

PEARCE, D.: 'The Global Commons', in: PEARCE, D. (ed.), *Blueprint 2: Greening the World Economy*, London: Earthscan Publications, 1991.

ROSE, A.: 'Equity Considerations of Tradeable Carbon Emission Entitlements', in: UNCTAD (ed.), *Combating Global Warming: Study on a Global System of Tradeable Carbon Emission Entitlements*, New York: UNCTAD, 1992.

STERN, N.: 'The Marginal Valuation of Income', in: ARTIS, M.J. and NOBAY, A.R. (eds.), *Essays in Economic Analysis*, Cambridge: Cambridge University Press, 1976, pp. 209-254.

STERN, N.: 'The Theory of Optimal Commodity and Income Taxation: An Introduction', in: NEWBERY, D. and STERN, N. (eds.), *The Theory of Taxation for Developing Countries*, Oxford: Oxford University Press, 1987, pp. 22-59.

SUMMERS, R. and HESTON, A.: 'The PENN World Table (Mark 5): an Expanded Set of International Comparisons 1950-1988', *Quarterly Journal of Economics* (1991), pp. 327-368.

VAN DER PLOEG, F. and DE ZEEUW, A.J.: 'International Aspects of Pollution Control', *Environmental and Resource Economics*, Vol. 2 (1992), pp. 117-139.

WELSCH, H.: 'Equity and Efficiency in International CO2 Agreements', mimeo, Cologne University: Institute of Energy Economics, 1991.

WHALLEY, J. and WIGLE, R.: 'Cutting CO_2 Emissions: the Effect of Alternative Policy Approaches', *Energy Journal*, Vol. 12 (1991), pp. 109-124.

APPENDIX

Using the specification of the cost function (15) with $\alpha = 0$ and the marginal benefit function (17), it is immediately obvious that the optimality conditions (2), (11) and (8), respectively, can be written as:

$$\frac{1}{\beta_i} \ln(1 - r_i^{NC}) = w_i \theta_i^{NC} MB \tag{A1}$$

$$\frac{1}{\beta_i} \ln(1 - r_i^{FB}) = MB \sum_{j=1}^{N} w_j \theta_j^{FB} \tag{A2}$$

EFFICIENCY AND DISTRIBUTION IN GREENHOUSE NEGOTIATIONS

$$\frac{1}{\beta_i}\ln(1-r_i^{SB}) = MB\sum_{j=1}^{N}\frac{\tilde{\lambda}_j^{SB}}{\tilde{\lambda}_i^{SB}}\theta_j^{SB}w_j \tag{A3}$$

Taking approximations, and using the notation $w_i\theta_i = \tilde{w}_i$, we get

$$r_i^{NC} \approx -\beta_i\tilde{w}_i^{NC}MB \tag{A4}$$

$$r_i^{FB} \approx -\beta_i MB\sum_{j=1}^{N}\tilde{w}_j^{FB} \tag{A5}$$

$$r_i^{SB} \approx -\beta_i MB\sum_{j=1}^{N}\frac{\tilde{\lambda}_j^{SB}\tilde{w}_j^{SB}}{\tilde{\lambda}_i^{SB}} \tag{A6}$$

These equations imply some rather striking results. Combining (A4) and (A5) we get

$$\frac{r_i^{NC}}{r_i^{FB}} \approx \frac{\tilde{w}_i^{NC}}{\sum_j \tilde{w}_j^{FB}} \tag{A7}$$

and, for the special case where $\theta_i = \theta \;\; \forall i$ (i.e., the same constant rate of time preference for all countries)

$$\frac{r_i^{NC}}{r_i^{FB}} \approx \frac{w_i}{\sum_j w_j} \tag{A7bis}$$

Equations (A7) and (A7bis) state that (always) $r_i^{NC} < r_i^{FB}$. This is not surprising. What is striking, however, is that the ratio of the two percentage emission reductions, is independent of MB (the overall world benefit) and (still more surprising) of β_i. Cost differences play no role in this ratio. Of course, this must be seen as an illustration of the limitations of our specifications.

Analogous results are found for the other comparisons. From (A4) and (A6) we derive

$$\frac{r_i^{NC}}{r_i^{SB}} \approx \frac{\tilde{\lambda}_i^{SB}\tilde{w}_i^{NC}}{\sum_j \tilde{\lambda}_j^{SB}\tilde{w}_j^{SB}} \tag{A8}$$

and, for the special case where $\theta_i = \theta \ \forall i$,

$$\frac{r_i^{NC}}{r_i^{SB}} \approx \frac{\tilde{\lambda}_i^{SB} w_i}{\sum_j \tilde{\lambda}_j^{SB} w_j} \tag{A8bis}$$

Under normal circumstances (e.g., always in (A8bis)), these equations imply that within our model $r_i^{NC} < r_i^{SB}$ (which does not necessarily hold for all specifications!). This means that no country will 'exploit' the others so much that it could actually lower its own efforts in the second-best solution (and independent of the value taken for ε). The comparison of (A7) and (A8) again shows the importance of the distributional weights.

Let us finally compare (A5) and (A6). This results in

$$\frac{r_i^{SB}}{r_i^{FB}} \approx \frac{\sum_j \tilde{\lambda}_j^{SB}\tilde{w}_j^{SB}}{\tilde{\lambda}_i^{SB}\sum_j \tilde{w}_j^{FB}} \tag{A9}$$

and, for the special case where $\theta_i = \theta \ \forall i$,

$$\frac{r_i^{SB}}{r_i^{FB}} \approx \frac{\sum_j \tilde{\lambda}_j^{SB}\tilde{w}_j}{\tilde{\lambda}_i^{SB}} \tag{A9bis}$$

Equation (A9bis) can be interpreted easily. The efforts made by country i in the first-best solution (r_i^{FB}) will be larger than the efforts in the solution without side payments (r_i^{SB}, i.e., the country is spared in the latter solution) if the distributional weight for that country ($\tilde{\lambda}_i^{SB}$, i.e., including the marginal cost factor) is greater than the weighted average of these weights for all the other countries (where the weights are the shares in the total benefits). Basically the same interpretation follows from equation (A9), but there the possible differences in θ_i and hence, in the $\tilde{w}$'s, make the expression somewhat more complicated.

EFFICIENCY AND DISTRIBUTION IN GREENHOUSE NEGOTIATIONS

SUMMARY

We analyse the international aspects of the greenhouse problem. The equity versus efficiency trade-off is examined by reducing the set of instruments to the allocation of abatement efforts over countries without the possibility of side payments. The traditional cost-effective allocation of abatement efforts is no longer necessarily optimal. The trade-off is illustrated empirically by combining the available cost and benefit estimates in a simplified two-period model with 12 regions in the world. In a second application we follow an inverse optimum approach and compute the power weights implicit in actuel agreements.

RÉSUMÉ

Ce papier traite des aspects internationaux de l'effet de serre. Le problème est formulé comme la recherche d'un maximum pour une fonction de bien-être et nous montrons que cette formulation permet plusieures interprétations intéressantes au niveau de la dimension éthique et de la dimension négociation. Le conflit équité-efficacité est étudié par la réduction de l'ensemble des instruments, à l'allocation, entre les pays, d'obligations de réduction d'émissions de gaz à effet de serre. Les paiements latéraux ont donc été exclu comme instrument. Dans cette situation le principe traditionnel d'une allocation minimisante les couts de réduction n'est plus nécessairement optimal. Le conflit équité-efficacité est illustré empiriquement par un modèle à deux périodes qui combine, pour un monde subdivisé en 12 régions, les estimations existantes pour les couts et bénéfices. Dans une première application nous donnons une interprétation éthique de la fonction de bien-être social. Ensuite nous prenons une approche d'optimum inverse et calculons les poids de négociation implicites dans les accords internationaux existants.

ZUSAMMENFASSUNG

Dieses Papier handelt von den internationalen Aspekten des Treibhauseffekts. Das Problem wurde als Suche nach einem Maximum einer Wohlfahrtsfunktion formuliert, und wir zeigen, dass diese Formulierung mehrere interessante Interpretationen auf der Stufe der ethischen Dimension und der Unterhandlungsdimension zulässt. Der Konflikt 'Gerechtigkeit-Wirksamkeit' wird untersucht, wobei die Gesamtheit der Instrumente auf die Zuteilung von Verpflichtungen unter den Ländern, ihre Treibhausgasemissionen einzuschränken, begrenzt wird. Nebenzahlungen werden also als Instrument ausgeschlossen. In dieser Situation ist das traditionelle Prinzip einer Zuteilung, welche die Emissionseinschränkungskosten minimalisiert, nicht mehr notwendigerweise optimal. Der Konflikt 'Gerechtigkeit-Wirksamkeit' wird durch ein Zwei-Periodenmodell empirisch erläutert, das für eine in zwölf Regionen unterteilte Welt die bestehenden Schätzungen für Kosten und Gewinne kombiniert. In einer ersten Anwendung geben wir eine ethische Interpretation der sozialen Wohlfahrtsfunktion. Anschliessend benützen wir eine umgekehrte Annäherung und berechnen die impliziten Unterhandlungsgewichte in den bestehenden internationalen Verträgen.

[11]

JOURNAL OF ENVIRONMENTAL ECONOMICS AND MANAGEMENT 24, 87–100 (1993)

A Finnish–Soviet Acid Rain Game: Noncooperative Equilibria, Cost Efficiency, and Sulfur Agreements[1]

OLLI TAHVONEN,* VEIJO KAITALA,† AND MATTI POHJOLA‡,

*University of Oulu, Department of Economics, Linnanmaa, SF-90570 Oulu, Finland; †Systems Analysis Laboratory, Helsinki University of Technology, Espoo, Finland; and ‡ETLA—Research Institute of the Finnish Economy, Lönnrotinkatu 4B, Helsinki, Finland

Received September 3, 1991; revised December 22, 1991

This study analyzes cost effectiveness in environmental cooperation between Finland and the Soviet Union. It is assumed that the aim of both countries is to attain a given target deposition level at minimum possible sulfur abatement costs. Cost-effective cooperation is compared to noncooperative equilibrium and to the agreement on sulfur emissions between these two countries. It is shown that the agreement is not cost-effective, implies higher abatement costs than under noncooperation, and is strategically unstable. However, the cost differences and the incentives to cheat are small. The computations reveal that the main source of potential cooperation benefits is not asymmetrical emission transportation or differences in abatement costs but rather different target deposition levels for Finland and the Soviet Union. © 1993 Academic Press, Inc.

1. INTRODUCTION

Transboundary air pollution problems have received increased attention in environmental economic research. For example, Mäler [7] has studied the economic rationale of the sulfur agreement concluded between the European countries. He found that the usual form of international agreement whereby countries have agreed to implement uniform sulfur emission reductions leads to abatement costs that are much higher than the cost-effective solution (for earlier studies of transfrontier pollution, see [2, 8]).

The long border between Finland and the Soviet Union[2] constitutes an interesting case of transboundary air pollution problems. The high material intensity of the Soviet economy is reflected in high sulfur emission levels near the border. While the annual sulfur emissions for the whole of Finland total about 160,000 tonnes, the Soviet Union's annual emissions near the border in an area some 30% larger than Finland amount to about 651,000 tonnes. The Soviet emissions—and depositions—are particularly high in the Kola peninsula, in Estonia, and in the vicinity of Leningrad. In the Kola peninsula, trees of the species *Picea abies* and *Pinus silvestris* have died in an area of about 100 km^2. The recovery of these areas will take a long time because the optimal forest rotation in these latitudes is about 150 years. In spite of the unusual severity of these problems, the Soviet govern-

[1]The authors thank two anonymous referees for comments and suggestions which influenced the final form of this paper.

[2]This study was carried out before the independence of Estonia and before the political changes that occurred in the Soviet Union in December 1991. However, Section 6 contains a brief discussion on an acid rain game between Finland, Estonia, and Russia.

0095-0696/93 $5.00

ment prefers to use resources for solving other, perhaps even more urgent, problems, and the level of sulfur abatement costs is still zero [5].

Although there has not been serious forest damage in Finland, the acidification of forest soil proceeds and the sulfur deposition is above the critical load virtually throughout the country [6]. The level of sulfur emissions in Finland was reduced by 40% between 1980 and 1987. However, only 20% of the Finnish deposition is due to home emissions and the deposition is highest near the Soviet border. Finland aims to reduce her emissions still further but because the marginal abatement costs are about five times lower on the Soviet side of the border, environmental cooperation offers potentially large savings in terms of resources. In 1987 these two countries signed an agreement calling for 50% reductions in sulfur emissions throughout Finland and in the adjacent areas of the Soviet Union. In this paper we compute the noncooperative and cost-effective sulfur abatement policies for these countries and investigate the rationale and stability of the agreement. We find that the agreement is not cost-effective and that it implies abatement costs that are higher than those in noncooperative equilibrium. However, the differences are relatively small. In general, we can show that, with various target deposition levels, cost-effective sulfur agreements would be beneficial to Finland but not to the Soviet Union. The main reason for this is not an upwind–downwind situation or differences in marginal abatement costs but rather high Soviet target deposition levels for sulfur deposition. Together, our results raise the politically difficult question of side payments from Finland to her neighbor.

The paper is organized as follows. Section 2 gives an overview of the physical background and describes the data. In Section 3 we define the solution concepts to be used in the computations. Section 4 analyses the sulfur agreement between Finland and the Soviet Union. In Section 5 we show how the cooperative benefits vary with variations in the region-specific target depositions. Section 6 considers the gains from cooperation in perhaps the most probable case, where the Finnish deposition targets are low while the Soviet target depositions are higher. Section 6 also briefly analyzes how the independence of Estonia will change this game. Section 7 concludes the paper.

2. PHYSICAL BACKGROUND AND DATA

Let Q_i denote the annual deposition of sulfur in the seven regions under consideration, $_i = (1), \ldots, (7)$: (1) = Northern Finland, (2) = Central Finland, (3) = Southern Finland, (4) = Kola, (5) = Karelia, (6) = Leningrad area, and (7) = Estonia. The deposition in each of these seven regions has eight sources, the last being the sum of the natural background deposition and human-generated emissions from the rest of the world. Denote this exogenous deposition vector by B. Let the transport coefficient matrix $A = (a_{ij})$ indicate how the emission E_j in region $_j$ is transported in the atmosphere to be deposited in region $_i$. Now our transportation model can be expressed in vector notation as

$$Q = AE + B.$$

The transport coefficient matrix has been constructed at the Finnish Meteorologi-

TABLE I

The Transport Coefficient Matrix and Annual Exogenous Deposition Level, B_{8i} Year^{-1} (in 1000 tonnes of sulfur), 1980 and 1987

	Emitting region								
	NFI	CFI	SFI	KOL	KAR	LEN	EST	B_{80} year^{-1}	B_{87} year^{-1}
Receiving region									
NFI	.2	.017	0.01	.046	.012	.0	.0	27	26
CFI	.0	.3	.062	.011	.047	.036	.029	66	59
SFI	.0	.017	.227	.003	.0	.027	.038	38	35
KOL	.0	.017	.0	.286	.023	.009	.0	36	27
KAR	.0	.033	.031	.017	.318	.045	.019	65	50
LEN	.0	.017	.031	.003	.012	.268	.058	57	46
EST	.0	.0	.031	.0	.0	.018	.221	38	32

cal Institute [9] by applying the long-range sulfur transport model developed at the Western Meteorological Center in Oslo. The parameters of the matrix and the exogenous depositions are shown in Table I. Since most of the emissions in each region are deposited in the same area, the largest parameters in matrix A can be found on the diagonal. This matrix reveals that we do not have a clear upwind–downwind country situation. Rather, we have a case of reciprocal transfrontier externalities[3] (cf. [2]). Note also the decrease in the exogenous deposition level between the years 1980 and 1987.

Table II gives data on the total depositions and emissions. The total deposition and also the deposition per square meter vary considerably among the regions. The deposition per square meter is highest in the regions of Kola, Estonia, and Leningrad. The high level in the latter is partly explained by the high exogenous deposition from other parts of Europe whereas in the Kola region the deposition is mainly due to the high home emission levels.[4] The critical load deposition level varies from region to region in Finland but according to some estimates [6] it can hardly exceed .3 g(S)m^{-2} year^{-1}.

The cost functions $C_i(E_i)$ are defined as the minimal cost envelope encompassing the entire range of sulfur abatement options for region $_i$ in a given time period. The costs can be calculated for various sulfur reduction requirements ranging up to the maximal technologically feasible removal. In the HAKOMA project conducted by the Technical Research Centre of Finland, such regional cost functions has been constructed by applying an engineering approach in estimating the direct costs of sulfur reductions in both combustion processes in energy production and noncombustion processes in industries using inputs containing sulfur. The annual costs, measured in million Finnish marks, have been estimated on the basis of expected energy demands for the year 2000, and they include both capital and operating costs. The former have been obtained by assuming that existing plants

[3]If matrix A is aggregated to contain only two regions, i.e., Finland and the nearby regions of the Soviet Union, about 8% of the Finnish emissions are deposited in the Soviet Union and 6.1% of the Soviet emissions in Finland.

[4]The annual deposition levels per square meter are quite low in comparison with those in certain parts of Central Europe. One should, however, bear in mind that the environment in the north is much more vulnerable to acid deposition [3, 4].

TABLE II
Depositions and Emissions

	Q_{87} year^{-1}	Q_{g87} m^{-2} year^{-1}	B_{g87} m^{-2} year^{-1}	E_{80} year^{-1}	E_{87} year^{-1}
NFI	46	.47	.26	18	5
CFI	98	.57	.34	107	60
SFI	66	1.0	.53	167	97
KOL	131	.94	.19	362	350
KAR	95	.53	.28	85	85
LEN	88	1.03	.54	125	112
EST	60	1.33	.71	120	104

Note. Q_{87} year^{-1} = total depositions (in 1000 tonnes of sulfur), 1987. Q_{g87} m^{-2} year^{-1} = depositions per square meter (in grams), 1987. B_{g87} m^{-2} year^{-1} = exogenous deposition per square meter (in grams), 1987. E_{8i} year^{-1} = emissions (in 1000 tonnes of sulfur), 198i.

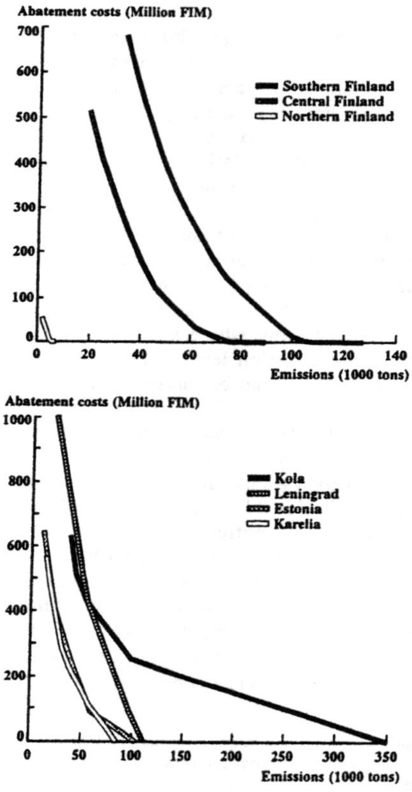

FIG. 1. The abatement cost functions in Finland and the Soviet Union.

are operated for 15 years and new plants for 25 years. The annual nominal interest rate used is 8%. Two main options for reducing emissions in energy production have been considered in constructing the cost functions. The first is sulfur abatement through in-furnace lime injection and flue gas desulfurization. The second is switching to the use of low-sulfur heavy oils in combustion systems. In calculating the costs for noncombustion processes, industry-specific costs per abated amount of sulfur have been applied.

The estimated cost functions are continuous, convex, and piecewise linear. They are depicted in Fig. 1.

3. SOLUTION CONCEPTS

To examine the economic logic of our problem we assume that the objective of both countries is to minimize the costs of sulfur abatement subject to region-specific deposition targets. This kind of cost-effective environmental policy is often preferred to other alternatives because no explicit consideration has to be given to the difficult problem of evaluating the damage costs of pollution. Critical deposition levels are explicitly mentioned in the Finnish–Soviet action programme. The parties have agreed that "they shall strive to reduce transboundary fluxes of air pollutants between the two countries so that the depositions, including those emanating from other European countries, shall not exceed the critical loads in areas near the common border" (Action Programme [1]). In what follows we analyze two explicitly mentioned environmental strategies. The first is an agreement between the neighbors which requires both countries to reduce the total sulfur emission levels by 50% from the 1980 levels by the end of 1995. The second is the Finnish long-run objective, which is to reduce the annual sulfur deposition below .5 g per m^2. We next define the solution and equilibrium concepts to be used in the analysis.

A cost-effective cooperative solution is an emission vector E which solves the problem

$$\underset{\{E\}}{\text{MIN}}\, C_{\text{FC}} + C_{\text{SC}} = \sum_{i=1}^{7} C_i(E_i)$$

$$\text{s.t.}\quad \hat{Q} \geq AE + B,$$

$$E_{\min} \leq E \leq E_{\max},$$

where C_{FC} refers to the Finnish and C_{SC} to the Soviet cooperative abatement costs, $E_{\min}$ and $E_{\max}$ are region-specific, technically feasible minimum and maximum emission levels, and $\hat{Q}$ is the target deposition vector.

The noncooperative equilibrium is defined as the solution to the problem where both countries minimize their own abatement costs subject to their own deposition targets while taking the emissions from their neighbor as given. Formally, the noncooperative equilibrium emission vectors $\tilde{E}_{\text{F}} = (\tilde{E}_1, \tilde{E}_2, \tilde{E}_3)$ and

$\bar{E}_S(\bar{E}_4, \bar{E}_5, \bar{E}_6, \bar{E}_7)$ solve the following minimization problems:

$$\min_{\{\bar{E}_F\}} C_{FN} = \sum_{i=1}^{3} C(E_i) \qquad \min_{\{\bar{E}_S\}} C_{SN} = \sum_{i=4}^{7} C_i(E_i)$$

$$\text{s.t.} \qquad\qquad\qquad\qquad \text{s.t.}$$

$$\hat{Q}_F \geq A_F E_F + B_F, \qquad \hat{Q}_S \geq A_S E_S + B_S,$$

$$E_{min} \leq E \leq E_{max}, \qquad E_{min} \leq E \leq E_{min},$$

$$E_S = \bar{E}_S, \qquad E_F = \bar{E}_F.$$

In addition to these two concepts, we use the same notation to define the agreement between Finland and the Soviet Union. Unfortunately, the interpretation of the agreement is not unique. The agreement requires that both countries reduce their total emissions by 50%. One obvious interpretation is that the 50% reduction strategy is assumed in each region. However, the wording of the agreement leaves room for interpretation where emissions are not reduced uniformly in the different regions. As a consequence, this strategy may create "hot spots" where the deposition per square meter may even increase. We assume here that if the countries observe the agreement they reduce emissions by 50% in every region.

Formally, the agreement can be defined as the solution to the problem

$$\min_{\{E_F, E_S\}} C_A = \sum_{i=1}^{7} C_i(E_i)$$

$$\text{s.t.} \quad \hat{Q} \geq AE + B,$$

$$(E_b - E)/E_b = \alpha,$$

$$E_{min} \leq E \leq E_{max},$$

where E_b is the emission vector in the base year and α is the agreed rate of reduction.

Because of an additional constraint, the agreement obviously implies abatement costs at least as high as the optimal cooperative solution. The interesting empirical question is whether the cost differences between the agreement and the optimal cooperative solution are considerable. If the difference is small, the agreement may be satisfactory as it is easier to manage (i.e. it may imply lower transaction costs) and it gives a superficial sense of fairness (cf. [7]).

4. ANALYSIS OF THE 50% AGREEMENT

To analyze the consequences of the 50% agreement we further assume that exogenous anthropogenic emissions will decrease by 50% from their 1980 levels by the end of 1995.[5] Below, we address the following questions: (1) What are the different deposition levels in different regions if the agreement is fulfilled, i.e., what is the implicit $\hat{Q}$; (2) does the abatement policy of the 50% agreement deviate

[5] It has been estimated that 70% of the background deposition is derived from anthropogenic sources [9].

TABLE III
The 50% Agreement

	Finland		
	Noncooperation	Cooperation	50% agreement
Soviet Union			
Noncooperation	175.10/817.56[a]	174.53*[b]/817.71	175.32*/817.49
Cooperation	174.30/817.77*	174.53/817.77	X
50% agreement	174.96/818.0*	X	175.32/818.0

[a]The first figure refers to the abatement costs in Finland and the second to the abatement costs in the Soviet Union.
[b]An asterisk next to a figure means that the deposition targets of the given country are violated.

from the cost-effective allocation of the abatement activities; (3) does the agreement deviate from the noncooperative equilibrium; and (4) how large are the benefits that the countries can gain by cheating their neighbors, that is, by deviating unilaterally from the agreement?

The results of the computations[6] are shown in Table III. Let us first compare the noncooperative equilibrium with the cost-effective cooperative solution. It can be noted that the Soviet Union loses and Finland gains from optimal cooperation. The strategy pair (noncooperation, cooperation) refers to the case where the cooperative policy has not been implemented in the Soviet Union but Finland has reduced emissions in compliance with the cooperative policy. As a consequence, the deposition targets are violated in Finland while the Soviet Union saves slightly in terms of abatement costs (FIM .06 million annually). Accordingly, Finland can slightly reduce her abatement costs (FIM .23 million annually) by applying the noncooperative policy if the Soviet Union maintains the cooperative mode. Now the target deposition levels are violated in the Soviet Union.

Consider next the 50% agreement. This implies abatement costs in both countries that are higher than the cost-effective costs and also higher than the noncooperative equilibrium costs. Again, both parties have an incentive to cheat their partner but the differences in the abatement costs in different cases are relatively small. Thus, from the point of view of game theory, neither the cost-effective cooperative emission vector nor the 50% agreement are equilibria in a strict sense since both parties have an incentive to deviate unilaterally from the agreement and to cheat their partner. However, the differences in abatement costs between the different cases are again small. Consequently, this means that the agreement might well be considered a satisfactory and safe agreement. If, on the other hand, one could be certain that the agreed target levels $\hat{Q}$ would also be applied during noncooperation, then the incentive for cooperation would be relatively weak. Indeed, given the existence of transaction costs one may ask why such an agreement has been made.

However, the analysis so far does not perhaps reveal the actual nature of the problem. The noncooperative solution has been solved here by assuming that the

[6]As our cost functions are piecewise linear and the constraints are linear, the optimization problems are solved by linear programming. Noncooperative equilibria are solved by an iterative process, which in all of our cases converges toward a unique equilibrium.

regional constraints for the depositions are the same as agreed by Finland and the Soviet Union. There is no guarantee, however, that under noncooperation these target levels would be applied. The abatement costs in the Soviet Union are quite high at the same time as the Soviet economy has not been developing as desired. Thus, there are economic grounds for believing that the Soviet Union will not fully implement the emission reductions laid down in the action program before the end of 1995. The implications of this are studied in Sections 5 and 6. The second problem is that the deposition levels will remain quite high even if the agreed emission reductions are carried out. In that case the deposition vector would be .30, .42, .74, .56, .38, .72, .92 g(S)m^{-2} $year^{-1}$. One way to solve this problem would be for the two countries to conclude an 80% agreement.

The solution of an 80% agreement in terms of regional deposition levels per square meter is .19, .26, .44, .29, .24, .46, .58 g(S)m^{-2} $year^{-1}$. The deposition levels in Southern Finland, the Leningrad, area and Estonia are still above the critical loads. However, because there are some minimum bounds to the emission level in each region, it is impossible to reach lower deposition levels by agreements that provide for uniform reduction. It turns out that in this case too a shift from noncooperative equilibrium to optimal cooperation would benefit Finland while the Soviet Union would incur some losses. The net benefits deriving from cooperation now amount to FIM 5.69 million annually, a sum which is, however, only .17 per cent of the noncooperative abatement costs. Comparing the 80% agreement with optimal cooperation gives the result that the agreement benefits the Soviet Union by FIM 26.34 million annually while Finland loses FIM 45.26 million annually. The total benefits deriving from optimal cooperation in comparison with the 80% agreement are again quite low, i.e., 0.6% of the abatement costs.

It seems that the magnitude of the cost savings from optimal cooperation increases when lower deposition levels are aimed at. However, the cost savings achieved by the cost-effective solution are not so dramatic (cf. [7]). The optimal cooperative solution may well imply high transaction costs, and thus noncooperative equilibrium or agreements providing for uniform reductions may be considered preferable. There may be several reasons for this. First, according to the transport coefficient matrix, the interaction between the two countries is not very strong. The highest coefficient between regions in different countries is only .047. If the size of the regions were smaller, the transportation coefficients near the border would be higher. This would increase the level of interaction and the magnitude of cost savings. There are some results which strongly support this view. In another paper Kaitala *et al.* [5] used only two regions, Finland and the nearby regions of the Soviet Union. With these larger regional units, the 50% agreement coincides with both the optimal solution and the noncooperative solution. The second reason for low differences in equilibrium abatement costs is the arbitrary target deposition vector implied by the emissions realized in the base year 1980. If some other base year were used, the cost differences might be completely different.

5. TARGETS SET ON DEPOSITION LEVELS

We next turn to study cases where both countries set some target deposition levels instead of emission targets. Finland has defined her goals quite clearly. Her

TABLE IV

Implications of Different Soviet Deposition Targets

Target[a] FIN/SOV	Optimum Costs	Noncoop. Costs	Cooperative Benefits	Noncooperative Depositions[a]
.45/.5	524.34/1299.1[b]	521.91/1301.72	−2.43/2.62	.24, .36, .45, .5, .37, .5, .5
.45/.6	658.93/672.47	658.92/672.49	−.01/.02	.27, .37, .45, .6, .38, .6, .6
.45/.7	714.69/515.63	1194.41/243.75	479.72/−271.9	.28, .29, .46*[c], .7, .38, .7, .7
.45/.8	714.69/503.86	1194.41/87.0	479.72/−416.86	.3, .29, .48*, .8, .39, .73, .8
.45/.95	714.69/497.17	1194.41/0	479.72/−497.17	.31, .3, .49*, .87, .4, .75, .94

[a]Unit: $g(S)m^{-2}$ $year^{-1}$.
[b]The first figure (million FIM $year^{-1}$) refers to Finland and the second to the Soviet Union.
[c]An asterisk next to a figure means that the deposition target of the given region is violated.

aim is to reduce sulfur deposition on Finnish territory to a level not exceeding .5 $g(S)m^{-2}$ $year^{-1}$. The Soviet Union, by contrast, has not set such deposition targets. Thus, in what follows we vary the Soviet deposition target from .5 to .95 $g(S)m^{-2}$ $year^{-1}$ while keeping the Finnish target fixed at .45 $g(S)m^{-2}year^{-1}$. We fix the Finnish target at slightly below .5 $g(S)m^{-2}$ $year^{-1}$ because our regions are quite large. This means that there will be some areas where deposition is below and some areas where it is above .5 $g(S)m^{-2}$ $year^{-1}$. In Northern Finland, in particular, deposition is much higher near the Soviet border than it is near the western border. Taking .45 $g(S)m^{-2}$ $year^{-1}$ as a target deposition level is therefore an attempt to approximate the real Finnish target. Note also that there are some minimum attainable region-specific deposition levels. These follow because of the exogenous deposition level and because there is some minimum attainable emission level in every region. Thus, although we assume that anthropogenic emissions will decline by 80% from 1980 levels, we cannot reach deposition levels below .45 $g(S)m^{-2}$ $year^{-1}$ in Southern Finland or below .5 $(g)m^{-2}$ $year^{-1}$ in Estonia. The results of this analysis are shown in Table IV.

Note first that the sign of cooperation benefits varies with variations in the Soviet deposition targets. If the Soviet Union aims at the lowest attainable target level, i.e., .5 $g(S)m^{-2}$ $year^{-1}$, Finland loses from cooperation and the Soviet Union gains. In that case the net gain from cooperation is negligible and only about .01 per cent of the noncooperative abatement costs. Note also that when the Soviet targets are low both countries can reach their targets without cooperation. In particular, if the Soviet deposition target is .6 $g(S)m^{-2}$ $year^{-1}$, the noncooperative solution and the optimal cooperative solution approximately coincide. However, if the Soviet target is .7 $g(S)m^{-2}$ $year^{-1}$, the picture changes considerably. Finland can no longer reach her target deposition in Southern Finland without cooperation. Now Finland gains significantly from cooperation while the Soviet Union experiences losses. The net gain from cooperation in terms of reduced abatement costs is now about 15% of the noncooperative abatement costs. When the Soviet target approaches .95 $g(S)m^{-2}$ $year^{-1}$ the Finnish noncooperative deposition in Southern Finland approaches .49 $g(S)m^{-2}$ $year^{-1}$. Accordingly, the Soviet noncooperative abatement cost approaches zero and the loss from cooperation approaches about 1/2 billion Finnish marks annually. The net gains from cooperation are no longer realized in the form of reduced abatement costs. In fact the abatement costs are higher in the optimal cooperative solution than in noncooperative equilibrium. The gains from cooperation are realized in the sense that Finland reaches her deposition targets.

This simulation reveals that potential cooperation benefits exists between Finland and the Soviet Union. However, substantial benefits cannot be attained with approximately equal Finnish–Soviet target deposition levels. With equal target deposition levels, the differences in marginal abatement costs in noncooperative equilibrium are relatively low with respect to the sulfur transport coefficients. If the target deposition levels differ, the differences in marginal abatement costs in noncooperative equilibrium are also higher, and thus in these cases it is optimal to change the regional allocation of abatement activities when the countries shift to the optimal cooperative mode. In addition, cooperation is called for when low Finnish targets are unattainable in the noncooperative game.

6. BENEFITS FROM COOPERATION WITH HIGH DEPOSITION TARGETS IN THE SOVIET UNION

To conclude our analysis, let us assume that the Soviet deposition targets equal the regional deposition levels of 1987. This means that the Soviet Union does not have to spend any money on sulfur abatement if Finland maintains or decreases her emission levels and if the exogenous deposition level does not increase. Under these assumptions the noncooperative policy of the Soviet Union is simply to maintain the current emission levels. Let us assume in addition that anthropogenic emissions decrease by 70% from their 1980 levels. Now we can easily compare the noncooperative abatement costs to cooperative abatement costs when the Finnish target deposition varies.

The results of this comparison are shown in Fig. 2. The symbol C_{FC} denotes Finnish cooperative costs, C_{FN} Finnish noncooperative costs, and C_{SC} Soviet cooperative costs. Note first that without cooperation Finland cannot reach a deposition target below .532 $g(S)m^{-2}$year^{-1} while with cooperation .430 g(S)m^{-2} year^{-1} is attainable. Between the target levels .88 and .655 g(S)m^{-2} year^{-1} it is optimal for Finland to reduce only her own emissions, and there are no potential gains from cooperation. Below the target level .665 g(S)m^{-2} year^{-1} optimal cooperation requires that Soviet emissions also be reduced. Down to the target level .532 g(S)m^{-2} year^{-1} cooperation benefits are realized in the form of lower abatement costs. At the target level .532 g(S)m^{-2} year^{-1} the cooperative abatement costs are 449.15 million FIM year^{-1} lower than noncooperative abatement costs. The share of Soviet abatement costs is 88.0 million of FIM year^{-1}. Thus although Finland has to pay the Soviet costs, her net gain is 361.15 million FIM year^{-1}, i.e., cooperation decreases the Finnish abatement costs by 31%. Finnish deposition levels below .532 g(S)m^{-2} year^{-1} can be reached only in cooperation. The proportion of Soviet abatement costs is substantially higher in optimal cooperation solutions. When the Finnish target is at the lowest attainable level, Soviet abatement costs are nearly 63% of the total minimum costs.

The optimal regional allocation of Finnish side payments is a question with practical interest. The Finnish authorities are now devising a scheme aimed at reducing emissions in the Kola region by about 90%. It involves both technical and economic assistance from Finland. In the present framework such a policy is not

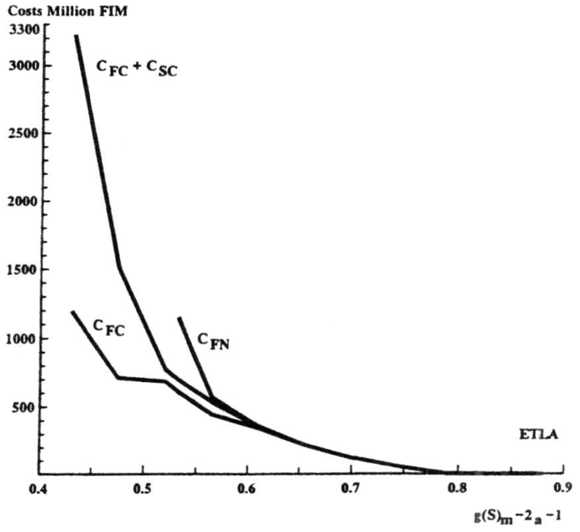

FIG. 2. Finnish cooperative and noncooperative abatement costs and Soviet cooperative abatement costs as functions of the Finnish deposition targets.

cost-effective. Above the Finnish target level .52 g(S)m^{-2} year^{-1} it is optimal to reduce Soviet emissions in Estonia only. Below .475 g(S)m^{-2} year^{-1} but above .43 g(S)m^{-2} year^{-1} Soviet emissions should be reduced in Estonia and in the Leningrad area. Only at the lowest target level should Soviet emissions be decreased in the Kola peninsula because of their contribution to the deposition in Southern Finland. The deposition target constraint of Northern Finland is not binding in any of these examples. However, there are at least two reasons that these results must be treated with caution. First, the whole of Northern Finland is treated as one regional unit. The deposition is not uniformly distributed over this region, being at least twice as high in the eastern part as in the western part. Thus using smaller regions in Northern Finland may give different results. Second, the deposition target should be lower in Northern Finland than in Central and Southern Finland because of its more vulnerable environment.

The political situation in the Soviet Union changed dramatically in 1991. Among other things, Estonia became an independent country. Thus there may now be three independent decision makers. As yet, we do not know how the 50% agreement will be interpreted in this new situation, nor do we know what will be the deposition targets in Estonia. In spite of these difficulties we have made some attempts to figure out the implications of this new situation.

Given that the agreement requires Estonia to reduce her emissions by 50% from their 1980 levels the stability properties of the agreement remain approximately the same. When the optimal solution is compared to the noncooperative equilibrium or to the agreement, it turns out that it is costly to Estonia but beneficial to

Finland and Russia. Estonia has an incentive to cheat in the optimal cooperative solution and may thus need side payments from Finland and Russia.

In the case where the target deposition levels of Finland are .45 g(S)m^{-2} year^{-1} and the targets of Russia and Estonia are .95 g(S)m^{-2} year^{-1}, the independence of Estonia does not change the noncooperative equilibrium. However, the independence of Estonia may lead to reductions in target deposition levels. Thus we study the case where Estonia and Finland aim at low deposition levels; i.e., $\hat{Q}_i$ = .45 g(S)m^{-2} year^{-1} is assumed for Finland and $\hat{Q}_i$ = .50 g(S)m^{-2} year^{-1} for Estonia while $\hat{Q}_i$ = .95 g(S)m^{-2} year^{-1} is maintained for Russia. When this case is compared to the case where Estonia was a part of the Soviet Union with .95 g(S)m^{-2} year^{-1} as her target deposition level, Finland gains considerably from the independence and lower target deposition levels of Estonia. Finland is now able to reach her targets in noncooperative equilibrium at a cost of FIM 713.29 million annually. Now Estonia inherits the previous role of Finland and cannot reach her targets in noncooperative equilibrium. However, the optimal cooperative equilibrium is now only about FIM 5 million more costly to Russia than the noncooperative equilibrium (cf. Table IV). Thus the role of side payments may diminish.

7. CONCLUSIONS

This paper has analyzed an acid rain game between Finland and the Soviet Union. Sulfur deposition is an acute and severe environmental problem in each country. Despite heavy local depositions, the sulfur problem has strong transboundary components—a significant proportion of the emissions is transported distances exceeding local dimensions.

We analyzed the 50% agreement by adopting the approach that the agreement implicitly includes targets for sulfur deposition. First, the cost-effective solution was analyzed under the assumption that the countries agree to minimize the joint costs of reducing sulfur emissions so that the targets for depositions are reached. Second, the costs of the current agreement on 50% reduction in sulfur emissions were determined. And third, the noncooperative game solution in which countries reach the same targets individually was analyzed. It was shown that the three solutions do not differ crucially from each other. This means that once an agreement is reached it is a safe agreement in the sense that no party has a strong incentive to cheat the partner, that is, not to observe the agreement. The opposite side of this property is, however, that there does not exist a strong incentive for environmental cooperation either.

The conclusions change, however, if we assume that it is highly uncertain what kind of environmental policy will be pursued in the Soviet Union. As was shown in Section 5, in the case where the Soviet Union does not use resources for abatement, Finland cannot reach the target levels she has set for deposition, and investments in the reduction of sulfur emissions become expensive. In this situation the potential benefits from cooperation are considerable. The problem is, however, that the Soviet Union loses from cost-effective cooperation while Finland gains. This means that the implementation of cost-effective agreements may entail politically difficult financial transfers from Finland to the Soviet Union. The need for side payments may, however, diminish if independent Estonia aims at lower target deposition levels than the Soviet Union did previously.

APPENDIX: SYMBOLS

A	sulfur transportation coefficient matrix
a_{ij}	fraction of the emissions released by region $_j$ that will be deposited in region $_i$
E	vector of emissions
$\bar{E}$	noncooperative emission vector
E_i	emissions in region $_i$
B	vector of exogenous deposition
Q	vector of depositions
$\hat{Q}$	target deposition vector
X g(S)m^{-2} year^{-1}	X grams of pure sulfur per square meter annually
$C_i(E_i)$	sulfur abatement costs in region $_i$
C_{FC}	Finnish cooperative abatement costs
C_{SC}	Soviet cooperative abatement costs
C_{FN}	Finnish noncooperative abatement costs
C_{SN}	Soviet noncooperative abatement costs
E_{min}	vector of minimum emissions in different regions
E_{max}	vector of maximum emissions
$\bar{E}_F$	noncooperative Finnish emission vector
$\bar{E}_S$	noncooperative Soviet emission vector
C_C	abatement costs of the agreed emission levels
E_b	emission vector of the agreed base year
α	agreed rate of sulfur emission reduction

REFERENCES

1. Action Programme 1989, Action programme agreed between the Republic of Finland and the Soviet Socialist Republics for the purpose of limiting and reducing the deposition and harmful effects of air pollutants emanating from areas near the common border, unofficial translation, 7 November 1989, Ministry of the Environment, Helsinki.
2. R. C. d'Arge, Transfrontier pollution: Some issues on regulation, *in* "Studies in International Environmental Economics" (I. Walter, Ed.), Wiley, New York (1976).
3. P. Hari, M. Holmberg, T. Raunemaa, and E. Nikinmaa, An approach to analyse the dynamics of environmental change and its effects on forest growth, *in* "Acidification in Finland" (Kauppi *et al.*, Eds.), Springer-Verlag, Berlin (1990).
4. S. Huttunen, J. Reinikainen, and M. Turunen, Wintering response of conifers to acid rain treatment under northern conditions, *in* "Acidification in Finland" (Kauppi *et al.*, Eds.), Springer-Verlag, Berlin (1990).
5. V. Kaitala, M. Pohjola, and O. Tahvonen, "An Economic Analysis of Transboundary Air Pollution between Finland and the Soviet Union," Discussion Paper 335, ETLA—Research Institute of the Finnish Economy (1990).
6. P. Kauppi, P. Anttila, and Kenttämies, K., "Acidification in Finland. Finnish Acidification Research Programme HAPRO 1985–1990," Springer-Verlag, Berlin (1990).
7. K. G. Mäler, International environmental problems, *Oxford Rev. Econom. Policy* 6, 80–108, (1990).
8. A. Scott, Transfrontier pollution and institutional choice, *in* "Studies in International Environmental Economics" (I. Walter, Ed.), Wiley, New York (1976).
9. J. P. Tuovinen, L. Kangas, and G. Norlund, Model calculations of sulphur and nitrogen depositions in Finland, *in* "Acidification in Finland," (Kauppi *et al.*, Eds.), Springer-Verlag, Berlin (1990).

[12]

KYKLOS, Vol. 47 – 1994 – Fasc. 4, 505 – 518

Voluntary Provision of a Public Good: Results from a Real World Experiment

WERNER W. POMMEREHNE, LARS P. FELD and ALBERT HART*

I. INTRODUCTION

Conventional wisdom in public finance has always been stating that the voluntary provision of a public good is not feasible due to the free rider behavior of individuals. However, a number of objections can be raised as to the theoretical and empirical validity of this presumption. For instance, when taking seriously AXELROD's (1984) idea of dynamic strategies, the typical neoclassical setting seems to be too narrow a conception, since it understands an individual's decision as a one-shot game. This might produce misleading predictions as to the extent of free riding, which, in effect, will be constantly overestimated[1].

Moreover, abundant empirical evidence on the questionable validity of the neoclassical claim is encountered when the actual behavior of individuals is looked upon. The strong version of the free rider hypothesis maintains that *each* citizen's optimization calculus is dominated by the free rider attitude. However, there exist a good many experiments (BOHM, 1972; PALFREY and ROSENTHAL, 1988; VAN DE KRAGT, DAWES and ORBELL, 1988; MESTELMAN and FEENY, 1989; BAGNOLI and MCKEE, 1991) suggesting that this hypothesis cannot be sustained, since participants voluntarily revealed a considerable part (often more than half) of their assumed true willingness to pay for the public good under concern. Of course, the hypothetical nature of most experiments might cast some doubt on their reliability. But even in some cases, in which real situations were simulated, the strong free rider hypothesis was rejected

*The first author is affiliated to both the University of Zurich and the University of Saarland, the others to the University of Saarland. Helpful comments on an earlier version of this paper have been provided by GEORGE BITTLINGMAYER, ROGER D. CONGLETON, BRUNO S. FREY, ANSELM U. RÖMER, GEORG SEECK and PHILIPPE THALMANN.

1. A rigorous game-theoretic model in line with AXELROD's argument has recently been advanced by GAITSGORY and NITZAN (1993).

(SCHNEIDER and POMMEREHNE, 1981). A similar conclusion can be arrived at by studying more or less unique events in reality. For instance, WEISBROD and DOMINGUEZ (1986) point out that the voluntary support of non-profit organizations in the United States is only compatible with the basic axioms of standard neoclassical theory under very restrictive assumptions. A different kind of evidence is provided by OSTROM (1990) who scrutinized a number of cases where people exploited common property resources over a long period of time. As a surprise for any standard neoclassical economist, no excessive exploitation was observed, i.e., under specific institutional settings, people did not adopt a complete free rider position and did not increase continuously the use-up of the resource.

In this paper we report on a 'real world experiment' regarding the voluntary provision of a public good. The conditions under which we studied citizens' contribution behavior were quite unique: As will be shown in section II, there was no real alternative but to donate in order to ensure the provision. In section III, potential determinants of the individual contribution decision will be discussed and subjected to an econometric test of their empirical validity. In section IV, some concluding remarks will be offered.

II. UNIQUENESS OF THE SITUATION

It so happened that the community of Kleinblittersdorf, which is located in the German State of Saarland directly at the border to France, was once faced with the following situation: In February 1987, the French sister community Grosbliederstroff, situated in western direction just across the river Saar, planned to erect a waste incinerator in a derelict area within the community. With west winds strongly prevailing in this region, the people of Kleinblittersdorf felt menaced by the pollution which was to be expected from the waste incinerator. Public meetings were organized to notify the citizens of the potential toxicity of the pollutants. Apart from those health-related aspects, prospective losses in real estate values were widely discussed. At all these meetings as well as on other occasions, both representatives and citizens were engaged in several kinds of protest actions, such as writing petitions and appealing to people to sign up against the incinerator. As a result, 16,000 legal objections in total were presented to the Prefect in Metz (the capital of the French Département Moselle) in 1988. All protest activities, however, were rendered ineffective in the end.

Ultimately, it turned out that the chances of success in preventing the waste incinerator through legal action and political pressure were nil. In this situation, clearly, no other options were left but to negotiate directly with the French community of Grosbliederstroff in order to find a mutually beneficial solution.

In June 1987, Robert Jeanrond, the mayor of Kleinblittersdorf, came up with the plan to buy the derelict and polluted land from the French municipality and to look for an investor who was willing to operate a less pollution-intensive plant. And, in fact, a supplier of automobile parts was found to be the most promising investor among a number of candidates. Jeanrond persuaded the sister community, Grosbliederstroff, which also perceived benefits from this less pollution-intensive investment project, to sell the area to him for the symbolic price of one Franc. Thereupon, public meetings were held in Kleinblittersdorf to inform the citizens about the plan which required a total of DM 3,500,000 to be collected.

After explaining carefully the expected (relative) benefits of the new plant with respect to health as well as real estate, Jeanrond suggested that each citizen contribute either DM 800 or ten percent of the prospective loss in real estate values to be resulting from the erection of the incinerator. The appeal was repeated several times, both in the newspapers and at various meetings. In order to organize the collection and the administration of the donated money, a club was founded. This club received financial contributions from June 1988 on.

But why was it not possible to raise the required amount through variations of the community's budget, for instance via increasing the rates of local business and real estate taxes? Well, the project itself would have required a total of DM 3,500,000, a sum equivalent to no less than 20 percent of the overall budget of Kleinblittersdorf. Therefore, the option of increasing local tax rates was not feasible in the short run, due to the sheer magnitude of the amount in question. Moreover, compared to the local business and real estate taxes of the neighboring municipalities, Kleinblittersdorf's tax rates were already quite impressive, which means that increasing the local tax burden was beyond consideration even in the longer run. Furthermore, it was not possible to let the municipality's deficit go up, due to the strong fiscal constraints imposed by the *Kommunalaufsichtsbehörde*, a state authority supervising local budget affairs. Cutting down on current local expenditures was not feasible either, because the bulk of the respective items consisted in compensation of resident public employees or in other spending necessities (like social and housing assistance), which could not be reduced in the short run. Finally, local government investment expenditures were not eligible for being lowered, because they were, as usual, earmarked for long-run purposes, and, in addition, subject to immediate control by the *Kommunalaufsichtsbehörde*.

Thus, the provision of the public good (i.e., the prevention of the public bad) was totally left to the citizens' internal bargaining. In fact, individual bidding took place to a considerable extent. By July 1990, a total of DM 3,525,955 had been collected.

In summer 1991, a university research team interviewed a sample of randomly chosen inhabitants of the community of Kleinblittersdorf. The main objective of the questionnaire was to come to grips with people's actual motivations to contribute or not.

III. ANALYSIS OF CONTRIBUTION BEHAVIOR

1. Theoretical Considerations

The fact that a considerable number of citizens did, in fact, contribute is not easy to explain as such. Neoclassical theory itself qualifies, in first instance, the relevance of the free rider problem to the effect that small group size can overcome the difficulties. Given the fact that more than 5,500 households would have been affected by the construction of the incinerator, this argument, as we think, hardly applies to the case under consideration.

However, conventional economic theory has more arguments at hand than just small group reasoning. According to OLSON (1965, pp. 45ff.), not only the ease of organizing collective action plays a crucial role, but also the size of the stakes and the homogeneity of the effects in question. Certainly, the latter arguments could have been important factors in the actual setting. The citizens' health state would have been unambiguously damaged by the operation of the waste incinerator, and this effect would have been almost the same for all people in Kleinblittersdorf. Avoiding an incinerator like this creates significant benefits accruing to each household. The damage would have been grave also with respect to real estate losses. Therefore, in most extreme cases this scenario could have constituted a private good setting for those seriously affected. According to OLSON's (1965) view, the stakes are very high in such a situation, whereas group size is very small. As a consequence, individual losses in the case of non-acting would be so high as to outweigh the cost associated with participating in collective action. Thus, the higher the expected losses in either of the two assets, the more likely, ceteris paribus, a person can be expected to feel caused to contribute[2].

2. This cannot be said of potential effects of different levels of household income, since it is only the long-run aspects which matter in such a situation.

In order to circumvent the negative health effects of the incinerator, the individuals may alternatively have the option of exiting the community. Although exit does not allow for escaping any losses in real estate, given the incinerator has been erected, it permits in any case to avoid any health-related impacts. The younger an individual, the more attractive this option should be, ceteris paribus.

These considerations complete the decision set of standard theories of REMM (resourceful evaluating, maximizing man; BRUNNER, 1978, p. 661). Such a thing as a particular free rider attitude should not make any difference, since, according to the conventional wisdom of neoclassical economists, literally all individuals are assumed to have a perfect free rider predisposition[3].

Evidence from related areas, however, suggests that framing individual decisions according to a narrow conception of man does not capture all of the relevant factors. In the case of tax evasion, for instance, an area which is in a similar fashion characterized by strategizing (and thus potential free riding), applying the neoclassical paradigm to actual behavior generates obvious paradoxes. As ALM, MCCLELLAND and SCHULZE (1992) point out, explaining tax compliance by employing ALLINGHAM and SANDMO's (1972) narrow neoclassical approach requires a totally implausible risk aversion coefficient to grasp the full size of actual tax payments[4]. In extending the set of explanatory variables, ERARD and FEINSTEIN (1993) obtain more reliable results by including psychological factors. In a more general way, HIRSCHMAN (1982, pp. 79ff.) criticized the neoclassical approach to human behavior in a context of collective decision making by emphasizing the importance of non-material influences on peoples' actual behavior. There is room for the potential influence of such aspects in our context, too. Psychic costs may be seen in a person's affinity to the community he belongs to. The longer an individual has been living in a municipality, the more affectioned he is with the fate of the latter, because he has been gathering 'sunk costs', so to speak, that produce some kind of cognitive dissonance in the end (AKERLOF and DICKENS, 1982).

3. For a good illustration of the behavior of 'rational fool', the creature of neoclassical economists, see SEN (1977).
4. Applying a conventional (isoelastic) utility function and inserting actual averages for the relevant economic variables [marginal tax rate, magnitude of fines and (objective) probability of detection] yields an equation where the unknown (relative) risk aversion parameter must exceed the value of 30 in order for compliance to exceed the 90% level in the United States. For Switzerland, POMMEREHNE and FREY (1993) calculated that the respective value of risk aversion has to take on a value of even 122.5. Field evidence for both countries, however, suggests that it ranges between 1.5 and two (see, e.g., MORIN and SUAREZ, 1983; SZPIRO, 1986).

In like vein, factors which can be categorized as more or less 'sociological' might also have affected citizens' decision to contribute[5]. The longer an individual has been a member of a community, the stronger the perceived pressure to participate in collective actions.

Apart from this informal network of social interrelations, on a local level there exists also a well established formal frame for organizing collective action. The fact that we observe these frames in reality might not be due to chance. Rather, formal political institutions might have been created in order to deal with problems of time-inconsistent individual behavior and thus to arrive at pareto-superior outcomes – an idea which is blatantly neglected by neoclassical economists. We expect that such formal and informal determinants of 'embeddedness' will strengthen individuals' incentives to contribute to the provision of a public good, ceteris paribus.

Carrying our reflections one step further, we might think of attitudinal factors as additional determinants of peoples' preparedness to donate. Getting rid of the presumption that all individuals are predisposed as free riders we might consider it quite plausible that 'participation altruism', as MARGOLIS (1982, pp. 21ff.) puts it, causes people to behave in a non purely egoistic manner to some extent.

2. *Empirical Implementation and Econometric Results*

The implementation is grounded on a random sample of 400 households in the municipality of Kleinblittersdorf. Somewhat more than half of this sample consented to participate in an interview. 201 questionnaires were completed after all, representing some 3.5 percent of the total number of households. The design of the survey was guided by the idea of capturing the determinants of the preparedness to contribute, as well as of the intensity of contribution.

Our basic model, which refers to the traditional neoclassical approach to human behavior, in first instance includes measurable costs or damages that are avoidable by collective action aiming at the prevention of the incinerator. Regarding health-related damage we asked the participants to assess their initial personal health status on a scale from zero (for a 'very bad' state) to six (for an 'excellent' state)[6] and, in addition, the health status they were expecting if the

5. Again, in the context of tax evasion, the validity of this argument is established by JUAN; LASHERAS and MAYO (1993).
6. This question was directed at the actual health status (with no incinerator in operation). In the following it is assumed that this health status would not deteriorate as a consequence of the

incinerator was erected. The variable HLOSS reflects the difference between the two ratings, i.e., the deterioration of the health status the citizens associate with the incinerator. Consequently, the variable takes on values from zero to six, with zero meaning no deterioration and six meaning very strong deterioration. We also asked participants who owned or expected to inherit real estate to provide an estimate of expected loss of real estate values (in percentage terms). Since the (historic) values of their real estate were also recorded[7], the variable ELOSS reflects the natural logarithm of the expected financial loss associated with the decline in real estate values. For both loss variables a positive influence on the individual contributions is expected. Moreover, since it makes a difference whether a marginal deterioration of health occurs when a person is in a state of good health or bad health, we include the initial health state (HSTATE) as an additional variable. We expect that a respondent with an initial state of excellent health contributes less, ceteris paribus, than one with an initial state of poor health[8]. The same reasoning applies to real estate values as expressed in log terms in our setup (ESTATE).

The differential effects of group size could not be tested for obvious reasons. Regarding exit as an alternative to participating in the contribution drive, sampling among those who decided to stay in Kleinblittersdorf is, of course, liable to the theoretical objection of a preselection bias[9]. However, when comparing migration data for Kleinblittersdorf to those of a large number of other municipalities (with a similar sociodemographic structure) well before as well as after the announcement of the plan to erect the incinerator, we did not find any evidence of the actual relevance of the exit option.

The least squares estimation results for the basic model are presented in column (1) in *table 1*[10]. This estimate excludes the real estate value (ESTATE) since the value of Pearson's coefficient of correlation ($r = 0.74$) suggests strong collinearity between this variable and real estate losses (ELOSS)[11].

operation of the automobile supplier's plant.

7. We got the impression that most respondents stated the assessed value of their real estates rather than the (potential) market value. This is not too surprising since the first is a well known component of the yearly tax declaration while the second may be rather unknown unless respondents try to sell the respective estates.
8. This means that we are assuming an increasing marginal disutility due to deterioration in health status.
9. For the same reason age cannot be considered as a reliable variable.
10. As the dependent variable can take on zero values, the contributions were slightly corrected upwards by an infinitesimal amount in order to keep the estimation approach (which is based on log terms) manageable.
11. The same does not hold for HSTATE and HLOSS, referring to Spearman's rank order coefficient, which amounts to 0.41.

VOLUNTARY PROVISION OF A PUBLIC GOOD

Table 1

Econometric Results for the Contribution Function[a]

Equation	(1)	(2)	(3)	(4)	(5)
Deterioration of health status HLOSS	1.74* (2.39)	1.15 (1.61)	1.15(*) (1.77)	–	1.06 (1.64)
Initial health status HSTATE	-1.13 (-1.59)	-0.97 (-1.42)	-1.29* (-2.07)	–	-1.14(*) (-1.84)
Natural logarithm of expected real estate losses ELOSS	0.33** (5.23)	0.29** (4.66)	0.14* (2.44)	–	0.13* (2.19)
Information scale INFO	–	4.54** (3.99)	2.41* (2.19)	–	2.31* (2.12)
Natural logarithm of living years in the community LTIME	–	–	1.30 (1.35)	2.68** (2.90)	1.25 (1.31)
Natural logarithm of number of children NCHILD	–	–	4.73* (2.34)	5.41** (2.70)	4.93* (2.46)
Participation in the meeting MEET	–	–	4.48* (2.11)	7.73** (3.90)	4.78* (2.27)
Appeal to donate DM 800 DON800	–	–	7.72** (5.66)	8.17** (5.90)	7.34** (5.39)
Appeal to donate 3% of real estate values DON3PERC	–	–	0.67* (2.54)	0.81** (3.00)	0.69* (2.63)
Participation altruism PALTR	–	–	–	–	0.23* (2.14)
CONST.	-7.79	-23.01	-24.22	-24.67	-22.84
R^2	0.16	0.23	0.42	0.36	0.43
Adjusted R^2	0.15	0.21	0.39	0.34	0.40
d.f.	197	196	191	195	190
F value	12.77	14.29	15.07	21.90	14.28

[a]The dependent variable consists in the natural logarithm of contributions (the mean of absolute contributions is DM 647.45, s.d. is DM 1,439.17, maximum is DM 10,895.78).

Notes: The numbers in parentheses represent the t-value of the respective coefficient. Two stars indicate statistical significance at the 99% confidence level, one star (in parenthesis) indicates statistical significance at the 95% (90%) confidence level. R^2 (adjusted R^2) corresponds to the coefficient of determination (corrected by the degrees of freedom); d.f. provides the degrees of freedom, and the F-value indicates the statistical significance of the estimate in total.

The coefficients of the two variables related to the expected decline in health and real estate value have the expected positive sign and are strongly significant. The coefficient of the initial health status has the expected negative sign, but falls short of the 90 percent confidence level by a narrow margin (significance at the 89 percent level). However, the narrow economic model explains only 15 percent of the variance of the contributions.

The performance of this basic model is somewhat better (adjusted $R^2 = 0.21$) if we take account of the information state as a conditioning variable, in line with STIGLER's (1961) extension of the traditional economic framework. The respective information variable (INFO) consists in the sum of dummy indicators of the knowledge of four events relevant to the contribution drive: (i) the establishment of a club to coordinate the collection and administration of the contributions; (ii) calculation and elicitation of the overall amount required to prevent the incinerator; (iii) the information that real estate values were down already by some 30 percent; (iv) presentation of the mayor's calculation of the necessary preparedness to contribute as discussed before. Thus, the information variable ranges from zero ('uninformed') to four ('fully informed') and should have a positive sign if we assume that people with poor information are not fully aware of the dangers. This hunch is confirmed in eq. (2) by the positive sign and strongly significant impact of our information variable[12], though the coefficients of the two variables related to health effects lose somewhat in statistical significance.

As a point of departure from our enlarged basic neoclassical model, let us now look at the other potential determinants which will have a positive impact on the intensity of contributing because they create a particular kind of embeddedness into a social network.

Informal components of psychic costs are represented by the variables LTIME, NCHILD and MEET. The first of those variables is recorded as the natural logarithm of the number of years an individual has been living in the municipality of Kleinblittersdorf. The second variable calculates as the log of the number of children in the respective household. We expect a positive coefficient for both variables, since the degree of affinity should be influenced in a positive way by the length of membership in a community and since 'investment in children' is associated with gathering another type of sunk costs.

12. As can be seen from the changes in the beta-coefficients F (not shown here) between eq. (1) and (2) (from 0.35 to 0.30 for ELOSS, from 0.18 to 0.12 for HLOSS and from -0.12 to -0.10 for HSTATE) as well as from the respective coefficient of INFO (0.26), maximization behavior seems to be guided by subjective considerations, i.e., assuming objective rationality is not without problems.

MEET stands for a dummy variable indicating participation in the general congregation (of June 1, 1988). There it was stated that, in order to raise enough money to prevent the construction of the incinerator, the necessary contribution of each citizen should be DM 800 on the average.

Formal embeddeness is reflected in the problem-related activities of that political institution which is responsible for acting in the interest of the community, namely the mayor. Right at the beginning of the fundraising efforts, Jeanrond appealed to the citizenry to donate DM 800 (DON800) or 10 percent of the assessed (30%) downfall of real estate values (DON3PERC). The effect of each appeal was asked for in the interview. In case a respondent stated that he was guided by the mayor's appeal to contribute DM 800, the log of the ratio of the respective household income to the amount of DM 800 is calculated indicating the ease or the degree of liquidity with which this sum can be contributed. Otherwise DON800 takes on the value of zero. In case a respondent reported having been influenced by the second appeal, this is processed by calculating the natural logarithm of the monetary amount corresponding to the requested three percent of the respective real estate value. Otherwise, DON3PERC is set to zero. In both cases we expect a positive sign.

The estimation results for this model which includes 'non-economic' costs are presented in column (3) of *table 1*. There is, evidently, a marked improvement in the performance of the econometric estimation (increase in adjusted R^2 from 0.21 to 0.39). The coefficients of all additional variables have the expected positive sign and are, with the exception of LTIME, strongly significant. The most important variables according to the level of statistical significance and to the beta-coefficients are the political institutions[13].

The relevance of formal and informal embeddedness can also be demonstrated by the results for eq. (4) which represents the influence of 'non-economic' factors in isolation. All variables are strongly significant and have the expected sign on their coefficients. Perhaps most strikingly, the goodness of fit (adjusted $R^2 = 0.34$) markedly surpasses that of the economic model, even in its extended form [adjusted $R^2 = 0.21$ in eq. (2)].

So far, we have been speaking of costs, i.e., restrictions on human behavior, in general. Attitudinal influences were captured, among other not explicitly specified influences, in the constant term due to the implicit assumption that all people have a free rider predisposition (which produces perfect collinearity with the 'true' constant term). Now we are going to relax this assumption by

13. The beta-coefficient for DON800 (0.34) exceeds the others by far; DON3PERC (0.15) reveals the same quantitative impact as ELOSS, the most important 'economic' variable.

introducing explicitly the variable PALTR, a proxy for participation altruism. A good indicator of the intensity of this attitude consists in a variable which provides evidence of the general donation behavior of an individual in the past. By asking peoples' former overall contribution to a number of large scale projects (such as environmental improvement, aid to developing countries etc.) we, in fact, capture the degree to which participation altruism was prevalent in the subjects of our sample. The amount of donations is related to the corresponding person's household income (as a logarithm function) in order to get a measure of the degree of voluntary participation[14]. PALTR is expected to have a positive impact on contributions, which is confirmed by eq. (5) in *table 1*.

Although the coefficient on PALTR has the expected positive sign and is statistically significant at the 95 percent confidence level, the goodness of fit is improved only slightly compared with eq. (3). Moreover, the impact of the so far dominating variables remains unaffected by this extension of the model[15].

In order to check the predictive quality of the models, we split up our sample into two halves by a random procedure, so as to be able to carry out the estimations with one subsample and to use the other subsample in order to control for the respective forecasting performance. The estimated coefficients differed only slightly from those in *table 1* (full sample), with all signs remaining unchanged[16]. As indicators of the predictive performance we chose three commonly used measures (GREENE, 1990, pp. 197 ff.), as indicated in *table 2*.

Table 2

Predictive Quality of the Models

Equation[a]	(1)	(2)	(3)	(4)	(5)
Root mean square error	15.35	15.69	13.62	12.73	14.07
Mean absolute error	13.50	13.48	11.55	11.36	11.66
Theil's inequality coefficient U[b]	0.83	0.85	0.74	0.69	0.76

[a]The equations refer to the same sequences of models (with the respective variables) as given in *table 1*.
[b]The higher this coefficient the poorer the predictive quality.

14. The mean of this ratio (in absolute terms) is 0.063 (s.d. = 0.092) overall and 0.075 (s.d. = 0.096) only for those who donated a positive amount.
15. Maximum likelihood specifications of the final econometric model produced mainly the same results (precise estimates can be obtained from the authors on request).
16. The estimation results can be obtained from the authors on request.

The values of all performance indicators support the basic idea that, besides economic factors, political and other reasons play a crucial role. The more weight is given to non-economic variables [with a maximum in eq. (4)], the higher is the predictive quality.

IV. CONCLUDING REMARKS

In the paper we looked at the actual behavior of individuals in a real world public good setting. In contrast to the strong version of the free rider hypothesis we observed that people contributed to a considerable amount, namely DM 3,500,000 at a population size of 16,000 (or, equivalently, 5,500 households), to the provision of a public good.

In-depth analysis of potential determinants of the individual contributions reveals the indisputable importance of economic factors. People are apparently guided by the desire to avoid financial as well as health damages. However, confining the analysis to merely economic factors distracts attention from other motives that are rooted in the social network as well as the political frame. From our case which, we admit, may correspond to a unique situation, we could even infer that the latter ones are perhaps more relevant to a citizen's decision than the narrowly defined economic reasons.

REFERENCES

AKERLOF, GEORGE A. and WILLIAM T. DICKENS (1982): The Economic Consequences of Cognitive Dissonance, *American Economic Review*, Vol. 72, 307-319.

ALLINGHAM, MICHAEL G. and AGNAR SANDMO (1972): Income Tax Evasion: A Theoretical Analysis, *Journal of Public Economics*, Vol. 1, 323-338.

ALM, JAMES; GARY H. MCCLELLAND and WILLIAM D. SCHULZE (1992): Why Do People Pay Taxes? *Journal of Public Economics*, Vol. 48, 21-38.

AXELROD, ROBERT (1984): *The Evolution of Cooperation*, New York: Basic Books.

BAGNOLI, MARK and MICHAEL MCKEE (1991): Voluntary Contribution Games: Efficient Private Provision of Public Goods, *Economic Inquiry*, Vol. 29, 351-366.

BOHM, PETER (1972): Estimating the Demand for Public Goods: An Experiment, *European Economic Review*, Vol. 3, 111-130.

BRUNNER, KARL (1978): Reflections on the Political Economy of Government. The Persistent Growth of Government, *Schweizerische Zeitschrift für Volkswirtschaft und Statistik*, Vol. 114, 649-680.

ERARD, BRIAN and JONATHAN S. FEINSTEIN (1993): The Role of Moral Sentiments and Audit Perceptions in Tax Compliance, Unpublished Manuscript, Carleton University.

GAITSGORY, VLADIMIR and SHMUEL NITZAN (1993): A 'Folk-Theorem' in a Dynamic Game of Private Provision of Public Goods, Unpublished Manuscript, Bar Ilan University Ramat Gan.

GREENE, WILLIAM H. (1990): *Econometric Analysis*, New York: Macmillan.

HIRSCHMAN, ALBERT O. (1982): *Shifting Involvements. Private Interest and Public Action*, Princeton, N.J.: Princeton University Press.

JUAN, ANA DE; M.A. LASHERAS and R. MAYO (1993): Voluntary Compliance and Behavior of Spanish Taxpayers, Unpublished Manuscript, Instituto de Estudios Fiscales, Madrid.

MARGOLIS, HOWARD (1982): *Selfishness, Altruism and Rationality: A Theory of Social Choice*, Cambridge: Cambridge University Press.

MESTELMAN, STUART and DAVID FEENY (1988): Does Ideology Matter? Anecdotal Experimental Evidence on the Voluntary Provision of Public Goods, *Public Choice*, Vol. 57, 281-286.

MORIN, ROGER A. and A. FERNANDEZ SUAREZ (1983): Risk Aversion Revisited, *Journal of Finance*, Vol. 38, 1201-1216.

OLSON, MANCUR (1965): *The Logic of Collective Action: Public Goods and the Theory of Groups*, Cambridge, MA: Harvard University Press.

OSTROM, ELINOR (1990): *Governing the Commons: The Evolution of Institutions of Collective Action*, Cambridge, MA: Cambridge University Press.

PALFREY, THOMAS R. and HOWARD ROSENTHAL (1988): Private Incentives in Social Dilemmas: The Effects of Incomplete Information and Altruism, *Journal of Public Economics*, Vol. 35, 309-332.

POMMEREHNE, WERNER W. and BRUNO S. FREY (1993): The Effects of Tax Administration on Tax Morale, in: B. GENSER and H. WECK-HANNEMANN (eds.), *International Political Economy of Taxation*, Konstanz: Sonderforschungsbereich Internationalisierung der Wirtschaft.

SCHNEIDER, FRIEDRICH and WERNER W. POMMEREHNE (1981): Free Riding and Collective Action: An Experiment in Public Microeconomics, *Quarterly Journal of Economics*, Vol. 96, 689-704.

SEN, AMARTYA K. (1977): Rational Fools: A Critique of the Behavioral Foundations of Economic Theory, *Philosophy and Public Affairs*, Vol. 6, 317-344.

STIGLER, GEORGE J. (1961): The Economics of Information, *Journal of Political Economy*, Vol. 69, 213-225.

SZPIRO, GEORGE G. (1986): Über das Risikoverhalten in der Schweiz, *Schweizerische Zeitschrift für Volkswirtschaft und Statistik*, Vol. 122, 463-470.

VAN DE KRAGT, ALPHONS J.C.; ROBYN M. DAWES and JOHN M. ORBELL (1988): Are People Who Cooperate 'Rational Altruists'? *Public Choice*, Vol. 56, 233-247.

WEISBROD, BURTON A. and NESTOR D. DOMINGUEZ (1986): Demand for Collective Goods in Private Non-Profit Markets: Can Fundraising Expenditures Help Overcome Free Riding Behavior? *Journal of Public Economics*, Vol. 30, 83-95.

SUMMARY

According to standard economic theory, voluntary provision of a public good is, at least in large group settings, hampered by people's presumed free rider disposition. In this paper, actual behavior of individuals in a non-hypothetical situation with large group characteristics was subjected to empirical testing as regards the validity of the neoclassical claim. In the case under consideration, the citizens of a municipality indeed overcame the free rider problem by voluntarily contributing on a large scale. It was found that 'economic' factors such as avoiding individual losses were important motivations, but political and other reasons also played a crucial role.

VOLUNTARY PROVISION OF A PUBLIC GOOD

ZUSAMMENFASSUNG

Gemäss der traditionellen ökonomischen Theorie wird die freiwillige Bereitstellung eines öffentlichen Gutes durch die annahmegemässe Freifahrerveranlagung der Wirtschaftssubjekte erschwert, zumindest wenn es sich um eine grosse Gruppe handelt. Im vorliegenden Beitrag wurde das tatsächliche Verhalten von Individuen in einer nicht hypothetischen Situation empirischen Tests unterzogen, und dies insbesondere im Hinblick auf die Verlässlichkeit der neoklassischen Behauptung. Im untersuchten Fall überwanden die Bürger einer Gemeinde tatsächlich das Freifahrerproblem. Es stellte sich heraus, dass 'ökonomische' Faktoren wie etwa das Vermeiden von Verlusten eine bedeutende Motivation darstellen, dass aber auch politische und andere Gründe eine entscheidende Rolle spielen.

RÉSUMÉ

Selon la théorie économique standard, la mise à disposition volontaire d'un bien public est, du moins dans le cadre d'un large échantillon, entravée par la présomption selon laquelle les individus sont prédisposés à se comporter en passagers clandestins. Dans cette contribution, le comportement réel des individues dans une situation non-hypothétique, présentant les caractéristiques d'un échantillon important, a été soumis à des tests empiriques en ce qui concerne la fiabilité de l'affirmation néoclassique. Dans le cas considéré, les citoyens d'une commune ont effectivement surmonté le problème de passager clandestin en offrant volontairement leur contribution dans une large mesure. Il s'est avéré que les facteurs 'économiques', tels que le fait d'éviter des pertes individuelles, constituaient une motivation importante, mais que des raisons politiques et d'autre nature jouaient également un rôle crucial.

[13]

ELSEVIER Journal of Public Economics 63 (1997) 331–349

JOURNAL OF PUBLIC ECONOMICS

The voluntary provision of a pure public good: The case of reduced CFC emissions and the Montreal Protocol*

James C. Murdoch[a], Todd Sandler[b,†]

[a]School of Social Sciences, University of Texas-Dallas, Richardson, TX 75083, USA
[b]Department of Economics, Iowa State University, Ames, IA 50011-1070, USA

Received June 1995; final version received January 1996

Abstract

This paper applies the theory of the voluntary provision of a pure public good to the behavior of nations to curb chlorofluorocarbon (CFC) emissions during the late 1980s. By devising an empirical test, we determine that these cutbacks in emissions are consistent with Nash behavior. When taste parameters are controlled, the relationship between emission cutbacks and national income is nearly linear as implied by the theory. If the sample is purged of potential outliers, then the linear relationship results. A significant taste parameter is the extent of political and civil freedoms, while a marginally significant parameter is geophysical position in terms of latitude.

Keywords: Public good; Montreal Protocol; Ozone shield; CFCs; Nash equilibrium

JEL classification: H41; D62; Q20

1. Introduction

In recent years, there has grown an increased awareness of transboundary pollution that places environmental assets at risk both globally and

* This paper was prepared under a cooperative agreement between the Institute for Policy Reform and the Agency for International Development (AID), Cooperative Agreement No. PDC-0095-A-00-1126-00. Our research was also funded by the National Science Foundation, grant SBR-9222953. Comments from two anonymous referees are gratefully acknowledged.

† Corresponding author. Tel. 515-294-5783, Fax: 515-294-0221, E-mail: tsandler@iastate.edu

PII S0047-2727(96)01598-8

regionally. Traditional nation-state jurisdictions need not coincide with the economic domain over which the economic impacts of consumption and production activities extend. Globally, manmade pollutants have degraded the stratospheric ozone shield, the oceans, the atmosphere, and the biodiversity of the planet; regionally, these pollutants have harmed aquifers, rivers, lakes, soils, and forests.[1] Many transboundary pollution problems share two common features: strategic interactions among nations and public good properties. Strategic interactions occur when the choices or the beliefs for these choices of two or more nations are mutually dependent in a significant fashion. To account for these interactions, a game theory formulation is often presented (see Barrett, 1994; and Sandler, 1993). Public good properties arise when the benefits (costs), derived from limiting (not limiting) the pollutant, provide consequences that are nonrival and nonexcludable to a set of nations. In the case of the stratospheric ozone, the release of chlorofluorocarbons (CFCs) and other halocarbons thins the shield that protects plants and animals from harmful ultraviolet radiation. This thinning has consequences for countries worldwide and is, thus, nonexcludable. Furthermore, one nation's increased exposure to enhanced ultraviolet radiation does not lessen the risks to any other nation; hence, nonrivalry is clearly present.

The purpose of this paper is to analyze *cutbacks* in CFC emissions *that, in large part, preceded* the ratification and institution of the Montreal Protocol on Substances that Deplete the Ozone Layer. It is our contention that the Montreal Protocol was initially enacted because it codified reductions in CFC emissions that polluters were voluntarily prepared to accomplish as the scientific case against CFCs grew. We investigate empirical predictions derived from the theory of the voluntary provision of public goods,[2] and find that the data are remarkably consistent with these predictions. That is, when tastes are controlled, the relationship between emission cutbacks and national income is nearly linear. A linear relationship is statistically significant if three outlier nations are removed from the sample. Our analysis is noteworthy because it provides the first statistical application of the group self-selection process as derived from the modern theory of the voluntary provision of pure public goods. If this latter theory is to prove useful, then empirical applications, such as the one here, need to be put forward.

Our findings suggest that the Montreal Protocol may be more symbolic than a true instance of a cooperative equilibrium, since nations' CFC

[1] See Helm (1991) and Sandler (1992) for analyses of a host of global and regional transboundary problems.

[2] On the private provision of public goods, see Andreoni (1988), Bergstrom, Blume, and Varian (1986), and Cornes and Sandler (1984, 1996).

reductions prior to the treaty taking effect appear to fit the predictions of a single-shot Nash equilibrium. By examining the data qualitatively, we provide further evidence that CFC cutbacks were voluntary, because these reductions characterized both ratifiers and nonratifiers, were at levels greater than the initial mandate, and displayed a large standard deviation.

This study differs from an important analysis by Congleton (1992), who related the ratification of the Vienna Convention of 1985 and the Montreal Protocol to political and market institutions. As such, Congleton did not explicitly account for public good attributes and did not include gross national product (GNP) levels of the participating nations.[3]

2. Background

2.1. The Stratospheric Ozone Shield

Despite its small concentration in the earth's atmosphere, representing less than one part per million, ozone absorbs much of the ultraviolet radiation (UV) of the sun and, thus, protects all living organisms and their DNA from UV's harmful effects. Any dissolution of the stratospheric ozone shield would not only increase the risk of skin cancer to humans, but would also threaten food supplies by adversely affecting phytoplankton at the base of the marine food chain. Disastrous consequences could result. The Environmental Protection Agency (EPA) estimated that the implementation of the Montreal Protocol of 1987 could save the United States $6.4 trillion by 2075 in reduced costs associated with skin cancers (EPA, 1987a, 1987b). In the absence of the Protocol, skin cancer incidence was based on an annual growth of CFC use at 2.5 percent through 2050. The long-run cost from cutting CFC use, as mandated by the Protocol, was estimated to be between $20 and $40 billion during the 1989-2075 period, given these projected growth rates (Morrisette et al., 1990, p. 16). For the United States, net gains would come from cutbacks in CFC emissions.

In 1985, the British Antarctic Survey presented evidence that an alarming 40 percent drop (from 1964 levels) in the springtime atmospheric concentration of ozone took place over Halley Bay, Antarctica, between 1977 and 1984. This so-called "hole" in the ozone layer of the stratosphere then drifts northward during the summer and mixes with other air masses, thus allowing the depletion to be shared worldwide on a more or less equal basis.

[3] Congleton (1992, p. 419) included GNP *per capita* in two of the six empirical models, but later dropped the variable, because of concerns that CFC regulations could affect GNP. Given the small percentage of GNP that is related to CFC production and consumption, we chose to ignore any such simultaneity.

The uniform mixing during the summertime reinforces the pure publicness of ozone depletion on a global basis. As the scientific case against CFCs mounted and the depletion process became understood, the main producer nations were motivated to curb emissions even if they had to act alone. The rapid development of CFC substitutes (e.g., hydrofluorocarbon) meant that there was little opposition to limiting CFC production by the CFC producers (Morrisette et al., 1990).

2.2. *Montreal Protocol of 1987*

Just prior to the discovery of the Antarctic ozone hole, nations negotiated the Convention for the Protection of the Ozone Layer in Vienna on 22 March 1985. This precursor to the Montreal Protocol mandated the ratifiers to study the harmful effects of CFC emissions on the ozone layer. Nations were committed to monitor the ozone layer, to exchange scientific findings, and to develop domestic programs for limiting ozone-depleting substances (see the U.N. Environment Programme (UNEP), 1991 for treaty texts).

On 16 September 1987, the Montreal Protocol extended the Vienna Convention by setting explicit limits to the emission of ozone-depleting substances, particularly CFC-11 and CFC-12. The Montreal Protocol entered into force on 1 January 1989, and included the following features: By 1 July 1993, ratifiers must reduce their annual consumption and production of CFCs to 1986 levels. For subsequent years until 1 July 1998, this annual production and consumption cannot exceed 80% of 1986 levels. Thereafter, it could not exceed 50% of 1986 levels. Beginning in 1990, the ratifiers must ban the import of ozone-depleting substances from nonratifiers; starting in 1993, a similar ban would apply to the export of these substances.

Ratifiers of the Montreal Protocol were automatically considered to be parties to the Vienna Convention. During 1989, the ratifiers were only obligated to return to 1986 emission levels; this fact becomes important for interpreting the empirical findings. Developing nations had a great inducement to ratify the Protocol, because they could delay compliance by ten years, gain technical and financial assistance, and be exempted from trade sanctions. If a developing nation qualified for these special treatments, it is referred to as an "Article 5" country.

During 1990, scientific evidence indicated that the thinning of the ozone layer had worsened and that a large hole had opened over the North Pole. On 29 June 1990, the Montreal Protocol was strengthened with a set of amendments (UNEP, 1991).

3. Theoretical Considerations

The theoretical model draws from the work of Andreoni (1988), Andreoni and McGuire (1993), and others, who used a subscription model of public good contributions to identify contributors. This model is extended by allowing for a non-normalized price of the public good. We assume that a nation's preferences for a global public good, G, is represented by a quasi-concave, strictly increasing utility function,

$$U_i = U_i(y_i, G), \tag{1}$$

where y_i is the ith nation's consumption of a composite private good and G is the total amount of the public good available for consumption, so that

$$G = \sum_{i \in C} g_i \, . \tag{2}$$

In Eq. (2), g_i is the ith nation's contribution to the public good and C denotes the set of contributors ($g_i > 0$). Total contributions can also be written as $g_i + G_{-i}$, where G_{-i} is the sum of contributions from contributors other than nation i, so that

$$G_{-i} = \sum_{j \neq i} g_j . \tag{3}$$

We normalize just the price of the private good and write the ith nation's linear income constraint as

$$w_i = y_i + pg_i, \tag{4}$$

where w_i denotes national income and p is the per-unit price of the public good. A full-income budget constraint follows from adding pG_{-i} to both sides of Eq. (4) to give

$$w_F^i = w_i + pG_{-i} = y_i + pG, \tag{5}$$

where w_F^i denotes the ith nation's full income – income plus spillins of public good benefits. To derive the nation's demand for the total amount of the public good, we depict the nation as solving the following problem:

$$\max_{y_i, G} \{U_i(y_i, G) | w_i + pG_{-i} = y_i + pG; G \geqq G_{-i}\} . \tag{6}$$

In Eq. (6), the inequality constraint indicates that the ith nation is a contributor and, hence, a member of C only when $G > G_{-i}$, so that $g_i > 0$. Noncontributors choose a G that equals G_{-i} and contribute nothing. The Kuhn-Tucker first-order conditions imply the following continuous demand function,

$$G = \max\{f_i(w_i + pG_{-i}; p), G_{-i}\} , \tag{7}$$

for the pubic good. When contributions are positive, the nation's demand for G is $f_i(\cdot)$; otherwise it is G_{-i}. A Nash equilibrium results when we have a vector of individual contributions, g_i, that maximize utility in (1) subject to (4) and to the best-response level for spillins, G^*_{-i}. This equilibrium is unique provided that all goods have positive income elasticities, which we, henceforth, assume.

When the stratospheric ozone shield is considered, g_i denotes the reduction in ozone-depleting CFC emissions and y_i represents all other goods. To maintain tractability and facilitate analogy with the public goods literature, we analyze only the nation's behavior with respect to current emission policy. Although this approach ignores dynamic stock adjustments, it is consistent with the language and articles of the Montreal Protocol.

To distinguish contributors and allow for heterogeneous tastes, we must put some structure on the taste pattern. Following Andreoni (1988, pp. 64–66), we allow nations' tastes to differ according to a taste parameter, Θ, so that

$$U_i = U_i(y_i, G; \Theta), \tag{8}$$

where Θ is used to *index* the various (finite) types of nations and may be a vector of exogenous parameters. For a given Θ, nations' demand for the public good can be rank ordered by income so that $g_i > g_j$ when $w_i(\Theta) > w_j(\Theta)$ owing to the assumption of income normality (Andreoni, 1988). The taste parameter, Θ, orders contributors among different taste classes. For a given income, this parameter is greater when the nation's taste for the public good is greater. We can utilize the result in Bergstrom, Blume, and Varian (1986, Fact 4) to identify the critical income level, w^*, conditional on p and Θ, below which no nation contributes. Specifically, a nation's equilibrium contribution, g_i^*, is[4]

$$g_i^* = \begin{cases} w_i/p - w^*(p, \Theta)/p & \text{if } w_i > w^*(p, \Theta), \\ 0 & \text{if } w_i \leqq w^*(p, \Theta), \end{cases} \tag{9}$$

where critical income $w^*(p, \Theta)$ equals $f^{-1}(G^*; p, \Theta) - pG^*$ and $f^{-1}(\cdot)$ is the inverse of $f(\cdot)$. Eq. (9) indicates that pollution cutbacks are a linear function of income with a slope of $1/p$. It also follows that all contributors within the same taste category consume the same amount of the private good, which equals $w^*(p, \Theta)/p$, and allocate their remaining income to the public good. This last result is not as unrealistic as it might seem, since, for a given Θ, $w^*(\cdot)$ might be quite high. By including taste parameters based on geophysical location, freedom indices, and other considerations, we have a

[4] This follows from examining total equilibrium contributions, which implies

$$G^* \geqq f(w_i + pG^*_{-i}; p, \Theta) \quad i = 1, \ldots, n,$$

with equality for $g_i^* > 0$. To derive Eq. (9), we invert both sides of the above equation, add pg_i^* to both sides, and rearrange terms.

fair number of classes. When population is included in Θ, each nation is a class unto itself; when it is not included in Θ, there are still numerous classes. By (9), there is a critical income level for *each* class of nations. Type Θ nations will contribute whenever their income exceeds $w^*(p, \Theta)$.

Eq. (9) indicates that a nation's demand for a global public good depends on national income and taste attributes. For instance, the Θ parameter could relate to the country's geographical position in terms of latitude. Temperate and arctic countries may have a greater preference for curbing CFCs emissions than tropical nations owing to generally fairer-skinned populations and to greater springtime exposure at higher latitudes to ultraviolet radiation.[5] Population size is another taste parameter, since countries with larger populations are exposed to greater potential damage from the incidence of skin cancers. The number of such cancers is expected to be proportional to population size.

Tastes may also differ between autocratic and democratic regimes. Congleton (1992) theorized that autocratic regimes will do less to protect the ozone shield, insofar as these autocracies confront a higher relative price for pollution abatement than their democratic median-voter counterpart. Congleton also argued that autocracies are less risk averse and, hence, less interested than democracies in insurance-type actions that protect against contingencies such as ozone depletion. Given the relatively short-term nature of most autocracies,[6] he also hypothesized that autocratic governments would not be as concerned about the long-run consequences of ozone depletion. Olson (1993) characterized autocracies as maximizing tax revenues and maintaining their monopoly rights over these taxes. As such, autocracies should be suspicious of protocols that could impose taxes or else could mandate contributions to a Multilateral Fund used to provide technology transfer and financial assistance to others. Olson indicated that autocracies would provide public goods when their provision *augments* taxable income sufficiently to finance the goods and leave some net gain. No short-run augmentation in taxable income can be expected to arise from cutting CFC emissions.[7] Autocracies may, therefore, be less willing than democracies to support ozone protection. Within the group of autocracies or

[5] This exposure difference could be taken into account by using a technology function, $k_i(G)$, so that $U_i = U_i(y_i, k_i(G), \Theta)$. This extension means that cut-off income is now $wi^*(p, \Theta)$, which differs even within the same taste class. We avoid this complication by assuming $k_i(G) = G$ and letting the taste parameter adjust for different risk perceptions. There is no empirical data that would allow us to calibrate the $k_i(G)$ functions, especially since ozone concentrations vary greatly even over the same country (de Gruijl, 1995).

[6] Bienen and van der Walle (1989) provided evidence that African autocracies lasted only four years on average.

[7] Reduced CFC emissions will improve health and productivity in the long run, but since we are concerned with only a four-year span, income augmentation is ignored.

democracies, the theory predicts that the cutback in CFCs emissions will be related to income.

4. Empirical Results

4.1. Empirical Model

Eq. (9) provides the theoretical predictions that can be tested with observed data. When tastes differences are ignored, Eq. (9) suggests that if we measure the voluntary contributions (g_i) and the income (w_i) of countries and then plot these data with income on the horizontal axis and contributions on the vertical axis, the data *should* lie on either the horizontal axis ($g_i = 0$) or on a line beginning at w^*/p with slope $1/p$. If we limit our investigation to countries with positive voluntary contributions, then the data should lie on the straight line. This prediction is, in principle, testable, but a major obstacle is to measure g_i and w_i precisely. If we assume random errors in measuring g_i and w_i, then

$$g_i = \beta_0 + \beta_1 w_i + \epsilon_i \tag{10}$$

is a reasonable empirical model for the data-generating process described in Eq. (9) for Θ constant. β_0 and β_1 can be estimated with ordinary least squares (OLS). We can test how well the model adheres to the straight line by assuming that the ϵ_i is normally distributed with mean zero and standard deviation σ.

Although the regression model described in Eq. (10) provides a simple method for testing whether the slope, β_1, of the hypothesized line is $1/p$, it does not facilitate a test of linearity. One means to test linearity is to estimate the transformation parameter of the Box-Cox transformation (Box and Cox, 1964; Spitzer, 1982). With λ denoting this parameter, the model becomes:

$$g_i = \beta_0 + \beta_1[(w_i^\lambda - 1)/\lambda] + \epsilon_i\ , \tag{11}$$

requiring a nonlinear least squares estimator. A test for linearity is based on λ. If λ is equal to one, then the model is linear with respect to w_i.

According to Eq. (9), the linearity of the relationship between w_i and g_i only holds within each group of nations as defined by the Θ parameter. To implement an empirical test of this prediction, we need to measure the taste differences of nations. Let $\boldsymbol{\Theta}_i$ denote a 1 by k vector of observable taste measures and $\boldsymbol{\gamma}$ denote a k by 1 vector of unknown parameters. Then a statistical model based on Eq. (9) is

$$g_i = \beta_0 + \beta_1[(w_i^\lambda - 1)/\lambda] + \boldsymbol{\Theta}_i\boldsymbol{\gamma} + \epsilon_i\ . \tag{12}$$

If the Andreoni (1988) model is more appropriate, then we should see significance in the estimates for the γ parameters and more linearity in the relationship between g_i and w_i when we compare estimates of Eq. (12) to (11).

4.2. Data and Variable Definitions

Our primary measure of g_i is $DEMIT_i$, which is the change in the CFC emissions for country i from 1986 to 1989 (EMIT86 — EMIT89). In total, 61 nations had positive values for $DEMIT_i$, thus making a positive contribution to the protection of the ozone layer. To test for voluntary behavior, we include only these countries, whether they ratified the Montreal Protocol or not,[8] in the regression estimates. The data for EMIT86 and EMIT89 are reported in World Resources Institute (WRI)(1990, 1992). Since 1986 is the benchmark year for the Montreal Protocol and 1989 is before any emission reductions (contributions) are mandated under the treaty, $DEMIT_i$ is a satisfactory measure of *voluntary* contributions.[9]

To measure income (w_i), we use gross national product in 1985 (GNP85). For the majority of the countries, GNP85 is obtained from the *World Tables* produced by the World Bank (1990). For some nations, in particular those with nonmarket economies, GNP data are taken from the *World Fact Book: 1989* (Central Intelligence Agency, 1989).

We use three measures for the components of the vector ($\boldsymbol{\Theta}$) of taste variables. The first is GASTIL, which is the sum of Gastil's (1986) index of civil liberties and index of political rights. These indices are integers, with 1 representing the most liberties and rights and 7 representing the least. Thus, GASTIL takes on integer values from 2 to 14. A country with a value of 2 would be considered the most "free." Because it is not clear that freedom can be measured on a nominal scale, as assumed in the GASTIL measure, we define three dummy variables to measure freedom: FREE equals 1 when GASTIL is 4 or smaller, and 0 otherwise; PFREE (partly free) equals 1 when GASTIL is greater than 4 but less than or equal to 9, and 0 otherwise; and NFREE (not free) equals 1 when GASTIL is greater than 9, and 0 otherwise. The second empirical measure of tastes is based on geographical location, in which LAT is defined to equal: 1 for all countries located above the Tropic of Cancer; 2 for all countries between the Tropic of Cancer and

[8] The status of countries with respect to the Montreal Protocol is obtained from UNEP (1993).

[9] WRI (1990, 1992) do not report any nations with zero emissions in both 1986 and 1989 or with the same emissions in both 1986 and 1989. Thus, we do not have data on the countries with zero contributions and the only testable hypothesis is that the relationship between positive contributions and income is linear.

the Tropic of Capricorn; and 3 for the countries below the Tropic of Capricorn.[10] Dummy variables corresponding to LAT were also defined. Thus, L1 is 1 when LAT is 1, and 0 otherwise; L2 is 1 when LAT is 2, and 0 otherwise; and L3 is 1 when LAT is 3, and 0 otherwise. Because of the risks that a thinning ozone layer poses for human health, we include POP85, the population in 1985, as the third taste shift variable.

A summary of the empirical variables and their definitions is displayed in Table 1, while the raw data are presented in Table A1. Included are two additional variables: RAT equals 1 for the nations that ratified the Montreal Protocol before 1 January 1990, and 0 otherwise; while ART5 equals 1 for nations designated as Article 5 developing nations, and 0 otherwise. These variables allow us to *qualitatively* assess a cooperative model of emission reductions, which is the most likely alternative to the subscription model. There are four grounds for rejecting a cooperative model. First, only 38 of these 61 nations (some 54%) ratified the Montreal Protocol during the time period covered by our data. If emission reductions are simply a reflection of the treaty mandate and, therefore, assumed to be generated by a model of

Table 1
Variable Descriptions

Variable	Description
GNP85	Gross National Product in 1985, expressed in hundred billions of dollars.
EMIT86	CFC emissions in 1986, expressed in thousand metric tons.
EMIT89	CFC emissions in 1989, expressed in thousand metric tons.
DEMIT	EMIT86 — EMIT89.
GASTIL	The sum of the Gastil's indices of civil liberties and political freedom.
FREE	A dummy variable equal to 1 for GASTIL $\leqq 4$, and 0 otherwise.
PFREE	A dummy variable equal to 1 for $4 <$ GASTIL $\leqq 9$, and 0 otherwise.
NFREE	A dummy variable equal to 1 for GASTIL $\geqq 10$.
L1	A dummy variable equal to 1 if a country is located above the Tropic of Cancer, and 0 otherwise.
L2	A dummy variable equal to 1 if a country is located between the Tropics of Cancer and Capricorn, and 0 otherwise.
L3	A dummy variable equal to 1 if a country is located below the Tropic of Capricorn, and 0 otherwise.
LAT	Equal to 1 for L1 = 1; equal to 2 for L2 = 1; and equal to 3 for L3 = 1.
POP85	Population in 1985, expressed in millions.
RAT	A dummy variable equal to 1 if a country ratified the Montreal Protocol before 1 January 1990, and 0 otherwise.
ART5	A dummy variable equal to 1 if a country is an Article 5 country, and 0 otherwise.

[10] In cases where the latitude cut through a country's border, we coded the country based on where the largest area is located.

cooperative behavior,[11] we would expect a much larger percentage to have ratified. In fact, nonratifiers would have no institutionalized reason for reducing their emission levels as they were not party to the Protocol. If, however, emission reductions reflect a nation's voluntary subscription level, then the fact that a CFC-reducing nation is almost equally likely to be a ratifier or nonratifier is not unexpected. Second, recall that the Montreal

Table A1
Raw Data

Country	GNP85	POP85	DEMIT	GASTIL	LAT	RAT	ART5
United States	40.128	239.283	67.400	2	1	1	0
USSR	23.540	276.946	34.398	14	1	1	0
Germany, FR	6.708	61.035	15.991	3	1	1	0
France	5.379	55.170	14.922	3	1	1	0
United Kingdom	4.796	56.618	15.455	2	1	1	0
Italy	4.411	57.141	15.433	2	1	1	0
Canada	3.589	25.379	9.405	2	1	1	0
China	3.432	1040.04	6.066	12	1	0	1
Brazil	2.264	135.564	2.616	5	2	0	1
Germany, DR	2.081	16.644	4.404	13	1	1	0
Australia	1.831	15.758	4.276	2	3	1	0
Mexico	1.712	78.524	0.218	8	2	1	1
Iran	1.680	44.212	2.245	11	1	0	1
Spain	1.649	38.523	10.653	3	1	1	0
Netherlands	1.355	14.491	3.861	2	1	1	0
Switzerland	1.053	6.472	3.443	2	1	1	0
Saudi Arabia	0.991	11.595	0.475	13	2	0	0
Sweden	0.989	8.350	0.796	2	1	1	0
Nigeria	0.947	99.669	9.883	12	1	1	1
Indonesia	0.856	164.630	4.447	11	2	0	1
Belgium	0.836	9.858	2.671	2	1	1	0
Poland	0.774	37.203	2.025	11	1	0	0
Austria	0.684	7.555	1.852	2	1	1	0
Argentina	0.649	30.331	0.285	4	3	0	1
Denmark	0.578	5.114	1.372	2	1	1	0
Turkey	0.543	50.310	3.832	8	1	0	1
Finland	0.541	4.908	2.119	4	1	1	0
Yugoslavia	0.476	23.123	0.752	11	1	0	0
Colombia	0.384	28.418	1.272	5	2	0	0
Greece	0.358	9.919	2.746	4	1	1	0
Iraq	0.310	15.898	0.721	14	1	0	0
Egypt	0.309	47.578	0.168	8	1	1	1

[11] By cooperative behavior, we mean cutbacks beyond those that a nation was prepared to make on their own. As information about ozone depletion was revealed, some nations made voluntary CFC cutbacks.

Table A1 *cont.*

Country	GNP85	POP85	DEMIT	GASTIL	LAT	RAT	ART5
U. Arab Emirates	0.284	1.350	0.323	10	2	1	0
Israel	0.278	4.233	0.298	4	1	0	0
Kuwait	0.256	1.712	0.404	8	1	0	1
New Zealand	0.219	3.247	1.169	2	3	1	0
Portugal	0.200	10.157	2.716	3	1	1	0
Singapore	0.195	2.558	1.433	9	2	1	0
Chile	0.176	12.121	0.888	11	3	0	1
Ireland	0.171	3.521	1.074	2	1	1	0
Ecuador	0.109	9.378	0.669	5	2	0	1
Tunisia	0.085	7.261	0.359	10	1	1	1
Trinidad & Tob.	0.072	1.185	0.197	3	2	1	1
Cote d'Ivoire	0.065	10.252	0.471	11	2	0	0
Zimbabwe	0.053	8.406	0.389	10	2	0	1
Luxembourg	0.052	0.366	0.137	2	1	1	0
Uruguay	0.051	2.940	0.119	4	3	0	1
Dominican R.	0.049	6.416	0.325	4	2	0	0
Ghana	0.047	12.620	0.637	13	2	1	1
Panama	0.046	2.180	0.023	9	2	1	1
Afghanistan	0.040	18.087	0.993	14	1	0	0
El Salvador	0.040	4.768	0.225	6	2	0	1
Costa Rica	0.035	2.489	0.153	2	2	0	1
Honduras	0.032	4.383	0.089	5	2	0	0
Bahrain	0.032	0.425	0.038	10	1	0	0
Iceland	0.028	0.241	0.046	2	1	1	0
Nicaragua	0.025	3.272	0.220	10	2	0	0
Senegal	0.024	6.567	0.353	7	2	0	0
Barbados	0.012	0.253	0.061	3	2	0	1
Fiji	0.011	0.700	0.060	4	2	1	1
Liberia	0.010	2.178	0.067	10	2	0	0

Note: See Table 1 for the definitions of variables.

Protocol mandated that ratifiers achieve 1986 levels by 1 July 1993. However, for the sample nations, *the average percent reduction from* 1986 *to* 1989 *is greater than* 41% implying voluntary behavior. Third, there is the variation in the DEMIT data. The Protocol called for equal percentage reductions in CFCs; however, the standard deviation of DEMIT is greater than 17%. If a cooperative solution were responsible for the observed behavior, we would expect the standard deviation to be close to zero. Finally, there is the behavior of the Article 5 countries. Because the Protocol excuses them for ten years from complying with the mandates, it would not be unexpected if none of the Article 5 nations appeared in our data set. Surprisingly, 22 of these Article 5 nations are among the contributors. Moreover, their average percentage reduction in emissions is greater than 45%, which is somewhat greater than the overall average! We find it difficult to conceive that these figures correspond to a cooperative model, the outcome of which is the Montreal Protocol. We, thus, concentrate on using the subscription model as the basis for our empirical estimations.

4.3. Regression Results

Nonlinear least squares estimates of the parameters in Eqs. (11) and (12) are presented in Table 2. The estimates on GNP85 and LAMBDA are significant at conventional levels in all seven specifications. The coefficient on the GASTIL index is negative and significant in models 2, 4 and 6, indicating that nations with fewer political and civil freedoms voluntarily contributed less when the other influences are held constant. Designating NFREE as the left-out dummy variable, the estimates on FREE and PFREE re-enforce the GASTIL estimates. In particular, we find that the primary distinction is between the nations categorized as FREE and all other nations. The positive sign on FREE indicates that the conditional expected value of $DEMIT_i$ is greater relative to NFREE, while the essentially zero coefficient on PFREE means that the conditional expected

Table 2
Nonlinear Least Squares Estimates of the Box—Cox Model. (n = 61)

	Models						
Variable	(1)	(2)	(3)	(4)	(5)	(6)	(7)
INTERCEPT	3.160	4.022	2.631	4.366	2.904	4.372	3.137
	(9.95)	(7.72)	(5.25)	(7.83)	(5.21)	(7.82)	(5.12)
GNP85	2.535	2.493	2.446	2.327	2.326	2.423	2.429
	(10.39)	(10.46)	(10.11)	(8.98)	(8.89)	(8.63)	(8.57)
GASTIL		−0.137		−0.134		−0.116	
		(−2.05)		(−1.98)		(−1.64)	
FREE			1.129		1.134		0.957
			(1.81)		(1.77)		(1.43)
PFREE			−0.212		−0.094		−0.176
			(−0.27)		(−0.12)		(−0.22)
L2				−0.904	−0.651	−0.898	−0.656
				(−1.40)	(−0.93)	(−1.38)	(−1.28)
L3				−1.283	−1.343	−1.284	-1.341
				(−1.24)	(−1.29)	(−1.24)	(−1.28)
POP85						−0.002	−0.002
						(−0.88)	(−0.93)
LAMBDA	0.822	0.828	0.835	0.853	0.852	0.840	0.838
	(20.05)	(20.44)	(20.07)	(18.76)	(18.55)	(18.16)	(18.00)
R^2	0.95	0.96	0.96	0.96	0.96	0.96	0.96

Note: The dependent variable is $DEMIT_i$. Asymptotic t-ratios are in parentheses.

value of $DEMIT_i$ is the same for PFREE and NFREE nations. The effect of FREE is marginally significant, since the critical values for the t-statistics are 1.678 and 1.282 (0.10 level of significance) for a two-tailed and one-tailed test, respectively. Regardless of whether we use GASTIL or the freedom dummy variables, the findings with respect to these rights and freedom measures are consistent with the predictions of Congleton (1992) and Olson (1993).

The latitude dummy variables are included in models 4, 5, 6, and 7. At a 0.10 level of significance, the latitude effects are technically insignificant in these models. The northern latitudes are the left-out category; hence, the estimates on L2 and L3 are relative to L1. The negative signs mean that the expected value of $DEMIT_i$, conditional on income, freedoms, and population, is less for the middle and lower (southern) latitude countries when compared to the expected value of the northern latitude group. Somewhat surprisingly, POP85 is insignificant and negative in both models 6 and 7. The R-squares are very high for cross-sectional data, which may indicate an "outlier" problem that we investigate below.

We are particularly interested in the estimates for the Box-Cox transformation parameter, LAMBDA, whose estimate from Model 1 is significantly different than one. The asymptotic standard error is .04, thus yielding a 95% confidence interval of $.822 \pm .08$. Andreoni's (1988) analysis indicates that linearity between income and contributions may not hold over all nations, but should hold within subclasses defined by taste parameters. By examining the remaining six estimates for LAMBDA, we see some empirical support for this hypothesis. As the tastes of the nations are controlled, the point estimate for LAMBDA moves closer to one; but, the 95% confidence interval estimates never include one.

From a purely statistical point-of-view, the results concerning the Box-Cox transformation parameter provide sufficient evidence to reject the pure subscription model. At the practical level, we cannot ignore the fact that the point estimates of LAMBDA are very close to one. To better understand this finding, we estimated the linear models using ordinary least squares (OLS) and give the results in Table 3. The qualitative conclusions are essentially the same, when comparing the nonlinear estimates in Table 2 to the OLS estimates in Table 3. Notable differences are that the estimates on L2 are more precise and the POP85 point estimates are positive for OLS estimates.

How do the estimates of $\partial g_i / \partial w_i$ vary between the Box-Cox and linear specifications? For the Box-Cox model, the estimated derivative depends on the value of w_i. Based on Box-Cox model 7, the largest estimated derivative is approximately 5.07 for Liberia whose 1985 GNP equals approximately $1 billion, while the lowest estimated derivative is approximately 1.35 for the

J.C. Murdoch, T. Sandler / Journal of Public Economics 63 (1997) 331–349 345

Table 3
Ordinary Least Squares Estimates of the Linear Model. (n = 61)

	Models						
Variable	(1)	(2)	(3)	(4)	(5)	(6)	(7)
INTERCEPT	1.061	2.050	0.559	2.712	1.213	2.714	1.203
	(3.28)	(3.61)	(1.06)	(4.50)	(2.03)	(4.46)	(1.87)
GNP85	1.649	1.643	1.633	1.612	1.609	1.611	1.608
	(31.60)	(32.34)	(32.06)	(32.19)	(31.79)	(30.17)	(29.77)
GASTIL		−0.152		−0.136		−0.138	
		(−2.09)		(−1.91)		(−1.85)	
FREE			1.296		1.170		1.179
			(1.92)		(1.73)		(1.67)
PFREE			−0.422		−0.080		−0.076
			(−0.50)		(−0.09)		(−0.09)
L2				−1.568	−1.312	−1.560	−1.308
				(−2.47)	(−1.89)	(−2.42)	(−1.85)
L3				−1.680	−1.744	−1.675	−1.742
				(−1.55)	(−1.59)	(−1.53)	(−1.57)
POP85						0.0002	0.0001
						(0.09)	(0.05)
R^2	0.94	0.95	0.95	0.95	0.95	0.95	0.95

Note: The dependent variable is $DEMIT_i$. t-ratios are in parentheses.

United States whose 1985 GNP equals approximately $4 trillion. Using the linear model 7, we see that the estimated derivative is constant at 1.608, which lies within the range of estimates from the Box-Cox model.

From linear model 7, our estimate of p, the implied price of g_i, is $62.19 per gram. EPA (1987b) estimated that the social opportunity cost of reducing CFC emissions in the United States starting in 1989 ranged between $0.30 and $1.00 per gram in 1985 dollars. Our estimate should be interpreted as an estimate of the world *average* price for the 1986–89 period. One explanation for the size of this estimate is the fact that the cheap substitute compounds for CFCs were unavailable before 1989. As these substitutes were made available, the *marginal* cost of emission reduction fell substantially as is evidenced by the EPA estimates.

Heteroskedasticity is always a possibility with cross-sectional data. With White's (1980) general test for heteroskedasticity on models 2-7, we fail to reject the null hypothesis of homoskedastic errors. The hypothesis is rejected for model 1, indicating a specification error in the model that has no taste parameters. This result provides additional support for Andreoni's characterization of the theory, since the data appear to fit the statistical model when the taste parameters are included.

Because the ordinary least squares and the nonlinear least squares (NLS) estimators minimize the sum of squared deviations, they are sensitive to "outliers." To check the robustness of our primary conclusion (linearity between $GNP85_i$ and $DEMIT_i$), we analyze the coefficient sensitivity for model 7 of the OLS estimates using the diagnostic measures proposed by Belsley, Kuh, and Welsch (1980, ch. 2). A particularly relevant diagnostic measure is $DFBETA_i$, which shows the impact on the estimated regression parameter from dropping the ith observation. Focusing on the relationship between DEMIT and GNP85, we find two observations, China and the USSR, with $DFBETA_i$s that fall outside the acceptable bounds established by Belsley, Kuh and Welsch. Moreover, both of these observations and that of the United States are identified as influential by the diagonal elements of the "hat matrix" (referred to as leverage points). When the model is re-estimated with just the United States *or* the USSR *or* China removed, there is little effect on the estimates for LAMBDA. If, however, all three countries are dropped, the NLS estimate for LAMBDA increases to 1.192 with a standard error of 0.20 (t-ratio equal to 6.1). In this case, the 95% confidence interval contains one, and we cannot statistically rule out the linear model. This finding indicates additional support for our hypothesis of linearity; *the influential observations appear to be the cause of the slight nonlinearity identified by the Box-Cox model.* The primary problem is that the model overpredicts the actual value of DEMIT for the United States, the USSR, and China, when these countries are left out of the sample. Because they are three of the largest nations (ranked first, second, and eighth, respectively, in terms of GNP), their inclusion makes the functional form slightly concave in order to provide a better fit between the observed and predicted DEMIT values.

The Belsley, Kuh, and Welsch (1980) procedures provide tools for checking the role of individual observations in regression. They do not give guidelines for dropping data points. We argue that the 61 country data set is still the most appropriate for our tests. However, we feel some confidence in stating that the "true relationship" between income and voluntary contributions is nicely approximated by the linear specification.[12]

[12] We also tested the model with other shift parameters. In particular, we added the percent of GNP from agriculture *and* the percent of land area in cropland. Both measures are available from WRI (1990) and measure potential physical damage from UV radiation. Like POP85, the measures were insignificant in the OLS models. In the Box-Cox models, these additional variables reduced the significance of the GNP85 parameter, but left our overall conclusions unchanged. These additional results are available upon request from the authors.

5. Conclusions

Based on the theory of the voluntary provision of pure public goods, we have hypothesized linear relationship between CFC emission reduction and GNP within each taste class of nations in the absence of a cooperative agreement or treaty. Our regressions indicated that the variation in CFC emission reductions between 1986 and 1989 is, in large part, explained by GNP and two taste parameters – political and civil rights, and geographical latitude. A Box-Cox transformation test comes close to verifying that a linear relationship between CFC emission reduction and GNP is the appropriate relationship for the 61 sample nations. When three outliers are dropped from the sample, linearity is verified. Nations are seen as reducing emissions beyond treaty-mandated levels even prior to the Montreal Protocol taking effect. On average, 61 nations in our sample set reduced CFC emissions by 41.6% from 1986 to 1989, which is well in excess of the 20% cutback mandated by the Protocol from the year commencing on 1 July 1993. This finding suggests that the initial provisions of the Montreal Protocol are largely consistent with voluntary subscription cutbacks in CFC emissions. Additional support for the subscription model is gleaned from the raw data.

Researchers before us have distinguished the ozone depletion problem from other global commons problems, such as global warming. For example, Barrett (1992, p. 17) argued that "The Montreal Protocol may not have increased global net benefits substantially compared with the noncooperative outcome." Although our research results concur with this view, we have taken a different tack and applied an explicit voluntary theory of emission reduction to test empirically whether the Montreal Protocol, as initially formulated, may have been largely symbolic. Our conclusions are only with respect to the initial Montreal Protocol, and not its subsequent amendments.

A number of policy conclusions follow. First, the Montreal Protocol may be a poor blueprint for other global agreements. Each global commons problem has its own pattern of payoffs based on publicness. Currently, ozone depletion is associated with more-certain and more-costly consequences than problems like global warming. Second, the wealthiest CFC emitters may be expected to adhere to the Montreal Protocol without the need of an enforcement mechanism, because the net benefits from doing so are apparently positive. Self-interests motivate compliance. Third, an increase in the number of democratic countries is apt to increase the number of nations that will take steps to curb transboundary emissions (also see Congleton, 1992). Thus, increases in the Gastil indices, achieved after 1989 by the transitional countries of Central and Eastern Europe, may serve to increase compliance with the Protocol's provision. Fourth, foreign aid, which expands the set of CFC reducers or increases the GNP level of developing and transitional economies by more than the donation, should accelerate the adherence to the mandated reductions in CFC emissions. An environmental dividend can stem from foreign aid, because the preservation of environmental assets is a normal good.

References

Andreoni, J., 1988, Privately provided public goods in a large economy: The limits of altruism, Journal of Public Economics 35, 57–73.

Andreoni, J. and M. C. McGuire, 1993, Identifying the free riders: A simple algorithm for determining who will contribute to a public good, Journal of Public Economics 51, 447–454.

Barrett, S., 1994, Self-enforcing international environmental agreements, Oxford Economic Papers 46, 878–894.

Belsley, D. A., E. Kuh, and R. E. Welsch, 1980, Regression diagnostics: Identifying influential data and sources of collinearity (Wiley, New York).

Bergstrom, T. C., L. Blume and H. R. Varian, 1986, On the private provision of public goods, Journal of Public Economics 29, 25–49.

Bienen, H. and N. van der Walle, 1989, Time and power in Africa, American Political Science Review 83, 19–34.

Box, G. E. P. and D. R. Cox, 1964, An analysis of transformations, Journal of the Royal Statistical Society, Series B, 26, 211–264.

Central Intelligence Agency (CIA), 1989, The world factbook: 1989 (CIA, Washington, DC).

Congleton, R. D., 1992, Political institutions and pollution control, Review of Economics and Statistics 74, 412–421.

Cornes, R. and T. Sandler, 1984, Easy riders, joint production, and public goods, Economic Journal 94, 580–598.

Cornes, R. and T. Sandler, 1996, The theory of externalities, public goods, and club goods, 2nd Ed. (Cambridge University Press, Cambridge).

de Gruijl, F. R., 1995, Impacts of a projected depletion in the ozone layer, Consequences 1, 13–21.

Environmental Protection Agency (EPA), 1987a, Assessing the risks of trace gases that can modify the stratosphere, 7 vols. (EPA, Washington, DC).

EPA, 1987b, Regulatory impact analysis: Protection of stratospheric ozone, 3 vols. (EPA, Washington, DC).

Gastil, R. D., 1986, Freedom in the world: Political rights and civil liberties 1985 (Greenwood Press, Westport, CT).

Helm, D. (ed.), 1991, Economic policy towards the environment (Blackwell, Oxford).

Morrisette, P. M., J. Darmstadter, A. J. Plantinga, and M. A. Toman, 1990, Lessons from other international agreements for a global CO_2 accord, Resources for the Future, Washington, DC, Discussion Paper ENR91-02.

Olson, M., 1993, Dictatorship, democracy, and development, American Political Science Review 87, 567–576.

Sandler, T., 1992, Collective action: Theory and applications (University of Michigan Press, Ann Arbor).

Sandler, T., 1996, A Game-theoretic analysis of carbon emissions, in: R. Congleton, ed., The political economy of environmental protection (University of Michigan Press, Ann Arbor), 9, 251–272.

Spitzer, J. J., 1982, A primer on Box-Cox estimator, Review of Economics and Statistics 64, 645–652.

United Nations Environment Programme (UNEP), 1991, Selected multilateral treaties in the field of the environment, Volume 2 (Grotius Publications Ltd., Cambridge).

UNEP, 1993, Status of ratification of the Montreal Protocol: June 1993 (UNEP, Nairobi).

White, H., 1980, A heteroskedasticity-consistent covariance matrix estimator and a direct test for heteroskedasticity, Econometrica, 48, 817–838.

World Bank, 1992, World Tables: 1991 (Johns Hopkins University Press, Baltimore).

World Resources Institute, 1990, World Resources 1990-91 (Oxford University Press, New York).

World Resources Institute, 1992, World Resources 1992-93 (Oxford University Press, New York).

[14]

Economica (1997) **64**, 281–301

A Tale of Two Collectives: Sulphur versus Nitrogen Oxides Emission Reduction in Europe

By JAMES C. MURDOCH,* TODD SANDLER† and KEITH SARGENT†

University of Texas-Dallas; †Iowa State University

Final version received 25 March 1996.

A theoretical model of emission reductions is specified that accounts for voluntary and non-voluntary behaviour regarding the adherence to the Helsinki and Sofia Protocols, which mandated emission reductions for sulphur (S) and nitrogen oxides (NO_x), respectively. From this model, we derive an econometric specification for the demand for emission reductions that adjusts for the spatial dispersion of the pollutant. When tested for 25 European nations, the model performs well for sulphur cutbacks. Less satisfying results are obtained for NO_x because the model's assumption of a unitary actor at the national level is less descriptive. Collective action considerations indicate that sulphur emissions are easier to control than those of NO_x.

INTRODUCTION

In recent years, tremendous interest has been shown in the study of a host of transnational collective action problems including acid rain, global warming, desertification, deforestation and stratospheric ozone depletion (see e.g. Barrett 1993; Eyckmans *et al.* 1993; Murdoch and Sandler 1997; Runge 1990; and Sandler and Sargent 1995). In the present paper, we are particularly interested in collective action concerning acid rain and surface-level ozone, stemming from the emissions of sulphur (S) and nitrogen oxides (NO_x). European concern over these and other pollutants resulted in the formulation of the 1979 Convention on Long-Range Transboundary Air Pollution (LRTAP) and its later ratification on 16 March 1983.[1]

Subsequent protocols to LRTAP have placed explicit limits on sulphur and NO_x emission levels. A casual comparison of European emission data for sulphur and nitrogen oxides throughout the 1980s (Sandnes 1993, tables 1–2) tells a different story with respect to these pollutants. Most countries have met or exceeded the 30% mandated reductions from 1980 levels in sulphur by the end of the decade, while some of these same countries were having a difficult time in reducing NO_x emission levels.

Why are the two responses so different? This paper attempts to answer the question by analysing the factors behind these two seemingly similar, but different, collective action problems. An important message that derives from our analysis is to resist the temptation to lump together collective action problems even if they involve the same participants, because key ingredients—group size, the range of benefit or cost spillovers and/or selective incentives—may differ (Olson 1965; Sandler 1992).

This paper has five purposes. First, we formulate a theoretical model of emission reductions that includes both voluntary and non-voluntary behaviour regarding sulphur and NO_x pollution. Voluntary behaviour concerns emission cutbacks beyond levels mandated in a protocol, whereas non-voluntary behaviour involves meeting mandated cutbacks. Second, we specify an empirical model, derived from the theoretical model, that accounts for the spatial dispersion of emissions within the European sample countries. Third, in an effort to refute the theoretical model, we put the empirical specification through a battery of tests using EMEP (Cooperative Programme for Monitoring and Evaluation of the Long-Range Transmission of Air Pollutants in Europe) data for the 1980–90 period. Fourth, we explain the above-mentioned contrast in the two transboundary pollution problems. Fifth, we draw some policy conclusions regarding future protocols for sulphur and NO_x.

The analysis indicates that our theoretical model leads to an empirical representation that yields reasonable results for sulphur, but less satisfying results for NO_x. Sulphur emissions appear easier to control than NO_x, because a greater proportion of a country's emissions falls on its own territory and within the treaty's region. Moreover, sulphur pollution sources are more concentrated and include public utilities that are easier for a country to control. Strategic behaviour, whereby a country limits its cleanup efforts as others reduce emissions, characterizes both problems despite the enactment of conventions and protocols, but appears stronger for NO_x. In the case of sulphur, a greater demand for a cleaner environment comes about as income and political freedoms are enhanced. For NO_x, income has no clear-cut influence, whereas increased political freedoms inhibit pollution reductions owing to strategic behaviour at the individual polluter level. Our empirical results are in keeping with Barrett (1994), which demonstrated that treaties containing more than a few participants are unlikely to achieve much in cooperative gains. For large groups like those of the Helsinki or Sofia Protocol, Nash behaviour appears best suited to explain reductions.

This paper is of general interest because its theoretical and empirical techniques can be applied to a wide range of public good problems, drawn from environmental and public economics. Its analysis is especially germane for those problems where spillins have a spatial dimension—e.g. recreation, police protection, disease containment.

I. Background

When sulphur and NO_x emissions from electric generation, transportation and other sources combine in the atmosphere with water vapour and tropospheric ozone, sulphuric and nitric acid can form. These acids can later fall with the rain and degrade lakes, rivers, coastal waters, forests and manmade structures. This degradation can also stem from dry depositions of sulphur and NO_x, which lead to increased acidity of soils and water sheds. In 1980, sources of sulphur emissions were: 47·8% from power plants, 37·4% from industry, 10% from residential and commercial activities, 3·7% from mobile polluters (e.g. cars and trucks) and 1% miscellaneous (OECD 1990); sources of NO_x emissions were: 53·6% from mobile polluters, 23·5% from power plants, 15·4% from industry, 6·1% from residential and commercial activities and 1·3% miscellaneous. These differences in sources figure prominently in our interpretation of the empirical results.

In addition to acid rain, sulphur and NO_x emissions lead to reductions in ambient air quality that may cause serious human health impairments to susceptible populations—particularly the young and old. NO_x and volatile organic compounds (VOCs) are the primary precursors to tropospheric ozone in European cities (OECD 1990). Ambient levels of particulate matter (PM), which are potentially more damaging than tropospheric ozone, are also influenced by sulphur and NO_x emissions. Approximately 10% of emitted SO_2 is converted to airborne sulphate aerosol (Latimer *et al.* 1990), and up to 20% of the total PM mass is attributable to sulphates (Sisler *et al.* 1993). Similarly, some fraction of NO_x is converted to nitrates, which comprise up to 5% of PM mass. Given that recent epidemiology studies have found a consistent association between premature death and PM (e.g. Schwartz 1991), ambient and deposition aspects of these pollutants are harmful.

A variety of strategies are available for the control of sulphur and NO_x emissions. Both emissions can be limited through improved efficiency, especially in the case of residential and commercial uses, and increased conservation. Sulphur can also be controlled through the use of low-sulphur coal and oil as well as through flue-gas desulphurization for power plants. In the case of NO_x, emissions can be reduced in power plants by installing low-NO_x burners. Pollution from mobile sources can be curtailed by setting emission standards on vehicles and by increasing the rate of turnover of the vehicle fleet. New vehicles can incorporate newer emission control technologies.

Both sulphur and NO_x emissions pose a transnational pollution concern, because once released into the atmosphere these pollutants can remain aloft for days and can travel from their emission source to be deposited on the territory of a downwind country. Sulphur emissions can remain in the atmosphere for 0·01 to 7 days, while NO_x can remain aloft from 2 to 8 days (Alcamo and Runca 1986, p. 3). On average, sulphur pollutants travel shorter distances than NO_x pollutants and land nearer to home.[2]

To account for the transport of sulphur and NO_x among European countries, we rely on the transport matrix devised from EMEP measurements (Eliassen and Saltbones 1980) and reported for various years in Sandnes (1993). For example, a sulphur matrix's entries indicate the amount of sulphur deposited in country i (row country) emitted by country j (column country). By dividing each entry by the emitter's total sulphur emissions and then multiplying by the fraction of the country's emissions that remains in the study area, we generate a transport matrix in which each entry indicates the *fraction* of country j's emissions deposited on country i—denoted by α_{ij}. The diagonal entries of the matrix indicate the fraction of country i's emissions dumped on itself. Bigger nations typically have larger diagonal elements than smaller countries, so that they absorb more of their own sulphur pollutants. A similar matrix can be formulated for NO_x. Although emission entries can differ in the *untransformed* matrix by year, the transport matrix, when expressed in percentage terms, varies imperceptibly from year to year; hence, a single transport matrix can be applied to the subperiods of this study. We use the transport matrix for 1985 for the empirical estimates.

A decrease in ambient air quality is related to depositions, since PM is proportional to emissions, and ambient impacts are experienced as pollutants are transported to their sites of deposition. We must rely on EMEP's deposition transport matrix to represent ambient transportation, inasmuch as data are not directly available for this transport for the sample period or countries. Surely, ambient air quality is reduced in and around deposition sites. We should, however, point out that the concern over ambient aspects of sulphur emissions is a recent phenomenon and did not characterize the period under study. Nevertheless, we attempt to include its effects on the demand for emission cutbacks.

One international convention and two subsequent protocols are germane to our study. On 13 November 1979, the LRTAP Convention was adopted at a high-level meeting of the UN Economic Commission for Europe on the Protection of the Environment. The treaty was subsequently ratified on 16 March 1983 by Austria, Belgium, Bulgaria, Canada, Czechoslovakia, Denmark, Finland, France, East Germany, West Germany, Greece, Hungary, Iceland, Ireland, Italy, Liechtenstein, Luxembourg, Netherlands, Norway, Poland, Portugal, Romania, Soviet Union, Spain, Sweden, Switzerland, Turkey, the United Kingdom, the United States and Yugoslavia (UNEP 1991). For our sample, Canada, Iceland and the United States are left out owing to our focus on European deposition, while Liechtenstein is excluded because it does not appear in the EMEP transport matrix as the grid is too coarse; Turkey also is dropped, because the data are inconsistent between different sources. The signatories of LRTAP agreed that further study was needed prior to specific limits of emission reductions being mandated. On 8 July 1985, the Helsinki Protocol to the LRTAP Convention was adopted and committed ratifiers to reduce sulphur emissions by at least 30%, based on 1980 levels, as soon as possible or by 1993. The protocol entered into force on 2 September 1987.

In the case of NO_x emissions, protocols have been much slower. On 31 October 1988, the Sofia Protocol was signed, requiring reductions in NO_x to return to 1987 levels by 31 December 1994 (UNEP 1991). This protocol did not enter into force until 14 February 1991.

On 24 November 1988, the Council of the European Communities drafted a Directive (88/609/EEC) to limit sulphur and NO_x emissions from large combustion plants (Council of the European Communities 1988). The Large Combustion Plant Directive (LCPD) did not mandate any emission reductions until after the sample period for the European Economic Community (EEC). Since LCPD was not in force during the sample period, we focus on the two protocols as driving sulphur and NO_x reductions during the 1980–90 period.[3]

II. Theoretical Model

We present a simple model of voluntary and non-voluntary emission reductions of a pollutant. The underlying model is a Nash subscription model, in which an impure public good (emission reduction) is allocated by a set of countries that are emitters and recipients of a pollutant (e.g. S or NO_x), henceforth denoted as 'emissions'.[4] For modelling purposes, each country is represented by a unitary actor whose interests are those of the nation's citizens. This representation ignores the collective action problem at the national level, but we return to this issue in Section V.

The ith nation's strictly increasing, quasi-concave utility function is

$$U_i = U_i(y_i, \alpha_{ii}q_i + \tilde{Q}_i, E_i), \tag{1}$$

where y_i is the ith nation's consumption of the private numeraire good; q_i denotes the ith nation's reduced emissions between a base year and the current year of reference; α_{ii} is the fraction of the ith nation's emissions deposited on itself; $\tilde{Q}_i$ is the reduction of emission spillins for nation i; and E_i is a vector of environmental and political factors in nation i. (These spillins are pollution received from other countries). The term $\alpha_{ii}q_i$ indicates the reduced emissions of nation i that are no longer deposited on its soil.[5] In general, q_i can be decomposed into two parts: a voluntary reduction, q_i^v, and a mandated reduction, q_i^T. In the case of sulphur, the Helsinki Protocol mandated targeted reductions of 30% of 1980 emission levels, so that voluntary reductions can be denoted after 1987 by

$$(2) \qquad q_i^v = q_i - q_i^T = 0{\cdot}7 \text{ (1980 emission levels)} - \text{current emissions.}$$

Emission levels smaller than 70% of the 1980 emission level are considered to include voluntary reductions. By (2), total emission reductions in nation i, based on a base-year level, equal

$$(3) \qquad q_i = q_i^v + q_i^T.$$

If $q_i^T = 0$, all reductions are voluntary.

Reduced spillins of pollution deposition in nation i, derived from *other* countries may also be made up of both voluntary and non-voluntary emission reductions from neighbouring countries. Suppose that there are n countries in the model. Then these spillins are

$$(4) \qquad \tilde{Q}_i = \sum_{j \neq i}^{n} \alpha_{ij} q_j = \sum_{j \neq i}^{n} \alpha_{ij}(q_j^v + q_j^T)$$

for nation i, where α_{ij} is the fraction of nation j's emissions that fall on nation i. In (4), the index on the summation runs from $j = 1$ to $j = n$ but excludes i. These spillins equal the summed reductions in transported emissions that are deposited on nation i, but originate from other nations. Total deposition reductions, Q_i, in nation i equal $q_i + \tilde{Q}_i$, or the sum of reductions from domestic and foreign sources. If all of a country's emissions fall within the region defined by the model, then each country's emissions must be deposited either on itself or on another country within the region, so that $\Sigma_{i=1}^{n} \alpha_{ij} = 1$. That is, *column* sums of the transport matrix of the α_{ij} must sum to one. This highlights the complete divisibility of the pollutant among nations in the case of sulphur and NO_x depositions. Publicness arises from non-excludability, not non-rivalry. If, instead, 62% of a nation's emissions were deposited within the region and the remainder were dropped on downwind regions or dissipated into the atmosphere, then the column sums for α_{ij} would equal 0·62.

Nation i is assumed to face the following linear budget constraint:

$$(5) \qquad m_i = y_i + p_i q_i^v + p_i q_i^T,$$

where m_i is national income, the price of the private good is unity and p_i is the per-unit price of voluntary and non-voluntary reductions. The model is kept uncomplex—p_i does not differ between the two classes of emission reductions, and a parametric price is assumed.[6] With the use of equations (3) and (4), we can now state the maximization (subscription) problem for nation i:

$$\max_{q_i^v} U_i\left[y_i, \alpha_{ii}q_i^v + \alpha_{ii}q_i^T + \sum_{j\neq i}^{n} \alpha_{ij}(q_j^v + q_j^T), E_i\right]$$

$$\text{subject to: } \begin{cases} m_i = y_i + p_i q_i^v + p_i q_i^T \\ \tilde{Q}_i \text{ and } q_i^T \text{ given} \\ q_i^v \gtreqless 0. \end{cases}$$

A number of remarks are in order. First, this is a Nash representation, so each nation chooses its optimizing response assuming the best-response level of spillins, $\tilde{Q}_i$. A Nash equilibrium results when each nation in the model is optimized, given its counterparts' best response, and would not unilaterally wish a different level of q_i^v. Second, if non-voluntary or targeted q_i^T exists, then it is exogenous. Third, the choice variable, q_i^v, can be positive, negative or zero; positive (negative) levels indicate greater (smaller) reductions than mandated. Owing to this last factor, the problem can be solved in two parts for positive and negative q_i^v; but in each case the Kuhn–Tucker conditions yield the same demand function. Fourth, exogenous factors include m_i, p_i, α_{ii}, q_i^T, $\tilde{Q}_i$ and E_i. As is discussed in Section III, E_i represents both environmental and political factors and acts as a shift variable. Fifth, if mandated levels are zero, then the choice variable is q_i, and q_i^T is no longer an exogenous variable. Furthermore, the target level would then not be part of spillins—spillins would be only voluntary. Sixth, ambient air quality is proxied by total depositions, Q_i. We could also add q_i by itself as a fourth argument to the utility function to proxy improved ambient air quality, but this addition would not change the demand equations in (6) and (7); hence it is not included here.

From the first-order conditions of the optimization problem, we can express the ith nation's demand for q_i^v, in terms of the exogenous variables, as

$$(6) \qquad q_i^v = q_i^v\left[m_i, p_i, \alpha_{ii}, E_i, \sum_{j\neq i}^{n} \alpha_{ij}(q_j^v + q_j^T), q_i^T\right], \qquad \text{for } q_i^T > 0,$$

and

$$(7) \qquad q_i^v = q_i^v\left(m_i, p_i, \alpha_{ii}, E_i, \sum_{j\neq i}^{n} \alpha_{ij}q_j^v\right), \qquad \text{for } q_i^T = 0.$$

Because the latter is a special case of the former, we focus our remarks on the empirical representation of the demand equation in (6). This equation applies to *each* country in the region (model). Taking a Taylor series expansion and keeping just the linear terms, we have

$$(8) \qquad q_i^v = \beta_0 + \rho \sum_{j\neq i}^{n} \alpha_{ij}(q_j^v + q_j^T) + \beta_1 m_i + \beta_2 p_i + \beta_3 \alpha_{ii} + \beta_4 E_i + \gamma q_i^T + \varepsilon_i, \qquad i = 1, \ldots, n,$$

where β_0 is a constant, the β_i are coefficients, ε_i is an error (remainder) term, and ρ and γ are coefficients.

To simplify notation, we revert to a vector representation where $\mathbf{q}^v$ is the $n\times 1$ vector $(q_1^v, \ldots, q_n^v)'$; $\mathbf{q}^T$ is the $n\times 1$ vector $(q_1^T, \ldots, q_n^T)'$, $\tilde{\mathbf{A}}$ is an $n\times n$ transport matrix, $\mathbf{X}$ is an $n\times 5$ matrix of parameters, $\boldsymbol{\beta}$ is a 5×1 vector $(\beta_0, \ldots, \beta_4)'$ and $\boldsymbol{\varepsilon}$ is an $n\times 1$ vector $(\varepsilon_1, \ldots, \varepsilon_n)'$ of error terms. The ith row of the $\mathbf{X}$ matrix is $(1, m_i, p_i, \alpha_{ii}, E_i)$. Finally, we must distinguish the $\mathbf{A}$ transport matrix from the $\tilde{\mathbf{A}}$ transport matrix. The latter includes zeros in the diagonal places, so that a country's own q_i^v appears only on the left-hand side of its equation. The remaining terms in $\tilde{\mathbf{A}}$ are the α_{ij}. Thus, the equation system in (8) can be written in matrix form as

$$\mathbf{q}^v = \rho\tilde{\mathbf{A}}\mathbf{q}^v + \mathbf{X}\boldsymbol{\beta} + \rho\tilde{\mathbf{A}}\mathbf{q}^T + \gamma\mathbf{q}^T + \boldsymbol{\varepsilon}, \tag{9}$$

where the targeted reductions affect spillins through the definition of spillins, and where these reductions have an independent influence owing to q_i^T in each country's optimization problem.

III. Empirical Model

Equation (6) is a representation of a country's demand function for emission reductions. We hypothesize that the data observed in the real world are generated from this type of behavioural relationship and that the relationship provides a good representation of past behaviour. To test this claim, we attempt to refute it. Our methodology involves using observations on the relevant variables to estimate the parameters of approximations to the function, such as the one presented in (8). These parameter estimates (the β, ρ and γ) can then be checked for logical consistency when interpreted as demand function parameters.

To estimate (6) for sulphur and NO_x reductions, we need data on these measures for the European nations that participated in the LRTAP (Convention on Long-Range Transboundary Air Pollution). We have 25 countries that generate useful observations for the study. At the present time, there is not enough annual data to estimate the demand function for each nation, implying that we must use the cross-sectional (or cross-national) data and estimate one demand function for the sample. Essentially, this approach requires that we assume that, with the exception of random errors, the demand function for each nation is identical, when controlling for measurable shift parameters. The estimated relationship must be interpreted as an 'average' equation derived from the sample.

Variable definitions

Measures of q_i^v and q_i^T. Emissions by country and by year are obtained from EMEP (Sandnes 1993). For a given year, the emissions of sulphur are denoted by the variable S*YY*, in which the *YY* represents the year; for example, S80 depicts the emissions of sulphur in 1980 for the country under consideration. The NO_x emissions are denoted by NO*YY*, so that NO85 denotes the NO_x emissions in 1985.

The dependent variable in our models represents the voluntary reductions (in '000 tons) of sulphur or NO_x emissions. With respect to sulphur, we need a measure of voluntary contributions before and after the 30% reduction target concluded at Helsinki on 8 July 1985. Because all reductions in emissions before the Helsinki Protocol are voluntary, we compute the q_i^v before the Helsinki Protocol as the difference S80 − S85 and refer to it as S80_85. To estimate demand behaviour after the Helsinki Protocol, we compute voluntary reductions as $q_i^v = 0{\cdot}7 \cdot S80 - S90$, which we refer to as S80_90. Our choice of 1990 as the ending year to compute the change is somewhat arbitrary; however, it is motivated by our desire to end the study period prior to the dramatic political changes in Eastern Europe and to provide some symmetry with respect to S80_85. Our qualitative conclusions are unaffected by this choice; i.e. using any ending year between 1988 and 1991, we generate the same qualitative conclusions.

Following the Helsinki Protocol, the target rate of reductions (q_i^T) enters the demand function as an exogenous variable. This value is referred to as *TARGET* and is the level of emission reductions specified in the Helsinki Protocol, i.e. 0·3 (S80). We emphasize that countries with high levels of emissions in 1980 will necessarily face greater targets. As *TARGET* increases, we consequently expect that, *ceteris paribus*, voluntary contributions will decrease.

For NO_x, we present estimates based on two measures of voluntary contributions. The first is NO85_87 = NO85 − NO87, and the second is NO88_90 = NO88 − NO90.[7] Technically, no targets existed for NO_x during the study period, so that all changes in emissions are viewed as voluntary. Still, several nations have ratified the Sofia Protocol, making it conceivable that the demand relationship shifted in 1988. Therefore, the results presented below facilitate an explicit examination of the model before and after the Sofia Protocol. The choice of 1990 as the ending period is again somewhat arbitrary, but provides consistency with the sulphur results.

Voluntary reductions in sulphur and NO_x, expressed in percentages, are presented for selected years in Table 1. We first focus on percentage reduction in sulphur emissions between 1980 and 1985 (*%SUL85*), based on 1980 emissions, in which the entire reduction, if positive, is voluntary. Ten of the 25 nations had achieved the subsequently targeted reductions at the time the Helsinki Protocol was adopted; another six (Denmark, West Germany, Norway, Portugal, Switzerland and the United Kingdom) had achieved a reduction of at least 23% by the end of 1985. Czechoslovakia, Hungary and the Soviet Union had already reduced emissions by 10–14% at the time of the treaty adoption. The overwhelming number of Protocol participants had met the treaty's mandate or were well on their way to meeting it by the time of adoption. Mean reductions were 20·59% prior to the treaty.

The second column displays the *voluntary* percentage reduction in sulphur emissions in 1990 based on 1980 emissions (*%SUL90*), where the 30% target is accounted for, so that positive levels indicate an over-achievement of the mandate. Fifteen sample nations had exceeded mandated levels by 1990 and another five were within 9 percentage points of the target.

A much different pattern of voluntary cutbacks for NO_x emerged prior to the Sofia Protocol. Voluntary reductions in NO_x emissions between 1980 and 1987 as a percentage of 1980 emissions (*%NOX87*) were positive for only eight of the nations in Table 1. It is also noteworthy that these reductions were much more modest than for sulphur on average. Overall mean reductions were −2·75%. Additionally, only a couple nations displayed a monotonic pattern of cutbacks from 1980 to 1987 when yearly observations are consulted (see

TABLE 1

PERCENTAGE REDUCTIONS IN VOLUNTARY SULPHUR AND NO_x EMISSIONS BY COUNTRY

Country	%SUL85	%SUL90	%SUL92[a]	%NOX87	%NOX90	%NOX92[a]
1. Austria	50·75	47·39	48·89	4·88	5·13	7·69
2. Belgium	45·41	16·38	15·89	32·81	−12·46	−12·79
3. Bulgaria	−12·88	−28·54	−10·98	0·00	9·62	34·38
4. Czechoslovakia	10·32	−8·79	−0·92	16·28	2·08	11·71
5. Denmark	23·89	30·18	16·02	−11·72	7·21	7·21
6. Finland	34·59	25·48	36·78	−2·27	−7·41	−10·74
7. France	55·96	32·25	28·96	10·59	−7·36	−11·04
8. E. Germany	−25·58	−41·63	−41·63[b]	−13·56	5·97	5·97[b]
9. W. Germany	24·98	40·57	40·57[b]	1·78	11·17	11·17[b]
10. Greece	−25·00	−55·00	−55·00	0·00	0·00	0·00
11. Hungary	13·97	8·11	8·11	−1·10	13·77	13·77
12. Ireland	36·94	−5·68	−15·59	−57·53	−17·39	−13·04
13. Italy	34·11	12·63	12·63	−14·86	−3·59	−3·59
14. Luxembourg	33·33	3·33	3·33	17·39	0·00	0·00
15. Netherlands	40·77	25·36	26·65	−2·01	1·25	1·97
16. Norway	28·57	31·43	35·71	−25·14	−1·75	−0·44
17. Poland	−4·88	−8·29	−3·07	−2·00	16·34	21·24
18. Portugal	25·56	−6·69	−6·69	30·12	−5·17	−5·17
19. Romania	0·00	−30·00	−30·00	0·00	0·00	0·00
20. Spain	34·04	0·24	0·24	11·68	0·00	0·00
21. Sweden	43·85	37·31	37·31	−2·86	6·26	6·26
22. Switzerland	23·81	20·79	20·79	−2·04	8·00	12·50
23. Soviet Union	13·05	3·12	3·12[b]	−23·44	−7·34	−7·84[b]
24. United Kingdom	23·97	−7·05	−7·05	−10·03	−7·27	−7·27
25. Yugoslavia	−14·88	−43·34	−43·34[b]	−25·71	4·55	4·55[b]
Average	20·59	3·98	4·83	−2·75	0·84	2·66

[a] For countries with identical emissions reported in 1990 and 1992, data were either extrapolated or estimated by Sandnes (1993).
[b] Based on the 1990 value because the country's borders changed in 1991.

%SUL85 =% reduction in total sulphur emissions from 1980 to 1985 as a % of 1980 emissions
%SUL90 =% reduction in sulphur emissions, beyond the 30% target reduction, from 1980 to 1990 as a % of 1980 emissions.
%SUL92 =% reduction in sulphur emissions, beyond the 30% target reduction, from 1980 to 1992 as a % of 1980 emissions.
%NOX87 =% reduction in total NO_x emissions from 1980 to 1987 as a % of 1980 emissions.
%NOX90 =% reduction in total NO_x emissions from 1987 to 1990 as a % of 1987 emissions.
%NOX92 =% reduction in total NO_x emissions from 1987 to 1992 as a % of 1987 emissions.

Murdoch *et al.* 1994, figure 2). By 1990, shortly after the adoption of the Sofia Protocol, all but nine sample nations had maintained NO_x emissions at or below 1987 levels. A positive, but small, mean reduction in NO_x emissions was evident.

Measures of m_i. To measure a nation's income, we used the gross national product (GNP), which poses some problems. Perhaps the most difficult problem is to find cross-nationally comparable figures. This is especially true in our case, because the sample of nations includes traditional market and non-market economies. Another problem is that there are many different sources for GNP estimates in the non-market economies. A third problem is that we want GNP estimates for different slices of time; thus, we need estimates comparable across nations and through time. Our approach is to use the estimates presented in World Resources Institute (WRI 1992, table 15.1), which presents the

1989 GNP in 1989 US dollars (*GNP89*), providing a cross-nationally consistent measure for 1989. To generate observations for other years, we utilize the average annual growth rate (*GR*) of constant GNP between 1980 and 1991 available in WRI (1994, table 15.1). For example, to compute the GNP in 1983 for country *i*, we compute $GNP83 = GNP89(1+GR)^{-6}$. The resulting estimate is expressed in tens of billions of 1989 US dollars.

Measures of α_{ii}. The fraction of a country's sulphur or NO_x emissions that falls within its own borders (*OWNSUL* or *OWNNOX*) is calculated from the 1985 Budget of Oxidized Sulphur or Nitrogen in Sandnes (1993). The budgets are matrices that show, for each country, the origin of the depositions on its soil. To explain the process for calculating *OWNSUL*, we consider the following example based on the actual data for Belgium. In 1985, Belgium's total sulphur emissions measured 226,000 tons. Of this, 66·1% (149,300 tons) fell within the EMEP study region. We can identify where 149,300 tons of Belgian emissions fell by examining the EMEP's 1985 Budget of Oxidized Sulphur: for example, 42,800 tons fell in Belgium itself, 23,800 tons in France and 24,700 tons in West Germany. To find *OWNSUL*, we first divide the country's deposition within its own border by the country's deposition within the study area. We then multiply by the fraction of the country's total emissions that fell within the study area. For Belgium, this calculation is 0·661 (428/1493) = 0·189. An identical procedure is used to calculate *OWNNOX*. *OWNSUL* and *OWNNOX* are appropriate measures for α_{ii}.

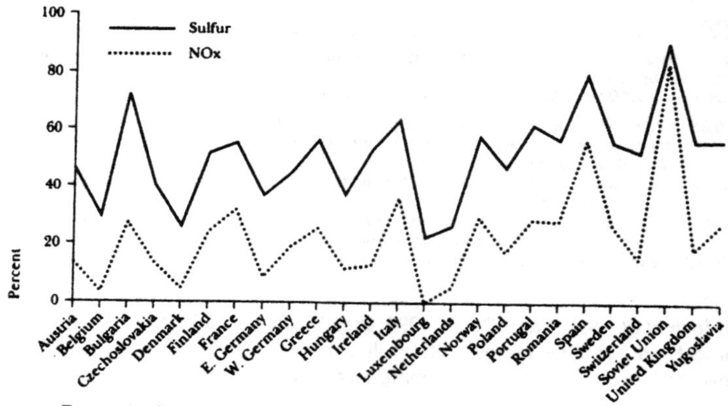

FIGURE 1. Percentage of depositions that falls within a nation's borders, 1988.

Figure 1 displays the region-specific α_{ii} values, measured along the vertical axis, for the 25 sample nations. For every nation, α_{ii} is greater for sulphur than for NO_x. Thus, self-deposition of pollutants is more characteristic of sulphur, and so there are more country-specific gains from reducing sulphur rather than NO_x emissions—i.e. selective incentives are greater.

Measures of $\tilde{Q}_i$. $\tilde{Q}_i$ indicates the amount of deposition reduction provided by other nations *to* country *i*, and denotes the spillins. As shown earlier, there are two components of spillins. The first ($\Sigma^n_{j\neq i}\,\alpha_{ij}q^v_j$) reflects the spillins from the voluntary reductions, and is indicated by $SPILL_i$, while the second ($\Sigma_{j\neq i}^{n} \alpha_{ij} q_j^T$) is a measure of the spillins from satisfying the target rate of emission reductions, and is represented by $TSPILL_i$. The computation of *SPILL* and *TSPILL* is based on EMEP's budgets for sulphur and NO_x, which in our case are 25 by 25 matrices. For example, assume that the fifth row of the matrix represents the depositions in Denmark and that the second column indicates the emissions from Belgium. Building on the earlier example for Belgium, we assume that the entry in the fifth row, second column in the Budget of Oxidized Sulphur is 1100 tons. This means that, from the 226,000 tons emitted by Belgium, 1100 tons fell within the borders of Denmark. Thus, the empirical realization of α_{52} is $1100/226{,}000 = 0{\cdot}005$, which implies that, when Belgium voluntarily reduces its emissions by, say, 1000 units, Denmark is expected to realize a reduction of 5 units of depositions.

Using a similar method, we can find a matrix of the α_{ij}. With zeros along the diagonal, this matrix is the empirical realization of $\tilde{\mathbf{A}}$ and allows us to calculate the voluntary reductions in spillins for Denmark or country 5 as $SPILL_5 = \Sigma_{j=1}^{25} \alpha_{5j} q_j^v$, where $\alpha_{55} = 0$. Alternatively, we can represent the calculation of the 25 by 1 *SPILL* vector as $\tilde{\mathbf{A}} \cdot \mathbf{q}^v$, where $\mathbf{q}^v$ is the 25 by 1 vector of voluntary contributions. The calculation is similar with respect to *TSPILL*.

Measures of p_i. We want a measure for the price of emission cutbacks in the various scenarios that reflects each country's energy pathway (i.e. its actual and anticipated pattern of energy generation), its level of emission reductions, and the marginal cost (MC) associated with the actual level of emission reductions. The Regional Acidification Information and Simulation (RAINS) model, version 6.1, of the International Institute for Applied Systems Analysis (IIASA) (1993) contains MC curves by countries for different years. For our pre-Helsinki estimates, we use the RAINS MC curves for each country to find the MC associated with the level of sulphur reductions in 1985, taken from Sandnes (1993). For just the Soviet Union, we calculate the relevant MC using the cost curve in Amann and Kornai (1987). We assume that MC, while different among countries, is parametric at the actual (equilibrium) level of emission cutbacks. For the post-Helsinki estimates, we employ 1990 sulphur reduction levels for the sample countries from Sandnes (1993) and the 1990 MC curves from the RAINS model to calculate the relevant MC levels for each country. Henceforth, we call MC levels for sulphur *MCSUL*.

We follow the same procedure for obtaining the MC measures for each country and different snapshots in time for NO_x. For the pre-Sofia period, emission cutbacks are based on NO85_87, which are then used in conjunction with the RAINS MC curves for 1985 to ascertain the MC levels for each sample country. (There is no RAINS MC curves for 1987.) For the post-Sofia period, emission cutbacks are based on NO88_90, which are then used in conjunction with the RAINS MC curves for 1990 to compute the MC levels for the estimates. These MC levels are called *MCNOX*.

Measures of E_i. E_i denotes the influences that shift a nation's emission reductions besides income, spillins, target, α_{ii} and price. One influence, explored recently by Congleton (1992), is the extent of democracy and/or freedom in the nation. The logic of this influence is that autocracies face a higher relative price for pollution abatement than their democratic median-voter counterparts. Moreover, autocracies are less risk-averse, making them less interested in policies to protect the environment. We attempt to control for this influence by using Gastil's (1989) index of civil liberties and index of political freedoms. Each index may take on an integer value from 1 to 7, with 1 being the greatest level of either civil liberties or political freedoms and 7 the least. We convert the sum of the two indices into a binary variable called *FREE*, which equals 1 for a sum less than or equal to 4, and 0 otherwise. Voluntary contributions are expected to respond positively to *FREE*. We use 1983 Gastil indices for the S80_85 estimates and 1988 indices for all of the other estimates.

A second influence that may shift the demand relationship is the potential for environmental damage caused by sulphur or NO_x emissions. For example, a country with the potential for large damages may demand more reductions to protect its resources. Thus, a nation with relatively large forest cover or a large susceptible population may desire more reductions to minimize the potential damages to their forests and exposed populations. To control for these influences, we examine two measures of potential damage. We consider *FOREST*, which is the percentage of a nation's land area in forest and woodland, for potential sulphur and NO_x deposition damage (UNEP 1993). For potential damages from ambient air quality degradation attributable to NO_x and sulphur, we employ a measure of the population most at risk—the proportion greater than or equal to 65 in age. This variable is denoted as $POP \geq 65$. For the S80_85 estimates, we use data from United Nations (1986, table 7), which give the sample country's proportion for a year between 1981 and 1984, with the preponderance of values for 1983. For the S80_90 and the NO_x estimates, we employ data from United Nations (1992, table 7), which give the sample country's proportion for a year between 1984 and 1990, with the preponderance of values for 1988 or 1989.

We are particularly interested in the third set of demand shift influences, i.e. international policy actions. We hypothesize that the countries that ratified the Helsinki and Sofia Protocols are more apt to have a different demand relationship when compared with the countries that did not.[8] To investigate this hypothesis, we formed two additional shift variables: (i) *HELSINKI*, a binary variable that equals 1 if a country ratified the Helsinki Protocol and 0 otherwise; and (ii) *SOFIA*, a binary variable that equals 1 if a country ratified the Sofia Protocol and 0 otherwise. While Sofia did not require a specific target rate of reductions for the time period under investigation, nor had it entered into force as of February 1991, the spirit of the Protocol was to encourage reduction in NO_x. Nations that ratified either protocol should demand more emission reductions.

Econometric model

Using the above-defined variables, we can re-specify the basic regression equation in (8) as

$$(10)\quad S80\_90_i = \beta_0 + \rho_1 SPILL_i + \rho_2 TSPILL_i + \beta_1 GNP_i + \beta_2 MCSUL_i + \beta_3 OWNSUL_i + \beta_4 GASTIL_i + \beta_5 FOREST_i + \beta_6 HELSINKI_i + \gamma\, TARGET_i + \varepsilon_i,$$

where S80_90 is the dependent variable and i denotes the country. In (10), the

ρ, β_i and γ are unknown slope coefficients, β_0 is a constant, and ε_i is an independent identically distributed random variable assumed to follow a normal distribution with a mean of 0 and a variance of σ^2. Equation (10) should be viewed as representative of our regression models; i.e. we estimate numerous similar expressions by changing the dependent variable and/or the set of independent variables. In the estimates, the GNP and MC variables are transformed by the square root function, since this transformation gives the clearest results and allows for a diminishing influence at the margin. Qualitatively, the results are similar without the square root transformation. The zero values for some MC values mean that we could not use a log transformation.

Our empirical task is to find estimates for the ρ, β, γ and σ^2. At first glance, it may appear that the method of ordinary least squares (OLS) is appropriate for estimating the parameters, but this is not the case. In fact, OLS would generate biased and inconsistent estimates owing to the $SPILL_i$ term, which is a weighted average of q_i^r, the dependent variable. Thus, values for S80_90 appear on the left- and right-hand side of the equation. But note that, for the ith observation, the *SPILL* term is a weighted average of the *other* (i.e. other than i) S80_90 values. Thus, the dependent variable is often said to appear in 'lagged' form on the right-hand side. This terminology is lifted from time-series models where the tth observation on the dependent variable is a function of the $(t-1)$st observation. In our case, we do not lag over time but over geographic space (i.e. countries). The *SPILL* term is therefore called a 'spatially lagged' dependent variable (see Cressie 1993; Anselin 1988). Intuitively, the problem with OLS is evident by solving for the dependent variable, because the resulting expression will have the β, γ and ε multiplied by the ρ_1 and the α_{ij} weights, making the model nonlinear in the parameters.

To get unbiased and consistent estimates, we appeal to the method of maximum likelihood (ML), which is appropriate if the ε_i follows the normal distribution. An analysis of the normal probability plot of the ML residuals (not shown) suggests that the normality assumption is reasonable for the models represented by equation (10).[9] Thus, we employ the ML approach as described in Anselin (1988, ch. 12) to estimate the parameters.

The ML parameter estimates for some alternative models of sulphur reductions are presented in Table 2, while the NO_x models are given in Table 3.[10] A quick scan of the two tables reveals that the sulphur data fit the models better than the NO_x data. In fact, approximately 62% of the coefficients in the sulphur models are statistically significant ($\alpha = 0{\cdot}10$, one-tail test) with the anticipated signs, while 23% are significant with the anticipated signs in the NO_x models. Despite 'looking good', we still must guard against making incorrect inferences in the sulphur models. Thus, we considered three sets of regression diagnostic procedures. The procedures were performed on model 5 presented in Table 2, because, as we argue below, it is one of the best models.

The first procedure involves visually examining the scatterplot of the ML residuals and normal probability plot. The second procedure is a test for heteroscedasticity. Using the ML residuals and the continuous independent variables, the Breusch–Pagan χ^2 equals 2·39. The p-value for the test is 0·793, indicating that we fail to reject the null hypothesis of homoscedasticity. Thus, there is little reason to doubt the constant variance assumption. Because only a fraction of the total land area in the Soviet Union is covered under the

Helsinki Protocol, we suspect that this country should not be treated like the others. For the third procedure, we re-estimated the model dropping the Soviet Union. The results are similar to those presented in Table 2, except that the GNP coefficient is insignificant and the $POP \geq 65$ estimate is more significant; hence, there does not appear to be sufficient evidence supporting the dropping of the Soviet Union.

IV. Empirical Results

In Table 2, the pre-Helsinki results generally confirm the model of voluntary behaviour that underlies our empirical specification. The negative and significant estimate on the *SPILL* term is entirely consistent with strategic (within-region) free-riding associated with the Nash assumption, whereas the positive

Table 2

Maximum Likelihood Estimates of the Sulphur Emission Reduction Regressions

(Asymptotic *t*-Ratios in Parentheses)

	Pre-Helsinki			Post-Helsinki		
Variables	(1)	(2)	(3)	(4)	(5)	(6)
SPILL	−1·911 (−11·65)	−2·104 (−12·87)	−2·807 (−19·48)	−7·039 (−35·97)	−6·265 (−33·12)	−6·520 (−36·71)
GNP[a]	65·986 (4·38)	72·961 (2·17)	83·144 (2·70)	93·682 (4·51)	77·973 (3·23)	70·574 (2·92)
MCSUL[a]	109·447 (1·12)	111·796 (1·12)	194·318 (1·96)	−28·121 (−0·48)	−25·091 (−0·43)	−7·450 (−0·13)
OWNSUL	998·322 (1·39)	1037·397 (1·43)	2535·826 (2·72)	729·516 (1·40)	650·112 (1·22)	1370·784 (1·89)
FREE	200·801 (2·00)	191·399 (1·66)	196·910 (1·87)	201·504 (1·95)	173·484 (1·65)	229·570 (2·14)
TARGET				−0·904 (−4·93)	−1·035 (−4·15)	−0·944 (−3·83)
HELSINKI				108·717 (1·76)	114·866 (1·82)	139·527 (2·22)
$POP \geq 65$		−4·680 (−0·20)	−25·413 (−1·14)		21·571 (1·03)	12·725 (0·61)
FOREST			−5·905 (−2·16)			−2·906 (−1·40)
Constant	−532·891 (−2·85)	−546·282 (−2·82)	−759·700 (−3·83)	−545·208 (−3·58)	−474·069 (−2·82)	−602·504 (−3·30)
−Log-likelihood	141·930	141·915	139·826	134·640	134·274	133·348

[a] Entered as the square root.

Note: Independent variables are as follows: *SPILL* is the sulphur deposition reduction derived from other sample nations; *GNP* is gross national product; *MCSUL* is the marginal cost of sulphur emission reduction; *OWNSUL* is the fraction of a country's own sulphur emissions deposited on itself; *FREE* is a dummy variable indicating political and civil liberties; *TARGET* is the required level of emission reduction; *HELSINKI* is a dummy for participation in the Protocol; $POP \geq 65$ is the proportion of population greater than or equal to age 65; and *FOREST* is the percentage of a nation's land area in forest. The pre-Helsinki models use the 1983 data for *GNP* and *FREE*; the post-Helsinki models use the 1988 data for these two variables.

income effect is consistent with the demand for emission reductions being income-normal.[11] On average, the estimates for model 2 suggest that, *ceteris paribus*, when depositions are reduced (i.e. when *SPILL* increases) by 1000 tons, emissions increase (S80_85 decreases) by approximately 2000 tons. This *partial effect* is dramatically different from the *gross* effect as measured by the correlation coefficient. For the pre-Helsinki period, the correlation between *SPILL* and S80_85 is just −0·05, suggesting no association. Model 2 indicates that the partial effect of a $4 billion increase in GNP is approximately 145,000 tons of emission reduction, in so far as GNP is entered into the model as the square root. The *FREE* and *OWNSUL* measures perform as expected, but the *OWNSUL* parameter estimates are significant only in model 3. In the case of *FREE*, political and civil freedoms apparently lead to greater environmental concern and larger emission reductions. *Ceteris paribus*, the average free nation reduced emissions by approximately 200,000 tons more than the average non-free nation in model 2.

MCSUL, *POP*≥*65* and *FOREST* do not perform as anticipated. While the *MCSUL* estimate is positive in all specifications, it is insignificant in models

TABLE 3

MAXIMUM LIKELIHOOD ESTIMATES OF THE NO_x EMISSION REDUCTION REGRESSIONS

(Asymptotic *t*-Ratios in Parentheses)

	Pre-Sofia			Post-Sofia		
Variables	(1)	(2)	(3)	(4)	(5)	(6)
SPILL	−14·163 (−28·66)	−20·347 (−50·65)	−20·187 (−50·02)	−17·170 (−23·46)	−15·789 (−21·77)	−16·435 (−26·35)
GNP[a]	−14·345 (−3·53)	12·280 (2·32)	12·127 (2·27)	4·882 (0·65)	10·099 (0·71)	8·566 (0·63)
MCNOX[a]	10·482 (1·05)	14·076 (2·23)	14·354 (2·23)	−2·576 (−0·16)	−1·91 (−0·11)	−9·821 (−0·56)
OWNNOX	−1797·460 (−2·15)	−725·308 (−1·25)	−844·840 (−1·06)	−119·645 (−0·08)	−87·967 (−0·05)	−2710·046 (−1·15)
FREE	38·705 (1·69)	−6·260 (−0·38)	−6·377 (−0·38)	−125·446 (−3·47)	−129·622 (−3·10)	−134·610 (−3·37)
SOFIA				−23·388 (−0·68)	−28·569 (−0·79)	−45·174 (−1·24)
POP≥*65*		−23·932 (−5·96)	−23·471 (−5·27)		−4·740 (−0·44)	4·155 (0·36)
FOREST			0·120 (0·24)			2·013 (1·55)
Constant	12·144 (0·52)	−32·934 (−1·98)	−34·220 (−1·96)	132·891 (2·81)	127·890 (2·54)	131·106 (2·73)
−Log-likelihood	110·60	99·72	99·69	121·82	121·76	120·62

[a] Entered as the square root.

Note: See Table 2 for variables' descriptions except for the following: *SPILL* is the NO_x deposition reduction derived from other sample nations; *MCNOX* is the marginal cost of NO_x emission reduction; *OWNNOX* is the fraction of a country's own NO_x emissions deposited on itself; and *SOFIA* is a dummy for participation in the protocol. The models use the 1988 data for *GNP* and *FREE*. *POP*≥*65* is from United Nations (1992).

1 and 2. This finding may indicate that the early rounds of emission cutbacks were not constrained by the estimates of MC, estimates that were not really available during this period. For the population measure, we find that both estimates are insignificant, suggesting that the pre-Helsinki contributions were not motivated by health concerns. Moreover, when alternative measures of the susceptible population (i.e. the proportion of the population less than 15 years old and the proportion of both younger and older populations) are entered, estimates are similar to those reported. Inclusion of the *FOREST* variable causes a large change in the *MCSUL*, *OWNSUL* and *POP* ≥ *65* estimates, perhaps indicating a multicollinearity problem. Since the *FOREST* coefficient is of the wrong sign, we are reluctant to draw conclusions from model 3.

For the post-Helsinki result, our theoretical characterization is also supported. The coefficients on *SPILL*, *GNP* and *FREE*, as well as on the additional terms, *TARGET* and *HELSINKI*, have the anticipated sign and are significant. *OWNSUL* has the correct sign and is marginally significant in model 6. *MCSUL* has the correct sign for the three post-Helsinki models, but is insignificant. The *POP* ≥ *65* coefficient exhibits the correct sign but is insignificant in both models. In contrast to the pre-Helsinki results, the estimates suggest, albeit weakly, that the private production costs and the public health benefits of reducing sulphur emissions are beginning to be considered at the national level. The *FOREST* coefficient again has the wrong sign and causes considerable instability to the estimates on *MCSUL*, *OWNSUL* and *POP* ≥ *65*. Consequently, we conclude that the *FOREST* variable should be excluded from the post- and pre-Helsinki models.

A comparison of the log-likelihood values gives little support in favour of a particular post-Helsinki model. We prefer model 5 primarily because we believe that the susceptible population is theoretically an important variable. Similarly, model 2 is preferred for the pre-Helsinki period. Henceforth, models 2 and 5 are viewed as the best representations of the data.

Ceteris paribus, nations that faced a greater target level of reductions are achieving less in voluntary reductions. In model 5, the *TARGET* coefficient indicates that, for every extra ton of required reductions, voluntary reductions fall by approximately one ton. In addition, nations that ratified the Helsinki Protocol appear more willing than non-ratifiers to make reductions beyond the targeted level. On average, ratifiers contribute approximately 115,000 tons more to voluntary reductions than non-ratifying nations. When comparing the pre-Helsinki (model 2) with the post-Helsinki (model 5) estimates, we find that the size of the spillin response increased quite substantially in the post-Helsinki sample. Apparently, emission reductions beyond the mandated 30% cut are subjected to greater strategic behaviour than the initial pre-Helsinki cuts. The slightly increased income effect may suggest that the post-Helsinki reductions are more discretionary, perhaps owing to the lack of a political constraint that mandates additional cuts.

In Table 3, the NO_x results offer much less support for our voluntary reduction model. The *SPILL* terms are still negative and of even greater magnitude, implying that the strategic response to foreign-originated depositions is greater with respect to the voluntary reductions in NO_x.

In the pre-Sofia specifications, the income parameter is significantly negative without the *POP* ≥ *65* term in the model. Inclusion of the susceptible population measure causes the GNP term to become positive and significant, but the $POP \geq 65$ coefficient is unexpectedly negative. The increase in the log-likelihood function value from −110·60 to −99·72 indicates that model 2 is statistically superior (p-value = 0·00) to model 1. Although the *FOREST* coefficient is positive as expected, its inclusion does not significantly improve the model. In model 2, *MCNOX*, *OWNNOX* and *FREE* disappointingly exhibit the unexpected sign.

The results are slightly different in the post-Sofia period, for which the coefficient of GNP and *MCNOX* are the right sign but insignificant in all three models. Similarly, *OWNNOX*, *SOFIA* and $POP \geq 65$ are insignificant. It is noteworthy that the *FREE* dummy variable is significantly negative, indicating that the nations with the greatest civil and political liberties voluntarily reduce emissions *less* on average compared with nations with fewer liberties. The *FOREST* coefficient is positive and marginally significant, but there is little statistical evidence favouring a particular model. For symmetry with the sulphur analysis, we prefer model 5 in the post-Sofia period.

A contrast of the sulphur and NO_x results yields several interesting insights. First, at the *supranational* level, we see evidence of strategic behaviour for both environmental problems. This lends support to our modelling efforts that cast each problem as a regional collective action problem. Second, the influence of political and civil liberties affects the two pollutants differently: liberties are supportive of emission reductions for sulphur, but are non-supportive for NO_x. In the case of sulphur, the major share of emissions stems from power plants that are government-controlled monopolies; in the case of NO_x, the major share of emissions come from a large number of small (mobile) polluters. Third, we see that the amount of a nation's emissions that fall within its borders (*OWNSUL* and *OWNNOX*) is much more relevant in the sulphur model. A relatively large fraction of a nation's sulphur emission falls on itself, while for NO_x the emissions travel much further or dissipate into the atmosphere (see Figure 1). The transferability of NO_x means a greater role for strategic behaviour at the supranational level, which is borne out by the larger absolute coefficients on the *SPILL* variable of NO_x. Finally, the treaty's effects are quite different. *HELSINKI* is a significant deterrent in the post-Helsinki period, because it had entered into force in September 1987 during the period under investigation, which goes through 1990. In contrast, the Sofia Protocol is not a deterrent and did not enter into force until February 1991, shortly after the study period.

V. Policy Implications

In Table 1, we saw that a majority of nations had either met or were close to meeting the 30% reductions (from 1980 levels) in sulphur emissions by the signing of the Helsinki Protocol. This suggests that, once a majority of nations can meet a given standard of reductions, the treaty is drafted and subsequently approved as others catch up. For many participants, the cutbacks already achieved served as a blueprint for the treaty stipulations. A similar kind of pattern regarding the Sofia Protocol emerged in the case of NO_x from Table 1. Since the reductions were slower to achieve and more modest, the stipulated reductions in the Sofia Protocol were also modest.

If this pattern of voluntary reductions preceding the framing of treaties continues, then a policy prediction follows from Table 1. In the case of sulphur, the percentage of voluntary sulphur emission reduction achieved in 1992 (*%SUL92*) is on average 4·8% *beyond* the targeted reductions of the Helsinki Protocol. Ten nations have achieved voluntary reductions greater than 15% *beyond* the 30% target. Thus, a new, stronger protocol should emerge in the next couple of years which will restrict sulphur emissions by another 10–15% from 1980 levels. In the case of NO_x, we can be much less sanguine. At the end of 1992, reductions from 1987 levels are 2·66% (on average) for the 25 sample nations in Table 1. Subsequent protocols on NO_x will take a longer time to achieve.

These predictions are consistent with some recent developments. The Large Combustion Plant Directive (LCPD) mandated stricter percentage reductions from 1980 levels for most of the EEC countries. When the LCPD was drafted at the end of 1988, ten out of twelve EEC countries had already met or exceeded the stricter reductions mandated for 1993. An eleventh country, Luxembourg, was near to the target; only Greece was some distance away. Even though the LCPD guidelines covered only about half of the sulphur emission sources, a pattern similar to the Helsinki Protocol emerged: nations achieved emission reduction levels and then drafted the treaty with these levels as targets. For NO_x inference is more problematic, in so far as combustion plants accounted for only 20–25% of emissions. Thus, it is difficult to compare the stricter requirements of the LCPD with the Sofia Protocol. Still, it is noteworthy that half of the EEC nations met or nearly met the percentage reductions for *overall* NO_x, whereas those mandated by the LCPD were for combustion plants alone at the time of the treaty drafting.

Our prediction of a stronger protocol on sulphur emissions is borne out by the Oslo Protocol drafted on 14 June 1994, but as of March 1996 still unratified. This protocol mandates stricter percentage reductions from 1980 levels than the Helsinki Protocol for most treaty countries by the year 2000 (United Nations 1994, p. 15). Unlike earlier protocols, percentage reductions vary by country in the Oslo Protocol. Countries with greater current reductions are given stricter targets, consistent with the spirit of our hypothesis. No stricter protocol for NO_x has yet been drafted.

Because a greater fraction of NO_x can be transferred *outside* the treaty region, there is a need for a larger treaty region if the externality is to be truly internalized. As a consequence, monitoring and evaluation activities need to be extended beyond their current boundaries. A similar recommendation does not follow for sulphur. Transnational liability assignments and a system of enforcement may be necessary if nations are to become more responsible about NO_x as a pollutant. These are not easy changes to engineer for transnational relationships that hinge, to a large extent, on national autonomy.

Another policy consideration involves control at the national level. For NO_x, nations must achieve greater control over mobile polluters. If increased demands for a cleaner environment are to be attained as a nation's income rises, then individual freedoms have to be traded off for more centralized control over NO_x polluters. For NO_x, unlike sulphur, policy must first be directed *at fixing the collective action problem at the national level.* Then attention can be focused on the second tier, where collective action is needed at the supranational level. If the first tier problem is not resolved, there will be little progress on the second.

Yet another consideration concerns inducements or selective incentives for some nations. The pattern of emissions and their reductions differs greatly among the convention members, owing to differing technologies and incentives (i.e. *OWNSUL* and *OWNNOX*). For example, the transitional economies have a difficult time cutting their sulphur emissions when compared with the other Protocol members. For the most part, treaties have viewed signers identically despite great differences in emissions and technology; mandated cuts apply in equal percentage terms to all. A degree of differentiation that changes over time may be supportive of treaty ratification. The Oslo Protocol appears to recognize this needed differentiation. Because the transitional nations tend to do more for curbing NO_x, a trade-off among pollutants might facilitate treaty ratification and compliance in the short run.

VI. Concluding Remarks

Two different experiences emerge when the econometric model is applied. For sulphur reductions, the model performs reasonably well, thus supporting our theoretical construct. Free riding does, indeed, characterize the ratifiers of the Helsinki Protocol. Increases in income and political freedoms augment emission reductions. This suggests that foreign aid and the promotion of democracy on behalf of the wealthier countries can bear a dividend in terms of a better environment for all. Voluntary cutbacks in 1992 bode well for greater mandated reductions being placed into future protocols.

For NO_x, the model performs in a much less convincing manner. This is probably due to the large number of small polluters whose unco-ordinated actions call into question our unitary decision-maker assumption at the national level. In fact, political freedoms appear to undermine the nations' actions to curb NO_x pollutants, thus lending support to this hypothesis. Thus, two collective action problems that have some similarities do not require the same policy prescriptions. In hindsight, the LRTAP Convention was properly designed when it provided for protocols to focus on separate pollutants. If all pollutants had been treated the same, much less progress would have been made for sulphur.

ACKNOWLEDGMENTS

This paper was prepared under a cooperative agreement between the Institute for Policy Reform and the Agency for International Development (AID), Cooperative Agreement no. PDC-0095-A-00-1126-00. Our research was also funded by the National Science Foundation, grant SBR-9222953. Comments from an anonymous referee are gratefully acknowledged.

NOTES

1. See UN Environment Programme (1991) for treaty and protocol text.
2. A longer unpublished version of this paper contains tables on the raw data and the transferability of the pollutants. See Murdoch *et al.* (1994, tables 1A–4A), which is available upon request.
3. LCPD applied only to combustion plants, while the Helsinki and Sofia Protocols applied to all sources of sulphur and NO_x emissions, respectively. In the case of NO_x, LCPD limits affected approximately 20–25% of NO_x pollution.

4. For alternative pollution scenarios, Nash equilibrium behaviour has been investigated by Barrett (1993) and Welsch (1993). These earlier subscription models did not include spatial dispersion, because it was not relevant to their problems.
5. Implicitly, we are assuming that reduced depositions are also a good proxy for improved ambient air quality, as stated in Section I.
6. The price or marginal cost of pollution reduction varies with the level of reduction. Thus, our model can be viewed as linearizing the budget constraint within a neighbourhood of the equilibrium, using the price associated with the equilibrating quantity. This is a standard procedure in applied studies (e.g. hedonic studies) for estimating a demand function when prices are variable.
7. In Murdoch *et al.* (1994, table 7A), we present the NO_x results with alternative definitions of voluntary behaviour. The results presented later are robust with respect to these alternative definitions.
8. The source for the ratification data is personal correspondence with the Treaty Section, Office of Legal Affairs, United Nations. These data are available in Murdoch *et al.* (1994).
9. See Murdoch *et al.* (1994). The normal probability plot is also called the normal *Q–Q* plot (Cleveland 1993, ch. 2).
10. The parameter on $TSPILL_i$ (ρ_2) is insignificant in all models (see Murdoch *et al.* 1994). Thus, we have dropped this variable when presenting the main results.
11. This is a partial measure that indicates the influence of reduced *SPILL* on voluntary reductions, holding all other influences constant. Since some of these influences are supportive of voluntary cutbacks, the negative estimate on the *SPILL* term is entirely consistent with nations having positive overall cutbacks owing to these other influences.

REFERENCES

ALCAMO, J. M. and RUNCA, E. (1986). Some technical dimensions of transboundary air pollution. In C. Flinterman, B. Kwiatkowska and J. G. Lammers (eds), *Transboundary Air Pollution: International Legal Aspects of the Cooperation of States*. Dordrecht: Martinus Nijhoff.

AMANN, M. and KORNAI, G. (1987). Cost functions for controlling SO_2 emissions in Europe. Working Paper no. WP-87-065, International Institute for Applied Systems Analysis, Laxenburg, Austria.

ANSELIN, L. (1988). *Spatial Econometrics: Methods and Models*. Dordrecht: Kluwer Academic.

BARRETT, S. (1993). *Convention on Climate Change: Economic Aspects of Negotiations*. Paris: Organization for Economic Cooperation and Development.

—— (1994). Self-enforcing international environmental agreements. *Oxford Economic Papers*, **46**, 878–94.

CLEVELAND, W. S. (1993). *Visualizing Data*. Summit, NJ: Hobart Press.

CONGLETON, R. D. (1992). Political institutions and pollution control. *Review of Economics and Statistics*, **74**, 412–21.

COUNCIL OF THE EUROPEAN COMMUNITIES (1988). Council Directive of 24 November 1988 (88/609/EEC) on the limitation of emissions of certain pollutants in the air from large combustion plants. *Official Journal of the European Communities*, **50**, 336/1–13.

CRESSIE, N. (1993). *Statistics for Spatial Data*, rev. ed. New York: John Wiley.

ELIASSEN, A. and SALTBONES, J. (1983). Modelling of long-range transport of sulphur over Europe: a two-year model run and some model experiments. *Atmospheric Environment*, **17**, 1457–73.

EYCKMANS, J., PROOST, S. and SCHOKKAERT, E. (1993). Efficiency and distribution in greenhouse negotiations. *Kyklos*, **46**, 363–97.

GASTIL, R. D. (1989). *Freedom in the World: Political Rights and Civil Liberties 1988–89*. New York: Freedom House.

INTERNATIONAL INSTITUTE FOR APPLIED SYSTEMS ANALYSIS (IIASA) (1993). *RAINS Model, Version 6.1*, Computer Program. Laxenburg, Austria: IIASA.

LATIMER, D. A., IYER, H. K. and MALM, W. C. (1990). Application of a differential mass balance model to attribute sulfate haze in the Southwest. In C. V. Mathai (ed.), *Visible and Fine Particulates*. Pittsburgh, Penna: Air and Waste Management Association.

MURDOCH, J. C. and SANDLER, T. (1997). The voluntary provision of a pure public good: the case of reduced CFC emissions and the Montreal Protocol. *Journal of Public Economics*, **63**, 311–29.

——, —— and SARGENT, K. (1994). A tale of two collectives: sulfur versus nitrogen oxides emission reduction in Europe. Mimeo, Iowa State University.

OLSON, M. (1965). *The Logic in Collective Action*. Cambridge, Mass.: Harvard University Press.

Organization for Economic Cooperation and Development (OECD) (1990). *Control Strategies for Photochemical Oxidants across Europe*. Paris: OECD.

Runge, C. F. (1990). Common property resources in a global context. Staff Paper P90-27, Center for International Food and Agricultural Policy, University of Minnesota.

Sandler, T. (1992). *Collective Action: Theory and Applications*. Ann Arbor: University of Michigan Press.

—— and Sargent, K. (1995). Management of transnational commons: coordination, publicness, and treaty formation. *Land Economics*, **71**, 145–62.

Sandnes, H. (1993). *Calculated Budgets for Airborne Acidifying Components in Europe, 1985, 1987, 1988, 1989, 1990, 1991, and 1992*. EMEP/MSC-W Report 1/93. Oslo: Norske Meteorologiske Institutt.

Schwartz, J. (1991). Particulate air pollution and daily mortality: a synthesis. *Public Health Review*, **19**, 39–60.

Sisler, J. F., Huffman, D., Latimer, D. A., Malm, W. C. and Pitchford, M. L. (1993). *Spatial and Temporal Patterns and the Chemical Composition of the Haze in the United States*. Fort Collins: Cooperative Institute for Research in the Atmosphere, Colorado State University.

United Nations (UN) (1986). *Demographic Yearbook 1984*. New York: United Nations.

—— (1992). *Demographic Yearbook 1990*. New York: United Nations.

—— (1994). *Protocol to the 1979 Convention on Long-Range Transboundary Air Pollution on Further Reduction of Sulfur Emissions*. New York: United Nations.

UN Environment Programme (UNEP) (1991). *Selected Multilateral Treaties in the Field of the Environment*, Vol. 2. Cambridge, Mass.: Grotius.

—— (1993). *Environmental Data Report: 1993–94*. Oxford: Blackwell Publishers.

Welsch, H. (1993). An equilibrium framework for global pollution problems. *Journal of Environmental Economics and Management*, **25**, S64–S79.

World Resources Institute (WRI) (1992). *World Resources 1992–93*. New York: Oxford University Press.

—— (1994). *World Resources 1994–95*. New York: Oxford University Press.

Name Index

9781138705210